Aloys Fleischmann (1880–1964)
An Immigrant Musician in Ireland

Aloys Fleischmann, Munich 1931, by Oskar Stohandl (1883–1943)

Aloys Fleischmann
(1880–1964)
An Immigrant Musician in Ireland

by
JOSEPH P. CUNNINGHAM
AND RUTH FLEISCHMANN

With an Essay on the Music
by Séamas de Barra

and Contributions by
Josef Focht, Andreas Pernpeintner
and Ursula Nauderer

CORK **cup** UNIVERSITY PRESS

First published in 2010 by
Cork University Press
Youngline Industrial Estate
Pouladuff Road, Togher
Cork, Ireland

British Library Cataloguing in Publication Data

ISBN-13: 978-1859-18462-2

Printed in the UK by J.F. Print
Typeset by Tower Books, Ballincollig, Co. Cork

www.corkuniversitypress.com

Contents

Acknowledgements

We would like to express our gratitude to:

Dr Elisabeth Boser, Director of the Dachau Art Gallery, for permission to reproduce paintings; Ursula Nauderer, Director of the Dachau District Museum, for having 'discovered' the Fleischmanns and done much to preserve Fleischmann's memory in his home town ever since, and for permission to reproduce old photographs; Andreas Bräunling, Municipal Archivist of Dachau, for help with research; Dr Josef Focht, Music Department of the University of Munich, for having 'discovered' the Fleischmanns and supported the research ever since; Dr Erich Pillwein of Munich for kind support in researching the painter Oskar Stohandl; Sabine Brantl of the Munich Academy of Fine Arts for help in researching the painter Oskar Stohandl; Gertrud Beckmann, née Rössler, Dachau, Tilly Fleischmann's cousin, for decades of hospitality; Hildegard Braceschi, née Schaehle, Weilheim/Bavaria, with her son Georg and daughter Paula Ader, for having permitted us to search among her papers for Fleischmann letters: in January 2009 we found sixty-two letters written to her father between 1912 and 1960; Elisabeth Peren and her son Alexander of Dachau for help with genealogical research; Josef Biersack, Maxhütte-Haidhof, for help in tracing the Fleischmanns of the Regensburg area; Andreas and Franz Dengl, cousins of Aloys Fleischmann's mother, Leni Deger, for providing photographs; the Gluck family, Dachau, for providing a Fleischmann letter of 1949; Florian Lang, Oberammergau, for material about his grandfather, Andreas Lang, who was interned with Fleischmann during the First World War; Dr Rudolf von Moreau, Munich, for information about his family; Hermann Windele, former mayor of Dachau and member of the Liedertafel Choir, for documentation of Aloys Fleischmann's father as founding member of the choir.

Thanks also to: the directors of the Archives of University College Cork: to the former director, Virginia Teehan for having taken the Fleischmann Papers into the care of the university, and for the invaluable support which she and her successor, Catriona Mulcahy, have given since then; Ciarán Mangan and John Smith for information about the internment camp in Oldcastle, Co Meath; Yvonne M. Cresswell of the Manx Museum and National Trust, Douglas, Isle of Man, for help in researching Fleischmann's time as internee; the priests of the diocese of Cork and Ross for help in researching Fleischmann's work at the cathedral: Dr Declan Mansfield, Administrator of the Diocese of Cork and Ross, Dr Tom Deenihan, Diocesan Secretary, Fr Tom Hayes, Fr Ted O'Sullivan, former Diocesan Secretary of Cork and Ross; Rev. Dr David Lannon of the Diocese of Salford, Lancs and Tom Flanagan; Denise O'Sullivan for copies of cathedral documents; Dr Myles Reardon of the Vincentian Archives in Raheny and Br John Brazil for information about the Swertz family; Regina Deacy for allowing us to read a draft of her thesis 'Continental Organists and Catholic Church Music in Ireland 1860–1960'; Cork City Libraries for permission to reproduce old photographs; the following for valuable information, assistance and permission to reproduce documents: Mona Brase, the late Patricia Cox, Julian Dodd, Dan Donovan, Adrian Gebruers, Charles Henchion, Aidan Kennedy, Maighread Murphy, Ann and Eoin Neeson, Íde Ní Laoghaire, Colum Ó Cléirigh, Madoline O'Connell, Patrick O'Connor, Máirín O'Rourke, the late Moira Pyne, Sister Cathy of the Presentation Order, Erika Roth, Martin Steffen, Michael Weedle.

We are under special obligation to those who have contributed directly to the biography: Séamas de Barra, whose essay gives the first scholarly assessment of Fleischmann's music and who has compiled an annotated catalogue of the works; Dr Josef Focht, Ursula Nauderer, Andreas Pernpeintner, whose essays present the context of Aloys Fleischmann's work in Dachau; former members of the cathedral choir and students of Fleischmann who provided material for the biography with accounts of their time with him: Seán Barrett, Bob Barry, Denis Bevan, Fr. Daniel J. Burns, Sister Marie Collins, Michael MacDonald, David McInerny, William Martin, Nicholas Motherway, Jerry O'Callaghan, Jack O'Donovan, Roibeárd Ó hÚrdail, Mary Sheppard, Rev. Patrick Walsh, Michael Weedle. We owe a large debt of gratitude to Max Fleischmann for his digital photography, Anne Fleischmann for recording and transcribing interviews, to Séamas de Barra and Dr Patrick Zuk for their expert advice so generously given, to Maria Cunningham, the Fleischmanns and Rainer Würgau for years of support.

To Mike Collins, Maria O'Donovan and the staff of Cork University Press we extend our best thanks for their most meticulous work, courtesy and friendliness.

Preface

JOSEPH P. CUNNINGHAM

Cantate Domino, canticum novum,
quia mirabilia fecit [Dominus]. (Psalm 98)

Sing ye to the Lord a new canticle
because He [the Lord] has done wonderful things.

This book was conceived at St Patrick's College, Maynooth, County Kildare on 2 February 1994, while attending a mass to mark the quadricentenary of the death of Palestrina, one of the great composers of contrapuntal music for unaccompanied chorus. Hearing Palestrina's great *Missa Papae Marcelli* in the Gothic surroundings of the college chapel brought me back some fifty years to my days as a choirboy, and particularly to my church music teacher and mentor, Herr Aloys Fleischmann, who was the first in my native city of Cork to perform this choral masterpiece, and who devoted his long life to the cultivation of the sacred music composed by the great masters of the sixteenth century.

The mass in Maynooth was celebrated by Cardinal Daly, and the music sung by the male college choir and the boys of the Pro-Cathedral Palestrina Choir, Dublin, while priests, seminarians and the general congregation joined in the singing of the Credo and Pater Noster in chant. During the sermon, the cardinal spoke of the life and works of Palestrina and of the place music has had in sacred liturgy down through the centuries – its importance, its development and its prospects. On the present state of church music in Ireland, the cardinal had this to say:

> There has been progress over recent decades, but it is partial and uneven, and sometimes changes intended as progress have been retrograde. We still have a prevalence of what has been called the 'four-hymn syndrome'; the quality of hymns and music in broadcast Masses both on radio and television is sometimes painfully embarrassing. Composers of sacred music need a deep understanding of – and a real feeling for – liturgy, just as much as they need musical talent, inspiration and skill.

In Palestrina's time, church music had also come in for criticism: the Council of Trent (1545–63) had even considered banning polyphonic music altogether from the church. Legend has it that it was the performance of three of Palestrina's masses, among them the *Missa Papae Marcelli*, which led the cardinals to vote unanimously against the proposed ban. The fact is, however, that this mass was written some ten years beforehand.

That six-part Palestrina mass was performed by Herr Fleischmann and the boys and men of the cathedral choir at a recital given in the Honan Chapel of University College Cork on 16 June 1934. Press reports on the recital stated that the rendering, like the work itself, was masterly. The choir was invited to broadcast the mass on many occasions over the years to come.

I sang for twenty years in the choir, beginning at the age of ten; I studied the organ with Herr Fleischmann, became his assistant, and during his last years helped with practices and services. This highly cultured man with his great love of all the arts was a formative influence in my life at a time when my mind was like a sponge; his example rubbed off on me and left me with a lasting interest in painting, the theatre and literature. The training he gave me and the opportunities created by his son made it possible for me to found and conduct a choir myself, which has been among the most rewarding experiences of my life. That is why I decided to embark on a biography so that he and his work for sacred music in Ireland would not be forgotten.

Jubilate Deo omnis terra,
servite Domino in laetitia. [Psalm 99]

O sing joyfully to God, all the earth
Serve ye the Lord with gladness.

Preface

Ruth Fleischmann

Joe Cunningham began to put his Fleischmann biography plan into action towards the end of 1994: he accepted the invitation of Wally McGrath, the editor of the *Cork Examiner* and the *Evening Echo,* to write a piece of some 4,000 words for the Christmas magazine, *The Holly Bough*. The illustrated article entitled 'The Herr and Cork's Most Famous Choir' was published in December 1994. Wally McGrath added a footnote announcing the author's intention of writing more extensively on the subject – in Joe's words: 'So he walked me right into it.' Joe then approached the family to ask for support with his project, in particular with the translation of the German documents among the Fleischmann papers. We were delighted to become involved. It had not occurred to any of us to undertake such a study, and we knew that Joe was the ideal person to do it, given his long association with our grandfather.

In 1995, Joe got down to work on the family papers in the archives of University College Cork. He transcribed everything relevant that was in English, interviewed all former choir members whom he could trace, travelled to Oldcastle in County Meath and to the Isle of Man to research our grandfather's time as an internee during the First World War, and to Dachau to see for himself where his choirmaster had come from. Joe thereby made contact with musicians and citizens of the town, which has turned out to be of great value and led to Fleischmann's works being performed again in his beloved native place.

It was not until my retirement in the late autumn of 2007 that I was able to concentrate on the project. I would like to thank Joe here for his immense patience with me. The whole family is greatly in his debt.

Introduction

ALOYS FLEISCHMANN (1880–1964)

Aloys Fleischmann was a Bavarian church musician and composer who emigrated to Cork in 1906, where he became organist and choirmaster at the Cathedral of St Mary and St Anne. He was a native of Dachau, a picturesque market town and artists' colony close to Munich, and the only son of a shoemaker. His father, a founding member of the Dachau Liedertafel Choir, took an active part in municipal affairs, and organised trade exhibitions documenting the local craft heritage. Aloys had seven years of schooling, began composing as a boy, and was admitted at sixteen to the Royal Academy of Music in Munich, where he studied the organ and composition under Josef Rheinberger. After his appointment at the age of twenty-one as organist and choirmaster to the parish church of St Jakob in his home town, he set up a choir school providing musical training to all the children in the two primary schools. He later founded a school of music in which friends from the Munich Court Orchestra gave free tuition and a Munich firm allowed his students to buy instruments at minimal cost. He revived an old Dachau drama tradition, putting on a nativity play every year for which he arranged or composed the music, three renowned painters providing costumes and scenery, the Munich Court Orchestra and choir supporting the local musicians, the undertaking financed by artisans, merchants and the town council. The plays were acclaimed in Munich, reviewed all over Germany and even in New York. His remarkable career in Dachau came to an abrupt end in 1906. The previous year he had married Tilly Swertz, a girl from Cork who had just graduated from the Academy of Music. She had relatives in Dachau, as her father had previously been organist there before he took a post in Cork in 1879. In 1906 Tilly's father unexpectedly moved to Philadelphia, leaving a family of nine in Cork to be provided for.

Ireland was still under British rule in 1906, but major reforms had been achieved by various nationalist organisations; these successes had inspired a revival of interest in the Irish language and Gaelic heritage, the

1

vigorous cultural movement paving the way for independence. The Fleischmanns soon found friends among these circles, among them Daniel Corkery, Terence MacSwiney, and the MacDonnells of Bandon. Fleischmann implemented the reform of church music prescribed by the pope in 1903 with a new repertoire of plainchant and seventeenth-century polyphonic music and the training of a boys' choir in place of the women who had sung in Swertz's mixed choir. The cause which Fleischmann took up in Dachau of giving the children of the poor the chance of a sound musical training was continued in Cork: the north parish from which the cathedral choirboys were recruited was one of the poorest in the city. He soon brought the choir to a high degree of excel-lence. His wife gave piano recitals and taught; he gave concerts with secular choirs. As in Dachau, music bridged class differences, but in Cork it also bridged political ones: they made friends among the gentry, the military, the merchant families of the city, as well as among those working in the language and literary movement. Terence MacSwiney was a frequent guest in the house and translated texts of Fleischmann's choral compositions. Fleischmann had not intended to remain in Cork once the Swertz children had finished their education. In the autumn of 1909 his wife went to Munich to give a concert and assess the prospect of their being able to return to Germany. Their only son Aloys was born in Munich in April 1910. In July 1910 the family came back to Cork.

When the First World War began in 1914, influential Anglo-Irish friends protected Fleischmann, but from 1916 to 1919 he was interned as an enemy alien, first in Oldcastle, County Meath, then on the Isle of Man, before being deported to Germany and not allowed to return to Cork until the autumn of 1920. Fleischmann was separated from his wife and child for nearly five years, living in a state of enforced inac-tivity while she did his work as well as her own; the man of solitary disposition used to roaming the countryside was locked up with hun-dreds and then thousands of strangers. Though for four years he could not play his instruments, the organ and piano, music remained to him: he had a choir and orchestra in the camps, for which he wrote ten works. Letters had to be short; they were censored and camp condi-tions could not be described. A grim picture emerged nonetheless; in his letters home the loneliness, anxiety, despair were evident but under control to comfort his wife. A letter written forty years later revealed the inner discipline which kept him alive.[1]

In the Free State, Fleischmann's field of activity was extended. He taught for nearly twenty years in the School of Music and for nearly forty in the diocesan seminary, St Finbarr's College, Farranferris (among his students were his son, Aloys junior, Seán Ó Riada, and the present Bishop of Cork, Most Reverend Dr John Buckley). He secured the purchase of a splendid Walcker organ for the cathedral; he broadcast on the newly established national radio, occasionally on the BBC World Service, and gave frequent recitals in the Honan Chapel of the university. He and his choir were known and respected throughout the city and beyond; he and his wife had the recognition and friendship of musicians such as Carl Hardebeck, Herbert Hughes, Richard Terry and Arnold Bax. He composed about four hundred works (which have now been catalogued and are here assessed for the first time). The inheritance from his mother allowed him to send his talented son to study in Munich; his son, Aloys, appointed to the chair of music in University College Cork, proceeded to set up organisations to promote music in the city as his father had done in his youth. But then came the anguish over the war, the fate of his country, the shame of his beloved Dachau now being a byword for Nazi atrocities.

The Fleischmanns lived to see their son continue their work for music in Cork and establish cultural links with continental Europe to an extent inconceivable in the first half of the century. During the 1950s, the Cork Orchestral Society (founded by Aloys Jun. in 1938) brought orchestras of world standing to visit Cork, among them the Vienna Philharmonic and the Bamberg Symphony Orchestras, and soloists such as Claudio Arrau and Yehudi Menuhin. The annual Cork International Choral Festival, founded in 1954 to promote choral singing in Ireland, brought hundreds of continental singers to the city. Fleischmann senior served on the festival's artistic advisory board from 1954–62, a time when numerous choirs were founded in the villages and towns of Munster, and whose standards rapidly improved through competing with choirs from all over the country and listening to the best from the continent. Among these choirs were several founded by former members of the cathedral choir and by Fleischmann students.

Fleischmann worked with dedication for over sixty years to give ordinary people access to their own creativity through music: for him appreciation, understanding and practice of the arts were the gateway to spirituality and thus a means of coming to terms with the suffering of life. He continued at the cathedral until he was eighty-one: his German savings had become worthless after the war and neither he nor his wife had a pension. For two years he was an invalid in the Incurable Hospital, where he died on 3 January 1964. His wife taught up to the day of her death, 17 October 1967, aged eighty-five.

IMMIGRANT MUSICIANS IN IRELAND

Fleischmann was one of the fifty continental organists brought to Ireland by the Catholic bishops from 1860 to 1960 to develop church music, all of whom made a significant impact on the cultural life of their communities. They were the first group of foreigners to have been invited in modern times by an Irish institution to take up appointment and residence in the country.

In previous centuries, those brought in had been mainly agricultural-
ists. Soldiers had been settled after the colonial wars, Scottish
tenant-farmers 'planted' and refugees from the Rhine-Palatinate granted
land in Munster in the hope of subduing unrest and promoting
Protestantism. In the eighteenth and nineteenth centuries religious per-
secution brought immigrants who settled in the cities. Protestant French
Huguenots were encouraged by the Irish parliament to move to Ireland:
several thousand settled in urban areas where they contributed much to
the textile and other manufacturing industries of the country. In the late
nineteenth century a small group of Jewish refugees fleeing from a
pogrom in Lithuania came to Limerick, where they eked out a living as
traders and peddlers.

Despite the depressed state of the Irish economy at the beginning of
the twentieth century, there had been some immigration: about 2,000
arrived from Russia, 1,200 from France and 1,000 from Germany. The
largest groups were to be found in Leinster but there were also sizeable
groupings in Ulster and Munster. According to the census of 1901, most
Germans living in Ireland were classified as domestic or hotel servants;
in addition to these 160 governesses and waiters, there were 115
teachers, 97 religious, 77 clockmakers, 46 students, 40 musicians and
others.[2] Many of the German musicians will have been in the employment of the Catholic church.

However, from the later part of the nineteenth century, Irish music-
teaching institutions also recruited continental musicians. The most
influential was no doubt Michele Esposito, the Italian professor of
piano at the Royal Irish Academy of Music in Dublin. He was appointed
in 1882, and stood at the centre of the musical life of the capital for
nearly fifty years. A tireless music organiser, he set about creating an
infrastructure for his art in the city. He initiated the Royal Dublin
Society chamber concerts, at which he often performed; he founded the
Dublin Orchestral Society, with which he gave regular concerts until
the First World War, gradually building up a following for symphonic
music. He composed a great deal in many different genres and much of
his music engaged with the Irish heritage. He was an excellent teacher;
among his composition pupils were Hamilton Harty, John Larchet and
Frederick May.[3] However, many of his talented students had to leave
Ireland to make a living. The city did not have a full professional
orchestra until the 1940s – the prospect of playing in the cinema during
silent films[4] was scarcely an attractive one. Larchet succeeded Esposito
at the Academy, also becoming professor of music at University College
Dublin. In his compositions he continued his teacher's commitment to
the Irish music heritage; he also emulated Esposito's active music-
making in the city with his work, for instance, as musical director of the
Abbey Theatre. Larchet, with others, embarked on the long and arduous

campaign to persuade the Free State government's Departmentof Education to have music taught in schools by properly trained teachers.

In Cork, two institutions recruited foreign musicians: the Catholic cathedral from 1870, and the Cork Municipal School of Music from its foundation in 1878. In Cork, as in other cathedral cities, the foreign organists and choirmasters also taught privately as well as in secular institutions. The Belgian cathedral organist, Léopold de Prins, performed at the opening of the School of Music in 1878 and taught there until 1889;[5] Hans Conrad Swertz was appointed professor of harmony at the school in 1882; the Swiss organist Theo Gmür and the German Heinrich Tils were already on the staff.[6] In 1920 the school appointed Carl Hardebeck as its director and professor of Irish music. The scholar, collector of folk music and composer came to Cork from Belfast; he was born in London of a German father.

Cork also had Italian musicians who did much for the musical life of the city. The organisers of the Cork International Exhibition of 1902 recruited a small orchestra of continental musicians, the city at the time not having one of its own, and invited Ferruccio Grossi of Milan to conduct it. He and his pianist wife were then persuaded to remain in the city: Grossi founded the Cork Orchestral Union and the couple performed and taught until the 1930s.[7]

The first government of the independent Irish Free State followed the example of the Catholic Church in looking to the continent, rather than to Britain, for the experts it needed to re-build and develop the nation. Probably the most significant engineering project ever undertaken in Ireland was the Shannon hydro-electric scheme designed to bring electricity to every part of the country. The German firm of Siemens-Schuckert was awarded the contract in 1925 by the government-appointed team of continental assessors. Between five and ten thousand Germans completed the scheme in 1929 and they were generally regarded with admiration and awe for the efficiency and dedication with which they conducted the huge task.[8] German expertise was also sought for the development of the Irish sugar and turf industries.

A similar policy brought the government to recruit continental expertise in establishing a school of military music in Dublin. When a request made to the French authorities was unsuccessful, the head of the School of Military Music in Berlin was consulted. As the German army had been disbanded at the end of the First World War, and the country subsequently de-militarised by the victors, most of the country's military musicians were unemployed. Fritz Brase was recruited from Berlin to direct the army's school of music and to set up military bands attached to the Curragh training camp, to the Southern Command in Cork, and to the Western Command in Athlone. He was assisted by

Friedrich Sauerzweig, who had come from Greifswald. The army agreed to purchase German instruments; the musicians were trained to play in 'philharmonic pitch,' whereas before independence all bands had used 'English High Pitch'.[9] The Army No. 1 Band with forty-four players was not only the first institution in Dublin to give regular concerts after the civil war, but due to the tuning of the instruments it became the nucleus of the Radio Éireann Symphony Orchestra. Brase's influence on the musical life of Dublin was therefore akin to Esposito's: he founded the Dublin Philharmonic Society soon after his arrival and conducted concerts organised by the RDS, performing works by Irish composers. Like Esposito, Brase's impact as a teacher was considerable; in addition he played a significant role in Irish broadcasting.[10] Indeed, the military historian John P. Duggan attributes the popularity of the newly founded Irish army to no small extent to its regular public music-making.[11]

The influence of the immigrant musicians in Ireland was far greater than their number, which gave rise to a certain hostility. German immigrants were targeted in a cartoon published in 1901 in D.P. Moran's journal, *The Leader*, entitled 'No Irish Need Apply'. It depicts two fat musicians ensconced in a building called 'Feis Ceoil', the inscription of which they have deleted and replaced with 'Musikschule'. In their school, Irish music is given only a minuscule place, whereas that of Mozart, Beethoven, Wagner and Esposito predominates. An irate Éire, in garb of Celtic design, equipped with war pipes and battle axe, is seeking admission, threatening force if necessary. In 1908 *The Leader* carried a letter to the editor complaining that Cork was 'absolutely the most foreigner besieged town in Ireland' and a letter from Annie Patterson, the founder of the Feis Ceoil, who defended the city's German musicians, arguing that music was international.[12]

The journal's sustained hostility to foreigners working in Ireland was no doubt partly motivated by the desire to secure jobs for the Irish. However, its targeting of the very small group of musicians among the German immigrants indicates that they were deemed to pose more than an economic threat. The charge levelled in the caricature is that these foreigners were not only in the country to make money, but that they despised Irish culture and the people who set store by it; that the music they taught was alien and was being imposed on an unwilling people at the expense of their own heritage. At the time of publication of the caricature there was already ample evidence of the interest taken by the immigrant musicians in Irish music – an interest indeed greater at the time than that of the majority of Irish people. As Esposito is specifically mentioned, it can be assumed that the creator of the caricature knew of his cantata *Deirdre*, composed in 1897, and of his many fine arrangements of Irish folk music. The foreign musicians in Ireland studied the country's musical heritage, the teachers among them included it in the curriculum for their students, those who composed paid tribute to it through choice of theme (Grossi's cantata, *Sarsfield in Limerick*), through choice of text for setting (Aloys Fleischmann's *Dán-Mholadhh na Ghaedhilge*) or choice of material for arrangement (Brase's *Irish Fantasias*). It is bizarre that a publication such as *The Leader*, an ardent supporter of the Irish language movement, should accuse Germans of all people of despising Irish culture, given the outstanding contribution of German Celtic scholars to the study and revival of the language.

The animosity towards Germans evident in the *Leader* cartoon became widespread during the First World War, in particular among the large loyalist, pro-British section of the population. When the war began in August 1914, strict censorship and intense anti-German war propaganda set in, most Germans were interned, the Irish Parliamentary Party supported the war wholeheartedly, and 100,000 Irishmen joined up during the first two years. Opposition to the war was exceptional until the threat of conscription, the huge war casualties, the lack of Allied victory and the rising of 1916 began to fuel disaffection, and scepticism arose about the veracity of the war reporting with its vilification of Germany. In Cork, loyalism was strong throughout the war. In 1915 the city fathers withdrew the freedom of the city from the Celtic scholar Kuno Meyer who, now professor of Celtic Studies in Berlin, had publicly advocated the German cause during a visit to the United States. In 1917 an anonymous piece of fiction called *The Germans in Cork* delivered a warning of what might await the Irish in the event of a German victory. After the conquest of Ireland, Cork's military governor, Baron Fritz von Kartoffels [potatoes], sets out to create order in the city with laws regulating every aspect of life, from obliging citizens to have scrubbed the footpaths outside their houses every day by 6.15 a.m., to the gassing of the insane, and the re-education of the idle poor in the now empty psychiatric hospitals. Germans, among them musicians, come in for special commendation for having served as effective spies for the fatherland while disguised as respectable, law-abiding residents of the city.[13]

With the end of the war such vituperation ceased. Controversy about the cultures, however, remained for a long time to come. The cultural nationalists adhering to the Irish-Irelander faction of the Gaelic revival movement had done dedicated, pioneering work to have the language respected, taught and used. Sometimes they sought to establish the value of the Gaelic heritage by denigrating that of other countries. One such person was the native speaker of Irish, writer and translator, founding member of the Gaelic League, Father Peter O'Leary, an tAthair Peadar. He set up libraries and night schools in his parishes, provided young speakers of Irish with a rich fare of Gaelic works, was learned in Greek and Latin literature, has been described as homely, humorous, witty and kind – yet he could write with painful ignorance and grotesque scorn about the English language and its literature.[14]

It was quite a different case with Father Christy O'Flynn, the charismatic Shakespeare producer, trainer of actors, curer of stammers, who was curate in the Cork cathedral from 1920–46. For a short period he studied the piano with Tilly Fleischmann, whose father he had consulted on an issue which was to remain a matter of concern to him all his life and which was to give rise to controversy with all three Fleischmann musicians. It was the question of traditional Irish music, *sean nós*, and the role of art music for the cultural development of Ireland. Father O'Flynn's mother had sung in Swertz's cathedral choir, so when as a boy he was puzzled by the difference he noticed between an Irish song he had heard from a street singer and the ballad 'A Nation Once Again', he put the problem to the choirmaster. Swertz responded that the street singer's traditional Irish song, the *sean nós*, was built, like plainchant, on the ancient modes whereas the ballad derived from the modern scale and had a strict beat. Swertz described the *sean nós* song as resembling the flight of a seagull with its free and natural rhythm and said he found it a more beautiful form of music.[15]

About twenty-five years later, during Easter Week 1924 when O'Flynn was a curate in the cathedral parish, he showed that he had adopted Swertz's theory about the affinity between the old Irish traditional songs and liturgical music. Swertz's son-in-law Fleischmann was now cathedral choirmaster and professor of music theory at the School of Music; Richard O'Donoghue describes the scene in his book on the priest:

> During Holy Week at Tenebrae, Father O'Flynn had sung the Lamentations of Jeremiah. He sang them in the traditional style of *sean nós* – from the heart. The poor people loved it and many of them were moved to tears. 'It was awful sad', they said. But Herr Fleischmann reacted differently. The choir saw him look to heaven, mutter something in German and plug his ears with his fingers.
>
> On Easter Sunday, after High Mass, by way of pulling the professor's leg, the Canon [Martin Murphy] said: 'Didn't Father O'Flynn sing those Lamentations superbly on Good Friday?'
>
> 'O mein Gott!' exclaimed the professor, 'please, do not call that singing: it was – murder! Father O'Flynn, he is a great artist, he has the drama, he has Shakespeare, and he has it all here'– he struck his heart – 'but when it comes to music – O mein Gott! He thinks he has it, but I tell you he has it not and he vill not listen to me. He is stubborn. Do you know vat I think, Canon? I think if der gute Gott in Himmel come down here on Good Friday and sing the Lamentation, Father O'Flynn would shake his fist and say: "You're wrong Herr Gott! You're wrong. You're only singing notes – you haven't got the emotions correct!'[16]

This is where they differed: O'Flynn was convinced that academic music training inhibited innate musicality, desiccated the natural instinct and paralysed the expression of authentic emotion. The education to which he was subjected in his youth was traumatic: 'You go in at one end like raw lumps of meat; you are forced through the Machine and you come out at the other end labelled "Sausage".'[17] He wanted children to love literature, to find inspiration and solace in it; he knew from his work with the poor of the cathedral parish how gifted they were; with his Cork Shakespearean Company he created an institution in which the talents of young people could blossom which the schools had done their best to smother. The actor and producer James Stack (also a member of the cathedral choir) wrote of him:

> Father O'Flynn literally took us off the streets of Cork and by talking to us about art and drama, and particularly about Shakespeare, he opened windows for us that we did not know existed. And he not only opened windows but he taught us how to see. You might say he exercised a hypnotic influence over us, and he filled us with such fire and enthusiasm that there was nothing we would not do for him. And he did it all without any encouragement from those in authority.[18]

For Father O'Flynn, the passionate advocate of the Gaelic tradition, Shakespeare was 'the dramatist par excellence' of universal relevance, the performing of whose plays could give actors and audience not only profound insight into the human condition, but also an uplifting sense of their own potential.[19] But the great masters of continental music he did not regard as having similar stature. For him the study of their works was irrelevant, if not damaging, for those interested in re-discovering and cherishing the musical heritage of the nation: 'Nothing written by Bach, Handel, Mozart or Beethoven can compare with the least of Irish folk-tunes', and notation and the music of instruments he considered 'enemies of native culture'.[20] In the *Leader* caricature of 1901 the immigrant German musicians were polemically represented as regarding Irish music as insignificant and irrelevant; what Éire was planning to do having gained admission to the school is not clear. Father O'Flynn would probably have counselled the elimination of training in any music other than Irish traditional. But his veneration and advocacy of the great dramatist of the neighbouring island is perhaps more astonishing than is his lack of appreciation of Shakespeare's continental counterparts in music.

The overwhelming prestige which Britain's artists enjoyed in Ireland at the end of the nineteenth century had constituted a daunting challenge to those seeking to establish Ireland's cultural independence. James Joyce expressed scant respect for Shakespeare and turned to

Scandinavia for his models; Daniel Corkery advised young writers to study the Russians. But all Irish writers were familiar with English literature; it provided the foundation for their new departures. The masterpieces of choral, symphonic and chamber music, however, were not generally known in Ireland in the first decades of the twentieth century: the immigrant musicians did much to redress that. They did not conceive of the two musical traditions as rivals or as being incompatible with one another. They arranged and performed Irish music with their choirs and ensembles, thus inculcating respect for it in their fellow musicians, students and audiences.

Aloys Fleischmann was the first music teacher of three people whose work for music in Ireland was significant. Pilib Ó Laoghaire was brought to a lifetime of choir-building in Munster by his early encounter in the cathedral with the great masters of polyphonic music, combined with his passion for Irish and its folk music. Seán Ó Riada studied with all three Fleischmann musicians; his journey back to the traditional culture of his family was circuitous, involving a protracted stay on the continent and immersion into a wide range of continental cultures. Aloys Fleischmann junior, proficient in Irish as in German and in the two cultures, set out from the beginning of his career to create and to foster an art music which was fed by the traditional heritage of the nation.

German Celtic scholars laid the foundations for the revival of the Irish language in the 1890s and, intimately connected with this, for the great flowering of the country's literature, both in English and in Irish, in the first decades of the twentieth century. The introduction of sacred polyphonic music, the development of Irish art music, the growth of choral music and the flourishing of traditional Irish music in the later part of the century had many origins: one of them was the influence of immigrant continental musicians. The achievement of the Celtic scholars is well known and documented. This biography of one of the immigrant musicians is the first of its kind – it is to be hoped that more will follow.

1. Youth in Dachau
1880–1906

Aloys Fleischmann 1904

THE MARKET TOWN AND ARTISTS' COLONY OF DACHAU

When Aloys Fleischmann was born in 1880, Dachau was known to Bavarians as an old market town and the summer residence of the Wittelsbach kings; it was known to painters and those interested in their work as an artists' colony, having been a centre of landscape painting since the middle of the nineteenth century. From 1933 the name took on a threatening connotation for all opponents of Nazism, being the location of the first concentration camp, which was established there in that year; from 1945 all over the world the name became synonymous with the infamy of the defeated regime.

Dachau is first mentioned in a document of AD 805 when it was donated by a noblewoman to the church – in 2005 it celebrated its twelve-hundredth anniversary. The town lies about twelve miles northwest of Munich, the centre perched on a hill 1,500 feet above sea level.

From the castle gardens there is a panoramic view over the surrounding countryside with Munich and sometimes the Alps visible on the horizon. At the southern foot of the hill beyond the river Amper there used to be extensive moorland dotted with small lakes and pools and covered by a blanket of almost twenty feet of turf. The name 'Dachau' means 'clay land surrounded by water': it derives from the locality rather than being the name of a settlement.[1] It was the extraordinary light and vivid colours to be found on the marshlands to the south of the town, and the charm of the hilly farmlands and forests to the north, which attracted so many landscape painters to the area.

The population of Dachau increased during the nineteenth century due to improved medical care[2] and the beginning of industrialisation. When Aloys Fleischmann was growing up in the 1880s, there were about 350 houses in the town and 3,000 inhabitants; by the time he was twenty the number had grown to 5,000. When his father was a boy, there had been about 200 houses and 1,300 citizens; when his grandfather was a child only 160 houses and 1,000 citizens.[3] The feudal privileges of the aristocracy were long-lived in Bavaria: serfdom was not formally abolished until 1808; restrictions on trade did not end until 1868. Dachau had long been a town of prosperous brewers, a centre of trade in agricultural produce and timber and home to a large variety of craftsmen. From the mid nineteenth century the modernisation process began to move from the urban centres and to have a considerable impact on the surrounding countryside. In 1862 a large paper factory was founded which catered for Munich's growing number of newspapers and publishing houses; in 1868 Dachau was linked by rail to Munich and Ingolstadt. This made it easier for the painters to travel to Dachau from Munich: from the 1890s to 1914 large numbers of distinguished artists came to paint and many to live. Literary accounts of the artists' colony increased its fame, bringing more writers, more painters, and also actors and musicians, until in 1900 it was said that every tenth person to be seen on the streets of the town was an artist. Over a thousand painters came to Dachau between 1840 and 1914.[4] It was, of course, the Dachau countryside as yet untouched by modernisation which brought them there and the attraction of a traditional way of life which was vanishing in the metropolitan centres from which they came. The train service, however, also brought industrially manufactured goods to the town which had previously been provided by the craftsmen, a development which began to threaten their livelihoods and the culture so esteemed by the newcomers.

FLEISCHMANN'S FAMILY BACKGROUND

Fleischmann's grandfather: a barber-surgeon

Aloys Fleischmann was born in Dachau on 24 April 1880. His father, also Aloys, was a master-shoemaker; his mother, Magdalena Deger (called

Leni), the daughter of the Dachau bookbinder, Josef Deger. Aloys was their only child, born twelve years after their marriage. The family were citizens of Dachau, being house-owners: Josef Deger had bought a house in 1835, which he transferred to his daughter Leni in 1867 so that her fiancé could set up a workshop in the town after her marriage.[5]

Aloys Fleischmann, the shoemaker, was born in the hamlet of Eisolzried,[6] a few miles to the west of Dachau, on 9 March 1844. His father, Franz Xaver, was a barber-surgeon who had come to Eisolzried from Fischbach, a village near Teubitz to the north of Regensburg. How he came to Eisolzried is not known, but he worked there as a barber-surgeon before marrying the previous barber-surgeon's daughter and being granted a licence to practise in 1843.[7] His wife had inherited 2,000 florins from her stepmother, and having paid the costs of the transfer of rights to the property, was left with just under 700 florins. The Patrimonial Court, acting on behalf of the aristocratic owner of the district, determined that Franz Xaver had to pay to be allowed to settle and practise as barber-surgeon since he did not fulfil the requirements for a dispensation.[8] It is not clear what that means. It may have been because he was born outside marriage, as was his wife. How he was able to train as a barber-surgeon is something of a mystery, as 'respectable birth' was one of the requirements for admission to apprenticeship.[9] Though being born outside marriage carried a stigma, it was by no means unusual. In Dachau in 1902, for instance, 231 children were born within marriage and 48 outside – that is 20 per cent.[10] The barbers living in rural areas did not have academic training but served a two-year apprenticeship and worked as journeymen for three years before taking their final examination. They supplied the only medical service available to most country people. They provided baths, acted as barbers, dentists, dressed wounds, set bones, bled, purged and sold ointments and lotions.[11] Franz Xaver Fleischmann married twice, his first wife having died one year after the birth of their son Aloys. Five children were born to the second wife, one of whom died in infancy. When the barber contracted tuberculosis, his two girls were sent at the ages of eight and six to a Munich convent dedicated to the service of the poor; the younger died of typhus there within two years; her father died three years later, in 1860, aged forty-nine. The elder girl, Anna, joined the order as Sister Genesia, where she fulfilled her duties as cleaner of the shoes for forty-two years before her death in 1912 after a long and painful illness.[12]

Fleischmann's father, a master shoemaker

Franz Xaver's son Aloys must have spent six years in school in Bergkirchen, served his apprenticeship (for which his father had to pay the master), become a journeyman for three to six years, done his five-year military service, and then taken his master examination. He was granted citizenship of Dachau on 3 January 1868. He married Magdalena

Deger on 14 April 1868. The house had been made over to her by her father, so Aloys was now a property owner through his wife, and so ful-filled the legal requirement for attaining citizenship in the town.

That year restrictions on trade were finally dropped, which meant the abolition of the craftsmen's guilds. In Dachau the shoemakers had been organised in a guild since 1561. Membership of the guild was obligatory to be allowed to practise the trade and attain citizenship. The guild regulated all levels of training from that of the apprentice to the master-craftsman; it regulated working conditions and pay, supervised the quality of the work done, and limited the number of apprentices to ensure the livelihoods of the members.[13] After the abolition of the guilds in 1868 anybody could set up a workshop. Times became difficult for the traditional craftsmen throughout Germany. As in Ireland, there was a crisis in agriculture in the 1880s and 1890s due to cheap imported American grain, which depressed prices[14] and caused serious hardship to small farmers – important customers for the craftsmen. Shoemakers were among the worst off of all craftsmen, but most were badly hit.

There is evidence that the Fleischmanns went through hard times in the 1880s. In an article written in 1905, the New York writer, Maude Barrows Dutton, describes a sad Christmas the shoemaker's son expe-rienced as a small child. She knew Fleischmann and must have heard the story from him:

> Soft snow was falling over the low red roofs and the cap-shaped church towers of Dachau, covering the village with Christmas white-ness. In a narrow street a child's face was pressed against the pane, and two sad eyes looked out through the storm to the house across the way, where the needled boughs of a Christmas-tree were silhou-etted against the drawn curtains. Now and again the curly head of a child danced by on the curtain, or a pair of tiny hands stretched up for a moment to light the candles, and each time the lump in the throat of the little boy who stood looking out into the night grew larger, and at last the hot tears sprang to his eyes and rolled down his cheeks. This year . . . there was no Christmas tree in his home, and his heart rebelled . . . until the next day, when, with his hand in his father's, he went out into the cold and stillness, followed the pathway down the village hillslope, and cut across the trackless fields to the woods. The storm had ceased, and the sunlight breaking through the clouds suddenly caught up tree after tree, changing their snow-decked branches into a blaze or iridescent colour. A hundred, a thousand Christmas-trees stretched out before the boy's eyes, and the pain in his heart was stilled.[15]

In 1884 – possibly the year of this incident – his father had the idea of founding a trade association for all the crafts in order to help them

withstand the onslaught of the new industrial manufacturing industries. The local newspaper of 1884 has not survived so unfortunately
there is no account of the founding, which would no doubt have provided a detailed description of the problems facing the crafts. In 1910
the Dachau newspaper reported extensively on the celebration of the
twenty-fifth anniversary of its founding, on the elaborate festivities to
which 400 guests were invited. In several speeches Fleischmann, the
senior master of the association, was commended for having been its
initiator, for having worked tirelessly in the cause of the crafts, and for
having helped to organise three craft exhibitions, in particular that of
1908, which was visited by Prince Ludwig,[16] the patron of the exhibition. Other speakers emphasised that it was due to the association that
there was now sufficient finance to provide adequate training for the
apprentices and thus a basis for a decent livelihood in the crafts; they
pointed out that the successful work of the association had given the
craftsmen back their self-respect and regained the esteem of the
public.[17] In 1908 in the local newspaper Fleischmann announced the
establishment of a vocational drawing school for apprentices where
they received tuition on Sunday mornings for a modest price.[18] He
remained active for his craft until the end of his life: in 1912 he participated in a referendum of Dachau shoemakers to decide whether a
compulsory shoemakers' association should be founded; he voted
against it and was the only one of the eighty-eight participants to add a
note explaining why he voted as he had. There were 118 shoemakers
altogether in Dachau and the surrounding area.[19]

Fleischmann was involved in many other fields besides those directly
related to his trade. He was given a medal for his years of service to the
Dachau Voluntary Fire Brigade; he was a founding member of the
craftsmen's health insurance association and, from 1900 until his death, a
member of the municipal welfare committee for the poor. He was an
elected member of the town corporation (*Gemeindekollegium*) from 1903
to 1908 and vice-chairman in 1908.[20]

In her book on the crafts in Dachau, Ingeborg Rüffelmacher writes
that the shoemakers were generally regarded 'as being especially open-
minded and imaginative people given to acting on their own initiative'.
In the fifteenth and sixteenth centuries they formed singing schools in
several towns in which they competed against each other as 'master-
singers'. The best known of these was the master-singer, poet and
shoemaker Hans Sachs of Nuremberg, the model for one of the central
characters of Wagner's opera *Die Meistersinger*. She reports that the old
Bavarian custom of 'hat-singing' was popular in Dachau, where three to
five singers vied with each other during their evenings in the inns to
produce witty verses to improvised tunes, the best being rewarded with
an expensive hat – hence the name.[21] Aloys Fleischmann was a sociable

man who enjoyed his *Stammtisch* or weekly evening in the tavern with colleagues and friends, and he was interested in music. He was a founding member of the Dachau *Liedertafel*, a choir established in 1879 by the schoolteacher, who conducted it. It was originally a male voice choir with thirty-one singers, most of them craftsmen. Many of the town's well-known painters joined, among them Hermann Stockmann, August Pfaltz and Hans von Hayek, as did the lawyer and writer Ludwig Thoma.[22] The name of the choir means 'Song Table': the choristers rehearsed in a tavern, where they treated themselves to good food, drink and talk after their exertions. Fleischmann's brother-in-law, Andreas Deger, was *Tafelmeister* or 'Master of Table Ceremonies'. The choir gave all sorts of public performances: they sang for celebrations of royal birthdays, to greet visiting dignitaries, to honour local citizens, at balls and receptions. In 1880 they travelled to a choral festival in Vienna, and in 1902 to one in Graz.[23] Their anniversaries were celebrated with style.

Fleischmann's choir membership and his work for the trade association brought him into contact with the artists who had come to live in Dachau. Some of them had developed an interest in the cultural heritage of the town and began to collect folk art, costumes, furniture and tools and to study and revive the traditions which were threatened with extinction due to the modernisation of rural life.[24] Many Dachau artisans were involved in this quest to record, preserve and pay tribute to the traditional crafts. A Museum Association was founded in 1903 by Hermann Stockmann (with Fleischmann's brother-in-law, Andreas Deger, on the first committee) to begin collecting artefacts for permanent exhibition. Due to the joint efforts of artists and artisans, the Dachau District Museum was founded in 1905 and housed in the castle.

During Fleischmann's time as senior master, the trade association organised three trade exhibitions: in 1887, 1901 and 1908. The 1908 one was a major event, which formed part of the celebrations of the 1100th anniversary of the founding of Dachau. Those celebrations should have taken place in 1905, but the municipal authorities had been unable to procure the necessary finance. The Museum Association and the Trade Association therefore had to disband their joint planning committee, which had consisted of six craftsmen (Fleischmann one of them), a brewer, a haulier, the doctor and the two painters, Hermann Stockmann and August Pfaltz. In 1908 the town decided to celebrate in style for a fortnight: to have a trade and agricultural exhibition, to establish an art gallery in the castle to house a permanent exhibition of Dachau painters, and to end with a *Volksfest* or funfair. The Crown Prince came to the town for the opening with an entourage of senior officials. He was greeted by a large assembly of royal officials, the corporation and council, the main families of Dachau, the nobility of the area, the clergy, various associations such as the Voluntary Fire Brigade, sports clubs, charity organisations – and by huge crowds. He visited the trade exhibition, the new art gallery and the museum before taking refreshments in one of the inns. Ten days later the funfair took place together with horse racing, an animal show, concerts and a torchlight procession. 60,000 people came to Dachau for the occasion by train, by bicycle and on foot.[25]

Fleischmann was involved in the organisation of the trade exhibition; indeed according to the newspaper report on the twenty-fifth anniversary of the trade association, it was primarily due to him that it took place and was so successful. The *Amper-Bote* of 10 September 1908 gave a long account of all the stands, including that of the shoemakers. It described the range of footwear exhibited, from the 'delightfully richly ornamented traditional women's shoes to the heaviest calibre of sturdy boots, the greatest variety being presented by *Meister* Fleischmann'. The 1908 celebrations were the culmination of many years of co-operation between the artists, the craftsmen and merchants of the town. Two institutions emerged from the joint efforts: the new art gallery making major works by Dachau painters available to the public, and the museum which documented and paid tribute to the traditional life and work of the local people.

FLEISCHMANN'S CHILDHOOD IN DACHAU

The earliest picture of Aloys Fleischmann was taken in his nursery school when he was about three years old, wearing a bib and looking none too happy. The kindergarten[26] was founded in 1883; that group of sixty children in the photograph may have been the first to be admitted. There is also a picture of him in his first class at school with the young teacher Lampl. Again, he is one of sixty boys, but now looks with assurance into the camera. Seven years of schooling were obligatory, beginning at the age of six or seven. He attended the boys' primary school, which was in the centre of the town next to the church and therefore called the *Kirchenschule* or church school.[27] There was no secondary school in Dachau at the time.

The boy must have often sat in his father's workshop, watching him and the apprentices. He might have gone along with his father to collect leather from the master-tanner up the hill, Jakob Rössler. It must have been interesting for him to watch the big cart-horses deliver their loads, to see the huge vats in which the leather was steeped for two years, and to watch the eight tanners at work. He saw the big cattle markets take place in the centre of the town, and the four seasonal markets attended by traders from all over the area. Everybody wore the distinctive Bavarian regional costume: Dachau had its own special tradition, which the visiting painters never tired of portraying. Children could play on the streets of the small town, the forests were not far away, the moorlands, the lakes and pools, the river and the weir offered a multitude of entertainments. As Aloys got older, he could explore the villages and hamlets of the area with their beautiful churches, and admire the monasteries and castles from outside. As a boy, he loved the brass bands that marched through the town on special occasions and made sure he stood nearby as they passed through the Augsburg Gate, the only remaining part of Dachau's mediaeval fortification, where the sound of the music was magnified tenfold as the band passed through the wide covered arch. The Gate was demolished in 1891 when he was eleven – his father had argued in vain in the town council against its destruction.[28]

Occasional glimpses of his childhood are to be found in his letters. From his bed, he heard the nightwatchman call out the hours as he passed through the street on his round of the town; sometimes the boy had terrifying nightmares in which a Dachau stone statue of a knight in armour appeared by his attic bedside complete with shining sword.[29] He once described how his mother taught him to count his blessings in the days when the family was going through very hard times, how on a dismal winter evening she comforted her dissatisfied little boy:

> 'Do you hear the storm that is howling outside? Do you hear the rain beating on the window and the slates falling off the roofs? And listen! how frightening the sound of the clock is as it strikes from the bell tower and resounds over the roofs through the dark night!
>
> 'You are sitting by the warm fire; you have food and a warm bed – do you realise what a blessing all that is? How many hundreds of poor people, who are even poorer than us, are outside in the storm and rain trying to find shelter? Who, when they have found a hut, have to beg for pity and food, have to move the hearts of strangers if they are to have a few hours' rest. Oh my immature, inexperienced boy, you don't know the world yet and how hard and cruel it is. Thank the good God, who still means well by us, and who has given us a warm fire and a warm bed!'[30]

The child went blind for a year after he had been vaccinated. During that time, his mother often brought him to the cathedral in Munich, where he forgot the pain in his delight at a set of small bells in the church which resounded to his touch. After he had undergone surgery, it was at Our Lady's altar of the cathedral that he was first able to see again.[31]

Fleischmann's attachment to his mother and his fond memories of childhood are evident in a letter written to her after he had left Dachau for Ireland, in which he assures her that he has not forgotten how she taught him 'the old poetic customs of our ancestors':

> Of course I remember how every year on the eve of the Epiphany, we two, I and you, and you and I went softly from top to bottom of

the house, from door to door, and how I, little rascal, with inimitable self-importance inscribed: K + M + B [for the three wise men, the kings from the East: Kaspar, Melchior, Balthazar] on the top of each door. Then the whole house was sprinkled thoroughly with holy water and swathed in enormous clouds of incense. The latter was in my opinion of greatest importance, as well as being the most entertaining part of the ceremony.

Of course I remember. I remember how we sat by ourselves in the bedroom on Sundays and feast days and how you read to me from the Bible, or how we chatted, and I tormented you with dozens of questions.

And if visitors came – ha, that was fun. I was soon put to bed, but the whispered conversation had often only just begun when from under the bedclothes an important statement or a question rang out. Or if father came home and brought me something.

I remember very specially the rosary on the eve of Candlemas[32] or on Christmas Eve when the little candles were lit and were so bright and beautiful. That did not make the prayers more fervent – how could it when every one of the many little candles had to be carefully minded at the same time? A quiet 'Oh!' escaped from my lips when, much too soon, often by the last Hail Maries or the Litany, some of the lights had already burnt dangerously low and, fluttering as if in pain at parting, their small souls were extinguished.

Some of these beautiful memories have sunk indelibly into my heart and gleam and sparkle there like stars in the heavens of my youth. I often lose myself, caught in dreams of that beautiful happy time, when every worry and some tears could take refuge in the folds of your apron; where all these big small things sought and found a haven, protection and comfort.[33]

Another memory was of being taken by his mother to the funerals of Wagner and King Ludwig II, Wagner's patron. Wagner died in February 1883 in Venice; his body was brought back to Germany and buried in Bayreuth. Aloys was then not quite three years old. King Ludwig drowned in Starnberg Lake in June 1886 shortly after having been declared insane:

I have a vague memory of seeing Wagner's coffin lit up by torches at the main railway station [in Munich]; I remember clearly and vividly the funeral procession of Ludwig II passing through Ludwig Street, his favourite horse draped in black following the coffin alone, the black clothes of the cloaked men, the weeping of the thousands, the sobbing of my mother for the king she adored, whereupon I wept copiously too until the sight of the splendid procession with kings, princes, courtiers, generals and so on transformed my pain into astonishment and allayed it. During his lifetime, I only saw him once (in Füssen) [in the Bavarian Alps] as he drove past with a man on horseback riding ahead – this man was of as much interest to me, a little lad, as was the king himself, who acknowledged our salutations. Two fairy-tale kings departed this world with them, leaving their colourful dreams behind to us.[34]

When he was eight he was brought to watch the centenary procession in honour of King Ludwig I of Bavaria, and vividly remembered the dramatic and disastrous ending of the celebration:

The splendid, indescribably magnificent procession passed through Ludwig Street, and ended with a calamity which caused a tremendous sensation. There were elephants in the procession, who took fright when a huge, fantastically formed dragon slowly crawled towards them, spewing fire. They fled, trampling people down in their panic and injuring them for life. Confusion, screaming, tumult and consternation ensued such as Munich had never before experienced. The escaped elephants were found after a long search in the old Royal Residence (Burgstrasse) where they were resting in the spacious hall, some of them sitting on the wide cool stone stairs. The frightened animals had been seeking shelter and, finding the extremely heavy oaken door locked, they pushed it open, smashing it like a matchbox. Having recovered and regained their normal calm, they allowed themselves to be led off like lambs by their keepers, who were attired as Moors.[35]

Fleischmann ends his account of the event by saying that he well knew that mediaeval hall with its faded frescoes on the high walls, as the wide marble staircase led to his uncle Simon's apartment, in which he had spent part of his youth: 'I loved the spacious old rooms with the splendid Blüthner grand piano, and revered my uncle and kindly aunt.' Dr Simon Trettenbacher must have had a very senior post in the administration to have lived in the former royal palace. Fleischmann may have been taken to live with the couple during the years of his parents' poverty.

All his life, Fleischmann was particularly attached to the feast of Christmas; in later years, it often brought back images of his childhood:

The sacred nights of Christmas are at hand! Memory is sitting next to me. I am wandering once again along the old paths and steps. The river Amper is beginning to freeze at the weir. I see myself again as a little fellow flying down Witches' Lane on the oak sledge. Or skating in elegant circles on the ice. I hear again the bells ringing from the high white steeples on Christmas Eve; am standing again under the little Christmas tree and the young heart is jumping for joy over an unforgettable magic box leading through extraordinary fairy-tale lands. Marvelling I once again see to the old crib in the church and throw the pennies saved with such difficulty into the tin box held by the coal-black Moor, who always nods his head in thanks. What a joy to be young! Everything is miraculous: the whole world enchanted. And then Midnight Mass, with the innumerable lighted candles, happy faces, heavenly singing accompanied by violins, trumpets, drums and organ! The great splendour at the altar, the solemnity of the ceremonies, the rising incense, the priests in their gleaming white and shimmering vestments, the splendidly deco-rated side altars. What magnificence in the middle of the night! Earth transformed into a paradise.[36]

He had recollections of being given treats by a neighbour, as he wrote to a Dachau acquaintance:

Your grandmother lived with her husband in the attractively painted little house opposite Rächl. She was always very fond of me right from my earliest years and showed her affection by inviting myself and my mother for tea with rum (no less!) on all my namedays, birthdays and feastdays. Those were wonderful afternoons for me, as the way to a small boy's heart goes through his stomach! She served us the choicest of cakes which she had baked herself, and wonderful tarts, pastries and biscuits, and I devoured all these delicacies like a hungry wolf. My mother often scolded me on the way home and said she was ashamed of me. I always resolved to restrain myself the next time, but I usually only remembered my good resolutions once the colourfully painted pictures on the plates stared up at me – devoid of their cake load! Then dear Frau Auer laughed heartily and said she was glad I was not suffering from 'lack of appetite', as she jokingly termed my childish gluttony. Now she is long since dead: but her kindness and the invitations to tea given to the privileged small boy have not been forgotten. Dead people whom we loved live on in our hearts as though untouched by the passage of time.[37]

In another account, he describes himself spending the days with his friends:

In my mind I often visit my old home and those years re-appear when the 'market', proud of its name, looked peacefully and stolidly from its height out into the world. That was in the old days when Mayor Scharl was still in office, when the character Jackl Strasberger cried out the public announcements of the councillors in the streets in a loud voice after ringing his bell, when schoolmaster Lampl swung his Spanish cane with gusto if he found an open Red Indian storybook hidden under the reader, when the steep Mountain Street was generally known as the 'Cow Mountain' and was in fact still enlivened by cows, when we boys romped and swam half the day long naked in the foaming weir, and on our way home roamed past the abandoned night watchman's hut on the Amper bridge and peeped in through the small half-blind windows. For on the wall next to the old clock with the broken face and the pendulum there hung the nightwatchman's horn, his spear and the wooden lanterns – all these things dating back to the days when Granddad married Grandma.[38]

But the boy often preferred solitude. The account of Fleischmann's youth in the New York journal, *The Bookman*, presents him thus:

> The boy grew up in the little village, spending long afternoons perched on the wall of the *Hofgarten* [palace garden], looking down over the unbroken moor to where the two towers of the Munich *Frauen-Kirche* [Our Lady's Cathedral] rise grey against the horizon; swimming the zig-zag course of the Amper river; hunting ghosts at midnight in the old castle on the hill; and wandering off for days at a time into the woods, where he told his heart out to the trees, and wrote his first songs, which he sang only to the birds.[39]

The writer, Maude Barrows Dutton, had become a friend of Fleischmann's and her report was based on extensive conversations.[40] However, it is hard to imagine that the solicitous mother of an only child would have allowed him to wander off at the dead of night, or to stay away from home in the woods 'for days at a time'. The exaggeration could have been his, or hers, or stemmed from a linguistic misunderstanding. Fleischmann himself gives a somewhat similar account of his solitary wanderings: in 1910 he wrote to his wife that he had just re-read Goethe's *Torquato Tasso*[41] and was reminded of his first encounter with the drama as a youth and of the inner turmoil that he struggled to come to terms with one evening

> . . . while walking in the direction of the sinking sun in my native place. At that time I chose the silent trees as my friends and trusted companions; the flames shot up over my head, and nobody could understand me. The fool's cap was not far removed from my lonely paths. In tears I searched and searched for the bridge, the links. And as today, I sought in vain. . . . I still vividly recall those places where my emotions overcame me and I found solace leaning against the splendid trunk of a huge tree; the indescribable impression remains with me to this day: the proud old trees – pines – and in the twilight the still visible silhouette of Dachau in the distance.[42]

STUDIES AT THE ROYAL ACADEMY OF MUSIC IN MUNICH

Fleischmann left school after seven years, probably aged fourteen; there is no documentation of what he did for the next two years. He might have started an apprenticeship with his father who, as a master shoemaker, was entitled to train young people – very often the craft was passed on from father to son. He sang in the church choir, and must have had a thorough musical training, because at fifteen he was commissioned by the Dachau Journeymen's Association (*Gesellenvereinigung*) to write a choral work.[43] The commission may have been influenced by his father, himself a choir singer and involved in all the craft organisations. But Aloys junior must have had music lessons as well as classes in theory and harmony, otherwise he could hardly have composed. He also knew Latin. His father might have arranged for his training; there were two relatively prosperous maternal uncles who might have taken the initiative – one of whom, like his maternal grandfather, Josef Deger, was an oboe player in the local territorial army band.[44]

The parish priest, Johannes Winhart, or the schoolmaster, Anton Ortner, probably supported him: both studied music at the seminary or college. Fleischmann liked and respected both, as he organised concerts in their honour when he had become church organist and choirmaster. He dedicated a work of his which was performed at the concert for Ortner in November 1904 to 'his dear former teacher in gratitude and admiration'. The schoolmaster played the violin in the orchestra for Fleischmann's first stage production in 1903.[45] Fleischmann's perform-ances were financed by a number of Dachau businesses, among them by the Ziegler family, wealthy brewers with a keen interest in the arts. Fleischmann had a standing invitation, not only to visit, but also to prac-tise on the grand piano and organ which they had in their villa; indeed he was treated almost as a member of the family.[46] They might have heard of his unusual talent when he was a boy, have paid for a teacher, and perhaps even helped him to get into the Royal Academy of Music in Munich. Maude Barrows Dutton writes that Fleischmann's songs were 'laid before'[47] the renowned composer and Academy professor, Josef Rheinberger. This could refer to Fleischmann's time as a student of Rheinberger's at the Academy when he submitted exercises and his own work, but it might also mean that somebody showed young Fleischmann's songs to the professor and that it was he who encouraged the youth to take up music and to apply for admission to the Academy. The Zieglers might have approached him: they had many friends in the Munich art world and would have been able to obtain access to anybody they wanted to meet. But the master-shoemaker might also have had the idea of sending his son's compositions to the master-musician. The youth might possibly have done so himself.

However it came about, in the autumn of 1896, when he was sixteen, Fleischmann passed the test for the preliminary two-year course at the Royal Academy of Music, which prepared students without a secondary-school music qualification for the Academy's entrance examination. His main instrument was the oboe; he also studied the piano, choral singing and harmony. In 1898 he passed the entrance examination proper to the Academy and began the full four-year course of studies. He studied the organ with the court organist Ludwig Maier, liturgy with the court conductor Josef Becht, counterpoint and composition with the composer Joseph von Rheinberger, score-reading and conducting with Hans Bussmeyer, who was also a pianist and Liszt pupil.[48] Among Fleischmann's minor subjects were piano and the history of music. In the course of his studies he read extensively in literature and philosophy, taking particular interest in Schopenhauer and Nietzsche.[49]

In 1896 there were only two young men from Dachau in higher education.[50] Fleischmann lived at home, travelling to Munich by train every day – there is no record of his ever having been registered as a resident of the city. He probably practised the organ in the church of St Jakob, as he was now training the boys' choir, deputising for the sick choirmaster and playing at the services.[51] On 25 June 1900 he conducted a choir concert in honour of the parish priest organised by the Catholic Journeymen's Association with choral music by Modlmayr, Kamerlander, Wagner and Franz Abt; on 19 March 1901 he conducted a choral concert for the same association in honour of St Joseph, with music by Mendelssohn, Schumann and Rheinberger.[52] But his main preoccupation was no doubt his studies. During these years '. . . each day found the boy before piano or organ for hours reaching into hours, and each night taking his place in the crowded ranks of the *Stehplätze* [standing room] in concert hall or opera house, learning his Bach and Mozart, Beethoven, Wagner and Brahms.'[53] He often walked the twelve miles home if he missed the last train, arriving in the small hours of the morning. The professors knew their students personally and kept a close eye on them, as Fleischmann describes: 'Once as I sat in the Court Garden Café with strawberries in front of me, Professor Becht passed and said laughing: "Don't eat yourself to death on that stuff – you still have a lecture to go to today!"'[54] That close relationship could have disadvantages. Fleischmann sometimes played in ensembles during the carnival season, which Academy students were strictly forbidden to do. On one such occasion, at a ball, he saw one of his professors waltz by close enough to recognise him; his teacher, however, was too preoccupied with his blonde dance-partner to notice him.[55]

In Rheinberger's composition class he won a prize and was sent by the Academy to Bayreuth to attend Wagner's operas *Tristan* and *The Ring of the Nibelungen*, living in quite unaccustomed luxury for the duration of his stay:

> I found friends there whom I had met during my studies: they were
> all foreigners, among them entertaining Kolukis from Athens. We
> lived like the nobility or indeed royalty at the expense of the state,

also enjoying the free-flowing funds of our colleague Jensen from Stockholm. We were kindly received in [the Wagner villa] Wahnfried by Liszt's daughter Cosima and [her son] Siegfried and paid our respects to the family regarded as saints in the world of music. We stood in homage at Wagner's grave; we were shown around the Festival Theatre and had the stage machinery explained to us.[56]

Fifty years later, in his account of that visit to Bayreuth, Fleischmann was still captivated by his experience of *Tristan*, that 'most splendid, most sublime, greatest, longest song of love ever created, which enthralls and enchants both heart and mind.'

Munich around 1900

During Fleischmann's youth, Munich was considered to be the cultural capital of Germany. It had a Royal family with a tradition of patronising the arts. The city had almost half a million inhabitants. Since his childhood Fleischmann had been familiar with the splendid Gothic, baroque and classical buildings. It was as a student that he got to know the state-maintained museums, art galleries, libraries and archives. He knew the city as a centre of the arts, and was perhaps less aware of the fact that it was a centre of industry. It was also an ecclesiastical centre, and he often attended high mass in the cathedral when the cardinal was present. The city was home to illustrious writers such as Thomas Mann and to a large community of painters. Fleischmann visited many exhibitions: those of the 'princes' among the artists, renowned traditionalist portrait painters such as Lenbach, but also modernists of the *Blaue Reiter* [Blue Rider] group such as Wassily Kandinsky, Franz Marc and August Macke, and he might have read of the many controversies between the various factions. He would have known that the Prince Regent had a particular interest in painting and liked to turn up unannounced in studios of painters of all types. He knew of the lively literary community, and heard of the storms caused by their more satirical representatives, two of whom ended up serving time in prison for blasphemy and for insulting the Kaiser.[57] He read the satirical journal *Simplizissimus,* which was produced in Munich, and *Die Jugend,* the journal of *art nouveau.* Munich was not only renowned for its impressive classical and modern architecture, for the priceless collections in its museums and galleries, but also as a centre of music. Though the citizens had been less than enthusiastic about King Ludwig II's boundless support for Wagner during his lifetime, after his death Wagner's works became a central part of the repertoire, the opera house performing them regularly before an enthusiastic public. Despite the fact that Munich audiences tended to be conservative, Fleischmann could nonetheless have heard works by Gustav Mahler, Anton Bruckner, Hugo Wolf and Richard Strauss. The court orchestra played in the opera house; in 1893 the Munich Philharmonic Orchestra was founded (for a time called the Kaim Orchestra after its founder), which was at first a private undertaking with its own concert hall. It gave regular concerts, some of which were *Volkskonzerte* with programmes of popular music, which drew large crowds, and also concerts with works by contemporary composers.[58]

FIRST POST: ORGANIST AND CHOIRMASTER IN
DACHAU'S CHURCH OF ST JAKOB

In 1901, the post of organist and choirmaster of Dachau's parish church of Sankt Jakob [St James] became vacant. At that time, Fleischmann had only completed three of the four years of his course of studies:[59] to be eligible he had to have graduated. His graduation certificate states that the Academy had agreed to allow him sit for his final examinations earlier than the regulations provided because of the position. His examiners were the two directors of the Academy, Stavenhagen and Bussmeyer, as well as Rheinberger and Becht. He received the best possible grade in all subjects, graduating with distinction in September 1901. He must have been one of the last students to have been examined by Rheinberger. On 28 November 1901 he was appointed to the post in St Jakob's and took up his duties on 1 January 1902 at the age of 21.[60]

Three days after his appointment, his revered teacher Rheinberger died. Fleischmann's grief was intense, and found expression in a lengthy epistle sent to his future wife: a letter of homage to the master. It reflects the mediaeval literature he been studying at the time, taking the form of a mystery play on the creation of outstanding talent and the high price to be paid for it. It is a song of praise to the musician, to his art as a divine process, his courage in withstanding enmity. It ends:

> Great Master, now you have gone: your playing is finished – the playing which for us was a revelation that carried us into a world now come to an end with you and of which only the blessed memory remains to us.
>
> Now you are listening to heavenly melodies, but your spirit is with us and your life and your enthusiasm for everything beautiful and noble will continue to live in us, together with in ineradicable gratitude: your memory will be sacred to us – dear Master, may you have beautiful dreams.

The new choirmaster seems to have plunged into his work with great zest. His first church service on New Year's Day brought him an appreciative notice in the local newspaper.[61] In June of the same year the paper describes a serenade, with songs by Mendelssohn and Rheinberger, which the church choir and its conductor gave for the parish priest outside his house to celebrate his birthday.[62] A few days later 'our active choirmaster' is commended for the Rheinberger Mass opus 126, which he performed with a three-part women's choir and organ accompaniment, and in November 'our tireless young choir-master' and his mixed choir are praised for an impressive performance of Rheinberger's Mass opus 159 and Bruckner's eight-part *Ave Maria*.[63]

Early compositions

According to Maude Barrows Dutton, Fleischmann began composing songs in his boyhood. In April 1903, for the first time, Fleischmann included a work of his own at a church service, at the mass for first communicants: a communion hymn for children's choir, organ and wind ensemble.[64] In 1904 he wrote an *Ave Maria* for voice and string orchestra (with a version for voice and organ), which he dedicated to Dora Ziegler, and which she performed 'most splendidly' as he noted on the manuscript.

He was also writing secular music, but as only some of the manuscripts are dated, it is not possible to give a chronology of his compositions. *Lieder aus der Jugendmappe* [Songs of Youth] was composed in 1898, the year he began the full course of studies at the Academy. Eight choruses for male voice choir were published in Vienna and also in Munich as opus 3, each one dedicated to a friend and patron, among them the Ziegler family, Baroness von Moreau and Count von Saedt.[65] On 12 August 1904 he dedicated his song 'Schliesse mir die Augen beide' [Close Both Mine Eyes] to his friend Tilly Swertz. On 13 November 1904 his *Albumblatt für Violine und Klavier* [Album Page for Violin and Piano] was performed at a concert in honour of his former schoolteacher, Anton Ortner, and dedicated to him. This work is lost.

The Choir School

Fleischmann was to continue in his father's and uncle's footsteps in embarking on a series of innovations to create an infrastructure for music in Dachau; he was also to follow their example in co-operating with the artists and merchants of the town.

He felt that the condition of music in Dachau was not what could be expected of a town of its size, and set out to provide the opportunity for musical training both for adults and children. At the beginning of his time as choirmaster, in January 1902, he founded a choir school, or *Singschule,* for children, giving daily singing lessons in the two primary schools to ninety-three pupils: 240 classes per year.[66] In the autumn of that year, he decided to expand the school and to provide singing tuition for adults. In the newspaper article announcing this, the public was invited to apply for auditions.[67] The school was a private association, with five Dachau citizens on the board[68] and Fleischmann the musical director. Because of the financial support given by these men, and later by the town council, tuition was at first given completely free of charge.[69] In December 1903, Fleischmann submitted a fifteen-page petition to the town council and corporation outlining the curriculum for the three courses given in the school. He wrote that, after almost two years, he now had three courses for girls and two for boys, with altogether a hundred children from the fourth to the seventh class being given six lessons a week. He makes three requests: firstly the assignment of a quiet room for the singing classes in the boys' primary school as the previous accommodation was quite unsuitable; secondly permission to take a fee of ten *pfennig* [pence] per month from each pupil in order to build up a music library and to save for a harmonium; thirdly that he be given appropriate payment for the annual examinations and for the additional work with the adults. His requests were granted.[70]

The origin of Fleischmann's nativity plays

Fleischmann had at this time become engrossed in the history and cultural heritage of Bavaria; his studies were to bring about a decisive development in his career. In August 1901 he stayed with relatives near Nuremberg, visited ruined mediaeval sites nearby and meditated in a lengthy epistle to his father on life in the mediaeval period, on the cruelties and violence which had led to the devastation of the area.[71] His interest in the Middle Ages was not sentimental or nostalgic. The letter he wrote a few months later to Tilly Swertz on the death of Rheinberger shows that he must have been reading ancient myths and mediaeval mystery plays, which he uses to pay tribute to his master. The parish priest may have introduced him to the literary heritage of the countryside, to the Bavarian tradition of Easter and nativity plays and the Dachau tradition. Since the Middle Ages, such plays had been performed to bring the stories of the bible closer to the faithful. In Oberammergau, in the Bavarian Alps, passion plays were initiated after the town escaped an epidemic of the plague in 1633, the text probably written for them by the monks of the nearby Benedictine monastery of Ettal. The plays were put on every ten years; Fleischmann no doubt attended that of 1900 and possibly the previous one of 1890. The Dachau passion plays go back to the seventeenth century; in the eighteenth century the schoolmaster and organist Kiennast brought the performance from the church to the square outside the town hall. In 1763 the princely government banned the plays, but Kiennast ignored the prohibition and had the support of the town council in so doing. After Kienast's death, the tradition declined.[72]

When Fleischmann took up his post, the Dachau dramatic tradition had become a memory. He was to revive it during the next five years with a different genre: nativity plays. These were major undertakings and marked a new phase in his development as a composer. Maude Barrows Dutton recounts how the venture came about:

With the end of student days he went back to his home in Dachau to be the musical director and organist in the church of the little village, where spring and autumn, dawn and sunset, birth and death, were still miracles. The boy had grown to manhood, but much of the child lingered yet in his nature, and sent him tramping through the woods for the first spring wild flowers or skating at moonlight on the black ice of the forest pool. Thus it was that with the approach of Christmastide there came over him the memories of that night long ago, the dusk, the storm, and the Christmas-tree across the way. The memory and the rebellion cost him sleep and long hours of dreaming, but finally from it was born the Krippenspiel at Dachau, the Manger Plays for the children of this Bavarian village at Christmastide.

In the annals of the village in the tenth century it stands written that there was given yearly at Dachau a passion play, and perhaps it was but the reincarnation in Aloys Fleischmann of this old dramatic spirit that led him to create his Manger Plays, and, quite unknown to himself, present them in the hall that stands now on the same spot where the Bürger Theater long since crumbled into ruins. This same dramatic spirit Herr Fleischmann found, too, was dominant in the children of the village, and it is no small part of his genius that he in no way sought to implant in his group of little players an outside polish, either of word or gesture, but rather to foster the instinct he found awaiting his touch.

Three years ago [in 1902] he called together a group of the village children, and, feeling his way, worked out with them the dramatisation of a fairy tale. The delight pictured on their faces and the response of their spirit to his, set his imagination afire, and the approach of the next Christmas found him again with the boys and girls about him listening as he read them the story of an old Miracle Play from the sixteenth century, and played them his music, into which he had woven the old hymn *'Heilige Nacht'* [Silent Night].

How contagious is the joy of children! The story of the *Krippenspiel* [nativity play] that they were to give at Christmas time spread through the village. It stirred the art colony that was found in Dachau, the Barbizon of Bavaria. Rumours of it even reached as far as Munich. Thus it was that in the third year, the composer, seeing ever higher than he could build, looked about and found others awaiting to help him.[73]

First Children's Festival and nativity play: Sonnenwende, 1903

For the following season, he decided to put on a dramatic Christmas tale in four acts entitled *Sonnenwende* [Solstice]. The text was by Anton Kohl, a priest from Ingolstadt, who had written it for his school; the music by Michael Haller was for three-part female choir, and was arranged for string orchestra by Fleischmann. He had rehearsed for months with sixty children of the choir school, aged from five to four-teen, and with forty adults in the choir and orchestra. This first Dachau *Kinderfestspiel* [Children's Festival] was performed on 1 January 1903, exactly one year after his appointment as church choirmaster and organist. Fleischmann was given financial support by Eduard Ziegler, the brewer, who was an accomplished zither player;[74] the painters Hermann Stockmann, Hans von Hayek, August Pfaltz and Hans Müller spent days producing the scenery; Frau Ziegler and the painters' wives made the costumes which the artists had designed, the children coming to the Ziegler villa for their fittings, which for weeks had been the headquarters of the undertaking. The newspaper reports that Dachau's most distinguished painter, Adolf Hölzel, played the violin in the orchestra, as did Fleischmann's former schoolmaster, Anton Ortner, and several members of the Royal Academy of Munich. Frau Ziegler sang some of the solos, and an Irish relative of the Rössler family, Fräulein Tilly Swertz of Cork, played the harmonium. The choir consisted of the ladies of the church choir and members of the Munich Court Theatre choir. The audience was enchanted and thanked the performers with thunderous applause; the evening concluded with one of the girls reciting a poem of thanks to all involved, the last stanza dedicated to the director, who was honoured with a laurel wreath.[75] The reporter claimed that the performance could be compared with the Oberammergau Passion Play. Two of the young Dachau actors involved in the play were to make names for themselves in later years: Anton Goldhofer became a distinguished violinist[76] and Agnes Straub, the girl who presented the wreath, a much acclaimed actress who specialised in classical roles and had her own theatre in Berlin for many years. Her performance at this play so delighted a number of court actors in the audience that they pre-vailed upon her father to allow her to study acting.[77]

Second Children's Festival and nativity play: Ein Altes Weihnachtsspiel, 1904

Fleischmann's 1903 venture was highly successful, attracting a large Dachau audience as well as many artistic visitors from Munich and appreciative reports in the local papers. This encouraged him to put on two plays the following January. One was a new year play by Ludwig Stark (a Munich professor) with music by E. Renner; the other a six-teenth-century nativity play adapted by Josef Beer, for which Fleischmann composed the music: *Ein Altes Weihnachtsspiel für Kinderstimmen, Harfe, Chor und großes Orchester* [An Old Nativity Play for Children's Voices, Harp, Choir and Large Orchestra].[78] This time the orchestra had thirty-six players, the Dachau musicians being augmented by members of the Munich Philharmonic Orchestra, the Dachau church choir by members of the Munich Court Theatre choir. Hans von Hayek, August Pfaltz and Hermann Stockmann produced the scenery, designed the costumes, and decorated the hall without charging a fee; the mill-owner Eduard Wittmann donated flowers and shrubs. The hall for the three performances was given free of charge by the owner and lease-holder, electricity for lighting donated by the municipal authority. The costs came to 2,000 marks; the brewer Eduard Ziegler, the newspaper owner and publisher Franz Mondrion and Hermann Stockmann guaranteed the venture against loss, a necessary measure as the tickets had to be reasonably priced to allow the people of Dachau to attend.

The national press was well represented at the performances. The Leipzig paper *Illustrierte Zeitung* of 14 January 1904 gave a detailed report reproducing two illustrations by Hermann Stockmann; it began with an outline of the history of drama in Dachau as the background to the current production:

> The love of drama, and in particular of religious drama, to which the Upper Bavarian people is so prone, was imbued with new life by the Dachau painters when in January of last year they put on a nativity play by Kohl. Its success spurred them on. This year they have revived a sixteenth-century folk-play, a 'Christ-Child Comedy', the main motifs of which were used in various plays in south-eastern and north-eastern Germany in the eighteenth century. The old version edited by Joseph Beer was taken for the performance. Choirmaster Alois Fleischmann, a gifted musician who was born in Dachau, provided the music, with effective compositions for children's voices, harp, choir and orchestra; the painter Hermann Stockmann took charge of the scenery, devoting loving care to the task and making the very most of the decorative aspect without losing sight of those great sublime features with which the old masters ennobled their heartlifting religious pictures.

> More than a hundred guests, among them many of the most eminent personalities of Munich's artistic circles, arrived on 3 January for the festive occasion, walked through snow-covered Dachau, past the white-frosted trees and the icy river Amper to the hall, which was already fairly crowded with Dachau men and women, the most 'genuine' of these having already taken their seats in the gallery, wearing wide pleated skirts of heavy cloth, bodices ornamented with silver, and lace bonnets covering part of the forehead. The Dachau Christ-Child (shown in our picture in his delightful costume) kept His word 'that everybody would see a very special and really lovely performance'. The introduction, a poetic New Year play called *The Turn of the Year* by Ludwig Stark, at once showed the evocative and picturesque art of Stockmann, assisted by Pfaltz and von Hayek, both members of the Dachau colony of painters. And every heart in the hall was moved by the festive solemnity.

(Fleischmann's first name is given in the usual German form: Alois. It was only in Ireland that he came to use the form more familiar to Irish people accustomed to the name of St Aloysius. His father, however, spelled his name 'Aloys'.)

Not everybody was enthusiastic about this novel form of folk-art. A Berlin newspaper, the *Berliner Tagblatt* of 7 January 1904, gave considerable space to an account of the performance, noted that the celebrated artist Professor Benno Becker and the architect Professor Thiersch had travelled from Munich to attend the play, but the report was in the main critical. It found Fleischmann's music distasteful, reminiscent of 'the bombastically ornate pomp and circumstances of Jesuit compositions à la Palestrina'. While the author conceded that the play on the whole dealt with the sacred subject with appropriate gravity, he regarded the 'rough peasant boys, glowing with health, acting out their roles to their hearts' delight, as somewhat grotesque'. The local newspaper, the *Amper-Bote* [River Amper Messenger], rebutted this criticism vociferously, defending composer and children. It ended its account of the plays with a tribute to Fleischmann, listing the many tasks he had to attend to in co-ordinating and overseeing the entire effort that went into the performances. The article concludes: 'Herr Fleischmann indicated wordlessly yet most eloquently what had motivated him to undertake this effort when, on receiving a laurel wreath at the end of the last performance, he took it and laid it at the feet of the infant in the manger.'[79]

It was, no doubt, due to the widespread publicity and remarkable success of the Children's Festivals and nativity plays that Fleischmann was given the distinction of being presented to the Prince Regent the following month, as the paper reported:

> We have heard that our choir master, Mr Alois Fleischmann, was presented to His Royal Highness Prince Regent Luitpold by the Imperial Councillor Ferdinand von Miller during the opening of the Schwind exhibition in the Artists' Residence in Munich. His Highness greeted Fleischmann most graciously and expressed his appreciation of the fact that there were still people who promoted and cultivated popular education and folk art so successfully in such a small place that they won the attention and admiration of the widest circles.[80]

Fleischmann, together with Stockmann, had been invited to lunch with the Prince Regent at his residence in Munich the previous week,[81] or as he put it in a letter to his friend: 'I was invited to pay my respects and make my deepest bow, which for me as a loyal monarchist was not only an honour but a pleasure.' He also noted that at the von Schwind exhibition, the kind words of the aged prince had been audibly prompted by von Miller.[82]

Miss Tilly Swertz

Some months later, the newspaper had more news about honours awarded in the capital to people connected with Dachau:

> At the last concert of the semester on the 14th of this month, the Royal Academy of Music in Munich had a prize-giving ceremony honouring particularly talented pupils, both male and female. Scholarships and medals were awarded. We are glad to be able to announce that among the students honoured with a medal there was a student who is a close relative of one of the families of this town. The student is Miss Tilly Schwertz [*sic*] of Cork in Ireland. She is a niece of the master-tanner, Mr Xaver Rössler, is in the women's advanced department, and was awarded a bronze medal. 109 women students are studying in this department.[83]

Tilly Swertz had been awarded the medal for her organ playing at her final examination. She had come to Munich to study at the Academy in the autumn of 1901. Her father, Hans Conrad Swertz, had held the post of church organist in Dachau from 1878–9. He was a native of Geldern in Rhine-Prussia, born there in 1858 as the son of a primary schoolteacher. He studied church music in Rome and in Regensburg (often given its Latin name, Ratisbon). During his first year in Dachau he fell in love with the daughter of the master-tanner Jakob Rössler, who was less than enthusiastic about the prospect of his only girl marrying an impecunious musician and a Prussian to boot.[84] So in 1879 Swertz accepted a post in St Vincent's church in Cork;[85] the following year he married Walburga Rössler. He became organist at Cork's Cathedral of St Mary and St Anne in 1890. He taught the organ, singing, composition and advanced harmony at the newly established Cork School of Music; he gave recitals, composed and had a number of choral works published in Britain.[86]

Swertz and his wife had nine children. The second girl, Mathilda – called Tilly – studied the piano and organ with her father and at the Cork School of Music, and was deemed good enough to be sent at the age of nineteen to Munich to study both instruments. She passed the entrance examination to the Royal Academy of Music in September 1901 and was accepted as an organ student by Josef Becht and for piano classes by Bernhard Stavenhagen, the director of the Academy and Franz Liszt's last pupil. Women had been admitted to the Academy since 1890 but were taught separately until 1918. When Stavenhagen left the Academy in 1904, she studied with Berthold Kellermann, also a Liszt pupil, until she graduated with the highest grades for organ in June 1904 and for piano in June 1905. She had been invited every year to play in the Academy's public concerts; in her final semester she played the Schumann Piano Concerto with the Academy orchestra conducted by Felix Mottl.[87]

During the first weeks of her stay, probably while she was visiting her mother's family in Dachau, she must have met the Academy graduate who had that year been appointed organist at St James's church – the post her father had held before he left for Ireland. In November 1901 he dedicated his long letter about Rheinberger to '*Meiner lieben*

Freundin' – 'To my dear friend'. She played the harmonium in the first nativity play of January 1903; Fleischmann's composition for the play of January 1904 was 'Dedicated in friendship to Miss Tilly Swertz'. In August he dedicated a song to her; that summer he visited Cork, probably to meet the family and to ask her father for her hand in marriage. If that was the reason for the visit, it was unsuccessful: no engagement was announced.

Third Children's Festival and nativity play: Die Nacht der Wunder, 1905

With the third nativity play, *Die Nacht der Wunder* [The Night of Wonders], Fleischmann achieved his greatest success in Dachau. The play was based on a Christmas legend by the Swedish writer of children's stories, Selma Lagerlöf (to be awarded the Nobel prize for literature in 1909), which had been published in translation in Munich in 1904.[88] It has a moving introduction in which the narrator recounts how one Christmas Day she and her grandmother are alone in the house, she being too young to go to church and her grandmother too old to do so; to alleviate their sadness, the grandmother tells her the story of miracles that occurred on the night of Christ's birth. The narrator underlines that her memory of the story is inextricably linked with the memory of the pain she suffered on the death of her grandmother when, with the dead body, all the tales and songs of her childhood left the house in a black coffin, never to return. Lagerlöf's Christmas tale can be imagined as taking place in a rural European locality – this together with the memory of Fleischmann's own sad childhood Christmas will probably have been the reason for the choice of the text which he and a Munich poet, Franz Langheinrich, the editor of the Munich journal *Die Jugend*,[89] decided to use as the basis of the play.

The third Christmas play was to be by far the biggest and most complex undertaking. For the first time it was not a purely local venture, which led, also for the first time, to some tensions and conflicts. It turned out to be costly. Fleischmann brought the Munich Philharmonic Orchestra to Dachau to support the local orchestra, the professional musicians being paid both for rehearsals and performances – they received five marks per head for each rehearsal. The Dachau choir was again joined by the choir of the Court Theatre, professional singers who had to be paid. The fees for the guest musicians came to 1,300 marks.[90] The municipal authorities were so short of money that they could not afford to celebrate the eleven-hundredth anniversary of the founding of Dachau, and were unable to provide funding for the nativity play. Guarantees against loss were once again given by friends and supporters: Stockmann, Mondrion and Ziegler were joined by the painter August Pfaltz, the brewer Adolf Hörhammer and the mayor Anton Mayerbacher (in a private capacity). All the

Dachau people involved gave their services free of charge. It was a huge communal effort. Stockmann and Pfaltz produced all the scenery, illustrations and costume designs for nothing, their wives again did the sewing and fittings for the children, ten citizens played in the orchestra without pay – among them an accountant, a brewery owner, a master clockmaker, a lawyer, a painter, a master saddler and three teachers. A mill-owner, a carpenter and a farmer donated the flowers, shrubs, and Christmas trees to decorate the hall; four young ladies spent days making garlands; six young men looked after the box-office and stewarding; the mayor's family business sold the tickets without taking a commission. The electricity company did not charge for the lighting and the Dachau paper factory made a donation of 100 marks.[91]

Lagerlöf's prose text was adapted by Franz Langheinrich, who added a verse prelude and epilogue, and rendered the dialogue in the Dachau dialect. A programme with the text and illustrations by Stockmann was printed and distributed to the press. Langheinrich insisted that it be done by a Munich company with which he had business contacts and which had promised him to do it free of charge; in fact it ended up costing a considerable sum. The Dachau publisher and printer, Mondrion, was incensed that he, a sponsor of the event, had been by-passed for the printing contract, and refused to pay what he regarded as unnecessary and excessive costs.[92] His conflict with Langheinrich led to some rather harsh critiques being published in Mondrion's paper, the *Amper-Bote*, probably written by Mondrion himself:[93] the criticism focused on the choice of text and the adaptation. Langheinrich was unwilling to have his text discussed and asked Fleischmann not to let anybody see the manuscript.[94]

The young conductor also had his tribulations with the orchestra from the capital. In a letter nearly thirty years later to his son about the difficulties beginners can have with professional orchestras, Fleischmann described his first rehearsal with the professional Munich orchestra:

> An orchestra never follows a young conductor! Indeed, they take pride in being as uncooperative as possible and joke about it afterwards among themselves. I recall an incident during the first rehearsal of my 'Night of Wonders' with the Harmonic Orchestra (Concert Orchestra) which confirms what I've just said. Towards the end of the rehearsal, the first horn kept playing f instead of f sharp. I thought it was a mistake and called out to him. I had them repeat it, but in vain – he played f. Time was pressing and I had to try and get finished. Once again I heard, instead of f sharp, f, and in addition yodelling! and I saw the gentlemen of the brass grinning furtively when I didn't rap on the rostrum and stop them. The rehearsal was over. The musicians packed up their instruments and the first horn was about to do likewise. I felt some disquiet as I had to an extent been made a fool of in the eyes of the orchestra. Suddenly an idea

shot through my mind. I went back to the rostrum, apologised for having extended the rehearsal somewhat, promised extra remuneration on that account and thanked them once again. To my regret, I said, there was one gentleman in their renowned orchestra from whom I had to withhold my thanks – everybody looked up with interest – namely the first horn. I didn't know the gentleman's name, I continued; I would call him 'Mr F' because he plays f so incessantly beautifully, and incidentally we don't go in for yodelling in Munich – the mountains is the place for that, for God's sake – roars of laughter. I said I would have to ask the gentleman to keep playing the last page until the fs turned into f sharps. The horn player became cherry-red in the face with anger and refused. (He spoke north German dialect: so I had hit the nail directly on the head.) He didn't have time. 'Very well, then,' I countered, 'I shall see to it that you don't get paid a penny for the rehearsal (5 marks).' Most of the members of the orchestra were standing around in groups, their instruments under their arms, eager to see what would happen. It was an embarrassing situation. The foxy-haired man, who was tall as a tree and about ten years older than I, slowly blew the water out of his instrument; still standing, he got the spittle out of both sides of the mouthpiece, clattered around on the valves, probably trying to work out what he should do. I waited patiently, and at last he sat down slowly at his desk – and played his part flawlessly.

This extremely risky and saucy lesson, which had been inspired by anger, could have been my undoing and cost me my neck. (In my time the orchestra played under Winderstein, Mottl, Weingartner, Zumpe.) If he had been a popular member of the orchestra, which thanks be to goodness he wasn't (I only heard about that afterwards, after the incident), the orchestra would have taught me a lesson which I would have felt in my very bones. When the storm piece was over, I praised his exquisite tone, his brilliant technique, and said to him that a 'mature artist' like himself should not play such tricks on a beginner. We parted friends: I shook hands with him. The groups broke up, their goodbyes were friendly and very respectful, and so everything ended satisfactorily. Leber, the solo violinist, now court conductor in Dresden, came down through the desks to tell me that they all liked the music very much and he warmly wished me success. All subsequent rehearsals went smoothly.[95]

So too, on the whole, did the performances. They were attended by many visitors: '. . . at all three performances of the play crowds came from Munich, until the road winding up the hill from the station was black with people, many of whom had to be turned away from the door for lack of room in the theatre.'[96] But there were also hitches, which Franz Mondrion's *Amper-Bote* described extensively. It complained that the time of the performance was changed only a few days before the opening, that the play did not last as long as the programme announced, that there was breaks when there was no music, that the stage curtains did not close properly, that the acoustics in parts of the hall were poor.[97]

The play was widely and on the whole very favourably reviewed in Munich, Berlin, Leipzig and Graz; visiting writers from London, Italy and New York deemed it of interest for their readers at home. All the critics found the scenery delightful; most were moved by the simplicity and naturalness of the forty children from the Dachau choir school – the only adult was the Florentine painter, Orelli, who played Joseph.[98] Where there was criticism, it came from close to home. A Munich paper, *Münchner Neueste Nachrichten* of 5 January 1905, regretted that Fleischmann had not simply arranged Christmas carols, and suggested that his music, inspired by Wagner and Liszt, was more suited to the concert hall than the nativity play and that furthermore only the bible or the old nativity plays should have been used and not a modern legend. That same paper published a long article the following day celebrating the performance as a new departure for the stage, paying tribute to the natural artistry to be found among the common people. The *Amper-Bote* had the last word on 14 January 1905 demanding, for the next time, a text closer to the people, who played such an eminent role in putting on the show.

These conflicts must have been unexpected and upsetting for Fleischmann. But he had the satisfaction of hearing great praise from the most competent critics – his eminent Academy professors who came to Dachau for the play, as Fleischmann described in a letter to his son some thirty years later:

> Kellermann, Becht, Maier praised the orchestra after the performance and said it sounded wonderful. Leber actually went so far as to say that he had not heard the orchestra play better under Weingartner than under my almost totally inexperienced hand. Dr Zumpe, who was then very old and taught the history of music at the University and at the Academy (he was once conductor of the court orchestra), was not sparing in his praise and he told me that Lachner said to him when he began: 'D'y know, Doctor, what it takes to be a good conductor? A big portion of cheek. But don't get me wrong: a cautious portion! That keeps the lads on their toes: keeps them fiddling and stops them tattling.' Laughing loudly at the good joke from his youth, he took his leave and thanked me for 'the wonderful evening'. He was then still the music pope of Munich, had a witty, sharp pen, and his operas and his 'Orchestral Cycle' were held in high esteem and unforgettable to me, as was the old gentleman himself, whose lectures, though he shook with age, sparkled with wit and amusing anecdotes.[99]

Maude Barrows Dutton describes Fleischmann as falling prey to a sense of dejection once the hard work, strain and elation of the performance were over:

The early grey twilight was falling over Dachau some three days later, and the young composer had closed his piano in despair and rushed down the stairs into the street. With the freedom from rehearsals and the excitement of the performance now outlived, he could see only the problems confronting future years and the failure ever to reach the border line of his ideal.

As he wandered down the hill's slope, the school door opened and a laughing, shouting crowd of boys tumbled out about him. In their midst he recognised three faces, swarthy yet, of the proud kings . . . who had absolutely refused to return to their natural selves again. A score of caps came off as the little urchins noticed the passing figure wrapped in his long cape and a smile broke over his solemn face as he responded with many a *"Grüss dich Gott"* [May God greet you]. His step grew elastic again, and he threw back his head to watch for the evening star just rising. The song that he had been trying in vain to catch all day sang itself calmly and sweetly within his ear. As he strolled along the familiar pathway to the woods, memory after memory flashed by. He saw himself a boy again, his hand in his father's, and felt again that pain deep in his heart because he had no Christmas-tree, and then there welled up within him the music of his *Krippenspiel*, born of this pain. He thought again of the children, the shepherd lads telling their riddles about the fire, and the dark-faced little princes coming across the moor. He saw again the little fellows who refused to have the black washed off their faces, and he heard the voices of the children as they pleaded with him after the play to promise them a part next Christmas. And then his thoughts spanned the years to come, when those boys should be grown to manhood. He saw their faces heavy and stolid now, their shoulders bent, their hands hard and callous as they went out to their work at sunrise and returned silent and weary in the evening. And he saw them turning back to their boyhood again as he so often did to his, particularly at Christmastide, seeing again that dim room, hearing the music and the simple story of 'The Night of Wonders'.

He paused for a moment as he stood before the forest pool looking down into its silent depths. A tiny pebble slipped from his fingers and fell into the dark water. He watched it sink, and then saw the circles rise upon the surface, one around the other, each one larger then the one before, until the last swelled and blended with the shadows of the pool, and then he knew again that a lifetime is but as the smallest inmost circle, and that only in the passing of generation into generation can one measure how his art has spanned the distance between human life and the boundaries of his ideal.[100]

Fleischmann's life had changed with the success of *The Night of Wonders*. As well as coming to terms with dissension among those involved in the plays, he found himself negotiating with impresarios on the issue of the rights to the plays. Emil Geyer, director of a theatre in

Düsseldorf and in Berlin, wanted to produce *The Night of Wonders* both in Düsseldorf and in Berlin for Christmas 1906, but Fleischmann refused permission as he would have had no control over the productions. Geyer tried to reassure the composer that the music would not be affected by his plans, guaranteed him 500 marks in royalties and held out the prospect of Fleischmann earning thousands and becoming famous overnight. Langheinrich was all in favour of the idea and urged Fleischmann to seize the opportunity on the grounds that the play would then be performed in many other cities and that this would create interest in his other compositions.[101] Fleischmann intended to publish the music and text, but Langheinrich had his own plans for publication. He did not wish to use the illustrations Stockmann had done for the play, but wanted to commission new ones by the painter Richard Pfeiffer. Because of these differences of opinion, nothing came of the project.

The reviews of the nativity plays and the publication of his choruses led to all sorts of new contacts, among them the acclaimed ballad writer and poet Agnes Miegel:

> Once, after a performance of one of the Dachau nativity plays, a pretty, bright-eyed young lady, slender as a reed, came up and introduced herself as Agnes Miegel of Königsberg. One could hear straight away from her speech, but also see from her manner, that she was from East Prussia. She wanted to know whether I would 'musically adorn' poems of hers. She said she did not have the poems with her, and asked whether we could meet in Munich to discuss the matter. We met several times. Her poetry was excellent, with regard to content as well as form. We were both very young, and we also spoke of other things. She invited me to Grünwald, where she was staying with an aunt. From there we often went off into the Isar valley. Shortly afterwards, Luise von Kobell offered me her father's poems and her own, as did Karl Stieler's daughter and others. A mixture of pride, shyness, awkwardness and a large portion of naivety accompanied me in this unexpected form of success.[102]

A further development seemed to herald a breakthrough for the young composer and the beginning of a brilliant career. Adolf Hölzel suggested to influential friends that Fleischmann should be invited to bring *The Night of Wonders* to Berlin. It was to be a charity performance, the orchestra of the Royal Theatre playing free of charge for the occasion. The president of Berlin's Academy of Art issued the invitation once Richard Strauss had approved Fleischmann's score:[103]

> The President of the Academy of Art in Berlin, Albert Dietrich, invited me to repeat *The Night of Wonders* there for the benefit of the de Ahna Trust. Richard Strauss, who was the son-in-law of General de Ahna, was involved and asked to see the score of the work to be

performed, which he received, saw, approved and even praised. In Berlin I had to present myself to the director of the Royal Theatre, Graf von Hochberg. I appeared before the great man armed with letters of recommendation from Oskar von Müller [cabinet secretary of Ludwig II], Gabriel von Seidl [the architect of Munich's museums], the court preacher von Hecher, Leo Samberger [distinguished Munich portrait painter] and Perfall [composer, Ludwig II's theatre director, founder of Wagner festival]. Everything went as hoped and I was charmed by his kindness. . . .

The old gentleman, Dietrich, received me with great warmth, told me about his teacher Robert Schumann, his experiences with Brahms and his operas and how he worked. He brought me around to his friends, from one splendid house to the next until late into the night. I enjoyed the generous hospitality and my young life to the full.

And so the time passed, and the agreed deadline was missed. I took it with a light heart. Friend Stockmann, however, who was already all set and looking forward to the performance in Berlin, was full of reproaches. On my return I was greeted as: Berlin rake, idler, night-owl, waster, even numbskull and clown, and a 'dreamer devoid of ambition'. (The latter was a saying coined by my teacher Rheinberger, which I used to hear if I hadn't prepared sufficiently well – Stockmann knew that and made stinging use of it.) When I flared up, he became more conciliatory and said it would all be postponed until the following year.[104]

Marriage to Tilly Swertz

Tilly Swertz graduated from the Royal Academy of Music in June 1905. In August she and Aloys Fleischmann announced their engagement. On 13 September 1905 they were married in Dachau's church of St James. The wedding took place despite the disapproval of the bride's father: the musician who had been considered an unsuitable match for the daughter of the master-tanner now regarded the son of a master-shoemaker as unsuitable for his daughter. But Tilly followed her mother's example and ignored the patriarch's wishes.

The couple had a somewhat unpropitious start to their married life. Fleischmann disliked fuss and crowds and had decided that the ceremony in the church was to be as simple as possible, with only the immediate family attending. But as soon as the bridal couple entered the church at nine that morning, the lights came on, the organ pealed out, the large church choir burst into song, and the couple saw that the church was full. Fleischmann was sure his wife had arranged this behind his back, and did not talk to her all day. In fact she was just as surprised as he was. They were married by an Irish priest, Fr John P. Donaghey.[105] The second mishap took place that evening. The couple had been invited to spend their honeymoon in Baron von Moreau's home, Schloss Kleeberg, close to Passau on the Austrian border. After their arrival, when dusk was falling, the sons showed them around the castle and led Tilly up to the belfry, telling her that it was the custom for the ladies to remove their hats. She did so, and to her horror found that bats which had been disturbed by the light were whirring around and became entangled in her hair. The Baron and Baroness were as indignant as Aloys Fleischmann when they found Tilly in hysterical tears. But the grandchildren were told that the rest of the stay was a happy one.

The School of Music

Just before his marriage, Fleischmann submitted a petition to the Dachau council and corporation for permission to found a school of music, lengthy extracts of which were published in the *Amper-Bote*; a month later he requested permission to have repairs done on the rooms of the boys' school used for the music teaching. In October 1905 the council approved his plans and agreed to finance them.[106] The plan to establish a school of instrumental music teaching had been announced at the founding of the Music and Drama Society earlier that year. Fleischmann now publicly explained the need, outlined his aims, and presented a detailed account of the curriculum.

The picture he gave of Dachau's musical life was gloomy: nowhere else in Bavaria in a town the size of Dachau was there such a dearth of good music and so little interest in it. Most of the members of the local orchestra also sang in the church choir, so when he needed all his singers for a big work, he had to hire instrumental musicians. In order to prevent the demise of the folk art of music, a wide range of music teaching had to be made available. This, he underlined, would benefit church, schools, the public and the family. As all classes were voluntary, music would be taught and learnt with pleasure and bring joy, which would strengthen the young musicians' hearts and minds as gymnastics trains their bodies, give them inner peace and composure, balance their thinking and rational processes, thus empowering them in their ability to be joyful, creative and mentally strong. Dachau with its 6,000 inhabitants had gifted children who deserved to be given the opportunity to develop their talents. The number of good musicians the school of music could produce might be small but they could exercise a beneficial influence on the life of the town out of proportion to their number. Young people trained in this art are capable of enriching church services, of contributing significantly both to the artistic life of the municipality as well as to family life both in times of joy and of trouble and sorrows.

There was an elementary class open to everybody from the age of seven who passed a simple ear test. Admission to tuition in the advanced class depended on the outcome of an examination; both groups received instruction in musical theory. Tuition was given over eight months, with two classes per week in groups of not more than three pupils. The holidays were listed and included the last three days of carnival. Special provision was made for adults. Fleischmann was very concerned to ensure that children from poorer families could afford to learn an instrument. He managed to negotiate special conditions with a Munich music company, which agreed to provide all instruments at exceptionally low prices, and to accept payment by instalment. The school charged a fee of seventy pfennigs per class; this was regarded as an instalment payment on the instrument so that students who attended classes for a year only had to pay five marks to became the owner of their instruments. Fleischmann succeeded in getting three Munich court-orchestra musicians to give all classes except the theory classes, which he gave himself. In his application to the town council, Fleischmann underlines that this enterprise was not regarded by himself or his Munich colleagues as a business venture and that the court musicians understood their participation as an act of friendship and support for him in his efforts to give children of all classes access to the art of music.

Fourth Children's Festival and nativity play: Krippenbilder, *1906*

The last nativity play which Fleischmann was to direct in Dachau was performed three times in January 1906. It consisted of the prologue and final chorus of *Die Nacht der Wunder* followed by five crib scenes with biblical texts and music by Michael Praetorius. These were called *Krippen-Bilder zur Erhaltung der Dachauer Kinderfestspiele* or 'Crib Scenes to maintain the Dachau Children's Festivals', a title indicating that they were endangered. Because of financial constraints, the orchestra was smaller, but members of the Munich Philharmonic Orchestra and singers from the Court Theatre Choir played and sang with the Dachau musicians. As always, the children from the choir school formed the children's choir; Stockmann and Pfaltz created beautiful backdrops and costumes, and a bevy of willing helpers saw to the many tasks involved in the organisation and creation of a pleasant ambience for a big production. The director of the drama section of the newly founded Music and Drama Society gave the readings. The actors played to full houses, and the critics in the capital were enthusiastic.

The Dachau Music and Drama Society

The week after the final performance of *Die Nacht der Wunder*, a further important step was taken towards creating an appropriate organisational infrastructure for the cultural life of Dachau. The town by now had its art gallery, its museum, its museum association to support it, and its school of music. On 15 January 1906, a society was established to facilitate the financing and organisation of productions such as the nativity plays: the Musikalisch-Dramatischer Verein Dachau [Dachau Music and Drama Society]. As was typical in Dachau, the founding committee comprised people involved in the arts, the crafts and commerce of the town. Von Hayek, Pfaltz and Stockmann were joined by their colleague Erich Engel, by the owner of a printing company Hans Findler, the school administrator Ludwig Heim, the builder Christian Hergl, the writer Georg Hirschfeld, the railway official Franz Kotschenreuther, the owner of the *Amper-Bote,* Mondrion, the teacher Ortner, the master-mechanic Bernhard Rollbühler, the priests Winhart and Wittmann, the master-chimneysweep Winter, the brewery owner Ziegler. Fleischmann was the musical director, the businessman Willi Grassl director of the drama section. The Society's aims were: 'to encourage and promote song, music, folk art and drama. Support for singing will be ensured through progressive training of choral singing for male-voice, female-voice and mixed choirs. The choirs will perform alternately and together with dramatic productions. Training in instrumental music is to be introduced.'[107]

Fleischmann organised a series of concerts in Dachau on behalf of the society,[108] of which only one programme has survived: that of 17 May 1906. It was a concert given by the choir and orchestra of the Music and Drama Society together with four soloists, who gave their services free of charge; two of them were Munich musicians who taught at Fleischmann's school of music. An interesting innovation is to be seen concerning the preparation of the concert: twice in the week running up to the performance Fleischmann was given half a page in the local newspaper to introduce the programme and present the works. It is an indication of the standing which these concerts, and their conductor, had in the town. The orchestra performed Mozart's Symphony K 201; this was followed by Tilly Fleischmann-Swertz playing Beethoven's Sonata No. 7; she was joined for Vieuxtemps' Ballade and Polonaise Op. 38 by the Munich violinist Anton Riebl and then she played Richard Strauss's Concerto for Horn and Piano No. 1 with Oskar Hieber of the Munich Court Orchestra. The second part of the concert consisted of works by Fleischmann: three songs for baritone and piano with texts by Theodor Storm and Peter Cornelius were sung by Josef Birchan accompanied by Tilly Fleischmann-Swertz, who then played the *Rhapsody for piano on an old Irish dance tune.* The concert ended with two choruses for solo voices, mixed choir and orchestra: 'Wanderers Nachtlied' (Goethe) and 'Über ein Stündlein' (Heyse).

DEPARTURE FROM DACHAU TO CORK

The year from the summer of 1905 to that of 1906 had brought Fleischmann much hard work, worry about the future of the plays, many organisational achievements, and considerable success with his performances and compositions. Probably around May 1906 he heard of a completely unexpected development, which was to change the course of his life. His new family in Cork were in serious trouble. His father-in-law, Hans Conrad Swertz, had decided to resign from his position and to take up a post as organist in Philadelphia. He left because of the reform of church music required by Pius X in his Instruction of November 1903, *The Juridical Code of Sacred Music*, known as *Motu proprio*. The Instruction declared church music to be an essential part of the divine service. This enhanced status for the music led to the exclusion of women from church choirs, as they could not be participants in divine service.[109] The Instruction required plainchant and classical polyphonic music of the sixteenth and seventeenth centuries (or modern composers in this style) to be put in place of the masses by Haydn, Mozart and Gounod. Swertz had built up an excellent mixed-voice choir in the cathedral and was loath to give it up and start all over again with boys voices in place of women's. The Instruction was differently interpreted by the American bishops, and women continued to sing in church choirs. However, this may not have been the sole reason for his departure. Swertz had lost a considerable amount of money on the stock-market and may have hoped to recoup his losses in America; lack of harmony in his marriage may have been a further reason.[110]

In 1906, eight of the nine Swertz children were still either at school or college; Tilly was the only one in a position to contribute to the family income, and her husband agreed to take on the responsibility of providing for her family. He had visited Cork once in 1904; in June 1906 he applied for his father-in-law's position and, on his appointment, gave notice in Dachau. The reason for his departure is given at the end of his letter of application for the cathedral post: he points out that his appointment would enable him and his wife to 'save the [Swertz] family from pending ruin and to help the children to finish their education'.[111] It must have been an extremely difficult decision to make, and one that caused great consternation and grief to his parents, who had had no warning that any such development was likely. They had had the joy of seeing their only son successful beyond all their expectations, happily married, living under their roof. The prospects for his future had seemed bright, their 'evening of life' untroubled: now they were facing old age alone.

Among the testimonials Fleischmann presented with his application for the post in Cork was one from the parish priest of Dachau, Fr Johann Winhart, who underlined how successful their choirmaster had been in training young singers, and how his nativity plays had 'brought great success and acknowledgement to him from the most distant parts of the kingdom'. Dr Sebastian Markle, professor of theology at Munich University, wrote that Fleischmann had performed a Rheinberger mass and several Palestrina motets at an ordination service 'which drew great admiration from all. My deceased colleague, Professor Dr Schell, was particularly charmed by the youthful conductor.' Dr Joseph von Hecher, royal spiritual advisor and court preacher, stated that he had known Fleischmann for a number of years, esteemed his compositions and considered him a 'splendid conductor'.

In announcing Fleischmann's departure, one of the Dachau newspapers wrote:

> Though quite a young man, he has attained a high reputation through his production of the Dachau nativity plays which were very favourably reviewed in a whole series of excellent papers and journals. Many will have pleasant memories of the musical family evenings he organised for the Dachau Musical-Dramatic Society. Dachau's flourishing School of Music owes its existence to his initiative. . . . He has also been successful as a composer. In all respects we lose in Herr Fleischmann one of our most talented sons and his unexpected departure will be deeply regretted by all.[112]

Before leaving Dachau in September 1906 Fleischmann arranged for a wind ensemble to play from the church tower every Christmas Eve as a tribute to the citizens and in honour of his mother: this was done every year, except during the two world wars, until the 1950s. They played a selection of old German Christmas carols which Fleischmann had arranged – Hermann Stockmann painted a delightful picture of this 'Turmmusik'.

Towards the end of his life, Fleischmann wrote on the subject of his departure from Dachau:

> When I left home in my young years I had no intention of spending my life abroad even if six times better conditions were to be found there. However, before it became possible for me to return in comfortable circumstances, there came the frightful storms of war, revolution, inflation, misery, suffering and tears. Since then I have been living in the past, dreaming of the old times, of the shadow play of youth, of the distant sun of home and one memory awakens another fed by homesickness, which accompanies every emigrant until the end of his life.[113]

Dachau from the south with River Amper
(*Dachau District Museum Collection*)

Shoemaker Aloys Fleischmann, his
wife Leni (at the top window)
outside his home and shoestore
(Schuhlager), Wieningerstrasse 22,
Dachau

The Augsburg Gate from outside the old walled town

Aloys Fleischmann
Dachau 1904

Aloys Fleischmann
aged about fifteen

Aloys Fleischmann
aged about six

Aloys Fleischmann aged
about twenty

The parish church of St Jakob around 1900

Fleischmann *(left)*, Maude Barrows Dutton and Andreas Lang, one of the passion play actors, 1905 in Oberammergau

Walburga Rössler, the tanner's daughter

Tilly Fleischmann's maternal grandfather, master tanner Jakob Rössler

Tilly Swertz as a student of the Royal Academy of Music in Munich 1901–5

Hans Conrad Swertz 1878 in Dachau

Hermann Stockmann's costume designs for the shepherd boys of Fleischmann's *The Night of Wonders*

The Dachau School of Music for
for Orchestral Instruments of 1905

ANDREAS PERNPEINTNER[1]

In the autumn of 1902, the year of his appointment as church musician to the church of St James in his home town of Dachau, Aloys Fleischmann founded a choir school, also termed school of singing,[2] in order to provide a sound training for new church choristers and to teach them the basics of musical notation.[3] Classes were held in the boys' primary school in a room allocated by the town council. Though lessons were at first given free of charge, at the end of the following year Fleischmann sought permission from the council to take a monthly fee of ten pfennigs per pupil in order to set up a choir library and purchase a harmonium. The participation of the pupils in the Dachau nativity plays was a significant achievement of the choir school. For the pedagogical context, it is striking that in these plays Fleischmann had trainee singers perform together with professional musicians.

In 1905 Aloys Fleischmann set up a further institution: the Dachau school of music for orchestral instruments.[4] He presented a detailed concept in the local newspaper, the *Amper-Bote*, which makes it possible to discuss the school in the context of early twentieth-century music pedagogy.

In founding the choir school before the school of music, Fleischmann followed traditional practice, as the music schools of Innsbruck, Graz and Vienna show.[5] This concept of beginning instrumental training after an initial period of choral training was still advocated in 1921 by the distinguished music pedagogue, Leo Kestenberg, in connection with the establishment of music schools for adult education, in his book *Musikerziehung und Musikpflege* [Music Education and the Cultivation of Music]. Kestenberg suggests founding the school first as a choir school, subsequently setting up an instrumental department – as Fleischmann had done almost twenty years previously.[6]

It is also striking that in the Dachau school of music all orchestral instruments were taught: students could learn all string, woodwind and brass instruments, as well as percussion. This was by no means generally the case in other music schools. But keyboard instruments were not included, although in the nineteenth century the piano was the main instrument studied by children, and in particular by girls, and constituted an essential element of domestic music-making. Institutions such as the piano academies of Johann Bernhard Logier had a decisive influence on the teaching of music. But as it was Fleischmann's declared aim to found an amateur orchestra in Dachau, his breach with the tradition of piano teaching was quite consistent.[7]

The teaching was not to be limited to practical skills but to encompass music theory. This, too, is consistent with the tradition in nineteenth-century schools of music of combining theory with practical training. But the re-evaluation of singing teaching in favour of teaching all aspects of music as a specialised subject also stood at the centre of school music pedagogical research in the early twentieth century.[8] Fleischmann's position on this was therefore consistent with the tradition of the music conservatories as well as corresponding to one of the main requirements of contemporary music teaching.

Pupils in the Dachau school of music were taught in groups selected according to standard: there was an elementary class, a department for advanced students and a theory class.[9] Practical classes were given in groups of no more than three (as was customary in Munich's Royal Academy of Music), whereas the theory classes were taken by all students together, though there was separate tuition for adults. This system corresponded in principle to a plan propagated in 1810 for the establishment of music conservatories in Germany.[10] However, the question of group tuition became an issue in the pedagogical reform movement of the early twentieth century, though Fleischmann's model was clearly the traditional form of teaching.

The quality of teaching was high, as three members of the Munich Court Orchestra joined the staff: Anton Riebl, Oskar Hieber and Franz Meier. With Fleischmann himself providing the theory and elementary tuition, the school of music of the small market town had a staff of four outstandingly well-qualified teachers.[11] Similar institutions in previous decades had of course also had teachers with appropriate qualifications: for instance the school of music of Passau's Music Society or the Fröhlich Musikinstitut in Würzburg. Such schools were often able to recruit musicians who had belonged to court orchestras and who were therefore able to provide good tuition.[12] On the other hand, there are examples of disturbingly poor-quality instrumental teaching in comparable institutions of the nineteenth century, not only with regard to private piano teachers but also in schools of music such as the Aschaffenburg school in 1820.[13] Fleischmann's music school can therefore be evaluated very positively. The standard of the teaching provided corresponded to that which music pedagogical strategists such as

Hermann Kretzschmar and Leo Kestenberg were campaigning to achieve for primary and secondary schools.[14]

In order to establish suitable conditions for the music classes, Fleischmann set down rules for the pupils of the school of music. He required 'good manners, good behaviour' and that students during classes 'should accept the instructions of the teachers without contradiction'. Such formulations have their origin rather in the old schoolmaster tradition than in the theories of the reform pedagogues.

Fleischmann was supported by the Dachau town council in a number of ways. Not only was he supplied with a room in the boys' primary school free of charge, but the council looked after the registration of students. This is of some significance. The Dachau school of music did not, like the Passau school, function under the auspices of a society, nor was it a purely private initiative: it was the private initiative of a dedicated church musician which was supported financially and administratively by the municipal authorities. Such co-operation was rather exceptional and shows the great openness of the Dachau councillors to the cultural advancement of the community.

Fleischmann sought to compensate for social inequality by making musical training and purchase of instruments affordable. He drew up a contract with the Munich company Holländer & Co. which established a branch in the school of music. It provided good quality instruments at extremely low prices and allowed purchase by instalment. It was Fleischmann's express intention to make it possible for children from less prosperous families to learn an instrument. This policy was quite unique at the time, and would be innovative even today. Assistance in the form of reduction of fees or scholarships was not unusual at that period.[15] Fleischmann, however, combined financial support with a motivational incentive, as diligent attendance of the courses led to the purchase of the instrument.

Equality also obtained in the Dachau school of music in a further regard: Fleischmann's views on music education for boys and girls were modern: he simply did not distinguish between them. That was most unusual at the time, given that at this period women did not have equal access to the universities, and that at the Munich Academy of Music – though they were admitted – they were called 'élèves' [pupils], the men 'students'.[16] At the time it was still widely held that girls and women were incapable of coping with the type of education given to men.[17] What is striking is that Fleischmann never mentioned the subject: he established equality of girls and boys in that it never occurred to him that they could be unequal.

In the formulation of his music-pedagogical aims, Fleischmann's modern approach becomes evident. In describing the desolate state of music in the town, he explained the need for a school of music in

Dachau; this was no doubt a tactic used to win over the local politicians, as it was an argument frequently employed to advocate the founding of such schools. With this school of instrumental music he pursued the aim of founding an orchestra, which would entail student concerts and lecture evenings, both of significance for the motivation of the learners.

Three aspects of Fleischmann's argument are central. First is the conviction that music can give children 'an inner composure which invigorates the spirit, leads young people . . . not only to reflect (and possibly to torment themselves), but brings them joy and psychological balance'. Secondly, he underlined the role of domestic music-making in this context, and thirdly he championed the strengthening of music as a living folk art.

These concepts are not new. The general educational value of music, of domestic music-making, of folk art and in particular of the folk song were esteemed by Pestalozzi with his emphasis on the ethical impact of music; domestic music-making played a considerable role in middle-class families of the nineteenth century, and the folk song constituted a vital element in the arts. But the links between these fields became very relevant in the early twentieth century. Folk art, the folk song and the idea of the education of young people through music are pivotal elements of the youth music movement, the influence of which persisted for decades. Fleischmann, however, went further. His emphasis on the emotional education arising through music on the one hand together with his requirement of competent musical training on the other combines the field of education through music with that of education in music.

There can be no doubt that the Dachau school of music derives from the tradition of schools of music and conservatories of the nineteenth century. Fleischmann indicates clearly that fundamental elements of his concept are oriented towards the system obtaining in the Munich Academy of Music, modified for the needs of the young students in the small market town of Dachau: for instance, the division into classes and group teaching.

But Fleischmann's institution was more than merely another music school organised after the traditional pattern. The early twentieth century was characterised by a number of new pedagogical departures.[18] Music teaching in schools was undergoing a period of fundamental reorganisation and developing away from pure singing classes towards the teaching of music as a full subject.[19] Music teaching institutions outside the school system were often more advanced in many of their concepts than the schools. It was a remarkable achievement of the twenty-five-year-old choirmaster to have founded a music-teaching institution of quality based on some of these principles and related in many ways to those of the youth music movement of the 1920s,[20] together with his innovative model of giving the children of the poor access to music, and treating boys and girls as equals. Despite its very short life, the Dachau school of music constitutes an interesting link between music school tradition and music pedagogical innovation. Aloys Fleischmann's concept withstands scrutiny based on advanced music-pedagogical concepts of the nineteenth century as well as those of the much later period.

Nativity Plays
in Dachau

JOSEF FOCHT[1]

Between 1903 and 1906 Aloys Fleischmann created four nativity plays in Dachau. Painters and writers with whom he was acquainted participated in the development of the concept of these stage productions, but the young, self-reliant and versatile choirmaster bore the entire responsibility for the music. This entailed composing new music, or adapting and arranging existing works, training the singers, rehearsing with them and the instrumental musicians, as well as directing the performances. The Dachau Nativity Plays or Children's Festivals were closely linked with Fleischmann's work for his post in the Church of St Jakob, his conception of this work, his music teaching and pedagogical views. There was a two-hundred-year-old tradition of religious plays in the town, but he succeeded in creating a new and very personal concept of religious music-theatre through the incorporation of broader contemporary artistic developments. When, in the summer of 1906, Fleischmann unexpectedly emigrated to Cork to take on his father-in-law's post as cathedral organist, the nativity plays in Dachau came to an abrupt end, and were gradually forgotten. Nonetheless his idea was to have a considerable impact in southern Germany; the Salzburg Advent Singing, for instance – a tourist attraction today among European festivals – stands in the tradition of the Dachau nativity plays.

THEATRE OF THE COUNTER-REFORMATION IN DACHAU

The market town and district of Dachau were part of the core territory of the Wittelsbach dynasty, which ruled Bavaria from the late mediaeval period to the First World War. That is why diverse cultural phenomena appeared there which were characteristic of Catholic Bavaria in general, and indeed of those parts of southern Germany outside Bavaria which had not been affected by the Reformation. Certain types of theatrical performances became popular which scholars of German literature and culture have called 'folk theatre'.

53

This type of theatre derives from the pedagogical counter-reformational programme of the Jesuits, whose influence in early modern times on Catholic schools in Bavaria was decisive. The performances were given at Christmas, New Year, on the feast of the Epiphany, during Holy Week and at Easter as well as at key periods of the school year. The lessons of the catechism were to be presented on stage not only for the children but for the Catholic population at large in schools, churches and municipal institutions. The plays were to be suitably devised, written and performed either by the Jesuits themselves or by appropriately qualified persons such as priests, teachers or organists. Borrowings were made, of course. Sometimes elements were adopted from older plays, such as St Nicolas plays, or nativity plays and pastorals going back to the Middle Ages, or from urban customs such as that of the 'Star Singers' (children dressed up as the Wise Men who go from door to door singing and receive money for charities).[2] The performances became popular and despite the religious subject matter, a tendency towards secularisation began to emerge by the eighteenth century.[3]

The poet and composer Johannes Khuen (1606–75) was a typical example. He was born in Moosach, at that time a village under the jurisdiction of the Dachau district court, today part of Munich. The highly talented son of a small farmer was admitted to the Jesuit school in Munich. On completing the course, he joined the order and read theology in the Gregorianum of the Munich Jesuit College; he studied composition with Georg Victorin (*c.* 1570–1639), the choirmaster of Munich's parish church of St Peter.

Khuen's song to Maria, 'Of our beloved Lady', the text and music of which he wrote around 1638, links the older tradition of processions with the catechetic education of the Jesuits and its religious piety. The song of over thirty stanzas names places in Munich associated with the veneration of the Virgin Mary which were visited during the processions of the 'congregationes' (confraternities) and praised in hymns. During the processions theatre-like rituals were enacted, though as yet with no distinction between actors and audience. (To this day, the song could serve as a guide for a tour of the old churches and sites of historical interest in Munich's city centre.)[4]

In Dachau itself too the oldest documents relating to clerical theatrical performances go back to the period of the Thirty Years War: in 1626 the Dachau schoolmaster Caspar Mader 'wrote a special play about the passion'. Further sporadic evidence occurs during the seventeenth century. Despite the principles of the counter-reformation educationalists, the theatrical productions always seem to have been initiated by individuals. The work of the organist and schoolmaster Franz de Paula Dionys Josef Kiennast (1731–83) is of particular interest. From 1751 he wrote several Lenten, passion and nativity plays, which were either performed in Dachau's parish church of St Jakob or on the marketplace outside the town hall. The plays were put on by the local confraternities or indeed by the citizens of the town. In most cases only the titles and brief summaries of these plays have survived, although they were probably all accompanied by musical interludes.

Not until 1763 does the archival documentation of the Dachau theatre performances set in, the reason being the sovereign's prohibition of clerical theatrical performances. The aim was to establish the separation of church and state advocated by the thinkers of the Enlightenment. As the citizens of Dachau were not prepared to abandon the clerical plays to which they had become attached, frequent conflict ensued with the government of Bavaria. Although the authorities re-enacted the prohibition of the performances several times, they took place in Dachau in 1764, 1770, 1774, 1775, 1779, 1787, 1791, 1797, 1798 and from 1805 to 1834 on an annual basis, with the last in 1836 and 1846.[5] The persistence of the citizens of Dachau is astonishing – and it corresponded to that of the people in other Upper Bavarian towns. It is also remarkable that the citizens in the municipalities repeatedly endeavoured to transfer the responsibility and trusteeship to theatrical societies which they established for this purpose. The first attempts took place between 1775 and 1791, and again between 1830 and 1846.[6]

A FRESH START FROM 1902

The next attempt to revive clerical theatre in Dachau was undertaken by Aloys Fleischmann. Exactly a year after he was appointed to the post of choirmaster in Dachau, at the beginning of 1902, a series of four nativity plays began, which were performed in the first days of January each year. He must have begun the preparations immediately after taking up the post.

The climax of the series was doubtless *The Night of Wonders*, for which he had no musical sources but produced the entire composition himself. Instrumental preludes, large-scale melodrama and a sweeping choral finale create a dramatic, indeed almost operatic effect. The actors, speakers, singers and choirs were accompanied by a large orchestra such as music from the romantic period required. The choirs were recruited from Fleischmann's school of music, the choir of the parish church of St Jakob and from among the citizens of Dachau; the orchestra consisted of Fleischmann's friends from his Academy days, members of the university and talented Dachau amateurs. The composer's wife, Tilly Fleischmann-Swertz, provided invaluable assistance in helping to prepare the performances, acting as repetiteur and playing the harmonium.

Many people from a wide range of professions collaborated with Fleischmann to produce the nativity plays. As well as the Dachau painter and book illustrator Hermann Stockmann, there were the artists Hans von Hayek, August Pfaltz and Erich Engel, and also lovers of art and the theatre in the circle of the brewer Eduard Ziegler, the publisher Franz Mondrion, the school inspector Winhart and the pastor, Fr Wittmann. These two groups came together on 15 January 1906 – just a few days after Fleischmann's last nativity play performance – to found a Music and Drama Society, the formal establishment of which, however, was preceded by at least five years of preliminary activities.[7] The aim of the society corresponded exactly to Fleischmann's ideas: 'It is the purpose of the society to cultivate and promote singing, music and traditional dramatic art. – The encouragement of singing is to take the form of progressive choir training of male-voice, female-voice and mixed-voice choirs which are to have the opportunity to sing in public in the context of drama performances. This will include instrumental music.'[8]

The significant innovations in Fleischmann's nativity plays are both conceptual and formal. In contrast to the baroque plays inspired by the Jesuits, the music is absolutely central: the text and stage activities are of secondary importance. A further innovation is the fusion of components in an artistic synthesis. In the *Night of Wonders* of 1905 different elements complement and overlap each other around the music at the centre: stage plot and scenery, costumes and props, libretto and illustrations by Hermann Stockmann. In the *Nativity Pictures* of 1906 Hermann Stockmann and August Pfaltz created tableaux on stage with texts from the Christmas gospel and choral works by Michael Praetorius, which Fleischmann incorporated into the framework of a musical synthesis. This synaesthetic and multimedia approach is not surprising. From the 1890s, the discourse of medical and psychological research on synaesthetics began to come into the public domain (with the work of, among others, Eugen Bleuler and Théodore Flournoy); it created interest in artistic circles in various European centres. In 1902 Beethoven became a fashionable topic in the visual arts – a trend which emerged in Vienna, for instance with Gustav Klimt's 'Beethoven Frieze' or Max Klinger's 'Beethoven Torso'. The Dachau painter Adolf Hölzel began his theoretical work on the musical aspect of the theory of colour and vocabulary of art around 1903; at the same time Wassily Kandinsky was classifying 'colour sounds' into 'colour symphonies'.[9] Composers also sought synaesthetics, light projections and 'colour pianos': Arnold Schönberg ('Die glückliche Hand' of 1909) and Alexander Scriabin ('Prometheus' of 1909) can be regarded as the most eminent examples. The question of whether Fleischmann was influenced by other artists or himself influenced others requires further research.

With regard to the type of performance: the sacred play of the old form was now taken out of the church and related municipal space and placed firmly on the secular stage – in the Ziegler Hall, the hall in the tavern of the Dachau beer-brewer Ziegler. Despite its religious material, the theatrical undertaking was completely secularised and professionalised: carried by a civic association, organised with a clear division of labour, tied in with the entertainment and media programme of the capital city, supplying the astonished audience with contemporary, 'modern' dramatic art. How well suited the Dachau nativity plays were to the Munich public only became clear to those involved in retrospect. On 18 January 1907 Hermann Stockmann wrote to Fleischmann, who at this time had already been living in Cork for six months: 'That place was very quiet this year where we used to put our muses into action. There was colossal lamentation in Munich; the people of Dachau do not seem to have noticed the loss. That is most instructive for the future.'

THE RECEPTION OF THE PLAYS

Hermann Stockmann was one of the founders of the Bavarian Association for Folk Art and Folklore, which was established in 1902. He brought the Dachau performance concept to Munich, where he produced the first of his nativity plays on 15 December 1907 in Munich's House of Artists. Further productions followed until the beginning of the First World War. During the 1920s and in the immediate aftermath of the Second World War, several southern German musicians and people involved in the theatre revived the Dachau model, which they adapted to their needs. Matthäus Roemer (1871–1954) set Ludwig Thoma's 'Heilige Nacht' [Holy Night] in 1924; Oscar Besemfelder (1893–1965) produced 'Weihnachtsansingen' [Singing Announcing Christmas] in the 1920s, and from 1945 to 1965. These soon fell into oblivion, but not the 'Salzburg Advent Singing' by Tobi Reiser (1907–74), which began in 1946. This religious meditation, steeped in music, with its contemplative Advent reflections, corresponded to a spiritual and emotional need of the immediate post-war period. It was broadcast on the radio and on television, immediately obtained high listener figures and sold many records. Its example was quickly followed elsewhere in the country. Today in Munich, as in many other southern German and Austrian towns and cities, hundreds of nativity plays are performed annually during the period of Advent and Christmas holidays, which – regardless of the different types of music, stage techniques and media employed – almost without exception look back to a common tradition, which began in Dachau in 1902.

Aloys Fleischmann's Home Town Dachau

Ursula K. Nauderer[1]

Aloys Fleischmann lived in Dachau, the town of his birth and his home, from 1880 to 1906. These were the years of his childhood, of his training as a musician in the Royal Academy of Music in Munich, and the years of his first successes as music pedagogue, church musician and composer. They coincide with the last years of the reign of King Ludwig II of Bavaria and the 'Prince Regent years' of his uncle Luitpold. Those determined the political, economic and cultural forces active during Aloys Fleischmann's youth in Dachau.[2]

During the reign of King Ludwig I (1786–1868), the grandfather of Ludwig II, Munich became an impressive city of art and culture and, together with Berlin, a centre of classicism in Germany.[3] Ludwig, an enthusiastic patron of the arts and passionate admirer of ancient Greece, was one of the most significant initiators of art in his period. He had the royal capital, Munich, re-designed along classicist lines by the architects Leo von Klenze and Friedrich von Gärtner.[4] As patron of the fine arts, he appointed Peter Cornelius to the Academy of Art, thus reviving historical monumental painting. With the building of the Pinakothek he created the largest art gallery of his period. From then on artists of all fields, from home and abroad, were drawn to 'Athens on the Isar', as Munich was called.

Ludwig's youngest son, Luitpold (1821–1912), was also deeply interested in the fine arts, in particular in painting. Although he did not actively influence cultural and artistic policies as did his father, during his reign a liberal and enlightened atmosphere prevailed in Munich, which allowed artists and those aspiring to that status to pursue their interests undisturbed. These were the years in which 'Munich shone'.[5]

The neighbouring market town of Dachau profited in a unique fashion from the rise of Munich as a centre of art, and Aloys Fleischmann was born during a highly interesting period of Dachau's history: since the end of the nineteenth century, Dachau, too, had acquired an outstanding, Europe-wide reputation as an artists' centre among those with an interest in culture.[6]

Johann Georg von Dillis (1759–1841), Ludwig I's artistic advisor and first professor of landscape-painting at the newly founded Academy of Art, was the first painter to come in 1820 with his painting class from Munich to the town separated from the city of the monarchy by an extensive peat bog. He was followed by Eduard Schleich the elder (1812–74), the 'father of southern German atmosphere painting' (S. Wichmann), by Carl Spitzweg (1808–85) and Christian Morgenstern (1805–67). The artists were greatly attracted not only by the wide, unspoiled moor landscape with its special flora and fauna, its unique light-effects and moods, but also by Dachau's alluring location on the first range of hills at the end of the great plain between the Alps and their northerly foothills. The German writer Ludwig Thoma (1867–1921) remembered his first glimpse of the town:

> One August evening [in 1894] I drove to Dachau with a friend. . . . As we came up the hill, and the market place with its gabled houses lay before me in tranquil relaxation after the day's work, I was overcome by a great longing to live in this peaceful place. . . . It did not take me long to make up my mind and I applied for a licence to practise in Dachau.[7]

The tranquillity of the place, the people's respect for what had been handed down and their determination to preserve tradition were offi-cially recorded by the Dachau district court. The royal court clerk of the neighbouring town of Bruck described the rural population of the area in 1875 as 'folk who have maintained unadulterated and unchanged their strange and therefore conspicuous costumes and customs and proudly keep them alive to this day in the midst of a civilisation which is levelling everything else.'[8]

The artists, above all the painters, who from the middle of the nine-teenth century came to Dachau in ever increasing numbers, found not only an attractive landscape but also people conscious and proud of their traditions. The eminently picturesque Sunday costumes of the wealthy farmers are recurring motifs in Dachau open-air painting.

Open-air painters belonged at this period to the avant-garde. The art students who fled from the confines of the Munich Academy of Art and stood for the new school of Pleinairism were in the majority. Many artists and students of art – among them a remarkably large number of women – visited Dachau, generally in summer, and signed on for the private schools of painting there.[9] The Academy professor, Wilhelm von Diez, came regularly with his pupils during the summer months. A number of artists took up permanent residence in the town, remaining for some years: among them Adolf Hölzel and Ludwig Dill. Hermann Stockmann and August Pfaltz remained for the rest of their lives. An artists' colony with villas and other artists' houses of various styles grew up after 1900 to the south of the town, close to the moor.[10]

Dachau was an ancient place of settlement; it was first mentioned in a document of AD 805. Due to its advantageous position on the trade-route between Munich and Augsburg, and the granting of privileges and market rights during the thirteenth and fourteenth centuries, it became a prosperous town whose citizens had been allowed to set up an autonomous local administration. Dachau was also the administrative centre of the district court and corresponding legal offices, and furthermore the seat of one of the Wittelsbach palaces. Architecturally the town was a typical old-Bavarian market place with town hall, church, school, official buildings and brewery inns grouped around the centre. Only one of the three town gates still stood in 1880, the year of Aloys Fleischmann's birth: the Augsburg Gate. On the highest point of the hill was the palace, overlooking the market; since 1790 only the west wing of the original four-sided Renaissance building remained.

The citizens of Dachau were mainly active in the crafts and in trade. There were generally close family ties with the rural population of the surrounding parishes. Many farmers who had handed over their land to the next generation moved to Dachau in their old age, supported by their young farmer sons.

The first industrial workers came to Dachau around the same time as the painters. In the second half of the nineteenth century a paper factory, a malt factory and a cardboard factory were established, all requiring increasing numbers of workers. In addition to artists' studios and homes, the building of small and very basic working-class houses began. The tranquillity of the market-town, which meant so much to the writer Ludwig Thoma, was gradually coming to an end.[11] The town had grown between 1850 and 1900 from 1,500 inhabitants living in 219 dwellings to over 5,000 in 506 houses. According to the statistics, there was an artist or an artist's atelier in every second house.[12]

The constant presence of artists in the locality had a considerable impact on the intellectual climate of Dachau.[13] Whereas the farming population and the workers generally took scant notice of the painting visitors, a section of the middle classes welcomed the stimulus which these artists from all parts of Germany and from abroad brought to the town.[14] A number of painters exercised a very decisive influence on the cultural life of Dachau through their personal commitment – in particular Adolf Hölzel, Hermann Stockmann, August Pfaltz and Hans von Hayek. They took an active part in the intellectual and social life of the community, and were fully integrated citizens.[15] 'These were Dachau's happy years before 1914,' as the artist Carl Thiemann wrote in his memoirs.[16]

Hermann Stockmann, a native of Lower Bavaria, was probably the artist who had the strongest sense of identification with the town that he had made his home. He had moved to the market town on the River Amper in 1898 and built himself a splendid house there, which he affectionately termed '*Spatzenschlößl*' [wee castle of the sparrows]. The story goes that during his first visit to Dachau Stockmann purchased an antique waistcoat in a tiny shop in the Augsburg Gate. From the very first day the artist took an interest in the cultural heritage of the town. The traditional legacy was then under threat and seemed doomed to disappear due to the relentless pace of change accompanying industrialisation – Stockmann sought to preserve what was unique in the culture of the region.[17] Accordingly, together with Dachau citizens and artist friends of similar views, he founded a folklore museum in 1905, the District Museum of Dachau, and three years later the Dachau Art Gallery.[18]

Aloys Fleischmann's father, a shoemaker, belonged to the circle of these open-minded Dachau citizens. His son therefore grew up during a time of manifold economic transition and radical change in a community which was culturally and intellectually innovative while retaining pride in its origins and heritage. This was the ground in which Fleischmann's special musical talent could take root before he embarked on the thorough course of training at the Royal Academy of Music in Munich.

During the few years of his activities in Dachau, Aloys Fleischmann revealed the enormous force of his musical inspiration. His work as choirmaster in the church of St Jakob, the founding of the choir school and school of music, his remarkable creative achievements, in particular that of the nativity play, *The Night of Wonders*, brought him an exceptional degree of respect and admiration as a very young man. After his departure from Dachau in 1906, what he had initiated either quickly shrank back to normal levels or disappeared entirely. The school of music did not survive once it had been deprived of the musical and pedagogic inspiration of his personality. It became clear that the market town of Dachau did not have the social or political resources to establish on a permanent basis something resembling the 1905 nativity play in dimension and quality.

All his life, Fleischmann remained closely attached to his home, even after the terrible and disastrous years of National Socialism and the horror of the Nazi concentration camp, which was set up in 1933 in close proximity to the town.

From the 1950s the memory of Fleischmann's nativity plays gradually faded away in Dachau. But Aloys Fleischmann was never forgotten by those who had known him, as the letter shows which an old lady wrote to Fleischmann's son in 1971: 'I will never forget your dear father. When I was in school he was our teacher in the choir school, which he built up. Later on, he was our conductor in the church choir. What a wonderful time that was. And now how far away.'[19]

The annual Christmas tower music which Fleischmann innovated after his departure from Dachau left its mark for even longer. Every

Christmas Eve, in honour of his mother and as a greeting to the citizens of Dachau, Fleischmann had Christmas music played from the tower of the church of St Jakob. The Dachau district judge and editor, Hans Seemüller (1905–85), wrote of it in his account of life in the town, 'The Old Dachau Christmas'. There is no mention of the origin of the custom, nor of the name of the initiator – the tower music had taken on a life of its own:

> Towards the ninth hour, when the candles on the Christmas tree had long been extinguished, something began to happen up on the tower of St Jakob. A gleam of light appeared through the hatch, disappeared, only to return again after a short time. Something mysterious had awoken up there high above the silent world. The deep chimes of the clock tower pealed out through the night and then the familiar Christmas carols, played on wind instruments, resounded far out into the Dachau countryside. . . . The carols rang out over the graves adorned with little trees and candles in the cemetery – at that time still so small – and some silent thoughts left the warm rooms to be with those who had had to take their leave. The tower music ended with the carol 'Silent night, holy night', and once again infinite stillness reigned until the midnight bells sent out their call to mass. Those old carols from the tower were heard down the years and down the decades, no matter how much the face and life of that town changed, which was now becoming ever bigger and noisier. They were heard in those years of Dachau's bitter poverty, when people without work and without hope stood at midday in the meagre December sun outside the Hölzl house, while hunger and despair had taken up residence in the small rooms of their homes. . . . Until the Big War came and, with it, death and horror sweeping around the world. Then all the lights went out, including the candles on the graves and anybody who still had lights for a Christmas tree lit them surreptitiously behind the blacked-out windows. The music from the tower was silenced as the sirens wailed throughout the fear-filled nights. . . . When at last the great dying had abated and the streets once again became bright, on the first Christmas Eve after the Big War, a few musicians passed through the overpopulated town. One of them marched ahead, carrying a lantern and the old songs were heard once more on the square outside the town hall. The people stood in silence in a circle, sunk in their thoughts. . . . This time, too, the music ended with 'Silent night, holy night' and, after the last tone had faded away, the people departed in the same mute silence in which they had listened. A Christmas tree, with lights, again stood outside the town hall, as in the past. The following day, a storm raged over the countryside and broke it. It was like an allegory illustrating that the world had changed, that something which could not be expressed in words was irrevocably lost and gone forever. Since then, the old songs have not been heard on the Holy Night: no longer do they

resound from the tower over the wide, sleeping Dachau countryside. . . . But for those who heard that music, it remains a memory
which they will never forget.[20]

2. The First Years in Cork
1906–14

Aloys Fleischmann 1910

As Fleischmann stood on the deck of the liner sailing up the estuary of the River Lee towards Queenstown on a July morning in 1906, he might have felt rather like Tamino in Mozart's opera, *The Magic Flute*, about to undergo the trials and ordeals required of him as a test of his fidelity to his beloved. One of Tamino's tests was his ability to remain silent: Fleischmann was going to have to learn to speak the language of his new surroundings. An only child, he was about to take up residence with a family of ten. Having made a name for himself in Munich's sophisticated art world with his imaginative stage-productions, he was coming as an unknown stranger to a small city in the poorest part of the United Kingdom. Having lived close to a flourishing centre of continental culture with a tradition of royal patronage of the arts, he was about to take up a post in a provincial city of a country just beginning to emerge from conquest and a degree of poverty no longer known in Germany. He was to learn how the city had fared under British rule, to become aware of a movement of cultural renaissance now developing there, and to contribute to it himself together with his wife. The period of test and ordeal was to be protracted and difficult; support and solace he was to find in the beauty of Ireland's coast and countryside, in the warmheartedness of his new friends, choristers and students and, above all, in the woman for whose sake he had given up his successful life in Germany.

CORK DURING THE LAST PHASE OF COLONIAL RULE 1879–1921

The end of colonial Ireland was approachig when in 1879 Fleischmann's father-in-law, Hans Conrad Swertz, came from Dachau to take up a position as organist in St Vincent's Church of Sunday's Well. It was the year in which the Land War began, which was to break the power of the landlords of Ireland and bring land reform, which by 1903 gave the peasants the right to purchase their holdings. During Swertz's first year in Cork, Charles Stuart Parnell became Member of Parliament for the city. Parnell, a Protestant Wicklow landlord, allied himself with the radicals of the Land League and turned the Irish Parliamentary Party into an efficient political instrument agitating in Westminster for land reform and for autonomy for Ireland under the Crown, for 'Home Rule'. The gradual undermining of the position of the colonial settlers or 'Ascendancy' had been under way for almost a hundred years. The decisive victory in the struggle to have the discriminatory legislation against Catholics repealed had come in 1829 with the Catholic Relief Act, the result of a protracted, efficiently organised mass movement of the peasantry led by the Catholic lawyer, Daniel O'Connell. But it had taken until 1840 before a Municipal Reform Act had removed barriers preventing Catholic merchants from becoming members of the Cork Corporation. The gradual introduction of democracy in Britain applied to Ireland also – an unforeseen consequence of the Act of Union of 1800. In 1867 all urban householders had been enfranchised.[1] Though this did not give the vote to adult members of their families or lodgers, the reform provided a solid basis for Irish nationalist parties; in 1885 the franchise was extended to rural householders. In the 1870s, living conditions for the poor of the city were still almost as bad as before the famine; low wages and intolerable working conditions had led in 1870–2 to strikes and riots.[2] There had been a smallpox epidemic in 1871 with 3,500 cases; typhus and tuberculosis were endemic. Six years later, due to over-crowding, lack of hygiene, lack of clean drinking water, the death rate had increased to 152 per 1,000 births.[3] (In 2009 in Ireland it was esti-mated to be 7.75 per 1,000). Such catastrophic conditions brought the city authorities to undertake major improvement projects. In 1878, the year before Swertz arrived, a Public Health Act was passed bringing compre-hensive sanitary laws; during the 1880s some hundreds of labourers' cottages were built. Thus the percentage of families living in tenements with one room per family had fallen by 1891 to 44 per cent; ten years later it was down to 12.6 per cent.[4] In 1898 the Local Government Act intro-duced elected county and city councils, thus removing one of the last bastions of landlord control of local administration.

The recovery of the Catholic church

The gradual undermining of the colonial structures in Ireland was reflected in the development of the Catholic church. During the eigh-teenth century the Catholic church had been banned from public life, the building of churches was forbidden and church services were severely restricted. In 1704 there were four Catholic priests in Cork and no Catholic church;[5] in 1786 there was one chapel in a back lane.[6] However, towards the end of the century the anti-Catholic legislation was no longer strictly imposed. The loss of the American colonies, the American-inspired activities of the Dublin parliament and the alarm caused by the French Revolution brought the British government to adopt more con-ciliatory religious policies. In 1795 the seminary of Maynooth was established; in 1799 the building began of Cork's Catholic cathedral of St Mary and St Anne; the religious orders of the Augustinians, Dominicans and Franciscans were tolerated in the city.[7] After the repeal of anti-Catholic legislation in 1829, the remaining official discrimination against Catholics was fiercely resisted, in particular the enforced payment of taxes by all households to the Protestant Church of Ireland. It was not until 1870 that the state church was disestablished and Irish Catholics and Presbyterians no longer had to pay tithes.

Ireland's first cardinal, Paul Cullen, had systematically built up the public presence of the Catholic Church during his time in office from 1849 to 1878. By the 1860s the bishops began to recruit organists from abroad as no Irish tradition of church music had survived the anti-Catholic repression; the fine Anglican church music to be found among the Anglo-Irish could not serve as a model. By 1870, the Cork diocese had recovered sufficiently from the bad times of the Penal Laws and the famine to become concerned about church music. The first continental organist appointed in 1870 to the cathedral was Léopold de Prins; he was succeeded by de Paine[8] in 1889 and by Hans Conrad Swertz in 1890. By the early 1900s there were about twenty-five German organists in Ireland, who brought the European tradition of sacred music to the country and built up choirs of high quality.[9]

The arts in Cork

When Hans Conrad Swertz came to Cork in 1879, the Opera House had been open for two years. There was no resident opera or drama company in Cork, no professional orchestra or chamber ensemble, but the city was visited regularly by many fine English opera and drama companies. Swertz attended Carl Rosa Company performances: he could have seen *Aida, Carmen, Lohengrin*.[10] From the 1880s the D'Oyly Carte Company brought Gilbert and Sullivan comic operas. Visiting professional companies brought a varied programme of drama, ranging from Shakespeare to the eighteenth-century Irish dramatists Sheridan and Goldsmith, and the plays of Oscar Wilde. The Opera House was very popular; seats at the top of the house – in 'the gods' – were cheap and there was a considerable working class following. The best known artists were often welcomed by large crowds at the railway station, who removed the horses from the carriages and drew the guests themselves to their hotel. On occasion, very special arrangements were needed. The celebrated actress Sarah Bernhardt was due to perform in Cork 1887 on her way to a tour in America; the liner arrived so late that cancellation of the show seemed imminent, but the management had her and the company brought up the river by tug and landed at the door of the Opera House: the performance began just one hour late.[11]

There was also much local musical activity at this time. Some of the more mobile groups operated close to the Swertz home on Dyke Parade: brass bands – both military and civilian – as well as fife and drum bands performed regularly in the evenings near the cricket grounds. That often inspired groups of ragged barefooted children to form bands of their own, to parade up and down the Mardyke singing and clattering with improvised instruments such as old pots and cans, combs and whistles, marching in perfect time to their raucous music.[12] Swertz no doubt preferred the orchestral concerts given by the Cork Musical Society, founded in 1869 by the organist of St Fin Barre's Protestant cathedral, Dr Marks, and those put on by the Cork Orchestral Union conducted by W.R. Atkins from 1875 to 1902. Members of these orchestras played on special occasions in the Catholic cathedral when Swertz performed masses by Mozart or Schubert with his choir.[13] The Cork Amateur Operatic and Dramatic Society was founded in 1883, directed by Theo Gmür, a Swiss musician, putting on light operas every year, including several performances of one by Gmür himself, until 1911.

The Cork Industrial Exhibitions of 1883 and 1902–03 were occasions of much musical activity in the city; for the opening concert in 1883, Swertz had trained a choir of 240 singers, who performed Mendelssohn's *Lobgesang* and parts of Haydn's *Creation*, as well as Irish airs.[14] For the Exhibition of 1902, as there was no longer a local amateur orchestra, musicians from continental Europe were invited to perform, among them the Berlin Philharmonic Orchestra;[15] Signor Ferruccio Grossi of Milan came with another group; he and his pianist wife were to remain in Cork, revive the Cork Orchestral Union, give concerts for ten years and teach until 1930.

Musical education was available from private teachers and from the School of Music – the first municipal one in the United Kingdom – which had opened the year before Swertz arrived and in which he obtained a post as professor of harmony.[16] Its stated aim was to provide sound musical education to all classes in the city.[17] However, as the funding provided for the school was small, students had to pay fees and instruments were not provided; nevertheless, children from widely differing social backgrounds signed up for classes.

Training in the fine arts was offered by the Crawford Gallery and School of Art. This institution opened in 1885 in the splendid building still used by the gallery today; it was financed by the brewer, William Crawford. It had a somewhat turbulent start, with crowds booing the officiating Prince of Wales at the opening ceremony and cheering for Parnell. Fees for the school were considerable, so most of the students were girls from wealthy families. However, from 1891 a scheme was set up to promote talented impecunious young citizens: apprentice plasterers, stonecutters, carpenters and masons could be admitted at half fees, the trade union paying the remainder, and eight scholarships were offered.[18]

The revival of interest in Gaelic culture

From the 1890s, all over Ireland the range of people interested in the arts broadened and amateur cultural activities increased considerably, taking a new direction. Up to then culture in the cities had been oriented towards London, professional companies and artists touring from Britain and inspiring local amateur activities to emulate them. Now, however, with the possibility growing that Ireland might be granted autonomy within the United Kingdom or 'home rule', interest in the nation's Celtic heritage became widespread. In 1884, during the Land War, the Gaelic Athletic Association had been founded, a sports organisation reviving Irish games, which soon became immensely popular and imbued its members with a strong sense of national identity. The work of German and Anglo-Irish scholars who had studied the older forms of Irish and its literature led to a revival of interest in the modern language, and to the founding by Douglas Hyde of the Gaelic League in 1893, an association established to de-anglicise Ireland culturally and to promote the study of Irish. A Cork branch was set up the following year. By 1900 Hyde had managed to have Irish put on the official school curriculum despite intense opposition from Trinity College; within ten years over half the country's secondary school pupils were taking the subject in their examinations.[19]

In 1901 The Cork Celtic Literary Society was founded by Terence MacSwiney, Liam de Róiste and Fred Cronin to encourage the writing of literature on Irish themes; it was followed by the Cork Dramatic Society in 1908 to provide a forum for Irish plays. Nine years previously, in 1899, the Irish Literary Theatre had been founded in Dublin by the Anglo-Irish artists Lady Gregory, Edward Martyn and Yeats; this was soon to become the country's national theatre, located in the Abbey Theatre. Martyn was exceptional in that he was a Catholic Galway landlord of a Norman family. He was a lover of music and 'the first to call attention to the beauty and value of the traditional singing amongst the peasants'.[20] Festivals of Irish music were begun in 1897 by people involved in the literary and language movement.[21] Edward Martyn took up the cause of reforming Irish Catholic church art: in 1899 he founded and endowed the Palestrina Choir in the Dublin Catholic cathedral and shortly afterwards initiated a studio for the manufacture of Irish stained-glass.

CATHOLIC CHURCH MUSIC REFORM ON THE CONTINENT

The efforts of the Irish Catholic bishops in the second half of the nineteenth century to improve the standard of church music were part of a European movement. In Belgium and in Germany scholars of liturgical music advocated a return to the older forms of sacred music, above all to the mediaeval tradition of Gregorian chant and to the polyphonic masters of the sixteenth century, to ensure that sacred music remained distinct from that of the opera and theatre. In the Bavarian city of Bamberg, the German priest and musician, Franz Xaver Witt, formed an organisation in 1868 to work for this programme: Allgemeiner Deutscher Cäcilienverein [German Cecilian Association] with its journal, *Musica Sacra*; it was granted papal approval two years later. One of the association's aims was reached with the founding in 1874 of a college of church music in Regensburg to provide appropriate training for church musicians. Five years later a similar institution was founded in Malines in Belgium (in Dutch called Mechelen), whose cathedral is dedicated to the Irish missionary monk, St Rombaut. The first Belgian organist to come to Cork, Léopold de Prins, and his brother Francis, organist in Limerick, set about putting these principles of the Cecilian movement into practice. They founded a journal, and when the Irish Society of St

Cecilia was established in 1879 with the approval of the Irish bishops, they supported it and its journal, *Lyra Ecclesiastica*, with enthusiasm. In 1888 the German cleric, Heinrich Bewerunge, was appointed professor of church music in Maynooth, and soon became the editor of the *Lyra*.

Hans Conrad Swertz was among the first graduates of the Regensburg college of sacred music, but he does not seem to have been an ardent Cecilian. His mixed choir in the cathedral was accompanied by an orchestra for major services and performed many nineteenth-century masses which were far removed from the austerity of the sixteenth- and seventeenth-century works recommended by the reformers.

The reorganisation of church music in Cork from 1906

On the feast of St Cecilia, 22 November 1903, Pope Pius X issued an Instruction on Sacred Music, a *Motu proprio*, adopting many of the principles of the Cecilian reformers as the official Vatican rules on music in church services. Gregorian chant[22] was declared the most authentic form of sacred music and therefore prescribed for parts of the services; the use of polyphonic music of the sixteenth century was encouraged; modern music was permitted, provided its 'excellence, sobriety and gravity made it worthy of the liturgical functions'. Singing was to be in Latin, solo singing not to predominate, the organ to be used in moderation, bands or orchestras were strictly forbidden, as were 'noisy and frivolous instruments' and the piano. Choir members were to wear ecclesiastical garb and to be hidden from the congregation. The bishops were instructed to set up a diocesan commission to watch over the quality of the music in the churches; they were urged to introduce a *schola cantorum* in all the main churches to train the parishioners, and to support or found where necessary colleges of sacred music so that the church herself would train her choirmasters, organists and singers.

The Instruction led the bishop of Cork, Dr O'Callaghan, to launch a campaign explaining the coming reforms to the people. He set up the Cork Episcopal Commission on Ecclesiastical Music. The cathedral organist and choirmaster, Hans Conrad Swertz, was appointed diocesan church music inspector, and asked to draw up a list of appropriate music for the diocese. Swertz adapted the Bishop of Salford's List;[23] it was published and circulated to all the churches of the diocese.[24] However, it may not have conformed altogether to the requirements of the Vatican. Swertz's son-in-law was to criticise it implicitly to the bishop not long after his arrival, writing that some of the modern composers on the list ought only be performed under exceptional circumstances.[25] If Swertz's implementation of the new rules was half-hearted and soon abandoned entirely, his son-in-law was to commit himself to them with dedication.

CORK AS PLACE OF EXILE 1906–10

The first years in Cork were difficult for Aloys and Tilly Fleischmann. Tilly had lived on her own in Munich from September 1901 up to her marriage in September 1905; she had lived with her parents-in-law in Dachau for less than a year, and was now back home with her mother and eight siblings. Her mother had not had a happy marriage: Tilly wrote towards the end of her life in a biographical sketch entitled 'Unhappy Youth' that her parents seldom agreed on anything and that they should never have married. Nothing is known about the circumstances of Walburga's separation at the age of 52 from her husband. Whether for her it was a calamity or a relief will probably have depended on how he was able to provide for the family. However, as Tilly and her husband were summoned back to Cork to help, the family's finances must have been precarious. Fleischmann's mother-in-law no doubt found it embarrassing to depend on the income of the son-in-law who had been rejected when he proposed to Tilly on the grounds that his father was a mere artisan. Walburga's mother in Dachau heard of the separation before her death at 82 in July 1906.[26] Although her daughter's marriage had lasted for a quarter of a century, she may have felt she was right to have rejected Hans Conrad, and Walburga may have come to agree with her and to have grim forebodings for the marriage of her daughter Tilly who, like herself, had ignored parental advice. In short: a complicated situation faced the new member of the family just arrived from Dachau.

It emerges from Fleischmann's letters that his relations with his mother-in-law were not good, and that he suffered from acute homesickness. He had left home before his mother's sixtieth birthday in September 1906; the eight-stanza poem he sent her for the occasion shows a painful awareness of her grief over their separation, and of her worries about his future and his happiness. He urges his mother to trust that 'He who in the past led the family out of poverty will continue to protect them', and thanks her for having given him what he values above all else: his wife. Another poem written for his parents to comfort them during the first Christmas without him also indicates a sharp sense of guilt over having left them. Occasional remarks in letters from German friends show that they were merely told he found the damp climate trying, having been used to the wintery snows and dry summer heat of the continental climate in Bavaria, but that he loved the landscape, and the poetry and music of the Irish.

Tilly began to teach in the autumn of 1906, having placed a notice in the local newspaper on 6 October announcing her qualifications; she taught in the family home at 15 Dyke Parade. Although warned that a solo piano recital would hardly attract an audience, she gave her début on 21 November of that year, playing Schumann, Chopin, her husband's *Rhapsody on an Old Irish Air*, and three pieces by Liszt. One of the pupils who was present at that recital wrote to Tilly's son seventy-five years later:

> I just cannot express my gratitude sufficiently for your parents. Your mother was an inspiring teacher and a really beautiful pianist. Never since hearing her play 'St Francis Preaching to the Birds' by Liszt have I heard anybody play it so well.[27]

Fleischmann friends in the Gaelic cultural renaissance

Through the Swertz family connections, the Fleischmanns had access to quite a wide circle of people interested in music, Hans Conrad having performed and taught in Cork for twenty-seven years. They became friendly with the young solicitor, John J. Horgan, whose father had been Parnell's Cork organiser and who introduced them to all sorts of people with artistic interests, among them the parish priest of Doneraile and novelist Canon Sheehan, and one of the activists of the co-operative movement, Lord Monteagle.

Many of their friends with an interest in music were involved in the new cultural movement exploring the Irish language and the Celtic heritage. Quite a number of them were to move from the cultural to the political field and to sympathise with or to join radical organisations seeking independence from Britain. Among these were the writer and scholar, Daniel Corkery, Mary and Terence MacSwiney, and William Stockley, professor of English at the university. Tilly knew the MacSwiney family from her schooldays in St Angela's, where Miss Mary had taught the elder Swertz girls. Her brother Terence was to become a major figure in the struggle for independence from Britain. He had had to leave school at the age of fifteen to support his family, and continued his education at night school, graduating from the university in 1907. He worked in the Irish language and the literary movements, and gradually became involved in militant nationalist organisations. He was arrested as Lord Mayor of Cork in August 1920, convicted of being in illegal possession of documents, went on hunger strike and died in Brixton Prison in London on 25 October 1920. His death brought the question of Irish independence to the attention of the world press and thereby to political leaders in the colonies such as Gandhi.[28] The Fleischmanns met MacSwiney soon after their arrival in Cork, when he had just graduated in philosophy while working full-time as a clerk to support his family. Through him, Tilly first became aware of the Gaelic heritage and cultural nationalist movement:

> When first I met him his family were living in very poor circumstances. He had a small job somewhere in an office.[29] . . . It was only then and from him that I got my first glimpse of Irish history and the Irish language and that the people of Ireland were longing for

freedom. We children in Cork looked upon ourselves as English – we were taught to look down upon the Irish language as being the language of our servants and of the 'common wild people'.[30]

MacSwiney used to visit the Fleischmanns at their home and liked the informal music-making. After the publication in 1907 of his first book, *The Music of Freedom*,[31] he began to collaborate with Daniel Corkery, both writing plays for the Cork Dramatic Society, which were performed in the Opera House in 1909. Corkery was a primary school teacher who in the early 1890s was dumbfounded to discover that Irish was a living language;[32] he studied it and soon became an enthusiastic and influential teacher and promoter of Gaelic. He found remnants of the vanishing Gaelic culture when he came upon 'old people in the Cork lanes who could tell stories about eighteenth century Gaelic poets and recite their work',[33] and from there embarked on his quest for the 'hidden Ireland'. All the arts attracted him: he took night classes at the Crawford School of Art with the painter Harry Scully;[34] he became friends of the Fleischmanns through his love of music: he went to all their concerts, started a school choir and played the cello in the Gaelic League's orchestra in Blackpool. Like Fleischmann, his father was a craftsman – a carpenter. Fleischmann felt at home with such people, and drawn to their cause, which in many ways resembled that which he had espoused in Dachau. He had learnt from his father and from the painters living in his town to esteem the heritage of the pre-industrial period and had set about studying and reviving parts of the literary and musical tradition – it was no wonder that he became friends with people like Corkery and MacSwiney.

But cultural nationalists were not necessarily people of modest means, or of native stock. On the heights of Montenotte overlooking the river Lee, Fleischmann found a fellow countrywoman and musician from Munich, Germaine Stockley. The Stockleys were among the first families to befriend the Fleischmanns. William Stockley had been professor of English at the university since 1905; he was Anglo-Irish, a convert to Catholicism, an enthusiastic supporter of the Irish cultural revival, and a man of radical nationalist sympathies. His second wife, Germaine Kolb, was half French and half German, a gifted singer who had studied with a pupil of Brahms. Her father was a well-known Munich landscape architect whose elegant villa was frequented by artists and the art-loving nobility of Munich. The Stockley home in Cork was a meeting place for those involved in the literary movement.

However, though there was much music-making in such homes, and the occasional public chamber music recital in the city organised by F. St John Lacy, the university lecturer in music,[35] Fleischmann sorely missed the great concerts of Munich. In 1907 he wrote disparagingly of the fare offered in Cork:

> ... the musical circumstances of the town are at a terribly low ebb,
> and the theatre, instead of being a temple of beauty and culture, and
> serving to make known the classical authors and their works, must
> be designated as an institution which demoralises and degrades
> taste.[36]

Work with the cathedral choir

When Fleischmann walked to the cathedral from 15 Dyke Parade, he
came from a pleasant residential area to one of the poorest of the city,
the 'marsh', where decayed eighteenth-century mansions had become
slum dwellings housing the poorest of Cork's poor. From there he
crossed the cast-iron North Gate Bridge with a panoramic view of the
river and ascended the hill towards Shandon past the laneways and
small cottages of the impoverished cathedral parish. Patricia Cox, his
wife's niece, remembered a story she heard from her grandmother,
Walburga Swertz, about his walk to work:

> That area was pretty tough when he first came to Cork, and appar-
> ently the local children used to catcall and shout names at him in the
> beginning as he made his way to his choir practices. But he com-
> pletely disarmed them by rolling pennies down the road, which they
> would pounce on, fight over, forgetting all about him in the excite-
> ment.[37]

The north parish, where the cathedral is situated, was a working-class
area in which tradesmen, craftsmen, skilled and unskilled workers
lived. Wages for working men were small, so hardship was common in
families with many children even when the father had employment. But
unemployment was endemic in Irish cities. During Fleischmann's first
years in Cork there was no state old-age pension and no unemployment benefit: charitable organisations run by the city's prosperous
merchants, and religious orders dedicated to the service of the poor,
sought to alleviate the distress. Father James Christopher O'Flynn was
to serve in the parish from 1920; he portrayed the people he knew so
well in sketches on the stage of the Opera House. He was struck by the
degree of solidarity to be found in the parish, by the fatalism and
resilience, by the sharp, irreverent wit, the gaiety, and by the sometimes
almost archaic outbursts of grief when death took a young man before
his mother.[38] Solace was provided by the church, by the public houses;
escape by the emigrant ships. A constant stream of young men left the
cathedral parish for the building sites and factories of Britain and
America or to join the British army, the girls who emigrated often going
into domestic service. The children of the parish were literate, being
obliged to attend primary school until the age of twelve; family circumstances then required the majority to begin their working lives. Music
was not at that time taught in primary schools, so when Fleischmann

founded the cathedral boys' choir in the winter of 1906, he began with children who had had no previous musical training.

The language must have been a major problem for the new twenty-six-year-old choirmaster. Notes of a speech he made to the choir for Christmas 1907 were written out in his wife's hand in phonetic script. He thanked his 'brave little band' for their 'fidelity to our noble cause':

> Almost a year has come and gone since a small boy hastened home to his parents, after a choir practice, with a great piece of news; bursting to tell it, he said: 'Mother, we have a funny man as our choir teacher now. He is small, has long hair, small little eyes, large feet and speaks nothing but German. At first we were all afraid of him, but we soon found out that he is a good fellow.'

> The boy is right: the strange man with the long hair, the small eyes and the large feet speaks German still and can drop it no more than the bird can drop its wings. Nevertheless we were able to work together steadily last year and now at the beginning of another year, I express my personal thanks for your unerring constancy and earnest endeavours. May you persevere during the coming year: that is my sincerest wish.

> There is much, much more that I would like to say to you, but my English words are all used up, so I sit down.

Fleischmann had had years of experience in Dachau training children to sing in choirs; he had himself known poverty as a child; he came from an artisan family as did many of the choirboys recruited from the parish. But in Dachau when faced with indiscipline, whether from the choir or the professional Munich orchestra, he had been able to respond using the local dialect to impress, amuse and win the group. What a daunting task it must have been to face a choir of perhaps forty boys and sixty men without an adequate grasp of that magic tool and weapon: language. Fleischmann once told a student of his: 'A choir is like a dog – it knows if you are afraid of it!'[39] If he had not in Dachau already learnt to overcome fear when rehearsing and conducting, he had plenty of opportunity during his first years in Cork to complete the process.

Plan for a Cathedral Choral Union rejected

The choirmaster not only had to win over his choir: the congregation at first did not take to the new type of music with the emphasis on Gregorian chant and works by sixteenth-century composers. In a long letter to the bishop of June 1907, Fleischmann describes the reaction of the public to the reforms of church music required by *Motu proprio*:

> Then not only from the pulpit, but in the school and press, the necessity of the reform was brought home to the people at large, and

explained in the greatest detail. Everyone had heard about it and was prepared for the coming change. The interest varied in kind and degree with different people. Nevertheless all were curious to see and hear for themselves the result of the revolution which was to be wrought at the cost of such sacrifice of time and money. This curiosity increased still more when the first unambitious practical attempt at the reformed church music took the place of the wonted pompous church music of the past – the great masses did not comprehend: 'Surely, this is not the much lauded new church music?' they asked. Even to this day they cannot understand that the grandeur and the brilliant splendour of the old music should be made to yield to these insignificant, though solemn tones. In short, people were disappointed. Incredulously they shake their heads when one speaks to them of the sublime and ethereal beauty of Gregorian chant, or of the powerful soul-stirring art of the old masters. . . . As sad as this may be for the connoisseur, it is nevertheless a fact that the majority of the people and most of the church choirs misinterpret and undervalue the immortal treasures brought to light again, and it is only their obedience to the Holy Father and his Lordship the Bishop that leads them to give up with gentle murmurs what through education and custom they have come to like.

Fleischmann feared that the rejection of the new repertoire was leading to falling numbers of recruits for the cathedral choir:

> As far as I have observed, it is hard to gain talented and persevering boys for the choir; the fact that many of their parents have to earn their daily bread by the labour of their hands, and that the boys are brought up so as to be able to support themselves as soon as possible, may partly account for the difficulty. Perhaps other things which escaped my notice have to be reckoned with too in this matter. However, I think I may maintain with certainty, that the general interest in this kind of church music, since the reform, with a few exceptions, is steadily decreasing. All this explains the small number of boys who are willing to be trained and offer their services.[40]

He therefore sought the bishop's permission to found a Cathedral Choral Union with men and boy singers who would be trained to perform sacred music outside the cathedral so that the public could learn to appreciate it. He hoped that in the long term such an institution could become the nucleus of a *schola cantorum*, or training college for performers of sacred music – in *Motu proprio* the pope had urged the founding of such an institution in every country. In the short term, he hoped the Cathedral Choral Union would secure a steady succession of new choir members willing to undergo the lengthy training needed. In his proposal to the bishop, he outlined in detail the purpose, activity and organisational form of the *schola*, including its statutes.

No written response from the bishop or cathedral administration has been found among Fleischmann's papers; the response, however, must have been negative as no such organisation came into being. In Dachau, all his innovations had won the full support of the municipal authorities, so it must have come as a severe disappointment that his ecclesiastical employers showed no interest in his analysis of the condition of sacred music in Cork nor in his carefully worked-out plans to familiarise the public with the reformed church music.

Some six months later, he was contemplating leaving Cork for a post in Germany, possibly in Berlin, which he had visited the previous summer. In February 1908 he received a testimonial from the cathedral administrator, Canon Richard McCarthy:

> Herr A. Fleischmann has filled the position of Choirmaster in the Bishop's Cathedral, Cork, since July 1906. During that time he discharged all the duties of that position in a most efficient and satisfactory manner.
>
> Herr Fleischmann came with the best possible recommendations as to character, training and professional abilities, and I am very pleased to say he has proved himself deserving of every word said in his favour. I would go even further and say he has not merely confirmed but materially improved the high reputation he brought with him.
>
> During the short time he has been engaged here he has brought our choir to a level of excellence it had not reached before, thereby winning the approval of all interested, but especially that of his Lordship our good Bishop.
>
> Success to a very marked degree has attended all Herr Fleischmann's work but especially in one particular – the training of the boys' voices – has he by his perfect method of voice culture shown himself a master in this department of vocal art and established himself as a most competent director of boy-choirs.
>
> I have just learned he is about to seek in his own country a position which will afford more scope for his brilliant attainments and while I regret anything like the thought of his severing connection with our choir I feel it is only due to him that I should further, as best I can, his very laudable efforts towards self-advancement. Herr Fleischmann has then my best and sincerest wishes for his well-deserved success.

Fleischmann had made friends with Baron and Baroness von Moreau in the course of his work in Dachau. Before Fleischmann left for Ireland, the Baron had been planning to offer him a post as musical director of a Calderon Society, which was to be a sort of Everyman Theatre producing folk plays with Christian content, concerts and oratorios. Von Moreau hoped that the Calderon Society would be financed by Munich's Catholic Casino – casinos had been founded in many parts of Bavaria in the later part of the nineteenth century as a source of funding for a variety of Catholic causes. The Calderon Society was founded in November 1906 in Munich, but by January 1908 it had become clear that the plans were not going to work out.[41] It is not known whether Fleischmann applied for a post in Germany the following month because of this, or because he had become dissatisfied with his employers, or with the cultural context of his work in Cork, or because he found his domestic situation difficult and decided to support the family from afar. However, he did not leave in 1908. If the position he applied for that year was indeed in Berlin, he was offered the post, but decided not to take it as he did not like what he had seen of the city.[42] Having been given a royal welcome during his 1905 visit to arrange the performance of his nativity play, he may have had false expectations when he returned two years later. For a Bavarian to adapt to life in the Prussian capital would perhaps, in those days, have entailed even more of a culture-shock than coming to Ireland.

Musical Director of the Cork Choral Union

It is also possible that a new opportunity to work for music in the city might have influenced his decision to remain in Cork. In mid-February 1908, Fleischmann was invited to become musical director of the Cork Choral Union. It had been founded in 1901 by Heinrich Tils for the purpose of bringing classical music before the public in two half-yearly 'grand concerts'. Foreign musicians continued to support the choir after Tils's departure for Dublin: the Fleischmanns probably attended the concert given in December 1906 under Signor Grossi's direction, at which his *Sarsfield at Limerick: an Irish Cantata* was performed by the choir and an orchestra of sixty-five players, augmented by the band of the First Battalion of the Gordon Highlanders. Six of the society's patrons had aristocratic titles; the president was Richard Beamish, the owner of the Cork brewery. At Fleischmann's first concert on 29 April 1908 the choir numbered ninety singers; the programme (which had been prepared in ten weeks) began with a 'Choral Greeting' composed by the conductor – that spring he wrote three of these. The concert combined Mendelssohn and Schumann choruses, Brahms and Schubert lieder sung by a guest singer from Dublin, and a transcription for violin and piano of Mendelssohn's Violin Concerto, Op. 64 performed by Theodore Lawson and Tilly Fleischmann, the latter also playing Brahms Hungarian Dances, a Liszt transcription of Wagner's 'Liebestod' from *Tristan and Isolde* and a Liszt Hungarian Rhapsody. Liszt made many transcriptions for piano of big orchestral works or operas to render these works accessible in the days before gramophone and radio. The second concert presented very much more of a challenge both to the choir and to the audience: it was a Richard Wagner evening, the first one to be given in Cork, planned for 9 December 1908, but postponed as Tilly Fleischmann became ill. Extracts from *Parsifal*, *Lohengrin*, *The Flying Dutchman*, *Tristan and Isolde* and *Tannhäuser* were performed, accompanied by piano (Tilly Fleischmann) and harmonium (her sister Rosa Swertz); Lena Munro from Dublin was again the principal soprano with T.J. Condon, the Cork tenor. The audience was small, it was thought due to the postponement; the concert was therefore repeated, but once again losses were incurred. The programme came in for criticism from some choir members which Fleischmann later termed 'stupid and impertinent'.[43]

With the work of the choir, however, he was extremely pleased. He sent a circular to 'my esteemed choir members' to thank them for the enthusiasm and perseverance which they had shown during the preparation of the Wagner concert. That, he wrote, was a feat on which the Choral Union could look back with pride and he with pleasure. He announced that in grateful recognition of their achievement he had composed a work that he dedicated to them, which he hoped they would enjoy singing at the next concert. This was *A Festive Ode*, his text – a tribute to Ireland – with text translated for him by Terence MacSwiney. Fleischmann wrote that he had taken on the Choral Union being convinced that in time he could bring it to a level which would command general respect and that he did not intend to deviate from the path on which he had set out. He described the works for the forthcoming concert which he had selected from among the rich and splendid treasures available, hoping they would meet with the approval of the choir. He ended by expressing his confidence that the insight into music afforded by thorough study would increase the singers' pleasure and discernment and inhibit the tendency to be judgemental; he requested them to give their energy in the coming season to the noble cause of improving artistic taste in Cork and developing music in Ireland.

It is clear from this how seriously he took his work with the Choral Union, that the criticism of his Wagner evening rankled, and how he saw his role as musical director of the choir: not as a provider of entertainment but as a pedagogue providing access to the arts both for performers and public. A further text written in German in preparation for the first rehearsal of the next concert shows how much trouble he took when introducing new works to the singers. Before talking about the composers and characterising the works, he spoke of the role of song in the world, and the power attributed to it from earliest times. He told them of the mediaeval German epic, *The Kudrun Saga*, partly set in Ireland, thus providing illustrative material from the choristers' own tradition about the role of singing in society and in the development of music. As he had done in Dachau, he saw his work for music as a service to a valuable musical heritage. This provided the basis for his friendship with people involved in the Irish cultural movement, and explains why Terence MacSwiney should have felt so drawn to his work that he translated Fleischmann's texts for his composition. Translation is perhaps not the right word: MacSwiney seems to have been inspired by the music to write his own text, as Tilly Fleischmann reported to MacSwiney's biographer:

> Terence had a very unusual artistic musical instinct. On one occasion he supplied the words for a choral and orchestral cantata with a German text without having any knowledge of the language. My husband played it for him several times. The musical rhythm of the German words straight away inspired him to compose an English text, which I enclose.[44]

At the fourth concert on 28 April 1909, the choir of ninety-five members was augmented by a hundred children's voices from the boys' cathedral choir and the girls of St Vincent's Convent school. The programme began with choruses by Anton Rubinstein and Fleischmann's teacher Joseph Rheinberger, then followed lieder by Cornelius, Richard Strauss and Humperdinck sung by Germaine Stockley. After sacred music for choir and solo alto by the seventeenth-century composer Albert Becker came Tilly Fleischmann's pupil Phyllis Scott with a Brahms Rhapsody; two light and humorous madrigals by the masters of sacred music, Gastoldi and Orlando di Lasso, ended the first section. Three works by Fleischmann concluded the concert. Two of these ('Wait! Oh be patient awhile' and 'The last March of the Goths' for male choir) had been performed by the Philharmonic Orchestra of Munich, by the Royal Opera Chorus and the Citizens' Singers' Guild in 1906, whereas the third piece, the 'Festive Ode' was given its first performance.

The week after the concert, Fleischmann was given a unanimous 'hearty vote of thanks' at the general meeting 'for his untiring efforts in the past to bring the society to the perfection which it has now attained' and the wish was expressed 'that he may long be spared to continue the good work which he is now engaged in'. He addressed the choir around the same time: [45]

> With our last concert we brought our second musical season to a close. I am delighted to be able to say, that without exaggeration, both concerts, but especially the last, were an eminent success. I was highly pleased with the rendering of the works and the spirit of the Choir. As I told you before, I do not mind what the public in general thinks of our performances. It does not influence me in the least

whether people appreciate us or not. I know, that our work is so good, that we could perform with success in any large continental town. Although our band is a small one, I am sure, it can do a great deal to spread good taste in Cork; this thought ought to inspire us to work with renewed effort next year and remain faithful to the noble aims of our Society.

During the long winter evenings we have passed many happy hours working together, in order to bring out the beauties and the character of the different masterpieces. . . .

We have made great progress since last year, and without doubt we shall make still more in the coming season. Who thought this time last year, that we could sing the 'Song of the Grail' and get so many knights to join us?

May we be filled with a similar enthusiasm next winter, and may the dove, which symbolises all that is beautiful and good, soar in our midst.

But the dove of peace was about to fly away and its departure to have a considerable impact on the lives of the Fleischmanns.

Conflict with the Committee of the Choral Union

On 7 May 1909, the secretary of the Choral Union invited Fleischmann to a meeting to discuss the possibility of an open-air concert in June, which 'would be the means of adding a few pounds to our funds'. Fleischmann must have taken this remark as an unwarranted reminder that his concerts had cost the society money and felt he was being put under pressure to give an additional concert. To the treasurer he sent a list of his expenses, including some he had incurred for the Wagner concert of the previous year which had not yet been repaid. The sum long overdue amounted to £2 13s., the equivalent today of about €230,[46] a not inconsiderable sum for a man supporting a family of eleven. In all, the society now owed him just under £17, in today's money €1,457. On 21 May he sent an irate letter to the treasurer:

I have considered the matter about the open-air concert once more and have decided to leave the matter *an open question*, until my accounts have been settled. I should not like to have the same experience as with the second Wagner evening (that the conductor, who had such an amount of work and personal expenses should get no remuneration whatsoever for his trouble, except stupid and impertinent criticisms and that the committee should give a singer £11 for a few songs). As I said to the gentlemen today, I shall only be too glad to help the Choral Union, as I have always done and to a considerable degree, since my connection with it, but I must say, I feel it very wrong, that you should take an advantage of my kindness.

The chairman replied by return of post:

Dear Herr,

I was sorry to hear your letter read at the meeting of committee today. It gave me both pain and surprise for if you remember, it was at your desire Miss Monroe was brought to sing at the Wagner concert and it was the illness of Frau Fleischmann which caused the concert to be postponed with all its attendant expense and loss that prompted us to repeat it, in order to try to pay our liabilities. However, we will endeavour to pay all your just demands tho you may have to wait a little time, until we can pay the balance, as we never intended to avail ourselves of your services without payment, and we are sorry that our relations *must* come to a close, as your letter leaves us no other course but to seek another musical director for our union and I beg to remain, with kind regards

Yours faithfully, Richard Blair, Chairman of CU

A few day later, Fleischmann received a letter from the secretary writing for the committee. He wrote that Fleischmann's refusal to conduct the open-air concert constituted the severing of his connection as musical director of the Cork Choral Union and that the committee had accepted his resignation with regret. The letter continues:

Since your connection with this Society, we have suffered a loss over each of our Concerts, and which loss we attribute to the pro-grammes not being arranged to suit the tastes of our supporters and after all you must bear in mind that the financial side is every bit as important as the musical side of a Society like ours who have to depend solely on outside contributions.

We are sure that it would be useful information to you to know that your predecessors took a much larger interest in our Society from a financial point as they often disposed of as much as from 8 to 10 pounds worth of tickets for our Concerts and our Complimentary list of tickets to the musical director was extremely small.

We have deducted the amount of 14/- charge in sortments a/c for copies of Peter Cornelius, Rd. Strauss, as the Committee have no knowledge of, and disclaim any liability of these copies.

For the Cork Choral Union
Hon Sec. John Gibbons

PS. Some of this music is absolutely useless to us as you claim it to be private property and which cannot be performed again.

On 29 May Fleischmann replied that the committee must be suf-fering from hallucinations, since he had neither refused to conduct the open-air concert, nor had he resigned from the Choral Union. He demanded that a general meeting of all members of the Choral Union be called so that he could put his case to them. He was subsequently informed that under the statutes a committee meeting had to be called first to prepare the general meeting, and he was invited to attend the former. On 3 June he wrote back, declining the invitation to attend the committee meeting, and reiterating his request that a general meeting be called. The committee wrote that they regarded his refusal to attend their meeting as a discourtesy, and sent a further cheque stating that his relationship with the Choral Union was thereby terminated.

On 10 June Fleischmann wrote:

> I most emphatically deny your statement that this action on your part terminates my connection with the Choral Union and please note for the information of your Committee that I still retain my position as Musical Director of the Cork Choral Union having been re-appointed to such by the members at the last general meeting assembled, and I have nothing further to add pending my interview with all the members of the special general meeting which I have already requested you to hold.

It is not known whether the general meeting was called. In the course of the autumn, Fleischmann must have secured the payment of the money still owed to him by having a lawyer's letter sent to the Choral Union, and then resigned.

Members of the choir were unhappy about the situation, as a letter indicates written on 20 January 1910 by two of them to another member who had come up with a peace proposal:

> Dear Mr Fielding,
>
> With reference to our conversation with you re the unfortunate state of things which has arisen between the Cork Choral Union and its late Conductor and some of its members, we gladly accept the suggestion you make and which we think is a very fair and generous one viz to pay the legal costs. Undersigned feel extremely gratified to be the means with you in arriving at an equitable solution.
>
> The Committee will accept and agree to the suggestion and will officially thank you for your kindly efforts at peaceful settlement and will ask you to convey to Herr Fleischmann our regret that this dispute should ever have arrived.
>
> It now only remains for us to receive Herr Fleischmann's acceptance of the conditions stated herein to finally close the matter.
>
> Yours sincerely
Thomas FitzGerald
William Doyle
on behalf of
Cork Choral Union

The conditions are not documented to which Fleischmann was to agree. On 15 February 1910 the secretary of the Choral Union wrote to the peacemaker:

> Dear Mr Fielding
>
> At a committee meeting held it was unanimously proposed that a sincere vote of thanks be accorded to you for your energy displayed and arranging so amicably our little matter. We feel very thankful to you and appreciate your kindness.
>
> Believe me to be
Yours very sincerely
John Gibbons

On 23 February 1910 Gibbons wrote to Fleischmann:

> Dear Herr Fleischmann
>
> I am instructed by my Committee to inform you that Mr Healy's account has been paid by this Society and trust now that all matters having been settled satisfactorily the good feeling which prevailed heretofore between the Choral Union and yourself will continue and I hope we shall all be good friends again.
>
> Yours very sincerely
John Gibbons

There is no documentation of any further work of Aloys Fleischmann's with the Choral Union. This unpleasant dispute may have been the reason why in September 1909 Tilly Fleischmann took the most unusual step of leaving her husband and home to stay in Munich alone where, despite being in the fifth month of pregnancy, she gave a concert in December, and where her child was born in April 1910. She returned to Cork with the baby in July 1910.

TILLY FLEISCHMANN IN MUNICH 1909–10

Tilly Fleischmann had left home for the first time at the age of nineteen to live alone in the land of her parents in order to undergo a rigorous course of musical training. She now set off alone from Cork once again, this time leaving her husband behind in the land of his exile, hoping to be able to arrange for their permanent return to Germany. Occasional remarks in the letters Fleischmann wrote to his wife in Munich provide indications as to why they had decided she should leave, but the matter will have been discussed exhaustively before she went and therefore does not figure as such in the correspondence. A number of aspects emerge: that they were not happy in Cork; that she felt her piano playing was not developing; that there was considerable tension between herself and her mother; that they believed personal contacts in Munich would increase their chances of securing positions, which they both now seem to have badly wanted. The idea was that they would invest in Tilly's reputation as a pianist. Through the concert agent Otto Bauer of Maximilianstrasse 5, arrangements were made for a recital in December 1909 in the Munich Museum Hall. She was to prepare for the concert in Munich, from time to time consulting her former professor, Berthold Kellermann. They hoped that a successful concert would open doors to her, help establish herself, if not as a performer at least as a private teacher, perhaps securing her a teaching post in one of the schools of music and that she would thus be in a better position to help her husband obtain something suitable.

No correspondence with Bauer or Kellermann on this subject was found among the Fleischmann papers, but the arranging of a concert will have required several months' notice and will no doubt have been underway before an unforeseen development occurred in July 1909. After nearly three years of marriage, Tilly became pregnant during a holiday at the seaside in County Cork. She may not have realised she was pregnant until August, possibly less than a month before her departure. They went ahead with the plans nonetheless. She did not live with her parents-in-law or her mother's people in Dachau, but on her own in Munich, giving her address on 17 September 1909 to the city registry authorities as Amalienstrasse 21/3rd floor, the apartment or house belonging to Rieger. It was the house in which Fr Donaghey had lived, the Irish priest who married them, so may have belonged to a friend of his. The concert took place on 8 December during a week full of musical events; her friends and acquaintances were delighted with it, there were positive reviews, but the main music critic gave it scant attention. Tilly was upset and dejected, could not face returning to Cork, and it was decided that she should remain where she was until after the birth of the baby. The child arrived on 13 April and was brought to Cork by both parents on 21 July 1910.[47]

The fact that the couple undertook such a plan, and in particular at such a time, indicates the urgency of their wish to leave Cork, the unconventional nature of their relationship, as well as Tilly's courage and independence in setting forth on such a venture. Fleischmann's letters written (in German) to Tilly during this time are quoted at some length in the following section. They give insight into his life in Cork, his work with the cathedral choir, his relationship with his wife, and his philosophy. It is a leitmotif of the letters that he and his wife had been endowed by their creator with the great gift of music, that it was therefore their mission in life to bring music of the highest excellence of which they were capable to the widest circles possible, and to foster talent wherever they found it. This sense of purpose, indeed of mission, constituted the foundation of their relationship and the bond that brought them through many difficult years.

The Swertz family in Cork

Conflict seems to have arisen between the Fleischmanns and Walburga
Swertz around this time. It is possible that the Choral Union conflict
might have triggered it. Walburga Swertz discovered that her son-in-
law's musical activities in the city were not only unpaid but that they
cost him money. She had experienced how in the 1890s her husband
had had to accept a reduction of his fees in the School of Music and
sometimes delays of months before he was paid for his work there[48]
and she may have been the driving force behind Fleischmann's rather
uncharacteristic efforts to recuperate the money owed to him by the
Choral Union. Whether this conflict led to Tilly leaving, or whether
discord arose because she had decided to leave, family relations in the
autumn of 1909 were so strained that Fleischmann left his mother-in-
law's house in 15 Dyke Parade after Tilly's departure for Munich,
moving into a house a few doors down at 12 Dyke Parade, where he
was lodged and fed by the Misses Fitzpatrick. He occasionally mentions
his mother-in-law in his letters, never has anything pleasant to report
about her and spent Christmas 1909 (his fourth in Cork) entirely on his
own. In an undated letter to Tilly, probably written in September 1909,
he describes his sense of liberation at being out of the house:

> Since I have been in this house, I have never had the feeling of panic
> or fear of life which so often overwhelmed and tormented me at night
> in No. 15, while you were asleep at my side. What a difference a
> healthy and friendly life makes and how much it can keep from one.

On 27 October 1909 he writes in a similar vein: 'Perhaps it is
because the morning sun is smiling so radiantly through the window
at me and the layer of ice which the foggy North laid around my heart
is beginning to thaw.' An undated letter, probably of the same month,
shows that there was no contact between Fleischmann and his mother-
in-law, and that he insisted Tilly sever relations as well. In the letter he
describes the circumstances leading to the departure from Cork of
Tilly's younger brother Xaver, the main force being his mother-in-law,
'the volcano', her third daughter, Elsa, taking her side:

> Xaver is really happy to have left, which is not surprising as the
> volcano was once again hellishly active, fully supported by Elsa. It
> was impossible to put up with, so R[osa] told me, which is why
> W[ally] and R[osa][49] came to me in tears to recover a little.

> I wasn't going to tell you, but I feel it is better to do so in the hope
> that you will at last understand my prohibition, which is: 'Do not
> write one more line to that house.' Should I once more hear that a
> postcard or anything else in your handwriting arrives at the house,
> and if I find out about it, do not be surprised if your letters remain

unanswered and you do not receive another line from me. So do as you are told!!!

I repeat: Xaver is glad to have left (he hates Cork) and he has great plans. Not a tear was shed, for they could all see the joy with which he broke out into the world and how delighted he was to be free at last. It was a merry farewell and there was not a trace of mourning. And you want to weep for him because he is at last moving towards the goals he so ardently desires to reach?[50]

It does not become clear from the correspondence whether he forbids Tilly to write home in order to protect her from further conflict and upset, or whether he does so because he regards himself as the injured party and requires loyalty from his wife in his quarrel with her mother.

The eldest of the Swertz children, Wally, was the next to leave home. She had graduated from the Royal University of Ireland in 1904 and been conferred with a Masters degree French and German in October 1908.[51] She then studied for a fellowship. She was not awarded the fellowship, but because of her excellent results in both modern languages was granted a scholarship of £100[52] – the equivalent today of £8,621. Tilly hoped she would continue her studies in Munich, but she chose the University of Bonn, where she also taught in two schools.[53] She would not have needed to do so unless she had given her scholarship money to her mother, thus reducing Fleischmann's financial burden. In November 1909 she visited her sister in Munich, bringing a present of a pearl brooch from her brother-in-law, who promised to keep the visit a secret from her mother.

Tilly Fleischmann's Munich concert

Apart from strained relations with her mother, there was another reason why Tilly left Cork: her husband describes it in a letter of 3 January 1910:

What drove you out of the narrow sphere of activity open to us here was not – I do believe you – ambition or desire for fame alone: it was a frightening prospect, the fear that you might fall back in your art, that you might slowly sink downwards. That feeling grew within you and developed, and you were filled with a longing for life which threw you into turmoil and instead of finding quiet peace, you were harried from doubt to doubt.

In Cork Fleischmann missed his annual nativity plays, his School of Music, his Music and Drama Society, but he was employed by a highly respected institution, for which he was doing innovative work. His wife, however, was not working within an institutional context, there was nobody to whom she could turn for further training and there were very limited possibilities of hearing music in those days before gramophones and radios, in a city with a modest range of public cultural activities. She had lived in a very different world for five years. But in taking on the 'mission' of trying to prepare the ground for their return to Munich, she was putting herself under enormous strain. Though she now had over twenty public performances behind her, the forthcoming concert worried her greatly; her husband constantly sought to dispel her fears and to comfort her:

> Remember that you have a sensitive audience and that you will be opening your heart to other receptive hearts, who do not want to have anything underlined for them, and who expect music, and not a witches' Sabbath or the arts of the devil: they want music which is beautiful, intelligently and sensitively played – and that, my despondent dear, you can give them, abundantly and splendidly.

In another undated letter he tries to calm her by playing down the role of the concert for their future:

> The best thing would be for me to send you a parcel of that couldn't-care-less feeling which I always have before such days. Don't give a toss about the people, and only be ambitious for yourself, that is: for your music! And then the audience will disappear into the darkness. Do not hope for success: play your superb works for yourself, for your pleasure: if you succeed in doing this during the first pieces, then you will have won! Remember, furthermore, that the concert is in no way of vital importance for you. Nothing depends on it, actually, when you think about it: *nothing*!!!!!! My appointment chances and so many other things have nothing to do with it! Play and allow your heart to speak and you will be satisfied with yourself. And that is the main thing.

Further strain arose over differences of opinion with her professor on questions of interpretation, Kellermann apparently brooking no dissent, insisting on the validity of his principles and on his authority as a pupil of Liszt's, deviations from his views considered 'arbitrary interpretation'. On 27 October 1909 Fleischmann writes:

> How does it happen that our greatest artists play their own works differently or allow them to be played differently at different times? Every day brings evidence of that. Why? Because as with a prism the light in their minds refracts differently every day, every hour.

But the following month she wrote that Kellermann was being most helpful.

Tilly was now in the fifth month of her pregnancy. The nervous tension of the preparation was such that she became ill shortly before the concert, as she had done the previous year before the Choral Union's Wagner evening, and she wrote to her husband in a state of complete despair. In response, on 4 December 1909, Fleischmann

questions the reason for her agitation and tries to put things in perspective:

> Play on account of yourself, for yourself, and all those groundless
> fears and despondency will, must disappear. The spectre which again
> seems to be tormenting you terribly should be given its proper
> name, and that is: vanity!! Ought I remind you how ridiculously
> despondent and desperate you were before the recitals in – Cork!
> How you played in fear and trembling before an audience incapable
> of distinguishing between a musical fly and an elephant!
>
> Give, without being concerned about praise or blame, what your
> good God gave you at birth and what you have achieved yourself
> through your tireless diligence. Can any more be expected of a
> mortal born of dust?
>
> Regard everything in the light of our beautiful and profound religion,
> which teaches us humility and holds up to us men and women who
> set themselves the highest and most difficult goals, and who, though
> derided, scorned and tormented by their fellow-men, nonetheless
> continued unerringly on their path. What are our sufferings and
> worries compared to such aims??
>
> Let every one of your notes in that sense rejoice, implore, lament and
> weep, and hearts will open to you and share with feeling your joys
> and pain. Be strong and firm in this thought, which will consecrate
> and bless you and give you the strength you need. . . .
>
> . . . Now my sweet, don't be despondent. You really have no cause to
> be so, and trust in God – He will not abandon you.

This letter may have reached her on 8 December, the morning of the
concert. The extreme tension she always suffered from before concerts
could have been the result of her first experiences of playing in public
for her father. She recounted to her grandchildren how, after one of her
first public performances playing the organ for Christmas mass in the
cathedral,[54] he reprimanded her for not having improvised during the
communion. The girl had been afraid to risk it. She went home in tears.
When they got back, her father produced a gold bracelet he had bought
for her to commemorate the occasion. She said she would have preferred a kind word at the right time. She may have internalised his
expectations of her: that nothing short of perfection was acceptable.

But Tilly and her audience were pleased with the concert. She had
played a Bach Prelude and Fugue, Beethoven's 'Moonlight' Sonata, a
Schubert Impromptu, a Chopin Ballade, two Liszt Concert Études and
one of his Ballades. Fleischmann wrote the following day:

> The telegram has been lying before me the whole day: 'Played won-
> derfully great success'. That is balm to my lonely heart! I was with

you in trepidation yesterday evening from beginning to end. . . .
Now the sky is bright again and the little pipe smoked by the fireside
once again tastes good.

He then presents a suggestion for her next project: that she should
study and perform works of contemporary composers such as Hugo
Wolf, Anton Bruckner, Richard Strauss, Ferruccio Busoni and César
Franck, as such recitals would attract the interest of musicians, and she
could hope to find herself a circle capable of upholding her. He must
have had misgivings about their choice of programme for some time:

> . . . one thing is certain: in Munich you should not sacrifice yourself
> and so much money for a programme which is certainly pleasant,
> but which cannot of its nature attract the interest of those people.
> For the public in the big cities is overfed with similar programmes
> played by *eminent* artists right through the winter.

A week after the concert, the reviews from the Munich papers arrived in
Cork. The review of the *Münchner Tagblatt* (*Munich Daily*) Tilly quoted in
her Press Notices:

> On Wednesday, 8th December, 1909, the pianist, Tilly Fleischmann
> Swertz, gave a Piano Recital in the Museum Hall. In the pieces we
> heard her play, especially in Beethoven's Moonlight Sonata, op 27,
> she showed great ability in the execution, and a fine musical con-
> ception. The audience was delighted with the artist's performance,
> and each item was greeted with loud applause.

Likewise P. Reber of the Leipzig journal *Neue Zeitschrift für Musik*:

> The outstanding quality of Frau Fleischmann's playing is her fine
> musical perception. Endowed with a strong individual perception
> she is well able to interpret the varied character of the Masters. She
> can adapt herself to the sublimity of Bach or Beethoven, the charm
> of Schubert or the refined delicacy of Chopin; she feels the sweet
> melancholy of Schumann, and she brings to the interpretation of
> Liszt more than mere brilliancy of technique.

But one of reviews left Tilly distraught; her husband called it 'a mer-
ciless dismissal'. It was in the *Münchner Zeitung* (*The Munich
Newspaper*) of 10 December 1909.[55] The section 'Münchner Musikleben'
(Munich Musical Events) contains accounts by Arthur Hahn of three
concerts and two piano recitals. The three concerts are reviewed; the
two piano recitals come last, with a mere four lines on each. Tilly
Fleischmann the critic finds wanting in emotional involvement; he
states that passages were 'often awfully blurred and unclear' so that, 'all
in all, the few better aspects of her playing were overshadowed and the

less pleasing predominated'. In neither case did he write a word about the pianists' programmes or about their personal background.

Tilly's teacher, Professor Kellermann, attended the concert and cannot have agreed with Arthur Hahn's damning comment, as he wrote his own account of the recital and allowed his former pupil to publish it in Ireland:

> At a piano recital given in Munich, Frau Fleischmann evinced not only a high degree of maturity as regards technique, but also proved herself a thoroughly accomplished artist in her conception and mastery of the different styles represented by a richly varied and difficult programme. At this recital all the pianist's fine qualities as a congenial artist prevailed: her rendering of the works of Bach, Beethoven, Chopin, Schumann and Liszt evoked the hearty applause of a numerous and appreciative audience.

In his response to the Hahn review, Fleischmann reminds his wife of the devastating early reviews of performances by Mozart, Beethoven and Liszt. A few days later he points out that she has much to be thankful for and that her concert had been praised by a musician whose judgement counts:

> What have you to complain and lament about, having been able to leave your sick-bed, as though through a miracle, and having found the strength to play your difficult programme in exemplary fashion? Is it because the masses have not heard much or enough about your triumph? Come to your senses and consider whether you are not showing ingratitude towards your God? Who was so gracious as to help you fulfil your wish? Is the recognition given to you by an honest, old and genuine artist not enough for you?

He tells her how, during his childhood when times were bad, his mother taught him to be grateful for what he had rather than complain about the shortcomings. He ends by writing of the blessing he values above all else:

> Continue to give me your love, your fidelity: what would your fame, your success be to me if I were without your love?
>
> What is it that makes us two so happy and stimulates your playing and mine?
>
> Why do I feel so rich when I think of you, as if I could live forever?
>
> Because the flame of our love is burning, is providing warmth, and is blessing us with consolation on our path.
>
> Beloved, . . . let me close with the simple words of my mother, who once said on a dismal winter evening: 'Be thankful to the good God – Who still means well by us'!!

They must have expected that she would have a joyful Christmas relaxing after the hard labour of the concert, relishing her success, and preparing for the next challenge: the birth of the baby. Instead she found herself in a state of turmoil, their hopes of her winning public acclaim in Munich having been dashed. It was Fleischmann's fourth Christmas in Cork. Earlier letters show that the memory of his childhood and of his parents had returned at Christmas time in Cork with an intensity which tormented him; he must also have been reminded forcefully and bitterly of his artistic triumphs with his nativity plays and of the hopes he and his family had harboured for his future. For the first time ever, he was alone for Christmas. The leitmotif of his Christmas letter to his wife, however, is tranquillity. He speaks of the sadness that at this time used to overcome him in Cork as belonging to the past, and there is indeed no trace of it in the picture he paints of his meditation on the family celebration in his old home. The underlying theme is that of the birth of their child:

You know that this time of year always saw me dejected and sad. This year I await the quiet days of the feast alone. I shall celebrate the beautiful feast in solitude! Strange to relate, my heart is tuned in gladness and serenity to the coming time of hope and joy! With equanimity and confident faith I shall put up my little Christmas tree thinking happily of you and of my parents.

Remember, darling: every little candle shining on the tree there, every golden nut that gleams there, every red apple beaming from the branches – all these small, rich splendours on the tree are this year not only shining, gleaming and beaming for you! Be glad with me! All the colourful glory which you will see – and which you should see with joy – will also be felt and experienced by our little heir! Especially on the days around the birth of our Lord, let much warming joy flow into your heart as a young mother, so that our slumbering child, whose eyes are still blind and whose hands cannot yet reach out towards the shining candle, may be granted the most beautiful and splendid gift of heaven: that of joy. Gloria in excelsis Deo: joy on earth to those of *good will*! Happy are they who at this time of grace are surrounded by love and are not deprived of the knowledge that they are faithfully remembered. Beloved, be glad with me! Let you light your little candle for me in the home of my youth where as a child I awaited with pounding heart the first bliss of the feast days, and I shall light mine for all of you in my quiet hermitage!

Carry the incense around the house for me, which I long ago used to carry with a feeling of great importance in an old, heated pan: I shall ignite mine and sacrifice to you who are far away.

Then, when in the late hours the bells ring out from the old steeple sending peace out over the roofs of my home, think of me and be cheerful and happy. For at this time, in the shining shimmer of the candlelight, amid the fragrance of the green fir tree, I shall be looking down into the depths of my childhood and thinking with gratitude of your love.

In this sense the quiet celebration will be for me an experience of peace and of joy, and the holy night will find me, too, among my loved ones, and not alone!

Tilly to give birth in Munich

After Christmas he writes about the next question to be decided: whether she should return to Cork or remain in Munich for the birth. This is bound up with their hopes for the future, but he leaves the decision to her and urges her to do what is best for her psychologically and physically and not to think about the money, though he is filled with sadness that all he can offer her is 'a modest, all too modest existence'. He explains that if she decides to stay in Germany he cannot join her unless he finds a post there:

> Now with regard to myself. My feelings and pride would never allow me to move to Munich if I did not have a post and had to depend on the compassion of our friends. To rely either directly or indirectly on their help would not only be undiplomatic but unwise, indeed stupid. In time we would find this weighed on us, and no matter how careful they were, we would feel it and bitterly regret it. Our creator did not make you nor me for such a role. As the years passed we would even come to despair of each other. Such plans and loose hopes bound together with cobwebs are pernicious.

He had just made a submission to the Prince Regent through a friend with court connections,[56] but says it could be years before they hear anything:

> I must repeat that without a post I cannot return with you, not even if you were to earn enough to keep us afloat reasonably well. The only way out without painful defeat, if Munich were to fail me completely, would be my home town Dachau! During the first year there would be a lot of derision and gossip, but I know that the following years would open their eyes for them! But this plan may take ten years to mature, so it is not to be even breathed to anybody, for it is a plan of very last resort!

> For you the first question is not so difficult, since as I have a secure position here, which I will maintain with all my strength, there may be the prospect that I could perhaps come to Munich for four to six months every year (for as long as I am here) and perhaps give lessons and soirées there.

If Tilly decides to return to Ireland for the birth of the baby, he suggests they consider living in a fisherman's cottage by the sea, but does not say how that could be combined with his nightly practices and services in the cathedral. He urges her to take the decision:

> And eliminate me completely: I can plunge into work as into a medicinal spring. Through you the greatest happiness flows to me and whether I have you at my side or must seek you far away, the knowledge of your love fills my chamber with riches.
>
> . . . May God, 'who still means well by us', grant us the blessing our modest life needs, and may your happiness as a young mother compensate you for the many things which I alas am not in a position to offer you. Good health is the greatest good and comprises all the joys on which the life of the soul flourishes. Knowing that you are in good health and that I am loved – can I ask more of my God?

Another letter suggests that they were hoping for a specific post in Munich, but he plays down her chances of influencing the outcome: 'Be guided by your own feeling for what you want to do – whether to remain there or to come to me. I am quite convinced that your presence in Munich will make no difference, absolutely no difference with regard to the decision about the post.' The decision that she should remain in Munich for the birth was probably taken in January 1910: 'I myself now believe it is best for you to give birth in Munich, that this will bring you greater calm and security. Because if you came back to 15 Dyke Parade you couldn't avoid scenes.'

Fleischmann's life in Cork

Throughout the correspondence, Fleischmann seeks to comfort, encourage and reassure his wife. All his accounts of his work and activities are cheerful and positive; if he did have to contend with difficulties, he does not describe them. On 21 November 1909 he writes:

> Buried in work, but happy! – and contented. My work brings me some great moments, and keeps me in equilibrium when the wings are about to take off on higher flights, and that is good. I now enjoy working with the boys (both big and small): they are transformed. Father Murphy is splendid; Father Leary is taking singing lessons so that he can sing Mass. My pupils – especially Rex! – are making great progress.

He had taken on his wife's pupils, and writes frequently about the remarkable progress her gifted sister Rosa was making, and that of her talented friend, Phyllis Scott. He clearly enjoyed their company, which he says 'grants me delightful insight into their innocent souls'. With another pupil he played Beethoven's symphonies arranged for piano duet; he said they were 'quite heavenly' and that he sometimes felt rather proud of himself.

He visited Phyllis's family regularly, also the Stockleys, a German pupil of Tilly's, Dr Orb, and the painter Seán Keating. Of the latter he writes:

> I often visit Keating; I am very much at ease in his dark painter's hermitage, and I feel that he is very pleased to see me whenever I come.

> My dearest, I now speak very good English, and sometimes, in order to hear good English, I go to the theatre – I understand every word, every shade of meaning! From now on you're not going to be able to lead me up the garden path any more!

> Was with Rosy today in *Samson*, and Eckhold was really good, at least far better than average. Puccini's *Tosca* – wonderful music, orchestra and choir here, really distinguished, rich and good. Have learnt a lot.

Another person whose company he enjoyed was a retired army officer, William Bauress:[57]

> Mr Bauress is a very assiduous, remarkable person of much talent, who reads the classics day and night. I am getting to know English literature through him. And we spend many pleasant hours at the fireside full of enthusiasm over the beauty of some works. I give him one German class a week. Sometimes I go out into the country with him for hours, mostly at dead of night. He is indeed a man of rich and noble character.

Despite all his teaching and his work at the cathedral, he applied himself to extensive studies with a rigorous daily work schedule. He writes about how he came to appreciate the music of Brahms through studying the lament for choir and orchestra of 1881, *Nänie*. The letter was written during a sermon at the Lent mission of 1910, the choirmaster taking a break from the service:

> Just a few quick lines to you. While the preacher is thundering outside and trying to terrify his listeners (we are having the mission) I am in the waiting room, trying to capture the sweetest words and tender emotions which I feel for you, my all.

> I had a remarkable experience this week. I have never felt very close to Brahms who, I used to think (or rather used to feel) was too academic a composer, and although I admired his works, I was not able to derive the warmth from them which could open up my innermost world.

> Every day I read scores for two hours, and happened to come upon his work for choir, *Nänie*, set to poems by Friedrich Schiller. I studied the work cursorily; I liked it very much and continued the following day and so on. Now I am so taken by it that I could play my fingers

to the bone on this wonderful music, that I could cry out with pleasure and pain when I even think of it. I am no longer standing in admiration outside the portals of Brahms's art: I have stepped into the holy of holies. What greatness, power, force. When these our gods bless one with the richness of their sublimity, send such flashes of lightning – such moments remain unforgettable and live on in us as glimpses of eternity.

He copied out the full text of Schiller's poem for her. This is followed by a long account of his reading and thoughts about Beethoven's 'Moonlight' Sonata, which she had played for her concert and which he greatly admires. The letter ends: 'May the inexhaustible fount which lies in this extraordinary work open itself up to you in its entirety, my dearest.' There are many such passages in the correspondence in which we see that the study of the arts is for Fleischmann a spiritual experience: this is the key to understanding his dedication to music and his commitment in the work with his choirs.

Brahms's lament was written after the death of his friend, the painter Anselm Feuerbach, and dedicated to the dead man's mother. Tilly must have feared that her husband's study of such music was motivated by unhappiness over her absence and probably said she felt sorry for him and tried to console him. In a letter of 5 March 1910 he rejects the idea that his pain is caused by her:

> Yearning is an agonising pain with which I was born and which cannot be healed. Whether you are here or there, or I there or here – I am always consumed by it, always. How often have I wished I was made of a harder wood, but nothing can be done about it. Nobody can get away from their own shadow.

> However, since I have been able to really work in depth, life has looked on me more cheerfully and happily notwithstanding. My treasure: consolation you cannot give me, but love, love!

> Consolation and pity are two brothers I do not want to meet any more. I would prefer to be hated by people than pitied: under no circumstances pitied. That hurts more than it helps. Consolation and pity are for me devalued coins.

Life cannot have been easy, alone in what was still very much a foreign land to him. But it is clear that the positive image conveyed in his letters to her is not only the result of his concern for her peace of mind, but also a product of his pride. He will not be pitied.

However, he had much to be proud of. In a letter written after Easter 1910, he describes the progress he has made with the cathedral choir:

> A long period of intensive work now lies behind me, which for the first time here has brought me genuine, substantial success. It is

success which derives from within and which has richly rewarded my efforts. I am even myself astonished at the ease with which both boys and men now approach new work which is unfamiliar to them. Yesterday for instance I rehearsed a new motet with them which demands the finest of nuances and sensitivity both from boys and men. Just imagine trying to finish a new motet in one rehearsal two years ago – it would have been impossible. I have indeed learnt an immense amount in recent times, and it is as though this were transmitted unconsciously to others.

What frightful dread I suffered when I had to face all those difficult tasks demanding diplomatic skills and the practical tricks of the trade! Now I have to laugh at myself: the chain of long adversity and hidden grief with which I used to be shackled now lies broken before me. The haze has lifted and with it that repulsive gloom which tormented my heart. In the glorious spring sunshine I now see clearly and brightly illuminated before me the hope-bringing words: In activity lies salvation!!!

I regard it as a good omen that it was Eastertide which brought me this precious insight. The festival of spring and the beginning of a new life and new blessings.

The picture of the early days in Cork which emerges here is a rather grim one. It is typical that he only describes such unhappiness once it has been overcome. This glimpse of his struggles with his work and with himself give a measure of his achievement in having within four years mastered a foreign language, trained the existing cathedral choir to sing a completely new repertoire and founded a boys' choir, bringing the untrained singers within a short time to a high level of excellence.

The second part of the letter shows Fleischmann on holiday after the exertions of Holy Week. What he terms 'doing nothing' turns out to be an intensive study of Goethe's dramas *Faust* and *Torquato Tasso*.

The whole week through I did nothing but lie in the sun and sleep long and well. During the best parts of the day I read *Faust*. *Faust*!! Sometimes it seemed to me as if heaven and earth would collapse in ruins. That was reading material for Easter, an overture to spring! It sweeps like a storm across the country and shakes everything in us and in our wretched artificial culture. Thunderbolts – oh for wings, wings to take us out of this misery and this small world!

. . . Almost too splendid for us poor mortals – such greatness hardly comprehensible.

He was also composing. At the end of February he must have sent his wife an organ prelude, the name of which she did not understand. He is surprised that she did not recognise the Liszt motif worked into it:

> . . . *Queril* is a Latin word which means cry of lamentation (the cry of
> the seagull). It is odd that you didn't recognise the mood of the first
> piano notes reminiscent of Liszt's old waltz, which I was thinking of
> when I wrote it down. I have written about a dozen such preludes,[58]
> partly because I felt an urge to do so, and partly as an exercise. Some
> of them have interesting harmonics. I was pleased to hear that you
> liked these few chords. I shall send some more later on.

A comical image of the hard labour of composing is given on the
occasion of Tilly's name-day, the feast day of her patron saint, Matilda, on
14 March. Catholic Germans of that generation celebrated name-days
more than birthdays. Fleischmann describes himself trying in vain to
think of an affordable present when inspiration comes in the form of a
print sent by Tilly's pupil and companion, Bertha Scherer, nicknamed
'Stützli' or 'little pillar' because of her great kindness to her teacher. It was
a painting by their friend Richard Pfeiffer, who had just been offered a
professorship at the Royal Academy of Art in Königsberg, and who was
just then painting a portrait of Tilly. The picture, *An die Nacht* [To Night],
had been published in the Munich *art nouveau* journal *Die Jugend*, which
was edited by Franz Langheinrich. The painting depicts Dachau at night:
it shows a man leaning out of an illuminated attic window overlooking a
patchwork of roofs of old half-timbered houses; he is gazing up at the
dark blue night sky covered in stars. Inscribed on the wall next to the
window is a poem,[59] which Fleischmann quotes in his letter and around
which he wove the song he was composing for Tilly:

> For the 14th of March
>
> For weeks I have been wondering what I could do to give my dear
> little wife who is so far away a small surprise for her name-day. I have
> been considering this and that, studying the catalogues: splendid
> instructive books and sublime works of sound and image passed
> before my mind's eye. I saw the big new elegantly bound Liszt biog-
> raphy, then works on Chopin and the marvellous book 'Robert and
> Klara Schumann' – not to mention all the pictures and music.
>
> Melancholy crept into my heart and thence the wish: Ah, if only I
> were a king or – a genius! With a sigh I sat down again and began to
> clatter away valiantly at the wooden foot pedals of the harmonium.
>
> The following morning I found a piece of home awaiting me, greeted
> by sunshine, sent by dear Stützli, on which the newly baked
> Professor dreamed his lovely dream.
>
> Again I sat down at the old pedals – it seemed as if 'the beautiful
> stars' were hanging directly over me, large and clear. A deep and
> blessed peace came over me, sent greetings to you, greeted your
> quiet kingdom and my queen – without a crown. When the stars
> departed all that remained to me were nostalgic wishes and these
> paltry tones that with their smiling ignorance demonstrate my own

powerlessness. But wishes they are, as only love knows them and implores their fulfilment: tones of nostalgia known to all who strive towards light.

These heartfelt and painful wishes together with this melody, this lament, are intended to speak to you of many beautiful things, things which have become lost, which have never been said.

Take as meant for you this quiet greeting from my home and the salutation which the creator of this splendid picture indirectly sends you. Thus united let us celebrate you on this special feast day in your cosy little room – you beloved sweet queen of my heart and my dearest without compare.

His song 'Night', Op., 26. No 1 for female voice and piano, is set to the text depicted in Pfeiffer's painting *To Night*; it was published by Augener of London in 1929.[60]

Some ten days later, about three weeks before the birth of the baby, he reassures her once again that the sadness and dejection of the first years in Cork have disappeared. He names a number of possible reasons for the release, but ultimately attributes it to the better under-standing of music attained through the discipline of his studies:

> I don't know whether it's my growing love for you, whether it's the warm sunshine of the young spring, the chorus of birdsong outside my window, or whether a curse has been lifted or a wish fulfilled. For the past few days I feel that a change has occurred, I feel uplifted by an indescribable feeling of happiness. As you know, success at my work didn't come easily in recent years; a leaden weight oppressed me and despite most favourable circumstances bound me and my mind and soul down. This weight has now been completely removed, and I find myself in a higher, purer atmosphere; the benefit of my long studies, which I pursue resolutely, is making itself felt. I feel I have taken a leap forward and that warms my heart. Fog has lifted; a large piece of the curtain that impeded my sight has fallen. It is as if a new door has opened on to one of the seven courtyards sur-rounding the high heaven of our art. Good luck to us, and a grateful glance to the skies.

The birth of their child

Fleischmann's pupil Phyllis Scott remembered him being extremely worried about his wife during this time, which (aged 17) she could not understand. But he keeps his fears out of the letters, ending this one with a message sent by the stars and the bells of St Fin Barre's Cathedral:

> Every evening the golden Plough brings me over to you. Listen! the bells of the Protestant cathedral are ringing – the magnificent sound echoes over the quiet roofs and fetters my thoughts in its enchantment.

Now my sweet precious treasure I shall close with these solemn bell chimes. May my fleeting words also ring out in your heart and speak to you of love – deep faithful love. Good night my sweet.

On her birthday, 2 April, he realises that the baby, like its mother, will be an April child, he himself being 'an April fool' as well:

That makes three April creatures – how could we not be lucky? There can be no doubt about it! According to the old beliefs of the people we are bound to be lucky, very lucky. And if luck doesn't come to us, then we will go and fetch it ourselves!

In fact their birthdays were to be exactly eleven days apart: she 2 April, the baby 13 April and he 24 April. In his last letter before the birth, he sends her his blessing, his fear of the dangerous days ahead kept firmly under control:

Now the blessed miracle of nature will soon be performed and both our hearts will be filled with new love, joy and happiness. May the hand of the Almighty protect and bless you during your hour of need.

My brave girl – you have so often proved yourself in life and have been strong: these anxious days will pass and you will recover, full of hope and joy.

She had a difficult birth, was in labour for three full days and suffered a great deal. She was moved to the midwife's nursing home for the birth,[61] where she stayed until the beginning of May. Having received the telegramme announcing the arrival of the baby, the proud father wrote ecstatically that he could shout, jump, sing his joy – but not write coherently:

Such miracles as these which are done unto us humans are too great for words. The feeling of happiness which has taken possession of me is so deep and so powerful that I have to remain silent, look upwards in silence and in spirit be with you, with you both, sharing your experience, your joy, your tenderness. . . .

The memory of my fears for you is still very much alive; it cuts my breath short and dries up the words that rush to the lips. You good, poor young mother! Please, please do keep telling me how you are and how the little one is – this great heavy weight of worry still oppresses me unspeakably. I beg you to take care of yourself and not to get up prematurely – do be careful!

Oh thou good quiet moon high up there in the heavens, dispatch my greetings for me! Oh ye innumerable radiant stars that look down like hovering angels, take my wishes and illuminate the cradle of my

son with your mild light and let his young mother dream of happiness and joy and of his bright future.

According to a note in Tilly's hand on the envelope of this letter, he sent
her a Mörike poem with it. It is not among the papers. It might have
been his New Year poem 'Ein Engelein leise' ['Like an angel softly']
which Fleischmann was to set later on. The baby was baptised in the
church of St Ludwig on 24 April 1910, his father's thirtieth birthday.
Thirty-five years later, he recalled the momentous moment when:

> . . . a telegram brought me the tidings that, after difficult labour, a son
> had been born to me. Deeply moved, I held it in my hands, reading it
> over and over again. Happiness, fear and worries overcame me
> simultaneously, alternating in my thoughts like the unstable April
> weather outside my window. What happiness! A son! I was the envy
> of kings and princes. Lonely stranger though I was, I went around as
> in a dream. But my fears for mother and child tormented me and
> subdued my joy; then came the worries about the future, for there
> were more thorns than roses growing along our path in those days.[62]

The young mother seems to have suffered a form of post-natal
trauma: shortly after the birth she sent her husband an angry note
accusing him of lack of concern for her, of indifference. In his reply to
this utterly unexpected charge, he describes the agony of mind he had
endured during this time, knowing that labour had set in, being without
news for so long and fearing the worst. His fears were well founded,
given the high mortality rate for women in childbed and given that so
many infants in his parents' families had died at birth or soon afterwards,
as had infants born to their friends. He writes in great distress:

> We have not had such a misunderstanding since we were married;
> indeed I can say that in all the years we have known each other
> there has never been such a serious misunderstanding between us
> as now – and that despite us both standing with joy and fear in our
> hearts on the brink of eternal remembrance!

> Don't you know me any more? Have I become such a stranger to
> you?? Are my ways, the world of my feelings, my emotions alien to
> you???

> What unfortunate delusion prevailed upon you to give credence to
> the incredible??

> How can a father whose first child has just been born to him be
> indifferent to such an occurrence? Who would not be deeply moved
> by such a blessed miracle and by the pain of a young mother? 'O vos
> omnes' I am forced to think of these words, which must move every
> heart profoundly, for such serious moments of life are deep and

mysterious as is life itself – the appropriate similes can only be found in the annals of religion.

Oh Tilly, I am inconsolable that you should unjustly attribute such an unpleasant attitude to me. I wept bitterly when I read your note. Do you consider me a barbarian? I cannot even indicate, not to mind describe the unutterable melancholy and nostalgia that overtook me when the first news arrived.

Can you really not put yourself in my situation, can you not under-stand what it means for me to know that you are in pain so far away and that I can do nothing, nothing except hope and hope from one hour to the next, and wait from one day to the next and try not to despair? Can you not imagine what it means not to be able to see my own child and not to be able to share the joy with you??

Indifference – !!! From between the lines of the telegram I read and felt that you had either been through an uncommonly bad time – or that such a time still lay ahead of you!!! Young Gebler, Frankgeld, Lemberger and others – all of them died after a few days. . . .

I was incapable of doing anything except brood and ponder. I ran to the post office; but turned around and went back. I wanted to write, not to congratulate you! Questions, questions – what had the telegram omitted to say? Questions burned in my heart. Could I write that?? No – only a few lines! No, otherwise she might think I was ill! In short, I simply cannot be made responsible for these days of torture: they were days of the most intense fear and terror and I went around as though out of my senses. Only with the arrival of the third telegram did I begin to think it was the truth and to feel joy. I reject your accusation: it is really unjust and has caused me unspeakable pain.[63]

The letters written in May are not among the Fleischmann papers, so it is not known how the conflict was resolved. However, the last letter written shortly before he left Cork to bring the mother and child home shows clearly that all was well again between them. It contains a dra-matic account of how his joyful anticipation of their reunion was brought to a sudden end by the death of an old woman in a room close to his:

I woke up this morning feeling unusually happy. . . . The sun was spreading its first rays, which fell in pink beams through my window. The twittering of birds enlivened the peace which still reigned supreme. I thought about my dream as I lay awake and dreamed on. . . . But then a low moan entered into my dream, such as one might hear from an injured person. The muffled sound from afar was repeated regularly; I sat up and listened, and vaguely remembered having heard that strange sound before. It was spine-chilling and I felt afraid and lonesome. Though the sun was flooding ever more strongly into my dark room, and the birds were singing at the tops of their voices as before, it was so strange that I felt utterly abandoned. An indeterminate sense of nostalgia affected every thought, every movement from the moment that undefinable sound destroyed my beautiful dream.

As I was trying to make out what this bizarre sound could signify, where it could be coming from, whether it emanated from an animal or a human being, I heard my name being called loudly. I was to discover all too soon in fright and confusion the place whence this uncanny lament had come.

Friend Death had crept into the house and had broken the heart of old Molly, who had woken unawares from a good sleep. After about ten minutes of weak resistance, she followed him into the kingdom of shades and death. All alone I watched her slowly weaken and by the time the others came back with the priest and the doctor, all was over, and she lay peacefully, almost smiling, on her pillows. Outside life moved on and people were hurrying past the door through which the relentless one had quietly entered, leaving silence and deep peace behind him.

May she hear all the lovely 'Irish Airs' beautifully played for her on heavenly harps which she so often played with rapt attention. May all the good wishes be fulfilled which I prayed at her bedside would be granted to her, deeply moved as I was by her fate. May she be shown around the heavenly kingdom by the little angels where she can now walk again without pain and without a stick, saved and liberated, and may she see all the splendours which are awaiting us too and have been promised to us. R. I. P.

Molly, infirm and living alone in Cork in her old age, must have been a traditional musician, perhaps the source of the Irish airs he used in his compositions. His prayer for her shows that he had already become assimilated in his new home: her own people could not have put it better. But perhaps assimilation just means arriving at the stage when you discover your own small town in the foreign one.

Death was also hovering over the Swertz family: Tilly's younger sister Rosa, of whom they were both so fond, was seriously ill and there seemed little hope for her, which 'terribly grieved' him. (She was soon to recover.) But nothing could keep him from setting out on his journey to Munich. The correspondence ends in a tone of exuberant optimism as the end of ten months of separation and the prospect of seeing his two-month-old son approaches:

Never have I faced the future with such proud confidence. I feel strength within myself: strength. Hard work has steeled me, allowed me to see what I am capable of, and that creates a feeling of jubilation like the tone of cast-iron bells. No farewell (Mr Bauress is moving to Dublin) and not even death with all its terrors and its

shattering power can daunt me and dampen the boisterous joy of
life which has now awoken within me and is impelling me forward
towards the time in my native place which I have so longed for.

The Dachau painter, Hermann Stockmann, who had designed costumes and scenery for his nativity plays, wrote in June to announce a
special welcome for the visitor in his home town:

We are delighted that we will soon be seeing you again. The salute
guns on the castle walls will be practising zealously as from today
and garlands of flowers one hundred and seventy six meters long are
being woven in Würmling forest. But I am not supposed to be
talking about this!

CORK BECOMING HOME 1910–14

Fleischmann made one last application for a post in Germany in 1911.
The only documentation is a testimonial given to him by the cathedral
administrator, and a note in Tilly Fleischmann's hand on the envelope
stating that it was for a position in Augsburg. He was not appointed,
though he had the small comfort of knowing that he had come very
close to being selected.[64]

The financial burden of supporting the Swertz family was by now
greatly reduced. By the summer of 1910 all the boys had left home: the
eldest, Hans Anton (called Tony), had finished his medical studies and
was in Trinidad; Xaver had graduated as an engineer and was in New
York; Ferdie was in Philadelphia, and Leo at sea. In 1910 Wally was
studying and teaching in Bonn; Elsa had married Chris O'Malley-
Williams in 1909 and moved to Dublin the following year. The two
younger daughters Rosa and Cressie were at home. Wally returned to
Cork in the autumn of 1910, and in 1911 was appointed to the first
chair of German at the university;[65] she was therefore able to support
her mother and the two sisters.

Surprisingly, the Fleischmanns nonetheless continued to live in No.
15 Dyke Parade with the Swertzes; in 1913 they all moved to Holmkliffe
on the Lee Road; in 1915 Guy's Cork Directory lists them all as living in
2 Clifton Villas in Montenotte. The most likely explanation of why they
still lived with Walburga Swertz is that they had together purchased a
house, which they could not have afforded on their own. Fleischmann's
regret and indeed sense of shame that he was not able to provide better
for his wife is a leitmotif of his letters and may have been at least partly
induced by their not having a choice in this matter. After 1910, he never
mentions his mother-in-law again in his correspondence and she does
not figure in the accounts he gives of the child's early years.

Progress with the cathedral choir

The testimonial given to Fleischmann for his Augsburg application by the cathedral administrator shows that his work was greatly appreciated and his personal dedication much admired. Canon Martin Murphy underlines the choirmaster's commitment, his work ethos, and his ability to motivate even 'the wildest boys':

> Herr A. Fleischmann was appointed Choirmaster and organist here some five years ago by my predecessor Canon McCarthy. I must say that he was especially fortunate in being able to secure the services of such a gifted musician. I have before me as I write Canon McCarthy's estimate of his worth and desire to endorse his statement in every particular.
>
> I am happy to be able to give Herr Fleischmann the highest recommendation as to character, ability and energy.
>
> Since I got charge of the Cathedral I have learnt to know him intimately and the more I know and see of him the better I like him and the more I appreciate his work. His Lordship the Bishop has frequently expressed his sense of indebtedness to him for all he has done for the Cathedral Boys Choir. He has brought this choir to a high pitch of perfection.
>
> His energy, punctuality, and the great interest he takes in his work have been admired, not only by the Bishop and Clergy here, but have won golden opinions for him from the laity throughout the city.
>
> All his duties in connection with the Cathedral Choir have been discharged in an eminently satisfactory manner. The boys' choir was practically founded by Herr Fleischmann. It has been his special work and thanks to his high professional abilities and training and to his intense application to work very marked success has crowned his efforts.
>
> Under his charge perfect discipline is maintained both among men and boys. I don't know how it is, but he seems to have the peculiar gift of getting all his choir to work with a will and under his influence some of the wildest boys grow steady and attentive at their lessons. In a word he has complete control over all the members of his choir.
>
> He has set an example of punctuality and love for work to us all; I have never known him to be absent or late even a minute from any practice or function at the Cathedral.
>
> I may add that he has a good knowledge of the Liturgy and rubrics of the church so essential to a Choirmaster.
>
> I do not exaggerate when I say that I have never met anyone so devotedly attached to his profession.

I should regret his departure from here extremely. It will be difficult to supply his place, but as he is going to his own country to a better position it would be unfair to put any obstacles in his way, and I wish him with all my heart the success due to his splendid abilities.

Cork 29 May 1911 (Eleulu)

Fleischmann continued his efforts to provide the citizens of Cork with the opportunity for active music-making outside the church.

Founding of the Filedha Choir

In 1912 Fleischmann founded a fifty-voice ladies' choir, the Filedha Choir, which gave concerts in the Assembly Rooms. It was almost a family undertaking, with all four sisters-in-law and his wife participating as well as his friends Germaine and Violet Stockley, and Rita Horgan. A programme design combining Celtic ornamentation with the Cork Arms was done for the choir by 'MM' in 1913 – this could have been Tilly Fleischmann's pupil, Muriel Murphy. The Filedha Choir was often joined by the men and boys of the cathedral choir. A concert given on 27 May 1914 included a 'Choral Greeting' by the conductor, and a work, 'The Kitten', for choir and female solo, the German text of which was translated by Terence MacSwiney[66] – it may have been a poem of the composer's. Tilly Fleischmann played Brahms's Sonata Op. 28 for Cello and Piano with Livio Boni of London; the concert ended with Wagner's 'Gralsfeier' from the opera *Parsifal*, the cathedral choir performing with the ladies. The concert was favourably received, the reporter from the *Cork Examiner* regretting, however, that 'while there was a large and fashionable audience present, the attendance was in no way worthy of the excellence of the entertainment'.

This was to be the last Fleischmann concert in Cork for a long time: during the first two years of the World War, he abandoned all public appearances in the hope of avoiding internment as an enemy alien.

Tilly Fleischmann's pupils

Tilly Fleischmann began to play publicly again some months after her return to Cork; the following year she gave a recital for the Liszt centenary; in February 1913 she played with the Dowse Quartet – these concerts were given favourable reviews in the London *Musical News*.[67]

She resumed work with the pupils who had been taught by her husband in her absence. Among them was the painter Harry Scully. He had been one of the first students of the Crawford School of Art, then studied in London and went from there to the continent, returning to Cork to teach in the school after he had become a member of the Royal Academy. He specialised in watercolours and in landscape painting, but he occasionally accepted commissions for portraits – his painting of the president of University College Cork, Bertram Windle, hangs in its Aula

Maxima. His work was exhibited in Dublin and in London. His piano teacher was presented with many of his paintings.

Tilly Fleischmann usually only accepted advanced students. She met a wide variety of people through her teaching, and developed friendships with many of them. There were Germans among them. One was Mary Hilser, the daughter of a German jeweller who had settled in Cork. Another was M. Orb, a physician who had studied the piano in the Conservatoire of Frankfurt with the Dutch pianist James Kwast; he had moved to Cork with his family to open a spa, St Anne's Hill Hydro, near Blarney. Mary Horgan, the wife of their solicitor friend and daughter of President Windle of the university, became a close friend, but her daughter remembers that she had to work extremely hard for her teacher nonetheless. The professor of economics, Timothy Smiddy, studied with Tilly Fleischmann until he was called away in 1921 to act as advisor to the Irish delegation negotiating the Treaty in London, after which he was sent to Washington as the first Irish ambassador to the United States. Students of very different political opinions met in Fleischmann's house. Tilly taught Victoria Kirkpatrick of Mallow, whose father was a colonel in the British army, and daughters of old Cork merchant families such as Geraldine Sullivan, Jennie O'Brien and Muriel Murphy, who were to become associated with radical opponents of British rule in Ireland. Muriel Murphy, whose family were wealthy Cork distillers, met her future husband, Terence MacSwiney, in December 1915 at one of her piano teacher's musical evenings.[68]

One of Tilly Fleischmann's clerical students, Fr Pat MacSwiney, was a cousin of Terence MacSwiney's. After his ordination, he was sent for three years on the English mission, when he studied under the eminent Gaelic scholar, Kuno Meyer, at Liverpool University, and took his MA in addition to carrying out his clerical duties. In 1914 he was brought home to become professor of Latin and Greek at the diocesan seminary of Farranferris, living in Montenotte near the Fleischmanns. He was also proficient in Irish, French and German; active in the Cork literary Twenty Club; lectured on literary subjects; developed a deep interest in music, especially in Chopin, on whom he did much research and planned to produce a study of his life and work. He became friendly with Corkery, the Stockleys and the circle involved in the literary movement, and almost a member of the Fleischmann family. He supplied translations for Fleischmann's works with German texts, and programme notes for Tilly's concerts.

The Fleischmanns' child

As a baby, Aloys junior was called Bubi (little lad) by his parents and their friends. In Dachau he was always called Alfi, perhaps to distinguish him from his father. As he got older, his parents' friends added the word 'óg' to his name, the Irish for young (pronounced with a long 'o' as in 'vogue').

Looking back in his mid fifties on the period of his son's childhood from 1910 to 1914, Fleischmann described it as one of 'happiness and contentment'. He wrote to Aloys Óg in 1945:

> Your mother's love, tenderness and willingness to make sacrifices knew no bounds. These cardinal virtues compensated us for the affluence we didn't have. So you grew and thrived to our great joy. Your young life filled the years with happiness and contentment for us. It made up to us to a large extent for the loss of our home.

Memories of Christmases with the baby came back to Fleischmann in 1932 when his son had left home to study in Munich and the first Christmas without him was approaching:

> On the third Christmas Eve of your life I held your little hand in mine. We left the bright house and went down Lacaduv avenue.[69] You were in the little grey trousers you owned and were wrapped in a small dark coat. We were walking along under the tall dark trees when you suddenly stopped. Startled and pleased you pointed to the bright stars over us: 'Papa, Papa look! Heaven is full of holes!' There was no end to the questions. The impression was powerful and lasted for a long time. It will have been your first conscious sight of the great mysteries of the worlds revolving over us.

> Another time on Christmas Eve when you still wore a little gown, and the bell in 'Holmcliff' indicated that the Infant Jesus had come at last, you came shooting down the long banisters like a flash of lightning before the eyes of the horrified nanny and off into the room with you. The big brightly lit Christmas tree hung with gold and silver ornaments and nuts, the colourful presents on the floor: a rocking horse, a playable piano etc etc – all were ignored and the heir to all these costly treasures disappeared at once under the table on which the Christmas tree towered resplendent. We looked at each other in concern as to the meaning of this; I felt a pang as I thought perhaps there was a weakness of the eyes which could not bear the army of bright lights. But not at all: without delay, off you crawled out into the dark corridor towards the hall door, repeating sorrowfully and with disappointment: 'Where is Infant Jesus? Want to see Infant Jesus!'. Only gradually was comfort found in the great variety of toys which no child's heart can resist. Finally the little Infant-Jesus-seeker fell asleep happily, his presents hung all around his cot. But the story of the disappointment over the Infant Jesus flying away without letting himself be seen and without staying for a chat was recounted to all our friends and spread afar. Your good Aunt Wally never tired of telling it.

One year when Christmas came, you sat in the evening when it was dark for hours at the big window on the balcony, and there was great joy and enthusiasm when you saw the right golden wing of a big angel who was among the Infant Jesus' followers disappear around the corner. On these nightly watches, you once withdrew your head quickly, held your hands over your hair and ran in greatest concern to the mirror in the bedroom. You looked long and carefully into the bright glass to see whether the dark night had dyed black the ash-blond hair of which Mama and the little fellow were so very proud!

The four good years of 'happiness and contentment' were to come to an end in June 1914 and to be followed by two years of anxiety; then came nearly five years of separation, and for Fleischmann imprisonment, ill-health, and despair.

Cork around 1900

The River Lee
(*Courtesy Cork City Libraries*)

Patrick Street
(*Courtesy Cork City Libraries*)

John J. Horgan and his
daughter Madoline,
*c.*1917

Mary Horgan *née* Windle

Terence MacSwiney and
his wife Muriel in 1917

Daniel Corkery

CATHEDRAL CHOIR SOPRANOS AND ALTOS.

The boys' cathedral choir; on the back in
Fleischmann's hand: 'My merry cathedral finches'

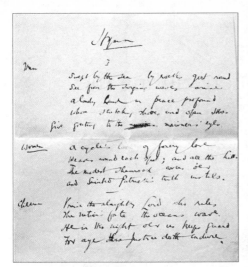

Terence MacSwiney's draft translation of
Fleischmann's 'Festive Ode', 1909

Tilly Fleischmann
in Munich 1909

The men's cathedral choir

A cathedral choir outing

Aloys Fleischmann in Dachau
visiting his grandparents, 1913

Tilly Fleischmann

3. Internment during the First World War

Aloys Fleischmann (*left*), Dr Heider, Oldcastle internment camp, 1918

FLEISCHMANN FROM 1914: AN ENEMY ALIEN

During his first eight years in Ireland, Fleischmann had to come to terms with the personal difficulties every immigrant encounters who must learn the language and adapt to the culture of the host country. From 1914 to 1920, however, the life of his family was determined by unforeseeable political developments. Ireland was under British rule, and with the beginning of the First World War on 4 August 1914, the German immigrant became an alien and was seen by the authorities as a potential threat to the realm. His situation as a foreigner from an enemy state was further aggravated by family circumstances.

Fleischmann was informed on 22 June 1914 that his father had died suddenly of heart failure in Dachau. He set out at once for Germany and arrived in time for the funeral. He remained with his mother until 30 July, arriving home on 1 August, three days before the declaration of war.[1] His sister-in-law, Wally Swertz, who had been spending the summer with relatives in Crefeld, did not leave Germany in time and was unable to return to Ireland. Fleischmann was taken into custody in Cork on 18 August, but released two days later when reputable friends had undertaken to guarantee for his good behaviour.[2] However, shortly afterwards the city of Cork was declared a prohibited area for aliens,[3] and the family was ordered to leave. They were given permission by the authorities to accept an invitation to stay with Colonel Kirkpatrick and his family in Mallow – the friendship with this influential Anglo-Irish family had arisen through music: the Colonel's daughter Victoria was a pupil of Tilly Fleischmann's. The Colonel intervened successfully on their behalf, as did the Bishop of Cork, the Lord Mayor, the High Sheriff, John J. Horgan and others: on 15 September the Fleischmanns were allowed back to their home at 2 Clifton Villas in Montenotte, Cork.[4]

On 7 May 1915 the British liner *Lusitania* was sunk by a German U-boat off the coast of County Cork and 1,200 passengers drowned. It looked as though Fleischmann's days of freedom were numbered. He submitted a petition to the Home Office seeking exemption from internment, reiterating his promise of appropriate conduct and compliance.[5] The exemption was granted, and for eight months the family was able to live a normal life. However, the exemption was withdrawn at the beginning of 1916. The British intelligence services were aware of the activities of the Cork republicans, as Mary Kirkpatrick, the Colonel's wife, indicated in a letter to Tilly Fleischmann: 'There has evidently been some trouble in connection with Cork which has . . . no doubt caused the stricter regulations which have now hit you so terribly.'[6] Some of those republicans were friends of the Fleischmanns. Fleischmann was arrested during the night of 4 January 1916. How the trauma of the scene had seared him is evident in a letter written to his son almost thirty years later on 13 April 1945:

> I shall never forget how you and your mother wept as we bade farewell, your little arms clinging to my knee and refusing to let me go until those brutal hirelings tore me away, taking me like a criminal before dawn at 4 a.m. to an unknown destination. The sound of that weeping and sobbing pursued me for years.

He was sent to an internment camp in Oldcastle, County Meath, and detained in the former workhouse with hundreds of other German civilian prisoners of war[7] – his prison number was 750.[8]

The reason for his internment, according to Major Price, the intelligence officer in the Dublin headquarters whom Fleischmann's solicitor contacted, was that he had sent a letter in November 1915 to his

mother in Dachau – it was a Christmas greeting.[9] A further twenty-two
charges of pro-German spying and sabotage were communicated by
the service to Colonel Kirkpatrick when he intervened on
Fleischmann's behalf. One of the allegations was that Fleischmann had
a wireless telegraph in his garden (it was a bird house); that he
frequented the coast with a telescope watching for submarines (he and
John Horgan used to go bird-watching with field glasses in
Oysterhaven); that he had been seen pouring poison into the River Lee
near the Cork waterworks.[10]

This time Colonel Kirkpatrick was unable to obtain his friend's
release. Fleischmann was to remain in Oldcastle for two and half years;
in May 1918 he was sent to a camp on the Isle of Man,[11] and though
the war ended in November 1918, he remained incarcerated on the
island until the summer of 1919, after which he was moved to London,
and from there deported back to Germany in October 1919, where he
had to remain until September 1920. He was away from home for
almost five years: his son was not yet six when he was taken prisoner
and was ten when his father saw him again in freedom.

CONDITIONS IN THE INTERNMENT CAMP

The prisoners were allowed to write two twenty-four line letters a
week, but were not permitted to describe the camp or their daily life.
However, they could receive parcels, and what Fleischmann asked his
wife to send him gives some idea of conditions. The buildings must
have been cold and spartan, as he wanted three blankets and a pillow
to be sent urgently, a warm knitted jacket, waterproof boots; he also
needed a wash bowl, a kettle and mug, cutlery, tobacco and books.
Provisions must have been very scarce, as Fleischmann always put the
word 'dinner' in inverted commas and had to have his wife send food
every week. Almost all his letters home were written in German.

He wrote in his first letter: 'The days are long; the nights inter-
minable. Twice a month I can see friends for fifteen minutes. The
journey from Cork and back takes two days!' The first to undertake the
onerous journey was the curate of the Cork cathedral parish, Father
O'Flynn. Two friends, Grace O'Brien and Mary Horgan,[12] also came in
January, but Fleischmann found the shortness of the visits so dis-
tressing that he was tempted to see nobody:

> When Märchen had left and the minutes began to revolve emptily
> again, I remembered what I had forgotten to say, and was ashamed.
> In my excitement I forgot to ask M how she and the family were, and
> didn't even thank her for all her goodness to you and to me! Thank M
> and John for me most heartily and explain to M that her firm

optimism so surprised and confused me that many questions and words remained stuck in my throat.[13]

When on writing home he describes his state of mind, he usually does so tersely: 'This week is over: it was hard. I feel as if I have lead in my bones and poison in my veins. Sleepless nights. A twilight life of torpor. An existence without substance, without aim.'[14] But in a letter to Muriel Murphy, he elaborates:

Dear Muriel, For your kindness, but especially for the time you give to my little lad, a thousand thanks. Everything is subsiding into mindlessness here. These are lost days in which mind and body run themselves into distraction along the walls. We meet fellow countrymen of all kinds. People from all corners and crevices of Germany and Austria. People with whom I share no interests, have nothing in common except the meaningless cycle of this restricted, desolate life. Mother Nature is kindly: sun and moon shine here too and touch faces and thoughts. Last night I dreamt of Brahms' 'Schicksalslied' [Song of Fate]. The sound was so clear and powerful that it woke me. I would need peace. I haven't been able to read ten pages. I don't mix with anybody, not with the 'virtuosos' either. In spite of all the parcels, I am only very slowly learning to cope in this curious ant heap. Farewell! Aloys[15]

During the long periods with no visitors, the stars were employed as messengers, as he wrote to Tilly and the Horgans: 'If you are together some evening and that Golden Chariot [the Plough], passes above you forming a great arch, then pack it with faithful and dear thoughts. On clear nights it always stops outside my window, with Mars at its side.'[16] His mother used a similar courier: she wrote to her son:[17]

Have received your letter: it is balsam on the wounds which the war has inflicted on us. That we have not been able to see each other for so many years. I send you thousands of greetings almost every day through the Evening Star; for Father used always say: this star shines on Alois as well as on us! Am most unhappy when we have an overcast sky and I cannot catch sight of my messenger.

Sometimes the stars mourn with him, as he put it to Tilly on New Year's Eve:

Am so glad that Christmas and that dark year 1916 are over. On Christmas Eve it was so silent and the stars looked down through a haze and their shimmer was as blurred as if they had tears in their eyes. For a long, long time I looked up to the quiet pilgrims on the heights. I comforted myself with the thought that every night leads to light, and tears and pain to joy, laughter and songs.

Pilgrims came from Cork too, though not often. The occasion of a visit from Tilly gave rise to a rare lighthearted letter to his friends Germaine Stockley and Mary Horgan:

> Dear, revered Schermen[18] + Märchen, Let me recount to you. At last I saw my long-awaited! After the first greeting I sat as though in the cinema. In Tilly's romantically rose-coloured cinema. Of you, good, faithful friends, I heard so much that I saw you before my eyes as in the old days, and that filled me with gladness and happiness. A thousand heartfelt thanks for everything. During the interval I wanted to get around to my fatherly admonitions. I began prosaically to talk of food, sensible clothes, strong shoes, when I noticed that Madame was keeping her feet demurely tucked in under the chair. Haha! a little hole in her stocking? (Oh blessed days of the pickenick [*sic*]) But no, she was hiding her tissue-paper shoes, for the world outside was swimming in floods of rain. [*in English*] 'Till, to get so wet is very detrimental and dangerous for you.' But unperturbed she continued: [*in English*] 'Nonsense; it is very satisfactory.' What can one do? I bowed my head and comforted myself with the thought that even Jupiter had to give in and change. Then I heard such nice things about Bubi that my heart leaped. I wanted to impress upon her the parable of the silent gold and speaking silver, but – the beautiful dream was already over. I fear the gold has already all been spent! When I got back, I re-read in a letter: 'Tilly is a woman of greatness'; in another: 'Tilly is a wonderful woman.' [*both in English*] What remains of the much admired lady for me, her poor old spouse?? Märchen, please go and inspect Tilly's collection of shoes. 1000 thanks for your great love.

Though Fleischmann's concern about his wife's health is treated here with self-irony and good humour, it provides a leitmotif in his letters. He calls her 'Griselda' – a character of Petrarch's and of Hans Sachs's who was subjected to the severest tests of endurance and obedience, and who withstood all tribulations[19] – and an 'Amazon'[20] because of all the work she was burdened with. She not only had to continue her work as a pianist, to cope with her teaching, but – qualified organist that she was – she was allowed by the bishop to take over her husband's work as organist, trainer and conductor of the cathedral choir. Though she was used to small boys as the elder sister of a large family, it cannot, nevertheless, have been an easy task maintaining discipline as a woman in such a position. Fleischmann's own enforced idleness must have been a particular torment to him under these circumstances.

A letter of advice to his wife on how to cope with the situation indicates his empathy with her grief and the comfort he derived from the memories of life with her and the child; it also shows how he himself sought to come to terms with his fate:

When the pain threatens to overwhelm you, go out of doors. Mother Nature is a good comforter (even in the worst of weathers). But take Bubi with you. It's not good for you to be wandering around alone in such hours, brooding and pondering. If I could take my child's hand and wander over the fields with him, and could hear him chatting, I think it would be like walking into the open heavens. . . . Am so glad to hear that you are reading the classics again to take your mind off things, even if only for ten minutes a day. Don't read anything tragic. I don't expect any long letters, Tilly, if you only tell me what you're doing, whether you're well or depressed: the slightest things are of interest to me. Let me live with you a bit! Your life is hard, I know. But there are many whose fate is a lot harder than ours. You have your boy, after all, and the hope of happy years. If you are tormented by suffering, weep it out of yourself: that brings relief; take your boy's hand and go out into the fresh air; then God won't abandon you, and you'll come home strengthened and calmed. Use every small pleasure, every ray of sunshine to strengthen yourself mentally and physically against trouble. Don't worry about me. Stay fond of me; be brave. I am. Who can say but that this terrible war mightn't collapse overnight?[21]

Two months later he writes: 'Dearly beloved Till, Your letter has made me happy and my troubled soul is beginning to become calmer. As after a confused dream, the words dance before my eyes until quiet, clear examination puts the pictures in position and orders them.'[22]

Fleischmann's son used to tell his children about a visit to the camp when he was perhaps seven years old, a visit which the detainee had looked forward to and prepared for months, but which ended in distress. The prisoner had spent weeks carving a ship for his child; the small boy was delighted with the present, but did not recognise his father in the alien surroundings and had indeed probably forgotten him. Having examined his present, packed it up again and tucked the parcel securely under his arm, he tugged his mother's sleeve and, to his parents' consternation, asked: 'Mum, can we go now?'

MUSIC AS CONSOLATION

Christmas was a painful time for the family:

Most beloved Till, The pleasure, the jubilation which will fill children's hearts over the coming days does not reach us here, but the thoughts – they do get to me with the thousands of burning heavenly lights, and they help me for the second time to celebrate the beautiful feast here alone. On Christmas Eve I will unpack all the old memories like Christmas presents – and will think of you. Your last letter, dear, good Till, was rather melancholy. Don't let your pleasure be dimmed by such a mood. All mourning must disappear when a

child's eyes shine in the candlelight! I am with you and am quietly
sharing your joy. Celebrate as in the old times. May my small presents contribute a little to your pleasure, and may my small friends
not completely forget me![23]

He is haunted by the Christmases of his youth in Dachau as well:

Most dearly beloved Till, heartiest thanks for your lovely Christmas
letter of 14.XII which sounded as beautiful and familiar as the E
minor chord of the old church bells hovering in the starlit sky of
Christmas Eve over the white, snow-covered gable roofs.[24]

Fleischmann conducted a choir and an orchestra in Oldcastle. He
had to copy by hand the music they performed; he arranged works of
the polyphonic masters, and also composed a number of new works. He
made sure that the prisoners at least had music at Christmas and the
work of preparing the concert helped to dispel the additional melancholy caused by the advent of what was supposed to be a festive season:

Am glad that Christmas is over. They were depressing days. On
Christmas Day I performed Goller's Mass in G together with my
Adeste. I set both for male-voice choir and string orchestra, the latter
with a solo clarinet. In spite of the over-full hall, it sounded good.
But the rehearsals, in which the sound was beautiful, gave me more
pleasure and compensated more for all the copying I had to do. Let
me have Goller's correspondence of the summer of 1913 in which
he talks about the liturgical synthesis of the arts, and in which he
invited me to Salzburg[25] – it must be somewhere among my papers.
I hope nothing of mine will get lost. . . . May the coming year be gracious to us, and open the gates.[26]

The gates remained closed for ever for one poor prisoner, who was
buried in the camp at the end of January 1917. Among the few papers
that Fleischmann brought home with him from his internment is a
photograph of the gravestone of an internee. Fleischmann wrote on the
back:

Franz Xaver Seemeier, prisoner in Oldcastle. On 28 January 1917 (at
5 pm) he was bayoneted by one of the guards when he was
searching along the barbed wire fence for some small thing he had
lost – he was within the walls on the west side. (The guard was
transferred and promoted to the rank of corporal). The physiology of
war!

The memorial stone was put up by us. Seemeier was an extremely
pleasant, peaceable and helpful person. 'Under the protection of
Erin, may the earth weigh lightly on you. R.I.P.'

THE DEATH OF WALLY SWERTZ IN GERMANY IN 1918

However, in the course of 1918, conditions were to become much more difficult for the family. Fleischmann's mother, Magdalena, had not written for a time. In April, he tells his wife of this, and warns her that her sister Wally may be ill:

> I now know that the long silence of my dear old mother was due to a serious illness; she wasn't even able to write and wanted to hide from me that she was ill so as not to frighten me. How that silence tormented me, I cannot describe to you. One just has to summon all one's strength and bow to it. Quietly accept the suffering God sends. She is now better again and sends her love to you and the little grandson. A strange uneasy feeling tells me it will be the same with Wally.[27]

Five weeks later, he confirms the bad news:

> I wrote to Wally every 3 weeks, sometimes more often. For 4 months Wally has not written to me: my letters remained unanswered. Nor did I get an answer from Aunt [Hans Conrad Swertz's sister, Mathilde Swertz of Crefeld]. (For a while I didn't notice, as the post is very slow). My good mother made a remark at the beginning of the year about Wally being sick and mother sent her balsam. I thought it was a passing problem, but when weeks passed without a sign of life from Crefeld, I wrote to mother (who keeps up a lively correspondence with Wally). I got the following reply: 'Dear A. I have news for you which will grieve you and Tilly. Wally is very seriously ill. It is difficult for me to have to tell you, for I know that you are so fond of Wally. I am sorry now that I didn't write sooner about her being sick: she has not been able to get up for a long time. But Wally strictly forbade me to tell you that she is ill, so as not to frighten you.'[28]

In fact, Wally had died four months previously, in January 1918, just before her thirty-seventh birthday; the family in Germany could not bring themselves to add to the troubles of the prisoner by telling him of her death. As there was no postal contact between Germany and Ireland, Tilly did not know about it either. Among Fleischmann's papers there is an account of how he heard of Wally's illness, of her death; a poem he wrote about her death indicates how much she meant to him. The paper on which it is written does not have the prison stamp but it resembles the camp paper.

REMOVAL FROM THE IRISH CAMP TO THE ISLE OF MAN

A further blow was to follow the next month. On 25 May 1918, the German civilian prisoners of war were removed from Oldcastle in County Meath and shipped to the Isle of Man. Fleischmann's registration number was 5,812;[29] his prisoner number as given on the letters: 32,342. The removal from Ireland meant the end of visits: the Fleischmanns were not to see each other again for over two years. A short visit was permitted every three months, but travel by sea was dangerous and costly. To Canon O'Sullivan of Cork cathedral Fleischmann mentions the difficulty of his departure from Oldcastle, and his worries about the political situation:

> I cannot tell you, Canon what awful hours of bitterest despair I have been through, with only here and there a calmer day, when I can think that perhaps there may be a little ray of hope left. I see the Hague conference is to be over in five days. I wonder if the proceedings will then be published? I am anxious about the outcome. I have meanwhile become more accustomed to the new surroundings. We all found it very hard to leave old Ireland and to take this change of air philosophically. It was hard for our families too. I feel still my boy's little hands around my neck.[30]

In his first letter to his wife he underlines the beauty of the landscape:

> The sea was so very beautiful and calm. A burning longing for you and our lad moved with me. . . . There is a view all round of a high chain of hills: the camp lies in a valley. The island seems to be very beautiful, as far as I could make out in the moonlight. For years I had wanted to see it. Now my wish has been fulfilled, though not quite as I had imagined.[31]

He could not tell her then about their traumatic arrival. He later recounted to his grandchildren that when the civilian German prisoners from Ireland landed on the Isle of Man, they were forced to walk in single file through a large group of women, who screamed abuse and jabbed them with hat-pins. There had been demagogic press reports about the alleged laxity of the prison regime in 1915, and throughout the war the stream of vitriolic articles castigating the savagery of Germans could rouse non-combatants to a degree of fanaticism seldom found among the soldiers.[32]

The history of the internment camps on the Isle of Man has been well researched and documented by the Manx Museum and National Trust. The first prisoner-of-war camp was set up near the capital, Douglas, in September 1914, and had originally been a men's holiday camp. It soon became unbearably overcrowded, and after a disturbance in November 1914 during which five prisoners were shot dead by guards, a new camp was established at Knockaloe on the west coast. By 1918, 23,000 detainees were living there in compounds, each of which held 1,000 men. Every compound had five sleeping huts with 200 prisoners per unit. 3,000 guards and 700 miles of barbed wire secured the three-mile camp circumference,[33] from which only a handful of prisoners ever escaped, and none for more than a few days.[34] Most of the internees were German, but there were also Austrians and some Turks, Turkey being an ally of Germany.

Fleischmann wrote home a few days after his arrival:

> The people flood past me as in a dream, and the pitiless truth is still covered up by the host of new phenomena. I have no idea what the people are like with whom I sit at table or share the dormitory. 'Who can count the peoples, knows the names of those who are together here?' . . . Lamentation and bemoaning are of no use: there is only one method – accepting calmly and with composure what every day brings by way of long suffering and short pleasures.[35]

He kept a magazine with a drawing on the cover of a prisoner standing in despair at the towering barbed wire fence of a camp,[36] which no doubt reflected his own experience. The anguish comes across in a letter written (in English) to his son in the autumn of 1918:

> My dearest Büblein, [little lad] you haunt me frightfully in dreams lately. Why is that? I was dreaming last night that you jump like a wild cat into my bed (every evening and very early in the morning) and we tease each another + play like in the old times – w[h]ere we even made gymnastic exercises on the organ bensh! Do you remember the lovely Mayfield walks? I shall never forget the evening where you and I went for a long, long walk – what a shock I got, as I found out that I went much to far, moreover that I was on the wrong road – after a while, happily, we discovered the right old way again. Late and tired we arrived in Montenotte, wet like drenched poodles! Do you remember? Tell me, wasn't it nice all the same? Often I think on this adventure – on those blesst + happy hours. Well my dear little boy, be good + obedient don't forget your papa who loves you so dearly – oh how desperately. I do long to be with you and your lovely mammy again.[37]

WORSENING OF CONDITIONS IN THE CAMP

From June 1918 the sending of food parcels to the prisoners was forbidden. Fleischmann told Seán Neeson that Jewish prisoners saved his life on the Isle of Man by sharing their food with him when rations were scarce.[38] The Quakers, who opposed the war, did all they could to alleviate distress and, from 1915 on, had helped provide books, tools, equipment and materials for the internees to work with and to start workshops in the camps.[39] As the cost of the war increased and its duration became unforeseeable, the camp authorities began to allow those prisoners who wished to do so to labour in quarries, on roadworks, construction works, bogs and farms; those with the required skills who could get hold of the necessary materials were permitted to set up workshops to produce clothes, shoes, furniture, baskets, carvings. American embassy officials visiting the camp in 1917 found about 1,500 men so employed. Many others worked in the camp administration as cooks, bakers, cleaners, gardeners. Improvisation was the order of the day. The renowned woodcarver from Oberammergau, Andreas Lang, produced exquisite pieces carved out of meat bones using a nail attached to a small block of wood. These he refused to sell to the camp officials: he made them only for his friends. [40]

Sports were allowed, and there was a great deal of cultural activity. The prisoners organised all sorts of educational classes for themselves; each compound had a theatre and an orchestra. Fleischmann had books sent to him: classical authors, especially dramatists, and he must have studied philosophical works, as he told his wife that he had 'freed himself from Schopenhauer's splendid theory of despair'.[41] He attended the camp performances: 'Was at a play and an operetta – first rate. The women's parts – absolutely masterly in presentation, language and song. Today B. Shaw's 'You never can tell'. 4 theatres and 3 orchestras try to alleviate the misery of imprisonment, and that is necessary.'[42] Fleischmann knew the other musicians. One of the conductors was Hans Adolf Winter, who had been working with the Moody Manners Grand Opera Company in London when the war began and became chief conductor of the Bavarian Radio Orchestra afterwards.[43] Fleischmann joined in the work for music in Knockaloe as he had done in Oldcastle, and directed a church choir and orchestra. When the prisoners left the camp, he was presented with a handwritten address of thanks for his efforts which was signed by a hundred choir members. He composed works for voice and orchestra for their concerts.

THE HEALING POWER OF SUGGESTION AS A LAST RESORT

Fleischmann suffered from bad health during his internment: in his letters home he does not mention it, but in 1957 he gave his son an account of his illness and of the unusual cure he effected through a combination of discipline and despair:

> During my four years of imprisonment I had seven (!) illnesses. Three were physical with typical symptoms; four were imagined.[44] We had twenty-six doctors in our camp who were strictly forbidden to have any professional dealings with us. We depended on the village doctor; he was a scoundrel who sold the medicine that was sent to him from Germany and treated us with coloured water. It actually worked for some poor simpletons who swallowed it down in good faith. (Simple-mindedness gives rise to miracles and is their never-failing source!) Every prisoner therefore had to be his own physician. The only remedies we had at our disposal were salt, vinegar, vermouth plants and warmth – the latter supplied by old newspapers and brown packaging paper. I was fortunate enough to have got hold of an old coal sack, which kept me warm during the winters.

By chance I met the Viennese psychologist Dr Ertl, a dignified old gentleman who stood next to me at the daily 'rag parade'. We called it the 'rag parade' as we were all lined up in rows and had to stand there in our threadbare and ragged clothing to salute His Highness, our commandant. Ertl turned out to be an enthusiastic admirer of Bruckner and Klose. One of his sons was studying music at the Academy and University of Vienna. Among his teachers were Professor Goller and Dr Springer with whom I had then been corresponding for years.[45] That was of course a welcome link and our relationship soon became closer. At that time I was suffering from lung pain with violent coughing and was spitting blood. He took a keen interest and was very helpful but had no access to medication of any kind. The place was so overcrowded that he was not even able to examine me. Like myself, he feared that tuberculosis was developing; he did not say so openly, but I knew it without explicit confirmation. I felt wretched and had a high temperature.

. . . One day Dr Ertl spoke to me about the healing powers of suggestion. He said that the mind forms and determines the body – astonishing to hear a free-thinker speak of 'faith-healing'! I gave a loud laugh. He was rather taken aback and said: 'There are more things in heaven and earth than are dreamed of in our philosophy!' He spoke of the incantation ceremonies of the Egyptians, of the sixth and seventh books of Moses and their healing incantations, of the force of suggestion exercised by the Siberian peasant and healer Rasputin. He expounded in a most scholarly fashion based on his wide professional experience on many issues which I unfortunately no longer recall, but I was particularly fascinated by what he said about the possibility of obtaining relief from suffering through auto-suggestion.

. . . So in my desperation, deprived as I was of all medication, I acted on the advice of this highly respected and renowned psychologist, and began daily auto-suggestion. I banned all pessimistic thoughts from my mind, paid more attention to my activities and behaviour, seeking to determine what was detrimental and what beneficial to my recovery. As one obsessed, I reiterated to myself over and over again: 'You will recover; you will recover completely. You will recover! You will recover in order to escape from this hell.' The impact was disappointing; my hopes dwindled and my patience was nearly exhausted. But I did not give up. The pressure on my lungs disappeared, so did the often excruciating pain, the coughing, the diabetes, and the paralysis of my right foot (this had been caused by a back injury which for months had made it impossible for me to move without a stick). A stay later on in the spa in Wiesbaden completed the cure. The four other imagined ailments disappeared like ghosts into the night. And so I did not end up (as many had expected) buried as a prisoner of war in the camp graveyard, but lived to see

you again, now a tall delightful boy, and your dear brave Mama, after
four hard and bitter years.[46]

The prisoners and their families were soon to need solace even more
than before. It was clear by July 1918 that the war was drawing to a
close, but they were informed that they would not be allowed to return
to Britain or Ireland. On 19 October 1918 Fleischmann was transferred
from Knockaloe to a smaller camp in Douglas. Only 16 per cent of the
prisoners were allowed to return to their place of residence in Britain,
and it took nearly a year before the appeal procedure was completed
and the other eighty-four per cent were sent back to Germany.[47] There
was virtually no chance that Fleischmann could return to Ireland, given
the trouble that was brewing there and the political affiliations of some
of his friends. Indeed, his wife had heard a rumour that she too might
be deported with her child.[48]

Only a few weeks after this terrible news, which had brought Tilly
Fleischmann to the verge of an emotional breakdown, she heard from
her husband that the flu had hit the camp:

> For 9 weeks there have been no distractions whatever. No church
> services, theatre, concerts. The halls were all turned into hospitals:
> the flu found its way here and wreaked great havoc. All my neigh-
> bours, those above and next to me got it – I escaped unscathed.[49]

They must have slept in two-tier bunks in the dormitories. During
the world flu epidemic, two hundred million Europeans were infected
and, between 1918 and 1919, twenty million died of it world-wide –
more than had been killed during the war. Fleischmann's brother-in-
law, Leo Swertz, who had been wounded twelve times during the war,
died of the flu in Charlerois in February 1918. The death rate in the
camps on the Isle of Man was high, as Fleischmann wrote many years
later:

> One needed a very tough constitution to survive, given the miser-
> able threadbare clothing we had. That is why in spring 1918
> hundreds died quickly and suddenly as if of the plague. The huts
> were full of enfeebled sick men who could no longer stand and were
> already marked by death. 'The more, the better!' laughed the
> Scottish soldiers, who guarded us 'Huns' full of hatred, their bayo-
> nets fixed. My good friend Andreas Lang was also among those who
> were carried away. Never to be seen again in this life, we thought.
> But as if by a miracle, Andreas, the woodcarver and High Priest from
> the world famous village, recovered and, like me, saw his home (and
> his beautifully painted old house in Oberammergau) again.[50]

AN UNCENSORED IMAGE OF CAMP LIFE

Fleischmann's son kept a diary in 1926 and 1927; an entry for 27 February 1927 describes an account his father gave of his internment. It seems to have been the first time the seventeen-year old heard of it:

> Pappi's one prayer was that he should not go mad and become like the poor lunatics who sat at mass and actually lived with the other prisoners! 350 men were partitioned in each court, having plank beds, wearing rags and getting loathsome food which they had to swallow in gulps to prevent nausea. A few times he was nearly strangled by madmen. Grafs [counts] and beggars, priests and lunatics were all mixed together. His diary he had to burn or it would have been taken by the authorities when he was freed.

Forty years after his internment, Fleischmann described the nightmare that was life there in a letter to his son:

> A person's life is worth nothing in such times and under such circumstances. It is of no significance whether an individual is healthy or ill, dies a natural death, opens his veins or hangs himself where thousands are oppressed and worn down by their fate, robbed of their livelihoods, torn from their families in all corners of the globe, all vegetating like packs of different animals behind barbed wire. Old and young, rich and poor, aristocrats and commoners, thieves, criminals, disreputable and honest people from all classes and from all over the world with white, brown, black, yellow faces, all indiscriminately rounded up, herded together and condemned. It was Babel with the pandemonium of foreign voices. An ant-heap in never-ending motion. All are strangers to each other, doubt the truth of what is said, are suspicious of people's accounts of their lives and background. Nobody is concerned about others; everybody carries his own burden and is silent, troubled and morose. The days are full of tumult and noise. The nights are mostly disturbed by quarrels, strife and fights. When the moon shines, the prisoners who have gone mad wail and howl for hours in their barracks on the hill near us. In our barracks the rats that scent our carefully hidden food swarm out in the darkness – rat hunts undertaken with shouting and commotion are not exactly gentle lullabies. A sad and miserable existence. Not a minute's peace by day or night. Dante's Hell is imagined: this was the real hell which constantly preyed on one's nerves, which drove those with less robust constitutions to madness and hanging. When I lay on my more than thin straw pallet on the damp stone floor, I often prayed: 'Those who have never eaten their bread with tears, who have never sat weeping by their beds – they do not know you, oh heavenly powers!' One has to have experienced such hours to be able to imagine them.[51]

When war ended on the 11 November 1918, there were 24,450 prisoners in Knockaloe Camp. On 16 January 1919 Fleischmann arranged a

Silcher a song for his choir in Douglas camp entitled 'Das Schifflein' [The Little Ship], words by Ludwig Uhland. But he remained in Douglas until 4 April 1919, when he was sent back to the larger camp of Knockaloe and later from there to a prison in London, where conditions were bad and the staff hostile. [52] A calculated provocation by the kitchen staff – they put rats' tails into the prisoners' soup – led to a riot with several deaths. Fleischmann rarely spoke to his grandchildren about his time in the camp, with the exception of a small number of stories: among them this. He also told them how appalled he had been the first time he saw the body of a man who had taken his life. After a while, to his greater horror, he found himself simply stepping over them and taking suicides completely for granted.

DEPORTED TO DACHAU IN POST-WAR CHAOS

Fleischmann was informed in October 1919 that he was to be deported to Germany, but that his wife was to be allowed to remain in Cork with her son, despite the 'troubles', the war of independence. Before his departure, he was allowed a brief visit to his brother-in-law, Dr Tony Swertz in London, possibly because of a back injury which had led to a paralysis of his right leg. Swertz brought him to a specialist, who diagnosed tuberculosis of the spine and gave him a few months to live.[53] No letters have survived from the last year of his imprisonment; no information has come to light from later correspondence as to how he reached Germany. Andreas Lang and his son had to go on foot and spent six weeks walking back to Oberammergau, never once being able to get out of their clothes. Fleischmann could not have accompanied them and must have travelled by train. When he reached the Red Cross central camp of Wesel, not far from the Dutch–German border, he was given a paper on 23 October 1919 entitling him to two days' bread rations and to travel by train to Dachau. He broke his journey in Wiesbaden to visit a friend, a doctor who was practising there – probably Dr Orb. On his advice Fleischmann went to the famous spa, and after five treatments in the hot springs, he was cured and 'able to jump like a goat for joy and high spirits'.[54] He had no further trouble for many years, though in later life he suffered from attacks of sciatica in the injured leg.

Life must have been an endurance test for Fleischmann's widowed mother during the turmoil of the end of the war, and she must have been overjoyed to have her son back again. He must have been appalled by the chaos and destitution he found in Dachau. A huge munitions factory had been built there during the war, which had employed about eight thousand workers, most of whom had come to the town because of the work and were not citizens of Dachau. The pre-war population of the town had been about 5,000. After the Treaty of Versailles, Germany was no longer allowed to produce military goods of any kind; the owners of the factory resided in Berlin and were either unable or unwilling to create alternative employment. The unemployed munitions workers remained in Dachau, having no prospects of finding work elsewhere. The German economy had ground to a halt; inflation was beginning to set in. In 1919 one US dollar was worth eighteen marks. By 1923, the dollar was worth over one hundred million marks. Fleischmann wrote:

> In 1920 after the First World War the German finances were bottom-less and at their lowest level. A possessor of a few hundred English pounds was, on German soil, a millionaire. A four- or five-storeyed house in the best streets of any city could be bought for four or five pounds. The price of a loaf of bread was 1,500 to 2,000 marks, for an egg 500 marks. The starvation and misery was frightful. A relation of mine wrote on the back of a 10,000 mark bank note a letter, saying it is cheaper to write this way than to buy notepaper.[55]

Under these circumstances, it was no wonder that the socialists and communists had a large following in Dachau, as they had in Munich, leading to a short-lived revolution in April 1919. Dachau was in the hands of the Red Army for a short spell. By the time Fleischmann arrived there, the leaders were all in prison. Right up to the 1930s, Dachau had one of the highest unemployment rates of Germany.[56]

The only surviving letter written to Fleischmann at that time is from his ten-year-old son, who was happily unaware of his father's plight:

> Dearest Pappy,
>
> I hope you are very well. We received your letter a few days ago, and thought it wonderful how narrowly you escaped the collision. We were at a great picture the other day. It was called 'Queen of Sheba', and it was beautiful. Is it the same picture that you said you saw in Germany? We went to Robert's Cove yesterday and we had a fine time. My shoes and stockings were swept away in the tide. One of our masters died the other day, and we had a big funeral for him. The whole school walked a part of the way with it, to his native place in the country. I do two pages of German every day and piano also. We are having an examination in a few days, and I am very nervous. I hope you are having a nice time in Germany.
>
> With love from
>
> Aloys
>
> P.S. (I typed the whole letter myself, and shall write the next one in German. Julia [the maid?] kept her promise also, and the house was not burnt down yet)

On 24 February 1920, Fleischmann wrote to the Home Office, Whitehall, London, asking permission to return to Ireland; this was granted more than five months later, on 3 August 1920.[57] He was issued a Bavarian passport on 25 August 1920, which was valid for one year and for one journey via Cologne and Rotterdam to London between 7 September and 7 October 1920. A Dutch visa in the passport is stamped and dated 9 September 1920, and a British stamp dated 10 September. His wife and son came to London to meet him; the family stayed with Tilly's brother, Tony Swertz.[58]

IMPACT OF INTERNMENT

Fleischmann had been a prisoner for four years, and away from his family for nearly five. Being locked up with strangers in a cramped, bleak, enclosed space for years on end, enduring loneliness, cold and hunger, must be a traumatic experience for anybody, but particularly so for a man who was something of a recluse with a pronounced love of solitude. He had missed five decisive years of his son's boyhood; he had been living a life of enforced idleness knowing that his wife had to cope with his work in addition to her own. The despair which he mentions in non-family letters did not disappear without trace; his son remembered him as suffering from moods of depression for many years, which he had not had before. Chance comments would occasionally give the family insight into that bad time. His daughter-in-law, for instance, once found him carefully transporting a spider from his study window to the safety of the garden; he explained that he had saved himself from madness in the camp by observing the extraordinary skill with which the small creatures wove their webs and the persistence with which they repaired damage done to them. His grandchildren knew him as a pacifist: they were not allowed to have toy weapons, and were surprised at his displeasure when he found them using bits of branches instead for cowboy and Indian games. He loathed the sound of planes and would mutter maledictions as they flew past. The children were disconcerted to witness the anger of their normally placid and cheerful grandfather at some of the stories they proudly recounted from their school history books in which slaughter of English soldiers by the Irish was presented as a heroic feat. Their mother's explanation made sense to them: namely that war looks very unheroic to prisoners locked up on account of it and that their grandfather had good reason to abhor war in all its forms.

Difficult though the years of internment were, Fleischmann had nonetheless been spared the battlefield, the massacres in the trenches, the horror of killing and facing death on a daily basis, of witnessing appalling mutilation and agony.

Oldcastle prisoner of war camp, painter unknown

Aloys Fleischmann
Oldcastle internment
camp,1916

Carving by Andreas Lang
of Oberammergau: a
memento of the Great War
1914–6

Right: The German passport
issued to Fleischmann for
his return to Ireland 1920

Tilly Fleischmann and
son: photograph sent to
the prisoner

Left: Andreas Lang of
Oberammergau when in Ireland in
the employment of the
Cooperative Movement as teacher
of wood-carving
*Courtesy of his grandson,
Florian Lang*

Right: Memorial stone, erected by
the German civilian prisoners of
war interned in the Oldcastle
camp, for Franz Xaver Seemeier,
born 1 December 1987 in Bavaria,
who was bayoneted by a guard
and died two days later, on
30 January 1917

Aloys Fleischmann
Jun.: photograph
sent to his father in
the camp

Tilly 1918

Franz Xaver Rössler (*left*), and
Fleischmann after his
deportation to Dachau in 1919

My dearest papa, my happy
days are thursday & saturday
mammy does not go out on these days. The
other days are not very nice, because I am
lonely. I am a great acrobat! mammy
does not know how I do it! would you
like to see me ? We have great fun at
school. fondest love & kisses from your
loving son aloys

Letter from Aloys Jun. to his father

Ivor Horgan (*left*), Tilly, and
Aloys Fleischmann Jun., 1918

Song arranged by Fleischmann for his camp choir
on the occasion of the departure of the prisoners
from the Isle of Man, January 1919

Signatures of the choir members on
the back of the song

4. Life in the Free State
1920–34

Aloys Fleischmann 1928

CORK IN 1920 DURING THE TROUBLES

Fleischmann returned to Cork in mid September 1920 after an absence of almost five years. He had to leave his mother on her own in a ruined country, her savings annihilated by the galloping inflation which was paralysing the German economy. In Ireland the war of independence had begun in January 1919: police barracks were being attacked by

131

republican insurgents, tax offices burnt down, British soldiers ambushed.
Taxes could no longer be collected, the courts could no longer sit, the
administration of the country was increasingly passing into the hands of
the rebels. In March 1920 a special force was sent to Ireland known as
the 'Black and Tans' due to the colour of their officers' improvised uniforms; in July 'Auxiliaries' were sent to support them. Their lawless
violence brought increasing numbers to join or at least help the rebels.
Republican ambushes and assassinations led to reprisals by the special
forces: in March 1920 the Lord Mayor of Cork, Tomás MacCurtain, was
assassinated. Terence MacSwiney was elected as his successor.
MacSwiney was arrested in August 1920 for illegal activities and sen-
tenced to two years' imprisonment. His death in October 1920 in
London's Brixton Prison after a long hunger strike attracted the attention of the world to the condition of Ireland. In November martial law
was imposed on Munster; in December the special forces burned down
the centre of Cork city, including the City Hall. As it had become clear
that the British could not win without resorting to an all-out military
campaign for which there was little support in Britain, a truce was nego-
tiated in July 1920, which was ratified in December. But it entailed the
partition of the island, the retaining of the British sovereign as head of
state, and the ceding of four Irish ports to British control. The majority of
Dáil delegates accepted this, albeit unwillingly; a large minority did not.
In June 1922 the hostility between the two factions erupted into a civil
war which was to last until May 1923. There were 4,000 casualties during
the civil war as against 1,500 during the war of independence. The worst
legacy was one of divisive hatred often within families, which smoul-
dered for decades. The civil war did further damage to the already
scarred infrastructure of the country, which was seriously under-devel-
oped even before the war of independence started. The first government
of the Free State thus faced a formidable task of reconstruction without
the prospect of receiving one penny in foreign aid or compensation.

When the fighting ended in the summer of 1923, the wreckage had to
be assessed. There was a sense of shock at the extent of the destruction:
not just the physical devastation of the country already so grievously
damaged by the war of independence, but a sense that the hopes and
potential for the future were in peril. This was coupled, however, with a
determination on the part of many working in the cultural field to make
every effort to salvage those hopes from the ruins, to heal the wounds of
the nation, to create a better life for the people, so that the destruction
and bloodshed would not prove to have been in vain.

<h2 style="text-align:center">A NEW START IN A NEW STATE</h2>

Fleischmann's joy at being reunited with his family in September 1920
was overshadowed by the troubled times, which also brought him

personal grief with the death of Terence MacSwiney. His death was of immense political significance, making it difficult for the British government to withstand the pressure of the American government for the granting of independence. MacSwiney's body was brought from the London prison to Cork, accompanied everywhere by vast crowds. His requiem mass at St Mary's Cathedral on 1 October 1920 was one of Fleischmann's first major services after his return from Germany.

The following month, Cork was placed under martial law. That winter young Aloys woke one night to see soldiers crawling past his attic window on their way to raid the house next door. He wrote in August 1921 to his grandmother with some understatement: 'I saw a lot last year, and was often not able to go to school. When our neighbour's house was on fire, I helped.' Fleischmann must have feared that his house too could be targeted, as his friendship with republicans was known to the intelligence service and his German nationality a source of suspicion.

The Fleischmanns lost one of their closest friends, Mary Horgan, who died unexpectedly in November 1920. They had called her 'Märchen', 'little Mary', but the name also meant 'fairy tale', a tribute to her radiant personality and great kindness. In 1915 Fleischmann had dedicated a song to her: 'Schlummerliedchen' [Little Lullaby]. A 'Märchen Circle' was formed, her friends meeting for music and readings she would have liked.[1] Another friend, the painter Harry Scully, left Ireland on the imposition of martial law. But the reunited family provided a haven for Fleischmann; he took pride in his ten-year-old son and courageous wife and found comfort in the friendship of Father Pat MacSwiney:

> On my return, I found you a keen little scholar, full of enthu-siasm and joy of life. Your teachers were full of praise, and your brave, tireless mother, who had brought you up so carefully despite great sorrow and many difficulties, rejoiced in proud dreams of your future. She had truly earned that reward for her unceasing efforts. Good Father Pat and I completed the small household up on the heights with the piece of garden outside the windows.[2] And down below, the River Lee patiently carried many a beautiful sailing ship into Cork harbour. Thus reunited, we watched the waves pass by like the years.[3]

The boy was now learning the violin from William Brady at the School of Music, and was much applauded at the school concerts.[4] He had long been studying the piano with his mother, though not always to the satis-faction of his exacting teacher, who had high expectations of him. He now began to learn the organ and the theory of music from his father, and to accompany him to his choir performances on Sunday mornings.

Tilly had become involved in a reorganisation of the School of Music two years before her husband's return to Cork. She was co-opted on to the School committee by the new members Terence MacSwiney, Daniel

Corkery, Father O'Flynn and Father Pat MacSwiney, with the task of drawing up a new curriculum. In November 1919 she was appointed head of the piano section.

Her husband's field of activity was considerably widened with the advent of the Free State. He was appointed to the teaching staff of the School of Music and took over the School Choral Society; he became music teacher in the diocesan seminary at St Finbarr's College Farranferris; he arranged for the purchase of a magnificent German organ for the cathedral, which greatly enhanced the quality of sacred music provided for the diocese; he extended his choir training to two towns in the county: to Bandon and Bantry; he founded the Bantry Operatic Society. The singing of the cathedral choir continued to attract musically-minded church-goers from all over the city to the cathedral services. The choir's recitals in the Honan Chapel of the university brought it a further academic following. The founding of the state radio in 1926, with a station in Cork from 1927, provided a national audience for the choir. Its participation in the Feis Maitiú in 1929 won it public recognition from the English composer Arnold Bax, leading to a lifelong friendship with the Fleischmanns. Two BBC broadcasts on the World Service brought letters from colleagues and former choir members now scattered across the globe. The inspiration for these activities came from Fleischmann's previous work in Dachau and in Cork before his internment; it now found a framework in an organisation presented to the public by Daniel Corkery in 1924: the Munster Society of Arts.

A CULTURAL MANIFESTO FOR MUNSTER: THE MUNSTER
SOCIETY OF ARTS

The Munster Society of Arts was founded in January 1924 by people who had been actively involved in the arts in Cork for many years, some of whom were also active in the political movement for independence. The cultural activities that had abounded in Cork during the early years of the twentieth century had come to an end with the onset of the Irish troubles. The founders of the Society were motivated by a sense of acute dismay at the stagnation in the life of the nation. Their first public document states: 'This Society has been founded for the purpose of developing and fostering the fine arts, now practically non-existent in our midst, or so feebly manifested as to be powerless as an influence in the social and cultural life of the province.' Corkery outlines the consequences of the stagnation in his press statement:

> We are a bookless people. We moreover lack both the fine arts and
> the fine crafts. We have no standards of drama. Generally, we have
> no standards in either learning or taste. Yet how little all this worries
> us! . . .

> We have all met the young priest, the young teacher fresh each from
> his training college. They are anxious to continue their reading, to
> keep up their studies, to explore more widely the realms that have
> been opened up to them. But flung into a land intellectually stag-
> nant, far from libraries, from discussion, from congenial companions,
> . . . they are hardly blameworthy if their impulses towards all this
> weaken down and finally die.[5]

Corkery deplores the fact that so many third-level students come
'from bookless homes' and are therefore disadvantaged at college; he
describes the disillusioned teacher 'who has ceased to be a student' as
'simply a menace' and states that there was virtually no cultural life to
which the new local men of property – those who had taken over the
lands and big houses of the Ascendancy – could be attracted and in
which they could play a role.

The society hoped to foster circles all over the province which would
stimulate local people to cherish and develop their culture. Corkery: 'In
no part of the world are the creative arts so dead as amongst us. To revive
them, we must hew in our own quarries.' This was to be done by promoting artistic regionalism, a 'provincial school' giving expression to the
specific features of the life and people of the province, by encouraging
the exploration of the Gaelic heritage in literature, the visual arts and
music, by providing a forum for local artists to present their work and by
instituting competitions in all fields of the arts to encourage discussion,
criticism and high standards. But the 'hewing in our own quarries' was to
be complemented by the study of what was being done elsewhere:
Article 10 of the constitution states that the 'Society shall endeavour to
bring the Art of other countries before its members by means of lectures,
exhibits etc.'.

The thirty-five first members of the society came from many walks of
life, from different countries, from different religious communities.
Among the twelve founders were the musician Dr Annie Patterson, the
writers Daniel Corkery, Lennox Robinson and Edith Somerville, the
painters W.K. MacDonnell and the American Daniel Veresmith, the president of the university, P.J. Merriman, Professors Alfred O'Rahilly, William
P. Stockley of University College Cork, and Professor Pádraig de Brún of
Maynooth. Fleischmann was a member of the council, of the executive
committee and of the music sub-committee. The contribution to the
latter by Cork's foreign citizenry was considerable: half of the ten
members were foreigners: Fleischmann, Germaine Stockley and Heinrich
Tils being German, Theo Gmür Swiss and Ferruccio Grossi Italian.

This documents that Fleischmann was at the heart of the cultural
life of his adopted city, fully integrated in the circle of activists seeking
to make the new Ireland a place worth living in. They hoped to foster
an environment in which the creativity of the people could come into

its own, and where conditions could be created allowing a life of interest, substance and dignity for all, including those living in modest circumstances. In Cork at that time, of the 80,000 citizens, one in nine was still living in a tenement, one in five in sub-standard housing, and the average life expectancy was less than fifty-eight years.[6] Conditions were worst in the centre of the city – in 'the marsh' – and in the cathedral parish.

FLEISCHMANN'S WORK AS ORGANIST AND CHOIRMASTER

A new organ for the Cathedral

The first change that Fleischmann sought to effect was in the cathedral. While in Dachau after his internment he had himself experienced the post-war economic collapse of Germany and had benefited from the extraordinary value of the English pound. Back in Cork, working with the old cathedral organ, which was now in an extremely poor condition, it occurred to him that the devaluation of the German mark provided a unique opportunity for the cathedral administration to buy a first-rate German organ for a fraction of the normal cost:

> Sixteen years I had been hoping for a playable organ. The old water-pumped organ which was in use at the time was serviceable no more, with its continual ciphering, hoarse and coarse tone, and it was very costly because of the endless repairs.
>
> The idea sprung in my mind that now or never we would be able to get an organ worthy of a Cathedral, through the unbelievably low standard of the German finances.[7]

The cathedral administrator agreed that Fleischmann should explore the options. The following summer he returned to Germany to the Wiesbaden spa, as he had not been well. In the course of his stay, he travelled to Ludwigsburg to the renowned organ builders, Walcker. In a letter to the Canon written in Wiesbaden, he continues to make his case for a new organ, underlining the special responsibility of the church towards the poor:

> My health has very much improved since I have been here and I have been well enough to go to several church ceremonies (I was also at church concerts). It was a great joy to hear a good choir with a fine organ and to witness the deep impression that they made, but my heart was sad when I considered that our choir was without this essential help.
>
> What pained me most however was to think that we have not the best means at our disposal in the church to carry out the musical part in the highest sense in liturgy as well as in art. Surely in Erin it

is more necessary than here to keep up a high standard for art in the church, because whilst here there are so many concerts, theaters, picture galleries etc open to everyone, in Ireland the church is the only place where a poor person comes in contact with art.

Can one still say as in olden times that the church is the mother of the arts?

. . . Since I have been away I have heard many choirs with boys' voices and I can truthfully say that none of them were to sound [sounded] as pure and good as ours, although the effect of some were more powerful on account of the excellent organ and the great space.

On our organ one can now hardly play and in a year or two it will be quite out of question to use it any longer. You were good enough to give me the power over £400. The estimate for repairing the old organ which was given [in] 1913 was over £1,000. . . . For the ordering of an organ from a second class firm I cannot take any responsibility. The estimate from one or two really first class firms that I can recommend comes to about £800-1,000.

As the opportunity will never again present itself, I am certain that you will agree with me, dear Canon, that it would be a great waste of money not to seize on it. The matter now lies entirely in your hands.

. . . If the Cathedral gets this instrument through your influence the city will enjoy in every way the privilege of having the best organ in the whole of Ireland.[8]

The negotiations were successful both in Ludwigsburg and in Cork, and the purchase of the organ was agreed. Many years later, Fleischmann gave an account of the ensuing saga:

The date of delivery of the Walcker organ was announced, and the ship with its contents came into Cork harbour. That very day a dock strike was declared. The strikers refused to discharge the cargo. Therefore the ship did not anchor, but went off at once to an unknown destination. I was in despair, and so was the Canon.

After thirteen months' uncertainty through pure accident news came that numerous cases, large and small, sent from Germany, were lying in all wind and weather on a quay in Belfast. At last the well-packed organ was found and arrived a second time in Cork, and was discharged at Albert Quay.

Mr Dowdall kindly lent his four horses, and in many shifts the big load was brought up to the Cathedral – in two evenings – and stored near the mortuary. So far all went well – but not for long. A deputation approached Canon O'Sullivan protesting that the people didn't want foreign organs. Rumours spread that the organ would be burnt, which in those years of political chaos was not out of question. Cautiously the Administrator posted a soldier in the yard, to guard

the cases during the night. A good while passed. The people's excitement about the foreign organ quietened down before the two men
sent by the Walcker firm arrived to put the organ parts together.
After three months their labour was complete.

Canon O'Sullivan announced from the pulpit that he would not ask
anyone to pay a penny for this magnificent organ: he would give it as
a gift to the Cathedral Parish. A heap of correspondence tells of the
excruciation, the ups and downs, the hopes, fears, the incomprehen-
sible difficulty and anxiety of this adventurous organ affair which
lasted two years, from 1923 to 1924.

With great solemnity, on the feast of St Cecilia 23rd November
1924,[9] the new organ was blessed during the High Mass by his
Lordship, Most Rev. Dr. Cohalan. The preacher was Rev. Dr Beecher
of Maynooth. He delivered a sermon on the Protector of the Musica
Sacra, St Cecilia. In the afternoon I gave an organ recital. The novelty
and curiosity brought crowds of people who filled the Cathedral.[10]

The splendid organ was Walcker's opus 2000.[11] It had 5,000 pipes,
some up to thirty-two feet high; there were four manuals: choir, great,
swell and solo, each manual encompassing five octaves (sixty-one
notes); the pedal organ had thirty notes. The instrument was equipped
with a dynamic crescendo roller pedal invented and patented by its
builders. It possessed exquisite stops, beautiful tone-colour, brilliant
volume. It was admired by all who heard it: by all visiting musicians,
including the musical director of Westminster Cathedral, Sir Richard
Terry, and was much appreciated in the parish and city. It was donated to
the cathedral by its generous and cultured administrator, Canon Michael
O'Sullivan.[12]

Creating a music library for the choir

Dublin's Pro-Cathedral[13] was fortunate in finding in Edward Martyn of
Galway a Maecenas who spent £20,000 on their choir, and later another
£10,000 – vast sums in the early twentieth century.[14] Fleischmann wrote
of him: 'Mr Martyn, though at the time an old and sick man, visited the
Cathedral several times to hear our choir, and was received by Canon
O'Sullivan with great honour.' Martyn presented the Pro-Cathedral in
Dublin with an excellent musical library of the Renaissance period. The
benefactors of the Cork cathedral did not have such means at their disposal, but their donations were very welcome, as Fleischmann wrote of
the gifts presented in the 1930s and 1940s:

> I was very grateful to Canon Martin Murphy, P.P., Bandon, when he
> presented us with thirty plainchant books. Prof. Stockley also gave
> us a motet by Marzello (score and 120 copies), Lord Monteagle
> (Protestant) a collection of Latin motets, the Italian composer

Montani a mass of his own, Dr Lyons a four-part mass, Sir Arnold
Bax his Mater, ora filium. Canon Cohalan[15] brought us back music by
Refice from his visit to Rome, Sir Granville Bantock sent us music by
William Byrd, and Canon Cullinane enriched us with the gift of the
big library press in the back sacristy.[16]

By far the greater part of the music used by the cathedral choir was
neither donated, nor purchased, but was copied by the choirmaster from
his own scores in countless hours of work.

The work with the cathedral choir through the year

As he had done in Dachau, Fleischmann sought to bring the highest
quality music to those who, he believed, needed, deserved and appreciated it most – to the poor. He explained this at some length to the
Cathedral administrator:

'By art we mean', writes a Catholic writer, 'the expression of man's
thought in a beautiful, enduring way, under the inspiration and in
the service of the church. Without art man would be little better than
a savage'. Not so much in Rome, London, or Dublin cathedrals
'where only better class people are to be seen' is it as necessary as
here, in our cathedral, to strive for the highest achievement in all
Catholic actions, where the bulk of the congregation consists of poor
people. From the cradle to the grave the church comprises everything for them, during their scanty existence. To lift their souls and
minds, they deserve only the best the church can give. Only the best
of the best is good enough, and due to them, when they seek refuge
in the church. It is prejudice as well as superficial mis-judgment to
think that these patient poor people do not care, or do not understand 'highbrow' church music, and therefore anything in this line
will do. As experience proves, Palestrina's, Vittoria's or Orlando's
music by its deep religious fervour lifts not only educated people, or
people of high society. A priest told me that during Holy Week he
heard around him, in the big gallery, women with shawls humming
Allegri's Miserere with the choir. Even a child possesses some sense
and feeling for beauty in the sphere of art. Among the poor lies the
hidden genius of the nation, and not among the over-estimated and
over-saturated upper class, with or without academic stamp.[17]

Bringing beauty and solace through music into the lives of the poor
of the parish was from the beginning the driving impulse behind
Fleischmann's work with the cathedral choir. That this was appreciated
is documented in many letters from former members of the choir who
learned through the choir training 'what a beautiful place a musical
world was to live in'.[18] The feat involved in training the choir, and in particular the boys, was described by Geraldine Neeson:

> He taught his choirboys, who as is the way of choirboys, looked like
> angels, but were as wild as colts, to produce a pure round tone and,
> supported by the men of the choir, to sing as well as any choir of its
> kind I have ever heard.[19]

The success of this purely voluntary choir seems to have been based
on the bond of affection and esteem between conductor and singers, on
Fleischmann's competence as a music pedagogue, on his belief in the
choristers' ability to produce outstanding quality, and on his gift of moti-
vating them to rise to the challenge.

On his return to Cork in 1920, Fleischmann was able to pick up
where he had left off, since his wife had maintained his method of
training the choir and the standard of singing. The choir consisted of
about a hundred voices: sixty boys, forty men. In addition, there was a
choir for the newly recruited boys – he used to refer to these as
'grasshoppers' and the trained boys as 'larks'. About every two years,
young singers were recruited. Announcements were made from the
pulpit during Sunday mass, inviting boys to apply for membership.
Fleischmann made a point of encouraging brothers and sons of choir
members to apply, as the choir tradition was already established in their
homes. Candidates were interviewed and given a simple voice and ear
test. The choir director insisted that boys could not join any other group,
such as scouts or altar boys: their time and efforts were to be devoted
exclusively to the choir. [20]

The boys' choir met on two evenings every week for an hour's practice, while the men's choir met once a week for an evening rehearsal
lasting an hour and a half. The choirs sang together every Sunday at
twelve o'clock mass: the Asperges at the sprinkling of holy water at the
beginning of the service and two or three motets during mass. When
new pieces were being added to the repertoire or special events
approaching, both choirs met for additional practices, often after Sunday
mass, though this was none too popular, as the members risked being
late for the afternoon football or hurling match. Attendance at practices
presented no great problem, however, because the boys and men had
few distractions in the home.

Choir practices were held in the library attached to the parish pres-
bytery, an old-world room with a harmonium, full of dust-covered
tomes and stacks of choral music. There was no heating and during
winter it could be very cold. The choirmaster's advice if complaints were
made was: 'Sing yourself warm, sir!' The new recruits met separately for
their first introduction to the rudiments of music and singing and were
trained to do simple sight reading of intervals. As soon as the 'grasshoppers' had a grasp of the basics, they were taught their first piece, which
was usually the Sanctus from the Gregorian requiem mass. When they
had mastered this, they learnt the Kyrie, Benedictus and Agnus Dei. They

were then ready to attend a practice with the 'larks' to rehearse the whole requiem. From 1920, Fleischmann started with this rather sombre piece of music because, each November, the choir sang the annual requiem for the Honan family in the Honan Chapel[21] of the university – the first public performance involving the new boys. The 'grasshoppers' looked forward eagerly to this event and particularly to getting the morning off school for the occasion. From 1916 the choir also sang in the Honan Chapel each October for the opening of the academic year in what was known as the Red Mass.

The choir then began preparing for the advent and Christmas season, learning sixteenth-century Christmas carols such as 'Puer Natus Est', 'Resonet in Laudibus' and 'Quem Pastores'. These were specially arranged by the director for the choir. His organ interludes between the verses were startlingly beautiful representations of the shepherd pipes – here the magnificent flute stops on the organ came into their own. The well known carols 'The First Noel', 'Once in Royal David's City' and 'Adeste Fideles', etc. did not feature very high in Herr Fleischmann's esteem. The offertory psalm for Christmas Day was *Tui sunt caeli*, but because of popular demand the choir did sing the 'Adeste', though in his own arrangement. A new element of the Christmas ceremonies was introduced after Fleischmann's return in 1920. The former Taoiseach, Jack Lynch, who was an altar boy in the cathedral in his youth, describes it:

> About the mid-twenties, midnight mass was introduced in the Cathedral (or the North Chapel as it is sometimes still called) where my brothers and I were altar boys. It used to be a very impressive ceremony. The Cathedral Choir, of men and boys, were directed and conducted by the old maestro, Herr Fleischmann, father of Professor Aloys Fleischmann, and their singing was augmented by the Cecilian choir (drawn from the girls confraternity). The male choir sang from its usual 'enclosure' at the Gospel side of the high altar and the female from the gallery, at the back of the Church. The synchronisation of the voices singing the usual Christmas hymns and carols was magnificent.[22]

The period between Christmas and Easter was a slack time for the choir without any great church feasts or festivals. Lent, the forty-day fast, was at that time strictly a penitential season: in all dioceses Lenten missions were held in all the churches, with thunderous sermons on hell and damnation delivered by the dreaded Redemptorist Fathers. Every church in the city was packed to the doors; in the cathedral even the choir loft was filled by the congregation. The congregational hymns and the benediction plainchant singing were splendid. During Lent the organ was silent: the choir sang all its motets unaccompanied, except on the fourth Sunday of Lent, *Laetare* Sunday, when the organ was allowed.

The old Easter rite was in use until 1957. The repertoire required for Holy Week and Easter was extensive and included some of the finest church music ever written. Many hours of practice were needed to prepare for this great festival. The cathedral Tenebrae services were renowned throughout the city. They began on the Wednesday evening of Holy Week, and continued the following day with a morning and evening service; there were two services on Good Friday, one on Saturday and two on Easter Sunday. It was a most challenging task for the choir to perform morning and evening each day with a different repertoire, and after Tenebrae each evening the choir had to practise for the following day's ceremony. But the full week of practice and singing was gladly undertaken by all the choristers. The Office of Tenebrae [darkness] was the name applied to Matins and Lauds sung during the evening of Wednesday, Thursday and Friday of Holy Week, at which the Lamentations were sung. All the lights of the church were extinguished one by one, as the Penitential Psalms were intoned, thus commemorating the darkness said to have come over the earth at the time of the crucifixion; the *Christus factus est* was sung, at the end of which the congregation clapped hands to represent the thunder that resounded when Jesus died on the cross.

The choir's two favourite pieces during Holy Week were the fiftieth psalm *Miserere mei, Deus* [Have mercy on me, O God] and the Fleischmann composition, *Canticum Zachariae*, also known as the 'Benedictus'. It was sung by the men's choir at the end of Tenebrae. After each of the thirteen verses, the church lights were extinguished one by one and the last verse was sung in darkness. In order to follow the music, the men used lighted candles. The last verse is: '*Illuminare his, qui in tenebris et in umbra mortis sedent: ad dirigendos pedes nostros in viam pacis*' [Enlighten those that sit in darkness and in the shadow of death; direct our feet to the path of peace]. The cathedral choir recorded this work for the BBC in September 1948 with the writer Sean O'Faolain introducing the programme.

There were no practices during the week after Easter. The next great feasts to be prepared were those of Pentecost[23] and Corpus Christi,[24] both moveable feasts which take place between May and June, and the *Quarant' Ore*, or forty-hour adoration of the Blessed Sacrament, which coincided with the feast of Corpus Christi, on which there was an annual procession through the streets of Cork, with benediction and sermon on the Grand Parade. Every house in the city, every street and laneway was decorated with papal and national flags and bunting. Every parish in the city took part; thousands of men and all the brass bands of the town marched. The celebrations lasted about four hours. During the procession along the streets the choir sang *Pange lingua* and *Ave verum*.

The *Quarant' Ore* ended the following day with the singing of Fleischmann's arrangement of the Te Deum.

The impression made by the church services is described by Niall Toibín, the actor, broadcaster and writer, who in his autobiography gives an account of his time in the cathedral choir.[25] It was the first encounter of this working-class boy with the great music of the Latin liturgy; his memories focus on the sense of calm which the polyphonic music gave him, on the drama which the music lent to the cathedral ceremonies, and on the enthusiasm and kindness of the choirmaster:

> He would be there, enthusing to a bunch of unruly ragamuffins, which most of the choir were, not excluding myself. Most of the kids in the choir were from families in the immediate vicinity of the cathedral.

> The music was entrancing. These days I regret, when I go to the Easter ceremonies, that you don't get the Vittoria and Palestrina Masses, and the Passion and all that. I can still sing, under provocation, Non morier, non morier, sed viviam et narrabo opera domini' or 'Si hunc dimittis non es amicus Caesari'. It was drummed into me, and it was so dramatic, so stirring, because you had sopranos, altos and tenors and bassi; you had 'the angels', as he called them, the women's choir, which couldn't fit into the space around the organ, in the choir stalls, but sang in the small gallery on the far side of the church. And he would flick his cupped hand up over the top of the partition, to bring the voices in. It was wonderful stuff.

> He was also very charitable – he gave away a lot of money, and I know that he helped out people in the choir. To my knowledge there were a few lads whose fathers weren't working, or were in England, whom he also helped.

> . . . I enjoyed being in the choir immensely. I loved the old-fashioned church music. Apart from any religious content or motivation at all, just to listen to it gives me a tremendous feeling of calm and peace; and the sung Masses, the full High Masses, were so operatic, so dramatic. And the Holy Week stuff, done with all the stops out, is scintillating theatre, whatever else. No wonder the churches were full.

There were many occasions for 'scintillating theatre' in the cathedral. Visiting clerical dignitaries were welcomed with much ceremony and no little pomp. The *Ecce Sacerdos Magnus* which the choir performed was usually one composed by Fleischmann. (One of the settings of this work was also in the repertoire of the Munich cathedral choir, and performed many times in the 1930s for the entry of the cardinal.) For very special occasions, the brass section of the Cork No. 2 Army Band performed with the choir, as Seán Barrett recalls, who sang in the choir until 1930.[26] Tilly Fleischmann played the organ so that her husband could concentrate on the conducting of the choir and army musicians. Such events were given full coverage in the Irish press, the extensive reports including an outline of the sermon, a list of the clergy and dignitaries in attendance and details about the music performed. Major national commemorations were celebrated by church and state alike. On 20 June 1927 at the Daniel O'Connell centenary some 30,000 people walked in procession through Cork's Grand Parade, led by all the clergy of the diocese. On 14 July 1929 the church celebrated the centenary of Catholic Emancipation. There was a pontifical high mass in the university grounds on the Mardyke attended by President Cosgrave, the Archbishop of Cashel, the university staff, the army, the diocesan clergy, the city corporation, with the Lord Mayor bearing the bishop's train. Sixty thousand people came to the grounds.[27] On 16 July 1930 the Papal Nuncio paid a visit to Cork. He was welcomed by huge crowds, and by all the dignitaries of the city. Fleischmann wrote a Te Deum for the Nuncio's liturgical reception at the cathedral.

In 1932 the Irish Eucharistic Congress celebrated the 1500th anniversary of St Patrick's coming to Ireland. This, too, was treated as a matter of state. In Cork, choir preparations began in September 1931. On 11 July 1932 there was a procession through the city, outdoor mass was celebrated by an array of bishops before the entire clergy of the province flanked by the city officials, the army, the university and tens of thousands of citizens. A special issue of the *Cork Examiner* celebrated the event. The sacred music performed by the cathedral choir enhanced the solemnity and grandeur of these occasions. The Catholic church did indeed enjoy a 'special position' in Irish society, as the constitution of 1937 was to proclaim. These public church celebrations constituted a triumphal reversal of British government policies towards the Catholic church during the colonial period.

AN EXTENDED FIELD OF ACTIVITY IN CORK

Professorship in the Cork Municipal School of Music

Both Fleischmanns served on the staff of the Cork Municipal School of Music for many years. In 1919 the School of Music was reorganised by a new committee, among whom were Terence MacSwiney (who became chairman of the School of Music Committee in 1920), Daniel Corkery, J.J. O'Connor, Father Patrick MacSwiney and Father Seamas O'Flynn. They established Irish music on the curriculum, introduced drama classes and sought to raise standards generally. Tilly Fleischmann was charged by the committee with the development of the syllabus and with the introduction of Irish music. In the face of some opposition, the committee managed to get the eminent collector and arranger of Irish folk music, Carl Hardebeck, appointed in the summer of 1919 as first

Head of the School and as professor of Irish traditional music. A deputation from the Discharged and Demobilised Soldiers and Sailors Federation protested to the committee at the appointment of somebody they considered a German, with the threat that 'the man who proposes the German will do so at his peril'.[28] Father O'Flynn put an end to the protest by threatening the former soldiers and sailors with a dip in the River Lee should they oppose the appointment. Hardebeck, though of German origin, was not a foreigner: he had been born in London, and lived in Belfast as teacher, organist and a composer. Though blind almost from birth, he spent many years visiting the Irish-speaking areas of Donegal, the Gaelteacht, recording in braille the songs of the countryside, and became a distinguished scholar and composer. His time in the Cork School of Music was stormy. Those that had elected him were no longer members of the committee: the school officials and he often clashed over matters of policy. He resigned after two years from the position of headmaster, partly because of this and partly because the school was not able to pay him what he had been promised. He remained at the school, however, as professor of Irish music. A special chair of Irish traditional music was created for him at the university, financed by the Cork Corporation. During the civil war, he resigned from both posts and returned to Belfast, moving later to Dublin. He always supported the Fleischmanns against the officials during his time at the school, and remained friends with them until his death in 1945.

In November 1919 Tilly Fleischmann was appointed to the professorship of piano in the institution in which her father had served for nearly twenty-five years. In May 1922 her husband became professor of harmony, theory of music, choral singing and a member of the school's consultive committee. In the course of the civil war, the government instructed the staff to take an oath of allegiance to the Free State; they refused, all resigned, and the requirement was subsequently removed.[29] Fleischmann was head of a music section and was thus accorded the title of 'Professor'. His wife was also head of her section, but the title does not appear to have been given to women. However, the posts were not full-time, and had no pension entitlements. In the 1920s there were close to 300 students from a fairly wide cross-section of the population.[30] Fees had been reduced since the founding of the school in 1878, and there were reductions if more than one child from a family attended. Fees charged per term of ten weeks for individual tuition from heads of department amounted to 2 16s. 2d. for a forty-minute period; the fees students paid for Fleischmann's group classes amounted to five shillings per term. Among his colleagues were Germaine Stockley and Seán Neeson for singing, Geraldine Sullivan (soon to marry Neeson) as assistant piano teacher, Theo Gmür, the Swiss organist, and William Brady for the violin.

The Choral Society attached to the School of Music was re-estab-
lished in 1921; the choir consisted of 130 members; Fleischmann
became director in the autumn of 1922. Among the society's patrons
were a number of university professors, city councillors, businessmen,
clergymen and the artist Harry Clarke. Quite a number of the choristers
had also sung in the Choral Union in the early 1900s. The School of
Music Choral Society gave the first of its many public concerts in the
Opera House on 18 March 1923. The programmes always included
works by Irish, English and continental composers of a variety of
periods, for instance Stanford, Field, Hardebeck, Hughes, Bax, as well as
Beethoven, Brahms, Schumann, Wagner or Rheinberger. A review of the
June concert of 1923 (one month after the end of the civil war) commended the efforts being made to overcome the 'chaotic state' caused
by the upheavals through which the country had just passed. The writer
pointed out that in such times

> music is the first to feel the existence of adverse conditions, and the
> last to recover its balance. Emerging from the troubles of the times, it
> is struggling to regain the far better place in public regard which it
> held in former times. All praise is due to those who have so bravely
> stuck at their hard task of keeping alive the spirit that fosters music
> and the kindred arts. . . . The choral recital which (for want of a more
> suitable hall) took place in the Lecture Theatre of the School of Art,
> was of much importance as showing what earnest efforts are being
> made to maintain a sound footing on the path of progress.[31]

But there were many obstacles to be overcome, most of them
deriving from the administrators on the Technical Instruction Committee, which governed the Schools of Art and Music. Only a few weeks
after the beginning of Fleischmann's work with the choir, he was
rebuked by the secretary of this committee for having placed an 'unau-
thorised' advertisement in the newspaper announcing the first practice
in the School of Art. The School of Music had been unable to provide
accommodation, so Fleischmann had organised it himself, which he was
henceforward forbidden to do.[32] A concert given at the Opera House in
1926 with the celebrated Australian baritone, Peter Dawson, led to
recriminations from School of Music officials over the type of programme chosen. Dawson had proposed a selection of light music for his
part of the concert, but accepted Fleischmann's suggestions of songs by
Mozart, Purcell, Sibelius and Tchaikovsky. For these he was accompanied
by the London pianist, Carlton Fay. The school choir sang Irish and
German folk song arrangements, and works by Wagner and Elgar. With
Dawson as one of the soloists they performed Mendelssohn's *First
Walpurgis Night*. The house was full and the concert very positively
reviewed. The choir rushed to the defence of its conductor and

threatened to leave the school unless the 'unmerited' and 'unfounded' criticism was withdrawn. The president and chairman of the Choral Society, C.F. Fielding, argued that

> we are not an entertainment Society but an Academic body whose first concern as representatives of the School of Music is the production of music by the best Masters, and in this ideal we naturally expected the unquestioning support of the School of Music Committee, especially as we have taken upon ourselves all financial risks and give the School of Music the credit of being associated with first class musical performances in public. The Choral Society felt . . . most pained by the reflections thereby cast on their esteemed conductor, who never spared himself in working for the honour of the School of Music and the Choral Society, and this we feel so strongly, that we have unanimously decided to suspend our attendances at the School of Music until the Committee be afforded an opportunity of examining for themselves the full facts.

> We regret having to adopt this course but we see no other practical way of meeting the unfounded criticisms which reflect on ourselves, not only as a Choral Society, but also on our Conductor and on the School of Music itself.

The matter was reported in the press, the protest was effective, the work continued, but conflict over the issue of quality and that of the powers of the officials continued to smoulder beneath the surface for the next ten years.

Music teacher at the Diocesan Seminary of Farranferris

St Finbarr's College of Farranferris was a boarding school providing secondary education to boys intending to enter the priesthood; pupils, however, did not have to be clerical students, and students from Cork city lived at home. At this diocesan seminary, the normally facultative subjects Latin, Greek and music were obligatory. Fleischmann taught there for nearly forty years; most of the priests of the Cork diocese were pupils of his, including the present bishop. No papers concerning Fleischmann's employment in Farranferris seem to have survived, but some former students have written or spoken to the authors about their music classes. From these accounts it becomes clear that most of the students came, if not from 'bookless homes', then from families remote from classical music. Some of the Farranferris pupils were aware of how onerous it was for their music teacher to have to deal with large classes of often unwilling students. Father Daniel J. Burns remembers Fleischmann's 'sense of dedication which sustained him in what was a philistine environment as far as art and music were concerned'.[33]

But that sense of dedication could lead to miscalculations, as Revd. Prof. James Good remembered in 1992, writing from his parish in the

Turkana Desert of Kenya:

> There was a memorable occasion in the Seminary when the students
> were barred from their once-a-term film in a city cinema due to an
> outbreak of measles. Herr Fleischmann announced that he could
> provide a replacement: a performance by the Cathedral Choir.
> So, barred from our favourite cowboy shoot-outs in the Savoy or the
> Palace, we sat in silence through several hours of four- and eight-
> part harmonies and pretended we were enjoying them. It would
> have hurt Herr Fleischmann to give the impression that he was less
> entertaining than our cowboys.[34]

Michael MacDonald did, however, develop a taste for the ancient
music during his time in the college. Of Fleischmann he wrote: 'His
great love was for Gregorian Chant with its cadences of simplicity which
he managed to get us, a bunch of raw children, to appreciate. This has
stayed with me for life. Compared with other teachers of his time, he
was a gentle person and a gentleman.'

Michael MacDonald gives an intriguing glimpse of the politics of the
diocese, which supplied priests – often republican sympathisers – to
minister in the British army, and appointed many with such sympathies
to high office in clerical institutions at home. Some of these republicans
were exclusive Irish-Irelanders in their cultural interests; for others continental Europe offered welcome access to the arts in bypassing
England, the predominant cultural monopolist and model-provider of
previous generations:

> In those days Canon Tom Duggan was president of Farranferris: a
> most wonderful, bad-tempered fellow who had been a chaplain to
> the UK army in the two World Wars. He was a strong republican,
> but when he was captured by the Germans, he would not spy
> against the British. Canon Duggan liked Fleischmann: both strong
> characters.
>
> Fleischmann and his son contributed much to Cork and represented
> a gateway to 'high music' other than the UK influence resented as
> foreign by the newly confident emerging republic's citizens, whose
> own music had been treated with contempt and scorn by the British
> as crude peasant music, God forgive them.[35]

Father Pat Walsh of Rosscarbery wrote an article on Fleischmann in
the Farranferris commemorative book published for the centenary of the
college in 1987; his memories highlight the hard life endured by the
muses in the institution, in particular by Polyhymnia:

> It was in the Junior Study Hall (the Juniora) that successive genera-
> tions of youthful collegians were introduced to academic life. The

Study Hall was post-Dickensian, but not very. On Sundays it acquired a different personality from its routine of class and prep. Sunday morning for singing with Herr Fleischmann – with a restless, captive group. Amid the stark furnishings of the place, incongruously positioned, was a harmonium. This intrepid instrument was more or less protected from marauders by a wooden case, solidly rather than artistically crafted.

The precarious life of this harmonium embodied, for me, the hazardous fortunes of the gentle muse in Farranferris. To be fair to the College, the attitude towards music there was hardly different from that found in most boys' school of the time. Interest in music was something boys inherited, generally, from their mothers. It was looked on like spots or acne. Far more desirable that boys should occupy themselves in knocking spots off one another on the playing fields. It was Herr Fleischmann's unhappy fate that he should have been the upholder of music in an environment scarcely favourable. That he persisted for almost forty years shows what a redoubtable character he was. However, there was a notional appreciation, at least, of what he was doing among the authorities.

The patience with which Fleischmann, on the whole, dealt with the restive pupils was noted, and those rare situations remembered when the teacher's tolerance was exhausted:

> Herr Fleischmann was a delightful person for those of us who knew him better. Though we were a scruffy lot, he had little difficulty in relating to us, despite the considerable separation in age and background. His patience as a teacher was limitless. Occasionally, when confronted by the indifference and unruliness of the general herd, there were eruptions. Then he was like a fine Bavarian beer, effervescence spilling over to the frightened glee of his tormentors.

Father Walsh was struck by Fleischmann's unostentatious piety:

> He was a spiritual man and a man of Faith, that Faith allied to much culture and reaching back through centuries of trial and endurance. He had a profound respect for priests and nuns. This merely reflected that high regard he had for the ecclesiastical structure and which, of course, most clearly manifested itself in a life devoted to embellishing Christian worship. In little ways he externalised his deep religious sense. During Benediction every Sunday he always played a little obligato while the Monstrance hung in blessing over our heads. Immediately afterwards he felt his way, ponderously, round the harmonium to kneel for the Divine Praises. A mundane enough exercise, perhaps, but performed with such reverence as to be still vivid in my memory forty years on.[36]

The Farranferris students who boarded in the college were expected
to attend mass on Sundays in the cathedral, so they became acquainted
with the full repertoire of chant and the sixteenth-century motets sung
by choristers who, unlike themselves, had trained voluntarily and had
been imbued with Fleischmann's commitment to sacred music of this
kind.

One of Fleischmann's Farranferris pupils was the future composer
Seán Ó Riada, to whom he taught the piano, the organ and singing. Ó
Riada's encounter with plainchant at school led ultimately to his developing a Gaelic form of church music – a combination of the Irish
traditional solo singing (*sean nós*) and plainchant – which he performed
in the church in the parish of Cúil Aodha, which his son fosters today
and which was taken up by the singer Nóirín Ní Ríain. What he learnt
about German culture is indicated in the tribute he paid to his teacher
with the *Four Hölderlin Songs* composed in his memory in 1964.

A short lived girls' church choir

From the beginning of his work in Cork, Fleischmann adhered most
strictly to the *Motu proprio* rules regarding sacred music. He also
accepted the rule excluding women from church choirs: his Cecilian
Choir was not part of the cathedral choir. He knew that in other countries this rule was not observed: his father-in-law in Philadelphia had a
mixed choir, as was quite common in the USA;[37] his friend Ludwig
Berberich had a mixed choir in the cathedral of Munich. In 1927 he
decided to found a girls' choir recruited from one of the girls' schools of
the city. It was not part of the main choir, but sang with it outside the
choir stalls. Mary Sheppard, a member of this choir, recalls:

> I had heard Herr Fleischmann's choir when I was at Mass in the
> church, but I did not get to know him until I was about fifteen years
> old. In 1927, when I was in school with the North Presentation nuns,
> we were invited to apply to join a new choir he was founding. As I
> loved singing, I did so; Herr Fleischmann himself tested each of us
> and I was among those accepted.
>
> From the very beginning I loved it. Herr Fleischmann was a most
> meticulous man and a very good music teacher. He always dressed
> in dark clothes, was clean-shaven, of medium height and very ener-
> getic. His wife, Tilly, dressed in black and wore her clothes long,
> regardless of fashion. She reminded me of the old Queen Mary: she
> had that gracious air about her.
>
> We had rehearsals every week in the church. Our place was at the
> top left side of the aisle near the altar from which the organ was
> visible. Herr Fleischmann taught us a full Latin Mass. He made sure
> we pronounced every single word correctly. On one occasion, when

Herr Fleischmann was pleased with three or four of us, he placed us in between the boy sopranos in the front row to sing seconds. We had no trouble in holding our own note in the line. We sang the Mass in Latin. It was beautiful. The people in charge of us had uniforms designed for us of lilac-coloured satin material, falling loosely something like the gowns students wear when receiving their degrees.

We respected and loved that man and it was very sad that some people did not like the idea of ladies singing in the church. Unfortunately, they soon succeeded in having our choir disbanded. The church wanted men only. Men held a very elitist position in the church at that time: women were treated as second-class citizens and were not allowed to take any active part in church ceremonies. The only ladies allowed inside the altar-rails were the women who washed the floors.[38]

Choirs in Bandon and Bantry, the Bantry Operatic Society

The priests in the Cork diocese (especially those who had been in charge of the cathedral administration) became well aware of Fleischmann's ability in the field of church music. When these priests were given parishes in the diocese, they usually called on him to come and help improve, advise and train the local church choir. This task Fleischmann undertook in Bandon and in Bantry. Canon Martin Murphy had been administrator in the cathedral from 1908 to 1917, and had become a good friend of Fleischmann's. When Fleischmann returned from Germany, the Canon was parish priest in Bantry, and often invited the family to visit. They stayed with him in the summer of 1924, a holiday described in glowing terms by young Aloys to his Dachau grandmother; Fleischmann stayed with the priest in the spring of 1928 to recover from surgery.

For the choir summer outing in July 1925 the cathedral choir went to Glengariff. They started out from Cork in the early morning, travelling by charabancs, complete with a half tierce[39] of porter (to lubricate the voices, we must presume). On the way they stopped off at Bantry and afforded the people of the town the opportunity of hearing the choir. At the noon high mass in St Finbarr's church, the choir performed to a large congregation, where they sang the *Missa Davidica* by Perosi, Pope Pius X's choirmaster at the Sistine Chapel in Rome. After the mass the choir proceeded to Glengariff for their outing. The interest aroused by the choir's visit was such that Fleischmann undertook to visit Bantry every two weeks to train the choir – a bus journey of eighty kilometres each way.

In addition to helping in the church, in 1926 Fleischmann founded and conducted the Bantry Choral Operatic Society. The following year its sixty singers began to give choral and song recitals in the local cinema, all proceeds of which were donated to the St Vincent de Paul charity. On 6 May 1927, in conjunction with the Dunmanway Dramatic Society, a recital and play, *Paid with His Own Coin*, were staged by the new group. Neither the programme nor the newspaper report mention the author of the comedy – it might possibly have been Canon Murphy. On 11 May 1928, a two-act opera was staged: *The Pied Piper of Hamelin*, text by Robert Browning, with a matinée for children.[40] The Bishop of Cork attended the performance. At a third concert on 24 May 1929 the Society performed the three-act operetta *The Jewel Maiden* by Gillington and Florian Pascal,[41] followed by a choral and song recital with music by Mendelssohn, Brahms and Wagner. The operetta was produced by Miss A. Crowley, a national school teacher, who also sang the main role.[42] Soon after this Fleischmann began evening classes for pianoforte and singing.[43]

Fleischmann stopped going to Bantry once Canon Murphy left. But the work he had begun there continued: the *Cork Examiner* of 15 January 1930 reports that the Convent of Mercy Dramatic Class had presented a miracle play *Nemesius* together with a concert and short comedy. A different national school teacher had trained the children, and a Professor O'Reilly conducted his orchestra with a new men's chorus. On 3 May 1930, the *Cork Examiner* carried an account of Bantry as a model for the country with its Improvements Committee and its Operatic Society, according to 'Leesider': both unusual in Ireland for a town of that size. *Hiawatha* by the English composer Coleridge-Taylor had just been performed there.

The cathedral choir had also been invited to Bandon to give recitals of sacred music for the parishioners, which at the same time gave the local choir an opportunity to sing with the cathedral choristers. Such a recital took place on 4 March 1928 in St Patrick's Church in Bandon, where Canon Cohalan (Bishop Cohalan's nephew) was parish priest, and the resident organist and choirmaster was Friedrich Gleitsmann-Wolf, who was also a gifted violinist. The first part of the programme consisted of organ solos played by Fleischmann, violin solos played by Herr Gleitsmann-Wolf, and sacred songs sung by a local soprano. The cathedral choir sang sixteenth-century motets of the Roman, Netherlands and Venetian Schools.[44] The *Cork Examiner* published a long and appreciative review on 7 March; the sole complaint was that the church was but half full.

Canon Cohalan was succeeded in 1930 by Canon Murphy, who was moved to Bandon from Bantry. Fleischmann continued to visit him in his new parish. Together they developed in Bandon a fine choir of twenty-one men and boys as well as a girls' choir who performed the music of the sixteenth-century masters.[45] Fleischmann came to Bandon once a fortnight, arriving at 6.30 p.m. on the bus from Cork and returning on the 9.30 p.m. one. If the practice ran too long he would stay over night with the canon in the parochial house, and return to Cork the following morning. This continued up to the time of the canon's death in 1938.[46] A year later, when the war began, all such activities had to stop as transport became restricted to a minimum due to the lack of petrol.

Nationwide audience with the advent of Irish Radio

The British Broadcasting Corporation was set up in 1922. The first Irish radio station was established in Dublin in January 1926 and given the name Dublin 2RN by the British Post Office.[47] It reached only a small part of the country, so the following year the Cork station was established. It was located in the old Women's Gaol, directed by Seán Neeson, and produced its own programmes until 1930. Though the two stations only broadcast for three hours per evening, and for two on Sundays, and the reception was sometimes poor, its impact was dramatic. In 1932 a much more powerful station was set up in Athlone, in the middle of Ireland. The Dublin station had an ensemble of seven musicians in 1926; ten years later it was given an orchestra of twenty-four players, which by 1948 had grown to sixty-two. The first three conductors were army musicians.[48] The number of radio licence-holders grew rapidly: in Ireland in 1926 there were almost 10,000. The Fleischmanns had a 'wireless', as they were called, in 1924; Aloys Óg wrote in his Christmas letter to his grandmother in Dachau that year: 'We are able to hear concerts from Berlin, Hamburg, from France, Spain and New York. Some are so clear you would think they are in the same room. The sea is the best sound carrier.' Music, talks, church ceremonies, news and sport were thus now delivered like the milk bottles to houses in places remote from cultural centres.

Public recitals and broadcasts played a large part in the work of the cathedral choir, amounting to four or five each year. The Honan Chapel was a frequent venue and an ideal place in which to perform as the acoustics in this beautiful church were excellent. The choir was also recorded in the cathedral and the Cork radio studio. These recitals were frequently introduced by Father Pat MacSwiney of Kinsale, an authority on sacred music. Father Pat gave a short account of the life and works of each composer and explained the text of the motet which the choir was about to sing. For a broadcast of 1936 Fleischmann's son performed this function to much acclaim. Síle Ní Bhríain of Radio Éireann sometimes gave introductions, as did James Stack, the actor and producer, who was a member of the choir.

All practices, performances, recitals and broadcasts started with the singing of an 'Invocare' or Invocation. This was the famous hymn to St John, *Ut queant laxis*, which Guido d'Arezzo used in developing his method of sight-singing around the beginning of the eleventh century. The initial pitch of each successive phrase of the tune (which Guido himself may have written) formed a series of ascending steps, and the syllables sung to these pitches – Ut, Re, Mi, Fa, Sol, La – became the basis of a system of mnemonics for the notes of the scale. *Ut queant laxis*, the origin of this fundamental teaching device, appropriately became the choir's signature tune.

The recitals and broadcasts were well received by the press; many letters of appreciation among the Fleischmann papers attest to the favour they found with the public interested in sacred and in classical music. Former members of the choir wrote from Britain, Ceylon, Gibraltar and Italy. Continental organist colleagues working in Ireland sent letters of congratulation to the choirmaster; acquaintances, friends and sometimes complete strangers from all over the country wrote to thank him for the beautiful music. Dr Annie Patterson, lecturer in Irish Music at University College Cork, wrote on 7 March 1924:

> I feel I must write to congratulate you *very warmly* on the admirable singing of your choir. They certainly showed the most careful and thorough training, and both my sister and self were much impressed with the vigour and heartiness of your conducting. It reminds us of some of our artistic experiences in the old days in London.

A member of the cathedral choir, Seán Barrett, remembers:

> The choir made a memorable broadcast from the radio studio in the old Women's Jail in 1927 and for a long time afterwards Bert [Fleischmann] would show us postcards and read us letters of praise from Germany. How strange it seems that reception on medium wave could be so good![49]

Many of the cathedral choir's recitals in the University's Honan Chapel took place at the invitation of the University Art Society, founded by Fleischmann's son in 1931. One such concert, given on 14 May 1932, was favourably reviewed by the *Cork Examiner*, the music critic regretting that this performance had not been broadcast:

> All the works were unaccompanied, a matter, perhaps, that would tend to exaggerate any defects, but there were none to need covering by an organ. There was perfect balance, perfect tuneness, and perfect modelling. One felt that the one drawback was that the intent listeners could not be multiplied a thousand fold so that the joy of hearing such a recital might be widespread.

The report ended with a list of the academics, clergymen and musicians among the audience; they included Dr Merriman, the president of the university, and his wife, the musician Lord Monteagle, the solicitor John J. Horgan and the politician Éamonn O'Neill.

The choir was often invited to sing in various churches throughout the diocese, and further afield. However, finance was the problem: the furthest distance travelled was to Killarney cathedral. Visits to towns in County Cork at the request of friends were occasionally possible. Once the bishop sought the choir's services outside the cathedral, and it accompanied him for the blessing and opening of a new chapel of the Convent of the Sisters of the Sacred Heart to Bessborough, Blackrock on 12 June 1932. Dr Doubleday, the Bishop of Brentford in England attended, in whose diocese was the parent house of the order. The visiting bishop spoke highly of Fleischmann's choir, as the *Cork Examiner* reported:

> I have had the opportunity of being present at the High Mass after the blessing of the Chapel, and I want to congratulate His Lordship, the Bishop of Cork, on the splendid choir he brought here to-day in order to carry out this function so well. I have heard a great many choirs in a great many churches, but I can say without fear of contradiction that this is one of the very best choirs I have heard singing High Mass at a function of this kind. While I give over my nuns to His Lordship the Bishop of Cork I should like to have some recompense and take his choir over to England to do a little work for us over there.

RECOGNITION FOR THE CATHEDRAL CHOIR FROM ENGLAND

Towards the end of the decade, Fleischmann's choir received public recognition of unique quality from the English composer, Arnold Bax. He first came to Cork in 1929 to adjudicate at the Feis[50] or music festival, having been invited at Tilly Fleischmann's suggestion.[51] He had spent long periods in Ireland during the first decades of the century, in Dublin and in Glencolumcille, having adopted the Irish name of Dermot O'Byrne, under which he wrote poems, plays and stories. At the Feis, the cathedral choir entered the plainchant and motet competition and had the distinction of being awarded full marks by Bax and Madame Bonfils. The adjudicators were reported in the *Cork Examiner* as having said that they had never heard a finer quality of boys' voices anywhere in Europe.

After his return, Bax wrote a letter to the London *Daily Telegraph* about the choir:

> While acting as adjudicator at the Easter Feis in the most hospitable city of Cork, I was given an opportunity of listening to the choir of the Roman Catholic Cathedral. They sang for about an hour – plain chant, rendered with devotional feeling, and works by Orlando di Lasso and other composers of the difficult and complicated sixteenth-century polyphony. These performances were a revelation to me, for I had no idea that Ireland, up to the present time, could show

anything indicative of such a high degree of musical culture. I was told that the singers were very tired after their arduous work during Holy Week and that at ordinary times they could do even better, but what I heard convinced me that this Cork choir could hold its own in competition with any organisation devoted to rendering similar music in any part of these islands. Particularly noticeable was the sweet and velvety tone of the sopranos. There was none of that slight out-of-tuneness which has always seemed to me to be an unavoid-able defect in boys' voices. The greatest honour is due to Herr Aloys Fleischmann, the organist of the Cathedral, and trainer of the choir. This gentleman is a very fine all-round musician and would be an inspiring influence in any musical circle in which he might be placed.

The *Daily Telegraph* letter of 4 May 1929 was reproduced in the Irish *Sunday Independent* the following day. What this public recognition meant to Fleischmann can be seen in the letter of thanks he wrote to Bax on 14 May:

Verehrter Meister [revered Maestro],

I hope the visit to Ireland has refreshed you. Its far-away-from-the-world people indeed deal with 'foreigners' very quaintly, don't they?

. . . We all felt very lonely after you had gone. Your visit was like a part of an Irish fairy tale. Your kind words have given the Cathedral Choir tremendous courage and several members including myself have received letters of congratulation from England, America, Italy and Germany.

This 'dull, lifeless music' is recognised at last after twenty long years' struggle and I don't know how to thank you for it.

He goes on to speak of the Irish, recognising their natural artistic talent, the damage done by the 'sad centuries' of foreign rule, and the need for justice and discipline to liberate the people's creativity:

I feel if these poor people got a fair chance and the experience, that only by hard work and endurance good things can be achieved, this gifted race would rise and become once more the first writers and bards of the world, as in the olden times, of which they always dream. It is unploughed land, hard to plough. The rubbish that comes constantly from across the water under the name of 'Art' has buried the natural taste and ruined the minds of the people. From the flame of these ancient sun-worshippers there is only left a spark in the ashes – love for a 'good tune' and a fairy tale. Tunes and fairy tales interwoven with the mysticism of the Catholic cult were the only ties which kept the instinct for music and poesy, more or less alive, through all their sad centuries.

. . .If you honour Cork again with a visit and you care to stay in our humble home, I assure you, you shall be always heartily welcome. Mit herzlichen Grüßen und guten Wünschen, auch von meiner Frau und Bubi, [with kindest greetings and good wishes, also from my wife and boy]

in Verehrung [Yours most respectfully] AF

PS I am just copying some of my scores and shall send them presently.

Fleischmann also sent Bax a number of scores by German composers whom Bax did not know. In Bax's reply of early June, his attachment to Ireland is very clear, as is his esteem for the cathedral choir:

My dear Alois (if you don't mind my so addressing you. I would like you to drop ceremony with me too). Thank you so much for sending the bundle of music which I find very interesting. I don't know any of it, and it appals one to consider the amount of music that has been written, doesn't it?

I have just been down to the country to see Henry Wood and find that my first symphony and a new work of mine are to be done at the Promenades. As these concerts are broadcast perhaps you might hear these things. It would comfort me to feel that an Irish friend was listening in.

I suffer from the most acute Heimweh [homesickness] for Ireland, and have done so ever since I returned. I expect to come back in September to Donegal, and I very much hope that I may see you all in Cork again too before the year is out. We have had the most lovely Monat Mai [month of May] here, a luxurious riot of flowers and sun-shine. I have done practically no work – the call of the sun has been too masterful.

I was so glad to see that just at the time that my letter about the Cork choir appeared in 'The Telegraph' Sir Richard Terry was praising the Dublin choir, and saying that Ireland took the lead of the world in Plain-Song. I wish there could be a festival of Plain Song and Elizabethan (or rather XVI century) church music covering all Great Britain and Ireland, and it would give me the keenest joy if Cork beat the world!!

I think I must talk to Terry about this, and see if it can't be arranged. (I believe the Sligo standard is quite high too.)

I shall be so glad to hear from you any time, dear Alois, and I am always mindful of your and Mrs Fleischmann's great kindness to me during those delightful days in Cork.

Yours

Arnold Bax

APPLICATION FOR THE SCHOOL OF MUSIC PROFESSORSHIP
OF ORGAN IN 1929

Not long after the cathedral choir's success at the Feis Maitiú, the position of professor of organ became vacant due to the death of the Swiss musician, Theo Gmür. Fleischmann applied for the post, submitting references from his Munich professors, assessments of his compositions by four German professors written in the mid-1920s, a list of his 120 compositions, and a covering letter dated 14 June 1929. In the letter he makes four points underlining his suitability for the position:

(1) that I have studied under the guidance of one of the greatest of organ virtuosos and organ composers, Dr Joseph von Rheinberger;

(2) that the lack of Irish organists is due to the fact that harmony, Catholic Liturgy and choir-training have always been overlooked, and these I propose to combine in my method of teaching;

(3) that in the absence of an organ in the School, I will supply a new organ with two manuals and pedals for purposes of practice and use in concerts and

(4) that since the knowledge of an up-to-date instrument is indispensable, the largest and most modern organ in the city (built in 1922) will be at the disposal of students.

Since the destruction of the organ in the City Hall during the burning of Cork in 1920, there had been no organ in a secular building in the city. His mother's legacy would have enabled Fleischmann to donate an instrument to the school, had he been appointed. It is surprising that he does not mention in his covering letter three further major points in his favour: his thirty years of experience as organist and choirmaster, his many organ recitals and his compositions for organ. The list of works supplied to the selection committee included thirteen organ works, as well as thirty-three sacred motets, thirty-five secular choral works, thirty-four lieder and the music for two nativity plays. There are further indications that the application was prepared in some haste: the pagination of the different sections of the application is not consistent; it was only partly amended by hand.

Fleischmann was not appointed. His application was returned to him, stamped by the school as of 15 June 1929, with an inscription on the envelope in red ink: '3 days late'. When Carl Hardebeck was head of the school, Geraldine O'Sullivan's application for a piano post also arrived late,[52] but Hardebeck was able to allow it be considered and she was appointed. No information has been found about the date when the post was advertised. The feast of Corpus Christi, with the public procession of clergy and choir through the city, took place on 30 May in 1929, an occasion requiring much preparation from the choirmaster. But Fleischmann may have hesitated to start preparing his application as it meant re-living painful periods of his life – he had to go through the papers for his three previous applications and thus re-visit the decision to give up his highly successful work in Dachau and his attempts to leave Cork in 1908 and 1911. It must have been a humiliating experience to be eliminated because of a minor breach of procedural formalities. Appointment committees have discretion to extend submission deadlines if they so wish: the officials' decision not to do so must have indicated clearly to Fleischmann that the school administrators had no interest in considering him for the post.

The successful candidate was Bernard Curtis, who had been appointed to the staff in 1924 as a teacher of organ under Theo Gmür.[53] Had Fleischmann become head of organ, as well as being the director of the school choir and the cathedral choir, the Cork School of Music might well have become a centre for the training of church musicians: a *schola cantorum* could have evolved such as was required of every country by the 1903 papal instruction on church music. As it was, Ireland had to wait a further fifty years before such a school was founded in Mullingar.

FAMILY LIFE

Life in the Fleischmann household was full of music, with a routine of constant work. The Fleischmanns spent their mornings at home: he in his study, composing, practising on the harmonium, studying scores, usually in the company of his dog and cat, all often enveloped in a cloud of sweet-smelling blue tobacco smoke. In the afternoons he went out to give his classes in Farranferris and, until 1937, in the School of Music; on several evenings each week there were separate practices with the men and the boys of the cathedral choir, as well as services for the various parish confraternities. There was a weekly choir practice with the School of Music Choral Society, often additional cathedral choir practices for the many special ceremonies and visits of church dignitaries, and rehearsals for the frequent broadcasts and performances given by the choir in the city. For over a decade, Fleischmann travelled once a week for an evening choir practice either to Bandon or to Bantry. On Sunday mornings he gave singing classes in Farranferris, had a sung mass in the cathedral, followed by a choir practice, benediction in the afternoon and benediction in Farranferris.

Many of his evenings were spent copying music for the extensive repertoire of his choir. The Cork cathedral had no Edward Martyn to endow it with a music library of the Renaissance period: the nucleus of the library went back to the years 1906–08, when Fleischmann had first become choirmaster and had to build up a collection of suitable music. He had to copy the music by hand from his scores, duplicating the parts with carbon paper and later with a mechanical copying machine. It was hard labour. In 1945 he described it to the cathedral administrator: 'the night-work of thirty-nine years, embracing eighty per cent of our whole musical library, comes to about 20,000 copies and scores. A quarter of it I had to renew several times, when the copies became torn and illegible, since, unlike the Pro-Cathedral copies, they are unbound'.[54]

He kept a picture on his desk of a mediaeval Irish monk copying in the scriptorium of his monastery. He also helped his son with such tasks: the piano scores of Aloys Óg's *The Fountain of Magic* and *The Golden Bell of Ko* are in Fleischmann's hand. It was indeed appropriate that Aloys Óg dedicated his *Four Masters* to his father, a work which celebrated the seventeenth-century Franciscan scholars who spent their lives copying and compiling the *Annals of the Kingdom of Ireland* from all the Gaelic documents that had survived the Tudor colonial wars.[55]

Tilly Fleischmann did not have to do housework, though she had to plan and supervise it, since the family had a housekeeper who lived with them – up to the 1950s most middle-class families were able to afford the very small wages paid.[56] Fleischmann often commended his wife for her energy and discipline. She spent the mornings working at the piano, always doing three to four hours' practice per day and before recitals up to five. She had about forty pupils in the School of Music, where she taught in the afternoons. The description given by Máire Weedle, who studied with her in the 1950s, no doubt applies also to the earlier periods: 'She was a very strong, awe-inspiring woman and very demanding. She "pushed" us students to the limits of our ability and got us playing works which many others would have considered far beyond our technical ability.' She gave recitals and broadcasts regularly until the 1950s. Among them was a Franz Liszt evening in the Abbey Theatre in 1923, and a Chopin recital in Cork and in Dublin for the International League in 1924, at which her husband accompanied Rita Wallace performing Chopin songs. Tilly played with the Brodsky Quartet in Cork the same year.

She was probably the first musician in Ireland to perform Bax. Tilly had first heard of him in 1917. She was told that an Irish poet called Dermot O'Byrne, a 'spoiled' priest and writer of rebel poetry, was composing music under the pseudonym of Arnold Bax. She was intrigued and wrote to a London publisher, who sent her songs and piano music by Bax. 'From that time onwards my husband and I procured as much of his work as could be got, and we followed his career with ever increasing interest and enthusiasm.'[57] In 1926 she and Rita Wallace gave a programme of modern compositions, which included Arnold Bax's *What the Minstrel Told Us: Ballad in E Minor*, her husband's *Rhapsody for Piano: Cuimhne ar Fheis Ceoil* [Recollection of the Music Festival], and Fritz Brase's Serenata 'Little Moira'. In November 1929, six months after their first meeting with Bax, Tilly and Geraldine Sullivan gave an evening of Bax works for two pianos; Bax songs were sung by Seán Neeson and the London singer, Doreen Thornton. The recital was introduced by Daniel Corkery. In January 1930 Tilly and the soprano Frances Allsom gave a recital in the Aberdeen Hall

Dublin of works by Bax, Vaughan-Williams, Delius, Scriabin, Debussy, Fleischmann's song 'The Awakening' and his *Rhapsody for Piano*.

The University Art Society invited Tilly to perform with the Kutcher Quartet in November 1932 and to accompany the celebrated German lieder-singer, Elisabeth Schumann,[58] in 1934. During this time Tilly gave a whole series of broadcasts from the Cork station, occasionally from Dublin, and in 1929 was the first Irish pianist to broadcast on the BBC. These performances took their toll. Playing in public never came easily to her: for weeks before concerts she suffered acute nervous strain, which never diminished with routine.

From their early years in Dachau, the Fleischmanns worked together, Tilly helping with the preparations for all the nativity plays and playing the harmonium at those of 1904 and 1906; she inspired some of her fiancé's music and performed it from their first joint concert in Dachau in May 1906. This pattern continued in Ireland. Tilly played the organ for major cathedral services, he sometimes gave her piano classes for her. She frequently accompanied singers giving his lieder, though in 1933 and 1934 he accompanied Rita Wallace at two recitals of his songs given in her residence before over a hundred guests. (Fleischmann wrote of this 'celebrated opera singer': 'She sang my songs with enthusiasm, ideal tone quality [*Tongebung*] and warmth.'[59]) Tilly enjoyed an unusual degree of independence in a period when wives were legally subject to their husbands' authority; her husband regarded her as his equal in every regard, as his letters to her document. During their sixty-two years of friendship, they worked for a common cause, shared the same high standards which they applied to themselves first but also to others, and were united in their dedication to and love of their art. On one occasion when Fleischmann agreed to allow somebody else to accompany the singer at a recital of his lieder, as he felt it would be too much for his wife, she was seriously incensed and insisted on doing it for him. However, the additional strain of the dispute about the matter brought on a serious pleurisy attack from which she did not recover for many weeks.[60]

They were often invited to visit friends, in whose homes informal recitals were given. They went to the theatre, to concerts and recitals, enjoying being listeners rather than performers. The radio brought them concerts from distant cities. In good weather, when he could spare the time, Fleischmann liked to walk along the quays by the river watching the ships which, until the 1950s, came right up to the city's first bridge, and to go for long walks outside the city by the Lee Fields. The family had occasional outings to west Cork visiting Canon Murphy, to Limerick staying with Lord Monteagle, and to the Dingle peninsula visiting the MacSwiney sisters. They often spent the summer holidays in a cottage in Oysterhaven. Fleischmann enjoyed good health on the whole, his sound constitution perhaps supported by the regular exercise of cycling or walking to and from work, up and down the hills and steps of the city.[61]

It is small wonder that the Fleischmanns' son, Aloys Óg, growing up in the household of such hard-working parents, should have adopted their work ethos as part of the natural order of things. He continued to be an excellent pupil. He went to school in the diocesan seminary of Farranferris from the autumn of 1923 aged thirteen, and though the youngest pupil in the school, won first prize for English and Latin. He studied incessantly and usually came top of his class at all examinations. On Sunday mornings he accompanied his parents to the cathedral, sitting on the organ bench, beside his mother if she played on special occasions, and watching his father conduct the choir.[62] He was given organ classes by his father and lessons in counterpoint and harmony; the piano classes with his mother continued to prove difficult. So he had a daily round of violin, piano and harmonium practice, together with exercises in music theory. He took one hour a day off during the week, did sports on Saturday mornings (at which he did not excel!) and spent Sunday afternoon with friends – the sons of John J. Horgan, Ivor and Joe, with whom he got up to all sorts of adventures about which his parents knew nothing. His first cousin, Patricia Cox, remembered him arriving to spend a five-week holiday at the seaside with her family carrying a suitcase of books to be studied. He had just taken his intermediate school examinations, at which he had obtained honours in six subjects, first place in Ireland for German and Latin and a scholarship from his school.[63] Her father therefore decided it was time for him to rest, confiscated the books and forbade all activities other than swimming, rowing and fishing – an injunction readily accepted by the young visitor. After the five weeks with the Williams family, he went with his parents to Bantry to stay for a fortnight with their friend, Canon Murphy, where he enjoyed swimming, walking, playing tennis, being taken for drives in the beautiful mountainous countryside and making a watermill, which he put into the stream running through the priest's garden. The Fleischmanns occasionally spent their holidays in London, where they visited Tilly's brother, Tony Swertz, and went to many concerts.

Young Aloys began to keep a diary in 1926 when he was sixteen, and kept it up the following year. A picture emerges from these of a closely-knit family, each of the three Fleischmanns operating independently in a field of their own but working as a team when it came to performance. Aloys junior helped his mother, for instance, by page-turning at recitals at which she accompanied another artist; from the age of fifteen he played the harmonium in his father's big concerts – suffering from much nervousness beforehand – and always helped to set up the halls for his parents' rehearsals and performances. He greatly admired their music-making and his father's compositions, was indignant if their work was not appreciated, and noted with surprise how stoically they reacted to the difficulties of creating a wide audience for classical music. His remarkable application to his studies came primarily from his interest in the subjects; it was also a matter of discipline which does not seem to have been enforced but to have come naturally, no doubt through the parents' example. But his industriousness was also strongly motivated by awareness of the family's modest finances and by a desire to contribute towards the family income. On his father's birthday, April 24 1926, as exams loomed, he remembered that the previous year he had not succeeded in winning a scholarship. He wrote: 'Imagine *losing* £80 last year by 10 marks out of 15,000! Could I get it next year what it would be for Pappi and Mammie!' He always seemed to enjoy their company and that of their friends, loved their informal recitals, at which he sometimes performed, and looked forward to the holidays when they would be together all day undertaking all sorts of interesting outings. His father kept a close eye on him, decided that daily diary writing was a waste of time and instructed him to make a weekly entry instead, which he did. He was 'caught' trying to compose one day, (April 29 1926) his father 'swearing'. 'He said I should learn something first and stop this "dilettantical" business. He is really right, but I love fishing around, and seeing what I can make.' The previous Christmas he had composed a prelude, which he played to the company at Corkery's; after his father's intervention, there is no further mention of compositions in the diaries.

Aloys Óg completed his schooling at seventeen with remarkable success, getting first place in Ireland in three subjects and second in another. He then began his studies at University College Cork, taking on two degree courses: that of Bachelor of Arts with English and German, together with the programme for a Bachelor of Music under Professor Lacy. In the summer of 1930, he graduated, aged twenty, with a first-class honours BA. He had done some composition during those years – two songs and *Movement for String Quartet*. He also followed his father's example in founding a small orchestra, which gave a number of concerts in the university. In the summer of 1931, he graduated with a first-class honours BMus. That autumn he signed on at UCC for a Masters degree and began work on a thesis entitled *The Neumes and Irish Liturgical MSS*. In November 1931 he founded the University Art Society, which was to arrange for many exhibitions, lectures and recitals by distinguished artists over the next fifty years. His father must have been most gratified to see his son with this society adopt the manifesto of the Munster Society of Arts, of which he had been a founding member. The inaugural lecture followed the lines laid down by Corkery in the previous decade about the need to encourage local artists 'to hew in our own quarries' while at the same time studying and engaging with the cultures of Europe.[64]

A letter from Fleischmann on the occasion of his son's twentieth birthday shows his deep attachment, but also his worry about the young man's future and the fervent hope that Aloys Óg would be spared the tribulations he had had to endure. As always, he wrote in German to the family:

> 13 April 1930
>
> My dear good son,
>
> All possible good wishes for your future on your twentieth birthday. –
>
> 'As you began, so will you remain' says a wise old proverb. You have begun well: continue to be good-hearted. Harbour no passion; be economical with your energy and you will reach your goal victorious and end happily in the dream-games of this existence.
>
> May God's protecting hand guide and bless you. Your happiness is our happiness!
>
> Hold fast to the principles of the faith – they are based on thousands of years' experience and history in the destiny of the human race. Only faith saves you from despair, and gives meaning and moderation to us who know we have to breathe on this revolving planet.
>
> Thank your mother very specially today. No sacrifice was too great or too heavy for her as she brought you up well and carefully. I am greatly moved as I think back on those days when you were very young and I see how devotedly and tenderly she looked after you and minded you herself. You will soon realise and discover how hard it is to come from modest beginnings and make life worth living. You are going *into* life – into your youth; I am going out of life – into old age. You are looking into the veiled beginning; I into the covered end. Both of us need courage!
>
> I have but one wish: may it be granted to me to be able to work until you can look without fear into the world's hard face.
> May your fate not be a hard one; and may you be spared much of what I was not spared; may your life be filled with joy, vigour and success.
>
> That is what we, your mother and I, wish you on the twentieth celebration of your birth, as well as much more which cannot be expressed – for you are our faith, our hope, and our love.
>
> Your father

At the age of twenty, the elder Fleischmann had also acquitted himself with considerable success at his studies and in his first post in Dachau; at fifty, he knew all too well that the achievements of young years could be quickly obliterated and how hard the face of the world could look.

The Swertz relations

Tilly Fleischmann's father, Hans Conrad Swertz, and her younger brothers, Ferdinand and Franz Xaver, never came back to Ireland after their departure for America; her contact with them was sporadic. Her father died of cancer in Philadelphia in July 1927. A letter from him written (in English) six months before his death to Tilly and her family provides some insight into his circumstances. It shows some uncertainty as to the size of his daughter's family; there is also a conscious echo of Cork ways of putting things:

> My dear children, Aloys, Tilly and Buby! That's all, I think!

> Although a little late, I wish you all the compliments of the season and a happy and very prosperous New Year! I did not feel so well of late and spent most of my holiday in bed, resting myself like. My nerves went back on me and I had lots of trouble with everything and everybody, the church, the house, some unscrupulous tenants and even with a few refractory and ungrateful pupils. But everything is coming out all right again, and in few weeks more I expect to see all my troubles ended. I suppose you heard, I bought myself a new Piano! It was built by an old New York firm by the name of Becker, and has a new Steinway action. Oh! It is beautiful; a semi-grand and the tone and action is superb! Do I not love to let my old fingers run over the keyboard. Oh yes! dear Tilly! I still can play, but not any length of time; my heart won't allow it. With the organ it is different; I could play and improvise the whole day long and feel no bad effects from doing it. Your occasional announcements and concert programmes give me the greatest pleasure and I am, as I always was, justly proud of you. –

> One great drawback in my work is my eyesight! It is getting very weak and I can neither read or write any length of time. Ferdie says, I must get new glasses! So I will after a little while. . . . This is the 6th letter I wrote today and I must stop now. So wishing you again every health and the greatest possible success, I remain yours

> very affectionately

> Hans Conrad Swertz

His son, Ferdie, lived in Philadelphia some miles from his house, whereas the elder son, Xaver, worked in New York. They told their sister that Hans Conrad had bought a large house, hoping to finance it by taking tenants. But, prone as he was to making rules, they never stayed long. Once he became ill, Ferdie and his wife came to see to him every day, until he had become so weak they felt he ought to be in hospital:

> I asked X. if he didn't think it best to send Father to this private hospital. Poor Father, when the doctor told him it would be $125 a week, would not hear of it, but when the doctor went away I telephoned to X. in New York and asked him to come over immediately and explain

to Father how we would be only too glad to pay the expenses of the hospital. So X. came over the following night and we both sat on the bed and told him how we were going to get the best attention and medical care we could get in Philadelphia for him. So he sat up in bed, put his arms around our necks and cried like a baby. That night he told us he had only $20 in the bank and that was the reason he did not go to the doctors earlier in his illness.[65]

Both sons underlined in their letters to Tilly how courageous, gentle and peaceful their father was in his last weeks. Hans Conrad left all his assets to his wife in Cork.

His two sons had a very difficult time during the long years of the depression. Xaver had started a company in New York, lost everything and went to work in Argentina; Ferdie died in 1933, having written home only days beforehand, with no mention of ill-health. Rosa Swertz, the gifted pianist Aloys and Tilly Fleischmann were so fond of, died in Dublin six months after her father, on New Year's day in 1929, aged thirty-seven. She had suffered a great deal of ill-health. She had married a Dublin man in 1919, lost her first child and had had an unhappy marriage.

MUSIC BRIDGING POLITICS AND CLASS

The Fleischmanns were never involved in politics, either German or Irish, but a number of their close friends were staunch supporters of radical republicanism. These included the MacSwiney sisters, William Stockley, Daniel Corkery, Seán and Geraldine Neeson. The Fleischmanns shared with them a love of music, an appreciation of the Irish heritage, as well as the willingness to work for cultural autonomy corresponding to the new political structures about to be established. But that was also the basis of their friendship with supporters of moderate nationalist policies such as John J. Horgan.

Tilly Fleischmann had not seen much of Mary and Annie MacSwiney during the war of independence. After Terence MacSwiney's death, Mary and his widow, Muriel, toured the United States extensively, winning American political support and funds for the republican movement. Mary had been elected during her absence to the second Dáil. She regarded the Treaty offered to Ireland in July 1921 as a betrayal of the cause for which her brother had died and was among the large minority that spoke and voted against it in the Dáil. She and her sister took the republican side during the civil war; Mary was imprisoned by the Free State, but released after a twenty-day hunger strike and international protests. When the bishops of Ireland excommunicated all republicans active in the civil war, she publicly accused them of abusing their ecclesiastical authority and of disguising their anti-republican political policies as religious dogma.[66] In

November 1923, she attacked the bishop of Cork for denying Christian burial to the republican prisoner, Denis Barry, who had died on hunger strike, reminding Dr Cohalan that he had officiated at the funeral of her brother. The bishop accused her of duplicity (in a speech reported verbatim on 28 November 1923 in the *Cork Examiner*): of having prevented a rising in Cork in 1916 by suppressing the Dublin order to the Volunteers, of having gambled on her brother's life by exerting pressure on him to maintain his hunger strike, believing he would be released and 'that she would share in a sunburst of cheap glory'. He declared that 'Republicanism in Ireland for the last twelve months has been a wicked, insidious attack on the Church and on the souls of the faithful committed to the Church'. He insinuated that Mary MacSwiney might have had knowledge of the concealing in a Cork convent of £100,000 which had been robbed by republicans from the Customs House in Dublin.[67] Outraged by these allegations, she began preparations to take the bishop to court for libel, although the penalty was excommunication for instituting proceedings in a secular court against a bishop without having permission from the church to do so.[68] After the end of the civil war and the defeat of the republicans, Mary characteristically continued to act according to her political convictions. She would not accept government grants for her school, since she did not recognise the legitimacy of either the first Free State government, nor that of de Valera, the republican leader of the civil war, who had abandoned his abstentionist policies and won the elections of 1933.

Tilly Fleischmann much admired the courage of those who had risked their jobs, their freedom and their lives for their cause and who were now prepared to put their principles before their pockets. But she did so without necessarily adopting those principles. Nor did her friendship with Mary MacSwiney, the bitter opponent of de Valera, prevent her from 'stealing out', when her husband was at the theatre, to join the huge crowds giving de Valera a triumphal entry into Cork during the election campaign of January 1933. She described the scene in a letter to her son in Munich:

> I think there must have been about 30,000 people to meet him. They had torchlights and tar-barrels and all the pipers bands, also working men's bands. It was well it was dark and there was nobody with me! I cried my eyes out. It reminded me so much of 1918, Terence MacSwiney and all those noble fellows who died for their country. The enormous enthusiasm too only made it the sadder – poor humanity – today rapturous and alive – tomorrow gone and silence. When the procession came around the corner it looked extraordinarily picturesque – the women with shawls, their hair flying wild in the wind, with torches in their hands, headed the procession. They looked wild, but determined. It reminded me of pictures that I have

seen of the French revolution! They were the only women that I
noticed. After them came thousands and thousands of men, all
singing and cheering. The streets were crowded with poor ragged
little boys who sang 'We'll crown De Valera king of Ireland'. . . . It is
very questionable if Dev will get a majority – all the money and business people (all the philistines) are against him and money is
powerful. He has all the poor and the thinking people with him.[69]

Neither the Fleischmanns' republican nor their pro-Treaty friends
(such as the Horgans) would have been too pleased with this classifica-
tion of de Valera's opponents and supporters. Her husband held that no
artist should 'meddle' with politics.[70]

The Fleischmanns remained on good terms with the MacSwineys.
They often visited them in their cottage in the Irish-speaking Gaeltacht
near Dunquin. There they enjoyed the company of the local people who
called to the house in the evenings, visited the Blasket Islands where
they met the great storytellers Peig Sayers and Tomás Ó Criomhthan,
visited the Gaelic scholar and mathematician, Professor Pádraig de
Brún, who had built a small cottage in Gráig on one of the most
splendid sites imaginable looking out over the Atlantic towards the
Blasket Islands on one side and over the sweep of wild indented coast
towards Mount Brandon on the other. They also called to 'An Bohán',
the hut, where students from Farranferris spent their holidays learning
Irish under the direction of their gentle teacher, the priest, an tAthair
Taidhg. Tilly Fleischmann gave frequent recitals in Scoil Íte, and later on
the three granddaughters were sent there.

In 1931 Tilly Fleischmann was able to help Mary and Annie
MacSwiney to re-establish contact with Terence's daughter, Máire Óg.
Terence's wife, Muriel, had never quite overcome the terrible ordeal of
her husband's fast and death. Like her sisters-in-law, she took the
republican side in the civil war, but was so scandalised by the Catholic
bishops' excommunication of all anti-Treaty militants that she never
crossed the door of a church again, nor would she allow her child to
receive any religious instruction or to attend a Catholic school. She
adopted the socialist theories of James Connolly, the leader of the
Dublin workers' movement executed after the 1916 rising, and went to
live in Germany. There, without warning, she left her five-year-old
daughter (who spoke no German) in a boarding school. Once the child
had recovered from the trauma of the desertion, and had learnt German,
she was happy there. Mary MacSwiney had been given joint custody of
the child by her brother. She was most worried about her sister-in-law's
development and the fate of her niece; Muriel had broken off all contact,
but Mary managed to find out where the child was. In 1931 Tilly and
Aloys Óg visited Máire Óg near Garmisch in Bavaria; the girl was now
thirteen and spoke no English. She remembers the visit:

My aunt Mary MacSwiney, who was very worried about my living abroad, used to ask friends who were visiting Germany to try to look me up. . . . I knew nothing about Ireland, not even where it was . . . but what did make an impression on me was how kind they [the Fleischmanns] were to take me out for the day. A photograph was also taken of the three of us, of which I still have a copy, me with my pigtails and little Bavarian dress. It was the Fleischmanns' visit that brought my aunt again in contact with me, and we started to correspond.[71]

Tilly Fleischmann brought the child to see Munich's Cardinal Faulhaber, at his request.[72] The following summer, Mary MacSwiney travelled to Garmisch with Germaine Stockley to see her. Muriel probably heard about these visits. The day after the meeting with her aunt, Máire Óg was informed that her mother was taking her away from her foster-family, with whom she had been very happy. On the advice of her foster-mother, she ran over to her aunt's hotel and asked to be taken back with her to Ireland. She was hidden in a taxi, driven across the nearby Austrian border; from there the three made their way to Geneva to the Irish legation, and from there to Cork. Her mother believed her daughter had been kidnapped, and brought a case for custody to the High Court in Dublin, which she lost. To Máire Óg's regret, they never met again.[73]

By Christmas 1923, the Fleischmanns' good friend, Father Pat MacSwiney, was no longer living near their house overlooking the river. Mary MacSwiney was the unwitting cause of her priest cousin being banished by his bishop from Cork city and sent to act as chaplain to a convent in the remote parish of Dunmanway. During the civil war in the autumn of 1922, Father Pat had, at her request, taken charge of a bag belonging to somebody whose premises were in danger of being raided by government forces. Father Pat deposited the bag in the Cork convent of which he was chaplain, where it was found by pro-Treaty troops. It contained £3,000. A year later, when the bishop publicly mentioned Mary MacSwiney in this connection, Father Pat wrote to the *Cork Examiner* to defend her and himself, since his role in the affair was known in the city. He wrote that he had complied with a request of Mary MacSwiney's to help a close friend of her brother's, and had been given a bag for safe-keeping, the contents of which he did not examine. Father Pat suggested that the money found in the bag could well have belonged to that friend, who might have withdrawn his savings, as bank deposits of republican sympathisers were known to be at risk of government seizure, and he deplored the unfounded attack on Mary MacSwiney's character.[74] Within a month, he was writing from Dunmanway, far from his friends, having to travel a considerable distance to hear their music, a luxury he could now scarcely afford:

My dear Alois,

I have so much to thank you for I do not know what to say. First
what you have done for poor Ireland – your beautiful fugue to St
Patrick. Like one of the old poet saints of Ireland your music kept me
happy company all my dreary way 'home' this morning. The music I
hear always comes back to me afterwards, and it is then I really hear
it in all its beauty. I thank you from my heart. Its sadness consoled
me and its merriment taught me another lesson in the beauty of
sorrow. And – to speak of lesser things – I also thank you for helping
an old Irish beggar [Father Pat himself] to pay his bills. May the God
of charity reward you and make you happy this Xmas.

With love and gratitude

Yours

P MacS

But Father Pat began to organise in Dunmanway: he established a
dramatic society there, which co-operated with Fleischmann's Bantry
Choral Society, and a Feis. He continued to study the piano with Tilly
Fleischmann, to write programme notes for Fleischmann recitals, to
introduce cathedral choir broadcasts, to serve on the committee of the
Cork School of Music and on the council of the Munster Society of Arts.

In 1927 he was sent as curate to Kinsale, under a very conservative
archdeacon.[75] The town was at that time in a dire state: the British military bases were gone, the fishing industry was dying; there was great
poverty and a sense of hopelessness. The priest visited the poor regularly; set up a vocational school, a creamery, housing schemes, help for
the travelling people; he revived the fishing industry, promoted Irish,
studied the history of the town, published scholarly articles on the
subject, and worked for years collecting material in order to set up the
regional museum of Kinsale, which opened some months before his
death in 1940. Indefatigable in his efforts to remove the causes of
poverty, to enable people to create lives worth living, to contend against
indifference and lack of concern, his source of strength was music and
conversations with friends on subjects close to his heart. Sometimes
duties were assigned to him which prevented him from attending concerts in Cork. On one such occasion, when he had been obliged to
officiate at a funeral in the country, he had missed Tilly Fleischmann's
performance with the Brodsky Quartet. He wrote to her:

> you could not have felt my sense of loss: no musician could ever
> sound the depths of longing which a mere ignorant lover of music
> like I suffer from. I would have given kingdoms, yea the whole world
> (were I not alas, as I am, only a beggar) to have heard this music. To
> you and A[loys] music is a science, an ideal art, but to me it is the
> only thing in life that satisfies the gnawing of my soul-hunger, the

terrible hunger of an untutored savage. Music alone makes me believe that even I have been moulded to 'the image and likeness of God' – as every Christian is supposed to believe.

His acute sense of deprivation illustrates the cultural stagnation of rural Ireland which Corkery spoke of when presenting the Munster Society of Arts, which Canon Sheehan had described with such feeling in *My New Curate*, and which George Russell had combated with his work for the co-operative movement and his journal *The Irish Homestead*. Like these three men, Father Pat never faltered in his efforts to cultivate the wasteland.

Father Pat was one of the many students of Tilly Fleischmann who became a close friend. Sinéad Ní Bhriain was another. She began her studies in 1912 after her return to Cork from an English Catholic boarding school. Young women from wealthy families often pursued studies in art or music, but these were usually undertaken as a pastime. Sinéad's commitment was serious. She was very gifted, and went on to become a performer, giving recitals in Cork and Dublin as well as broadcasts, which came in for much praise. She joined the staff of the MacSwiney sisters' school, Scoil Íte, as music teacher, and played a role in the city's cultural institutions, becoming honorary secretary of the Munster Society of Arts.

Geraldine O'Sullivan (later Neeson), who, like Sinéad, came from an old Cork family, took up her studies with Tilly around the same time. The association between their families was to last a lifetime. She wrote of Aloys Fleischmann: 'He was a wonderful man. Kind, generous, informed, sensitively artistic, very gifted, and with it all modest. . . . He gave to his acquaintances a wider vision and a deeper knowledge and a love for the enduring things.'[76] She had first got to know him as a teacher:

> One day Aloys took his wife's place and gave me a lesson. He opened up new vistas. He talked of music as a live thing; indeed, he talked of life as a musical thing. That lesson was the first of many spread over several years. . . . With the growth of this friendship I developed completely new horizons. Now, for me, art of all kinds acquired a significance and was no longer the 'eccentric' taste it was deemed to be among many of my friends and relatives. . . . Aloys was volatile and witty. He could also be very human. He had a profound respect and love for life and was a good companion, who could also drive one wild with his obstinacy, intolerance and impatience. But he introduced a bracing stimulant into every phase of life. It was to him I went with problems big or little, his gentle philosophy or, if he thought it was more suitable, his anger or biting irony often put me right.[77]

Geraldine Neeson was a woman of many talents: an accomplished pianist who broadcast, performed with her former teacher, accompanied and taught in the School of Music. She was involved in a variety of theatrical undertakings in Cork, from An Dún to the Little Theatre Society of the 1940s, and acted lead roles in many plays, for instance in Synge's *Riders to the Sea*. It was that Little Theatre Society which gave the first performance in Cork of Synge's *Playboy of the Western World*, forty years after its riotous début in Dublin. Her husband Seán was a Belfast man, a singer, an Irish speaker, a collector of Irish music, a man of the theatre, a music teacher, a member of the cathedral choir – and a republican. After the 1916 rising, he was first interned in Frongoch in Wales, then imprisoned in Reading Gaol, where he founded a choir, which his companions Seán T. O'Kelly, later President of Ireland, and Terence MacSwiney joined. During the war of independence, he was gaoled several times. Like his friends Corkery, Stockley and the MacSwiney sisters, he did not accept the Treaty: he joined the anti-Treaty forces. He was interned by the government troops, and released on Christmas Eve 1923. His wife wrote: 'A great welcome was given to Seán when he took his place, bearded and looking a little older, in the Cathedral Choir on Christmas Day.'[78]

Though most of the Irish landed gentry with an interest in the arts tended towards literature, a small number were musicians. The Kirkpatricks of Mallow were one such family. They had protected the Fleischmanns in 1914 after the British authorities had banished them from Cork as aliens. Through John J. Horgan, the Fleischmanns had become acquainted with Lord Monteagle of Brandon. He was of the Limerick Spring-Rice family and an influential supporter (and president) of the co-operative movement, founded by Horace Plunkett to free small farmers from the dominion of unscrupulous traders. When Monteagle died in 1926, his son and heir, Thomas, was in the British diplomatic service, where he had served with great distinction in Washington and then in Paris during the Versaille Treaty negotiations. His main interest, however, was music. On his return in 1930 to the family estate in Mount Trenchard, he devoted his considerable energies to the management of his lands and to his art. He played the piano in chamber ensembles, often attended concerts and recitals in Cork, performed there sometimes, and frequently hosted concerts in his home, to which the Fleischmanns were invited, both as performers and as guests.

In 1934, he wrote to Tilly Fleischmann from St James's Club in Piccadilly to explain why he could not stay with them for the Elisabeth Schumann concert in Cork, adding:

> If you think of it when you see her, would you remind her of the
> expedition we made some years ago to my old friend Mr Edward

Speyer in Hertfordshire, and how I accompanied her singing 'Das Veilchen' of Mozart from the original manuscript, which was one of Mr Speyer's most treasured possessions in his wonderful collection!

I am going to the Busch quartet concerts here. They are playing quite superbly – better than ever – and the E minor Beethoven (Op. 59 No. 2) on Monday was something quite unforgettable. We also had a delightful recital of piano and violin sonatas by Adolf Busch and Serkin on Saturday, including the C minor Sonata of Max Reger which I'd never heard before: a most interesting work, and they made it sound magnificent. This evening I am dining with Mrs Mormsey.

I have (very boldly) undertaken to play some solos at the concert which Mrs Horgan is giving in Cork on 13 April – and look forward to seeing you both then, and also to making plans for your next visit to Mount Trenchard.

I hope you have good news of your son in Munich.

Yours very sincerely

Monteagle

I do wish I could have come to your recital on 21 Feb. (what a lovely programme) – but was tied down at home just then and could not get away.[79]

Fleischmann described him as 'a dear friend'; he and his wife grieved at his unexpected death in 1934.[80]

Many close friendships remain undocumented as people who lived in Cork and whom the Fleischmanns met regularly had no cause to correspond with them. Germaine Stockley was an exception. She generally sent a little note of thanks after every concert or special church service on which she painted delightful miniature watercolour landscapes, usually writing in German to her compatriot.

In 1924, the Fleischmanns met another German who had come to settle in Ireland. Colonel Fritz Brase called to see the Fleischmanns during his first visit to the south to prepare for the establishing of an army band in Cork. He wrote (in German) to Tilly from Beggars Bush Barracks in Dublin:

Permit me to tell you how very pleased I was to have found in you and in your esteemed husband such splendid people, artists and – Germans. Permit me to say how your playing delighted me. Never shall I forget that evening, with darkness falling, the mood corresponding so well to your masterly performance of Liszt, which I was privileged to listen to alone. The hours spent with your husband revealed to me a truly German artistic soul; should the earnest efforts I shall make to cultivate his acquaintance be successful, I should profit greatly: very bitter experience of life has destroyed many of my ideals.

From then on cordial relations developed between the two families, Brase writing to congratulate them on broadcasts he had heard or concerts he had attended. The No. 2 Army Band was set up in 1926, with Arthur Duff as conductor. Duff gave Aloys Óg his first conducting lessons, often letting the music student rehearse in his stead with the army band.[81] The colonel was somewhat disappointed when young Fleischmann did not take his advice and opt for a musical career in the army. But he travelled to Cork for the first performance of Aloys Óg's Piano Quintet in April 1939; in his letter of congratulation assuring the young composer of his blessings for the road of life. In none of the Brase letters which have survived is there any mention of politics, Irish or German.

Letters have survived from two of the Fleischmanns' painter friends after they left Ireland. In his last letter, written two years before his death, Harry Scully told Tilly that he felt life was passing him by, that he was 'outside life':

> My dear Tilly,
>
> My very warmest greetings to you all. Very many thanks for your card and kind wishes – what memories it awoke. How I envy you and wish I could once again enjoy your circle. I am sorry for my long silence. I wonder do you realise that I am now a very feeble old man and, I am sorry to say, a back number. I have grown to dread writing letters, have really nothing to tell you except that I am keeping fairly well but having a different life, outside life, except for my solitary visits to the galleries here. I snatch an odd moment now and then in my wooden shed, but it's rather useless as I no longer have the staying powers and there are so many demands on my time – it seems a hopeless job.[82]

The stained-glass artist Harry Clarke probably made the acquaintance of the Fleischmanns in 1916 when he was working on his splendid windows for the Honan Chapel of the university. His father was an immigrant from England who had come to Ireland in the late 1870s now that the Catholic church was in a position to provide employment. The elder Clarke set up a successful church decoration business in Dublin; his gifted son studied art in Dublin and in France, then joining the stained glass department of the family firm. He loved the theatre, designed programmes for the Dublin Drama League and was a great admirer of the Abbey, as he wrote to Tilly Fleischmann when he asked her to look after his friend the actress Kate Curling during the company's visit to Cork in November 1927: 'I hope you like the players – I never tire of the Abbey – we go week after week and their work seems always fresh and spontaneous.'

He drafted the programme design for Tilly Fleischmann's Liszt recital in the Abbey Theatre in 1923 together with a little caricature of 'The

Critic'. Some months before the recital he had heard her play and had presented her with a drawing. The art historian Nicola Gordon Bowe describes it in her study of his life and work:

> It is in water colour heightened by gold. It was done on 23 August 1923 after he had heard his friend Tilly Fleischmann of Cork play Liszt's Valse Impromptu in A flat for him at her sister's house in Sutton. She had studied with Liszt's last pupil. Harry's little picture (5 x 3.5 inches), which he presented to her, shows Liszt's head and shoulders. He tears at his hair as he struggles with his composition – a tiny crinolined figure tied to his outstretched baton. Above, before a painted curtain, a girl personifying the Vivace Scherzando dances on a black stage, naked except for the large cloak which billows behind her; her wild mop of hair is picked out in gold paint. The drawing is initialled and inscribed: Franz Liszt *Vivace Scherzando* in Dublin.[83]

Another painter friend was Daniel A. Veresmith,[84] an American of German origin who lived for a long time in England, working as an illustrator and teacher of drawing, before moving to Doneraile. He first met the Fleischmanns at a recital by Tilly Fleischmann in December 1922, which he said left him 'in a regular "ferment", artistically and musically'; he was involved in the Munster Society of Arts from the beginning and heralds its advent just a year before it was officially established in a letter of 3 January 1923:

> So you may be sure I will appear on the scene again, on the stage or behind it, for Munster is going to be waked up, or *we* are, Artistically, Musically, Historically, Philosophically – not Metaphorically but Categorically! Mrs Veresmith and I have decided we want *Music*! And so we are coming in as soon as the evenings get a little lighter for a week or two, and see what we can carry off. Soon we hope the Society of Arts will be functioning. It will be a real pleasure to meet folk who are still 'students' aetat [even if close to the end], as Methusalah, and drink at the Fountain [of life and art].

Perhaps the Society did not transform life in Doneraile, for some years later he decided to return to England. In June 1926, before his departure, he wrote:

> I am having a 'clearing out' and so send you three little (very little) sketches. Two are old ones, and have a look of old masters and the other a late one, of an effect I am fond of. It was in our back yard. So I hope you will see what I have been driving at. They won't take up much space in your drawing room anyway.

One of the main subjects of the letters written after Veresmith had moved back to England is music. He had a fine voice, helped to train the

church choir in the Somerset village in which he now lived, and wrote
with indignation about the poor quality of the singing and of the music
there. In June 1929 Fleischmann had sent him some songs – probably
those just published by Augener:

> Your kind gift came safely. Now again do I feel amongst the brother-
> hood of Ideals! We are so poverty stricken as to musical people in our
> village that your songs came as a ray of sunshine. Particularly as I
> have been so sick of the things they are doing in our choir. In our
> hymn book there are so many fine church hymns taken from the past
> German and French composers, yet they sing the fearful rubbish
> composed by the *parsons* of the last 50–60 years, with words equal to
> the worst Moody and Sankey type. It is really 'unter'm Hund'
> [beneath contempt], as we used say in the U.S. It has been a curse to
> the English church. Why they can't leave the music to the musician,
> goodness knows. . . . Mrs Veresmith has tried the accompaniments of
> your charming songs, but she says they are too difficult. What they
> would say if I sang them at a concert here! I do not say I weep – I
> *curse*! And we have such a beautiful old church and see so many
> beautiful old buildings all round us here in this county.[85]

A further motif in his letters is how much he misses Ireland.
Although Ireland was the third country in which Veresmith lived and
worked, he writes of it as an emigrant might of his native place. He contrasts the way of life in his rural parish unfavourably with that of Ireland:

> I really would enjoy a good talk with you and Mrs Fleischmann, and
> I miss often the quick intelligence of the Irish people, also their *faces*
> for I have not see anything so *engaging* and unusual over here, as one
> sees in Ireland. All is orderly, fixed, stodgy and uninteresting, and
> *stubborn*, nothing wayward to tickle one's imagination. . . . When
> Ireland becomes *rich* through the Shannon scheme, and the people
> have money to foster *Art*, then we shall hear and see great things
> from the Irish people. Well, then we shall come over and *board* with
> some family (to escape the double income tax) and feast our eyes
> and senses on the Renaissance. Drop a line when you are not busy
> and give us the news.
>
> Kindest regards to Madame and Aloys and yourself with many
> thanks for your kind thoughtfulness for a parched soul![86]

The following year, in January 1931, he wrote: 'What a joyful thing
to see your well beloved handwriting again! . . . I don't know how
often I wish I were back in Ireland to "commune" in thoughts and talk
with you.' The last letter, written five weeks before his death on 22
February 1932, shows the strength of his bond with Ireland and his
Irish friends:

It was indeed a pleasure to get your postcard and to know you were in 'good shape' as they say in the U.S. Tho' our correspondence has such wide gaps, I do think of you often, because one's own friends don't consist of such sympathetic, artistico, musico people, and one often longs for a real good talk with some one who 'awakens and understands' as Browning says. I caught some of the broadcast from Dublin that while ago when your dear sposa played. I lost the first part because our Regional comes through badly but it was Beethoven, wasn't it? And the song 'Adelaide'? Just a link to join us together again. My Christmas was a washout. I went to bed just before and spent about three weeks, rather critical and very weakening in bed. So now to get rid of my trouble I am going into a nursing home for 'a coupla' days and get quit of it. Is it not a terrible thing to be familiar, oh so friendly and loving with people and then part for so long? 'Ach Scheiden thut weh' [parting is so painful] as the 'Schwalben heimwärts ziehen!' [as the swallows make their way home] There seems to be something wrong when we can't see each other, isn't there! All my days off and on in Cork were so vivid, and pleasant in my memory that thinking of this past seems unreal. I want to know how so and so is, how time has dealt with all friends yet there is no news agency to tell me. I think I could even fall on the neck of a crossing sweeper if he could. . . . Before Christmas I had about four weeks of choir masters teaching our boys a Communion service. I had to sing every note to them. Talk of 'Die Macht der Musik' – it was a case of 'Der macht die Musik', and no mistake. [The grammatical change brings a witty change of meaning: 'Die Macht der Musik' means 'the power of music'; 'der macht die Musik' means 'he makes the music' i.e. is in charge.]

Now dear friends take my heartiest wishes for your welfare in this coming year. If it is possible to write then you know how pleased I should be, if not, well then another Christmas card next Christmas will do as long as I know you 'are well and prosper' as Rip Van Winkle says.

Grüß Gott!

Yours D.A. Veresmith

The music makers of Cork all knew each other; many were friends who gave each other support and solace in the small world into which fortune had wheeled them and left them to contend against its confinements. Sean O'Faolain and Frank O'Connor in their autobiographies give us glimpses of the frustrations talented young Cork people endured who grew up far from the arts, whose families had no money to spare, and who felt intellectually starved and trapped in the small city devoid of the artistic heritage and tradition of culture to be found in the great cities of the continent, about which they read so much. O'Faolain began his studies at University College Cork in 1918 as a student of William Stockley. The young man chafed at the limitations of university and city;

although highly critical of Stockley as a teacher, he remembered with
gratitude the encounters with the professor outside the lecture hall:

> About twice a year he would invite a group of us to his home, a
> charming old house with wrought-iron balconies, overlooking the
> wide Lochs of the Lee at Tivoli . . . its pink-washed stucco front
> covered in summer by greyblue wistaria. There in his delightful
> drawing room upstairs he and his lively German wife would show us
> his pictures – he had some excellent Walter Osbornes – or arrange a
> play-reading, or she might play Chopin, or persuade her friend Frau
> Fleischmann, a highly talented pianist and most kindly woman, to
> play for us. The tea would be handed around ceremoniously, in old
> china on old silver, and they would struggle to draw us out of our
> shyness and awkwardness and lure us to talk as if we were not hob-
> bledehoys but the grown men and women we pretended to be. If
> only for these gestures of kindness, as well as for his natural courtesy
> and dignity, if only indeed for his picturesque appearance, bearded,
> always capped and gowned, I am deeply grateful to his memory and
> the memory of his wife Germaine.[87]

He realised later on that Germaine Stockley, having grown up in Munich
in a world of art, elegance and interest, might have found life in Cork as
restricting as he did. This is reflected in one of his plays. The main character of his comedy, *She Had to Do Something*, is partly modelled on
Madame Stockley. It was first given at the Abbey Theatre in Dublin in
1937, and portrays 'a lively Frenchwoman marooned in Ireland in a
provincial town', the troubles she brings on herself when she invites
Russian ballet dancers to perform there, and how, though defeated by
the scandalised clergy and their followers, she is not subdued.[88]

Frank O'Connor grew up in Cork in greater poverty than his friend
O'Faolain; both writers had the good fortune in their youth to have had
Daniel Corkery as their mentor and friend. O'Faolain acknowledged
with gratitude that Corkery 'had the highest literary standards and
imposed them on us constantly'.[89] O'Connor describes in his autobiography how Corkery introduced him to classical music and the pain the
process at first caused him:

> Corkery took me a couple of times to real piano recitals by Tilly
> Fleischmann and Geraldine Sullivan, but, though I read the pro-
> gramme notes like mad – they were usually by Corkery's friend,
> Father Pat MacSwiney – and pretended to myself that I could recog-
> nize the moment when 'the dawn wind wakes the sleeping leaves,
> and these, tapping at the window pane, rouse the joyous maiden who
> as been dreaming of her secret lover', it always turned out that I had
> just been listening to the climax in which 'Smiling, she leans through
> the window and plucks a rose for her hair'. It mortified me to see all
> those educated people who had no difficulty in distinguishing the

dawn wind rising from a girl plucking a rose for her hair and made me feel that life was really unfair.[90]

Corkery often went to the cathedral with O'Faolain to hear the choir and found Fleischmann 'a man after my own heart'.[91] But he had a colleague, Denis Breen, who did not share Corkery's affection for the choirmaster. Breen was unusual in several regards. He had a great love of music, and played for the theatre which Corkery had founded with Terence MacSwiney and others. An ardent supporter of the Irish language movement, Breen did not condone the disparaging of English culture to which narrow Irish-Irelanders occasionally tended and, rather exceptionally in Cork, he had no time for the Catholic church, as O'Connor reports:

> At Gaelic League meetings he roared down patriotic souls who decried English music and talked of the greatness of Byrd, Dowland, and Purcell, whom none of us had ever heard of. He also professed to be an atheist, which was rather like proclaiming yourself a Christian in modern China, and the defensiveness this had induced in him was reflected in everything he did and said. He had a great contempt for our little colony of German musicians, whom he spoke of as though they were Catholic priests, as 'bleddy eejits'.

Breen often 'battered a Beethoven sonata to death with his red eyebrows reverently raised', or, having 'hammered Hugo Wolff's *An die Geliebte* unconscious, he struck out the last chords as only a man who loved music could do it, scowling and muttering: "Now listen to the bloody stars!"' Those 'stars', whose musical authority he repudiated, spoke of him, according to O'Connor, with charity as 'a genius without musical training'.[92]

LINKS WITH GERMANY

During the bad years after the war, Fleischmann supported his mother in Dachau, sending food parcels and money. He also helped many others: among those known are the parish priest, the clerical editor of the local newspaper, and the director of the Munich cathedral choir, Ludwig Berberich. In 1923 Berberich wrote that he had found somebody to bring his letter to England who offered to post it there, that he could otherwise hardly have afforded to buy the postal stamp.[93] Fleischmann was only able to help, given his own very modest circumstances, because in Germany the rate of exchange for sterling was so good.

He frequently spent his summer holidays in Dachau during the 1920s, staying with his mother, and with Berberich in Munich, visiting old friends and using the time for study and composing. In a letter to his wife in Cork, he describes with sadness the changes he notices during a visit in August 1926, twenty years after he had left home. The removal of the ancient fountain outside the Fleischmann house brings back a wave of memories of his youth:

> Now I am under the roof on which my thoughts down through the years have so often rested like tired migrating birds. The old roofs and the tall, slender church steeple, whose shadow touches the gable like a sundial, stand pensively on the old square, exactly as in the old days when my young eyes saw these places in a very different light. A young boy greets me respectfully from the window of the house opposite – I do not know him: perhaps his mother or his father used to know me. I do not know him, just as the old people whom I met yesterday did not know me any more. Twenty years is a long stretch of time. At home in foreign parts – a stranger in one's native place!
>
> I wander through the streets and squares: much has changed, has been done up differently or renewed, and the graveyard has among its guests many dear friends whom I had intended to call on. And the old fountain diagonally opposite the house is – gone.
>
> The old fountain that offered a drink to the Roman mercenary, that sang in my sleep or in the restlessness of my nights when I lay behind the gable window high up above the earth and when confused, disquieting things stormed my sleep – then I used to hear its good, wise voice murmuring from the depths. Its murmuring seemed to me to be happiness and reassurance. I heard it when I sat with my head bent over books, or when it filled the pauses in my music. I heard it when the midnight hour rang out sonorously and eerily from the steeple, or when late wayfarers passed it; I heard it when the summer morning rose up and the birds began to try out their bright voices. I heard it in the death-filled autumn night, when everything died that was alive; I heard it in the stillness of winter when its pipes were protected with straw against the corrosion of the cold and the snow lay knee-deep on the street. Its murmuring was always there and its murmuring was always the good and faithful voice of home. Now it is no longer, the tireless donor, the old friend of my youth. What pain that brings.[94]

Fleischmann's presence in Dachau was announced in the newspaper, the *Amper Bote*, on 30 July 1926, so he subsequently had numerous callers coming to pay their respects. He visited his old friends and supporters among the painters and brewers of the town and his wife's relatives, the Rösslers. He still had an open invitation to use the piano in the house of the Ziegler brewers whenever he wished and often worked there. Ziegler's daughter, Dora, performed his Tagore songs for their friends. He writes to Tilly that his mother, who was to celebrate her eightieth birthday on 29 September, was well:

Dachau cattle market at the lower market place, 1890, by Karl Stuhlmüller (1859–1930) in Josef Reitmeier, *Dachau: Ein Kunstbilderbuch*, Dachau, 1995, p. 203

Midsummer clouds over old Dachau-Etzenhausen, 1908, by Georg Flad (1853–1913) in the exhibition catalogue Friedrich, Wichmann (ed.), *Dachau Ansichten aus zwölf Jahrhunderten*, Dachau n.d., p. 60

Sunny autumn day at the Dachau millstream, 1921, by Otto Strützel (1855–1930) in
Josef Reitmeier, *Dachau: Ansichten, Der Letzte Teil*, Dachau, 1982, p. 36

Midsummer clouds over old Dachau-Etzenhausen, 1908, by Georg Flad (1853–1913) in
the exhibition catalogue Friedrich, Wichmann (ed.), *Dachau Ansichten aus zwölf
Jahrhunderten*, Dachau n.d., p. 60

(*l.*) Aloys Fleischmann, shoemaker; (*r.*) Magdalena Fleischmann née Deger,
probably 1868 on the occasion of their marriage, painter unknown

Two young and three old Dachau women, 1908, by Josef Andreas Sailer (1872–1952) in
Josef Reitmeier, *Dachau: ein Kunstbilderbuch*, Dachau 1995, p. 54

Adoration of the Shepherds, 1905, by Ignatius Taschner
(1871–1913), in Josef Reitmeier, *Dachau: Ansichten, Der
Letzte Teil*, Dachau, 1982, p. 223

To Night, *c.*1910 by Richard Pfeiffer (1878–1962), in *Die
Jugend*, Munich 1910

That I found my old mother active and in good health I have already told you. I lead a quiet life. During the morning hours I work, in the afternoon I go visiting and in the evenings I usually sit over – a glass of beer! I am conducting a dogged stealthy struggle against the invitations which have increased since I was publicly welcomed (press cuttings enclosed).[95] This has disturbed my peace and quiet. H.H., the clergyman, has just called, full of all sorts of musical troubles. Kind regards to you from Prof. Stockmann, Bürgers, Zieglers, Rösslers, Hörhammers and Hayeks et al. I work a good deal in Zieglers' magnificent music room. The Steinway grand is still as good as ever: it sounds enchanting in this room which one could almost call sacred. Frau Ziegler is gradually recovering from her suffering and illness. Dora has a splendid voice: she is studying with Bossetti!

She sings some of my songs, which she likes very much indeed. I have really been very lucky with the Tagore songs: everybody likes them and they must be published first. Germans are quick to become enthusiastic and they give logical, well-substantiated reasons for their judgement, which does one good and stimulates. If I didn't have you and our beloved friend [Fr Pat MacSwiney] – I would come here.[96]

He also wrote of a visit to the science museum in Munich. This celebrated institution had been founded in 1903 by Oskar von Miller in order to present technology and the natural sciences to all classes of the people in an interesting and entertaining fashion; Fleischmann went to the planetarium:

I was in the German Museum a few days ago and was quite enraptured by the experience: by a demonstration of the science of astronomy from the first beginnings of the Pythagoreans up to our own time. I had had no idea of the degree of technical perfection of the instruments, nor had I been able to imagine the movements of the heavenly bodies as clearly as they were shown. This section of the museum is unbelievable and unique in the world. It is awe-inspiring to stand there in the midst of the movement of infinity and to see the millions of sources of light begin to dance.[97]

The gradual recovery are before frowned on after the devastation of the war is noted,[98] but the new fashions and music frowned on:

The church is being enlarged: wonderful plans – the back wall has already been removed. A new organ is also being built for the church (in connection with which my advice was sought). Despite the great shortage of money, minds are becoming active everywhere here: the intellectuals are not standing aside but getting involved. In the cafés, however, bobbed hair, short skirts and jazz prevail! . . .

Best regards from Mother, Uncle and Aunt. I miss you and Erin very much.

In May 1928 Fleischmann was invited to become a member of the Munich Bruckner Society and to write an article for its journal of sacred music, *Organon*. The Munich cathedral organist, Josef Schmidt, was chairman, and had put his name forward; Fleischmann agreed to both requests. The following year he was asked to promote the society in Ireland, and invited to publish a 'Music Letter from Ireland' in the journal. He obliged the secretary, Dr Alfred Zehelein, by sending him Irish folk songs for lectures at his school of music, and was then asked to translate an oratorio Zehelein had composed on Alfred the Great, which he probably declined – at least there is no further correspondence on the issue. It was through Zehelein that in 1931 he found a publisher for his *lieder aus der Kinderwelt*, though he had to contribute to the cost by buying a fixed number of copies.

The death of Fleischmann's mother

The last surviving draft of a letter to his mother was written on 12 January 1927. On 23 May 1928 he wrote to his uncle Thomas Deger, who had returned to Dachau with his wife Theres after his retirement and was living with his sister in Fleischmann's family home. He must have warned his nephew that Leni Fleischmann was seriously ill and asked for instructions for her funeral. In a letter, which Fleischmann said was the most excruciatingly painful he had ever had to write, he outlined what he thought appropriate, gave the text for the death notice and 400 mortuary cards, and said he wanted the funeral service and the reception for those relatives who had travelled to the funeral to be simple and dignified without unseemly fuss. He said he would, of course, attend should circumstances permit.

They did. He set off to see his mother for the last time in July 1928, as he describes in a letter to his wife of 15 July:

> At last I'm able to write to you in more detail. From the post cards you will have seen that I interrupted my journey several times so that I wouldn't arrive here too exhausted, as the heat was like hell fire; the journey seemed interminable. It was a difficult, sorrowful journey. The first meeting was quiet and tragic. I was as shocked as if I had seen a ghost: didn't recognise my own mother any more, so have the heralds of death disfigured her features. I could have cried out with the pain.
>
> When she heard me coming in, she tried to sit up and shaded her eyes with her emaciated hand.
>
> 'I can't see you any more; I only recognise you by your voice'; then she sank back exhausted onto her pillows. 'It's a long time that I've been waiting for you, and how I would have loved to see Tilly and Alfi again. But even if you had brought them with you I wouldn't

have been able to see them: my eyes have already been taken from me – I feel as if everything is a dream.'

Then she became quiet; and soon slow heavy breathing indicated that she had sunk into a deep sleep.

I looked around the room and sat down on a chair. Over the bed hangs a very old crucifix: at Christ's feet the mater dolorosa with swords through her heart. Not far from this our pictures: Bubi with the little cat. On the small table there are a number of medicine bottles, there is the sofa, chairs and all the furniture, and along the wall beside the bed there is a piece of dark red linen and embroidered on it: 'Lord, remain with me for the evening is nigh.'
Yes, evening is indeed close: the last sad, weak rays of sunshine are illuminating the end of an unfortunate human life.

I went upstairs to the little bedroom where I slept as a boy, where the bells of the high tower boom out the time. Often did I listen up there to the riot of the elements, observe the dazzling lightning as it flashed around the tower and tremble when storm and rolling thunder made earth and house shake.

Tonight the stars are shining down, the old roofs leaning peacefully on each other as in the old days, and a fountain is murmuring softly in the distance.

An acute sense of home overcomes me – my thoughts go back to the most distant years of childhood, to the days of that untiring love which once minded and cared for me. Soon it will cease and the bond be torn which has tied me to my home.

The two doctors are of the same opinion: cancer of the stomach and dropsy: a cure is out of the question. It is only a matter of time. Dr Engert thought last Christmas would have brought her the final release and is astonished that the disease is progressing so slowly. She is getting excellent care and that is necessary, for she can scarcely move and every drop of water has to be given to her. These are sad days that I experience here. . . .

She lived for almost a month longer, dying on 11 August 1928, some six weeks before her eighty-second birthday.

Fleischmann made arrangements for the Christmas tower music to continue which he had established as a tribute to his mother when he left Dachau in 1906. The local newspaper announced it in its Christmas Eve edition on 24 December 1928:

Tower Music

The lovely custom of having music on Christmas Eve from the tower of our fine parish church will continue to be practised this year, due to the generosity of our Dachau citizen, Cathedral Organist Fleischmann in York [*sic*] Ireland. This evening at 9 o'clock, beautiful old Christmas carols will be played from the tower of the parish church by the wind ensemble of Dachau Orchestral Society.

Performance of a Fleischmann work in Munich Cathedral

In August 1930, two years after his mother's death, Fleischmann was staying in Dachau in the old family home arranging its sale, now that his uncle Thomas Deger had moved back with his wife to the Nuremberg area, where he had worked all his life. The pain of giving up the house in which he had been born, of finally severing his roots in his native place, is not the theme of the letters to his wife which have survived. He writes home about memorable experiences: a guided tour of the upper regions of Munich cathedral given by his young architect cousin Franz Berberich, a service at which he played the organ, a meeting with colleagues, hearing his offertory prayer 'Ave Maria' sung before a huge congregation, and a meeting with the celebrated actress Agnes Straub, who had begun her career with a role in his Dachau nativity play of 1904. In his letter of 12 August 1930 he describes a visit to the Munich cathedral, the Frauenkirche, with Franz Berberich:

> I enclose some cuttings about Siegfried Wagner's death – a great loss for Germany and Wagner's art.
>
> . . . I have a lot to settle here and without a personal word some things wouldn't have been possible. Up to now I haven't been able to get any private work done, which I regret, as I hate every day which passes without my having been able to make some progress. I went only once to the theatre: to Ludwig Thoma's *The Moral*, which is a very amusing play – but entertainment of that kind brings me little: I am tired from all the running around, and what I need is the cathedral and the old masters whose works echo through the immense building – these are experiences which sink into my soul and move me to the core.
>
> This time I didn't go up to the tower [of Munich cathedral]. Instead I went with the architect Franz Berberich up to three of the attic structures [of the church] and looked down through the Gothic arches into the nave and transept. The roof truss has three levels and is twenty-one metres high! You can imagine the forest of trees when I tell you that 14,400 beams support the roof. You only realise the colossal dimension of the building when you see the incredible confusion of this steep triple division holding the old hollow bricks. All these old tree trunks and panels date from the year 1540 and are all in perfect condition. It was an age of heaven-storming faith which built this powerful bastion for eternity. The free-standing arches are a story of their own: they are suspended at intervals of eighteen to twenty metres between the huge pillars. They are about twenty centimetres thick, and seen from this height appear terrifying and you

get the impression you are walking on clouds. The naive poor people of the 'dark' mediaeval times indeed! One stands full of admiration before their works and the greatness of their spirit.

He reports that he was surprised to receive from the Dublin composer Harold White[99] an excellent critique of the three songs he had sent him. He then tells his wife about musicians he met in Munich: his friends the cathedral choirmaster, Ludwig Berberich, whom he visited at home, the cathedral organist, Josef Schmidt, and a composer from Vienna. He deputised for Schmidt, playing in the cathedral during one of the services. The two other musicians tried to help him find a publisher for his music. A performance of his offertory prayer is to take place in the cathedral for the Feast of the Assumption:

> At Berberichs' I met Prof. Dr Lutztheler of Vienna, whose compositions I have known for years. He is a most intellectual and kindly person who told me many interesting things. We were together a good deal. His big mass was performed for the first time yesterday (Sunday) and made a deep impression on me. He is highly modern, yet the vocal part is deep, effective and singable. The publisher Böhm (the top man in Vienna) I met there too, and he was extremely nice. I'm to send him something. Berberich and Lutztheler seem to have spoken to him on my behalf without my knowledge. I was astonished by his excellent judgement in musical matters. I found the cathedral organist Schmidt in great form: he seemed delighted when he glanced up from the keyboard and saw me standing there. We celebrated the pleasure of meeting again with a morning drink. He is still on holiday and I am playing the Thursday services. Last Sunday Lutztheler played his own mass: he was obviously very moved by the splendid volume of sound which filled the cathedral. He told me they don't have it in St Stephen's cathedral [in Vienna]. The cathedral choir impressed him greatly. Most members of the choir are on holiday and there were only forty-five present. But down in the nave you would think there were a few hundred. It is extraordinary what magical effect first-class acoustics can achieve. You're faced with a miracle of sound. Every tonal sequence in e or f always has determining appeal and is really inexhaustible in its diversity and hovers like the voice of a spirit through the Gothic sanctuary enveloped in half-darkness.
>
> Twice my 'Ecce Sacerdos' was played this year for the entrance of the cardinal. The cathedral choir like it so much, Berberich tells me. Next Friday, 15 August, is a high feast day here! A state holiday! Pontifical Mass. The programme: Bruckner's B minor Mass; Rheinberger's Graduale Assumpta Est Maria; Offertories (Gaudeamus in Maria): Ave Maria for eight-part choir by Alois Fleischmann. As you see, I find myself in good company and am naturally most curious to hear what it will sound like with these most noble neighbours.

Berberich once heard the Cork cathedral choir and wrote to Rome about it. He was highly critical of the quality of sacred music to be heard in the Vatican:

> Monsignor Berberich told me in his letters that he wrote to Rome about the performance and that he said more or less what Arnold Bax had said. Berberich did not get a good impression of music in Rome. 'Slovenly bawlers' he called them, who issue regulations for the world which they themselves ignore. No wonder, he says, that the Rome League are surprised by good performances, for you hardly find any in the churches of Rome, nor in St Peter's either.

A week later, on 21 August 1930, Fleischmann writes home about the performance of his work in the crowded cathedral:

> I met John and Ivor[100] in Munich – we were very pleased to see each other. John and the Consul came to hear the big Bruckner mass and my eight-part Offertories. It made a deep impression on them. The women's voices sounded as if they were coming from heaven, and I had to stand very firmly on my two feet when my music resounded through the immense expanse. My boyhood and youth passed by me with all their pleasure and pain, and I was most deeply moved. The cathedral was packed full; the three of us were standing in the middle aisle – we couldn't move back or forward. Bruckner's name acts like a magnet here to all music-lovers. We were told that of all distinguished Bruckner admirers, not a single one was missing. A large number of his friends had come and we heard French, English and Italian spoken. In the evening I attended Vespers. The members of the choir came to congratulate me and told me that they had taken to my music with enthusiasm and enjoyed singing my work so much, and had I been satisfied etc. I went back behind the organ and between light and shadow a few tears rolled down my cheeks. I thought of you two, who constitute my home in foreign parts. It seemed to me as though the huge pillars arching up to the heavens whispered: no man is so great that he does not become small in our embrace. And as the choir out in the front sang the psalms, I sat in a quiet corner in the twilight of the coloured windows, and verses carved in stone looked at me with everlasting eyes:
>
> 'Not what you suffer is decisive/On the scales of the highest life/But how you bear your earthly suffering/– That will determine how the judgement on you lies.'

He anchors his jubilation very firmly with the recognition that he is without a homeland: he calls his small family his home, but the country in which they live a foreign land. The lesson he bears with him from this extraordinary day in the cathedral is that the only success which counts is that of accepting and enduring the suffering which life has imposed on him.

However, fate had one further consolation in store for him during that visit to Dachau: an encounter with a performer of his nativity play of 1904 who had become an acclaimed actress. Agnes Straub, aged thirteen, had played the part of the Queen of Light. He went to the Munich Court Theatre to see her perform the leading role in Schiller's tragedy, *Maria Stuart*, and had a long talk with her after the play:

> . . . I saw Agnes Straub[101] as Maria Stuart – a character of daemonic scope. 'Germany's foremost dramatic tragedy actress.' I visited her. She was most sweet and said she owed everything to me and to Court Councillor Beck who gave her a contract to act in 'Maria Stuart' in Heidelberg after *one month* studying. I said it was a long way from the Queen of Light to the Queen of Scots. She remembered every detail clearly and said she has never studied any of her great roles with such enthusiasm as her first role in the Dachau Nativity Play. The audience in the Court Theatre already went wild with excitement after the first act: she got five curtain calls of her own. The end of the play was given in the programme as being at 11.15 p.m.; at 11.45 we were still standing in our rows: there was no end to the applause. It was an experience I will not forget as long as I live. She is a most modest person to talk to: she sets no store on her fame. She turned four reporters away when I was with her – and they had not just come from Munich – who were pushing for interviews. Her eyes have an extraordinary fire; she speaks with passion and one feels that every word is the fruit of experience. She told me about her life, which has been marked with much suffering. She would like to see the scene of her youth again and the hall in which we first performed. There are a number of actors from Berlin who would like to go on the trip to Dachau with her. I enclose some newspaper cuttings.

FLEISCHMANN'S SON IN MUNICH

Having sold his mother's house, Fleischmann for the first time in his life had assets to his name, and was therefore in a position to allow his son to undertake a course of postgraduate studies in Munich both at the Academy of Music and at the university. Aloys Óg completed his Masters thesis within a year, and left for Germany in September 1932. He had occasionally departed to the west of Ireland without his parents for a short holiday during his studies; now, for the first time since his internment, Fleischmann was to be far from his son for a longer period; for his wife it was the first separation. They and their young housekeeper, Madge, bade the traveller farewell on board the liner in Cobh. Fleischmann describes in his first letter how the acute sense of loss he suffered as he saw the ship depart was heightened by a series of images from his youth in that country to which his boy was now journeying:

My beloved good son,

Now you are separated from us, I have to take up the pen to communicate with you. The impact of the parting I cannot and do not want to describe to you. Only a very little, beginning, like Horace, in medias res. When I saw you standing high up on the ship and waved to you, my young life arose before me again. I saw myself rejuvenated in you – it seemed to me that I was once again standing at the beginning of my journey through life. An indescribable feeling of grief and joy quivered through me. My blood flowed hot and cold through my heart. Images arose out of the mirror-smooth surface of the water: images of my youth, of children, animals, friends, landscapes, houses; even the dead of my distant home were revealed out of the depths of the sea, rose and sank with the waves. My entire existence flowed by me as though from under a green, wet veil. With a fervent prayer in my heart that the waves may not bury as many of your joys and hopes as they have of mine, I saw you leave. We gazed after the floating giant who carried you on his back until he disappeared from our view into the east. Not until we were in the train on the way home did we feel more and more the emptiness, the loss. We became wordless, lowered our eyes sadly and all three wept for you.[102]

Fleischmann suffered a serious disappointment when he learnt that Aloys Óg had signed on, not for composition and organ, as he had hoped and indeed expected, but for composition and conducting. He realised that this meant his son would not become a church musician, could not succeed him at the cathedral, that he therefore could not count on being followed by somebody who would build on the foundations he had laid with such dedication: that there was a danger that his life's work would leave little trace. However, after some attempts to dissuade him, he accepted his son's choice.

Though Aloys Óg was most conscious of the sacrifices being made for his education, his father always made light of the financial issues and encouraged him to incur whatever expenses were necessary. As if to reassure him that they were not living at home on bread and water in order to be able to support him in Munich, he depicts the domestic comforts in which he had invested: 'In Mama's bedroom I have had a bedside lamp and electrical heating put in. The drawing room, library and study were also equipped with electric stoves and an electric cooker was put into the kitchen.' He then indicates that he can, by taking on further work, augment the family income: 'I have had some practices with a new nuns' choir in the Presentation Convent – so far it has been quite good. There is an abundance of work for me! Art seeks bread.' He describes his regular work with the cathedral choir: it was autumn auditioning time. A large number of new recruits had presented themselves from the parish, of whom only the best were admitted for training:

'Have accepted eighty new choirboys for preparation. Was very exacting in my selection: excellent voices and bright eyes were the criteria. At the moment I am studying with the choir: Ravanello's work, Vittoria's Ave Maria, Orlando's Tibi Laus, Palestrina's Exultate Deo etc.'[103]

Aloys Óg received much paternal counsel from his father about appropriate behaviour in Germany. He was reminded of the greater formality expected there of young people towards their seniors (no hands in pockets while speaking to them, respectful listening rather than talking considered appropriate) and the wisdom of holding one's tongue. The young man was admonished for rash judgement when he made a derogatory remark about Hugo Röhr, who gave master-classes in conducting; Fleischmann had in his Dachau days often seen him in the Opera House:

Röhr, the admirable practician, whom for over a decade I heard conducting the most difficult foreign operas – it was ignorance that led you to scorn him.

Many of your rather pointed judgements about people and things are circulating at the C.C.U. [Munich University] and, believe me, they will not be advantageous to you. You have been given *two* ears and only *one* mouth! I hope you will guard your tongue more in future. Bridle it firmly if it has nothing good to say![104]

Much encouragement and practical advice was forthcoming from Fleischmann when Aloys Óg wrote of the difficulties he was having with composition exercises and above all with sight-reading of scores, at which the students had to demonstrate their prowess to the professor in class, one after the other. He was expected to visit the old family friends:

Am glad you went to Zieglers: they are fine, delightful people and I always feel I am in good hands there. Go to visit Baroness Moreau, Georgenstrasse 4, and give her our greetings. Uncommonly pleasant, simple, noble people. The baroness was a delightful comforter for your mother when you were just a few days old and she was the first visitor! She knows how to take young people: has five sons of her own.[105]

On All Souls' Day 1932 Fleischmann conducted a requiem mass; the sacred music for the ancient feast day celebrating the dead left him in a melancholy frame of mind:

All sorts of ideas arise when one's heart or brain gradually become emptier and more desolate, like a bare, dead tree. Then one's footsteps follow their usual path, but one's thoughts take off with the migrating birds and fly over the earth towards unknown distant places. ('Father, where do the swans fly to?' thus one generation asks the other). Days and hours are now approaching in which one secretly envies those who only need a few feet of earth and who lie in a quiet corner under the symbol of the cross, resting after the pain of their gnawing homesickness. All Souls, feast of the dead and of the far-off!

Don't let me infect you with my sad thoughts. In you lie the justified hopes of youth, with countless prospects of blossoming spring, with the long bright days of summer, if you remain faithful to yourself. If I sum up the thoughts expressed above in one wish for you: namely that your autumn and your prospect of winter may be more consoling, brighter – you will, I am sure, be able to understand that.

He continues with reflections on musical form. His son had begun to send him the exercises in composition written for his professor; Fleischmann comments here in very general terms, neither praises nor criticises, and gives advice obliquely:

Your canons and harmony exercises have arrived. Your work interests me very much. In these and similar mathematical combinations, in tensions and reduction of tensions, in building up and resolution lies the secret of the *unified* force of the movement of thought. The boundlessness and diversity of a Bach, a Händel and the old musicians. Gothic cathedrals which appear, as it were, as new every day, at all times, and convey every mood without sentimentality. They do not eliminate lyricism: on the contrary, it glows like the sun shining through stained-glass windows and gives one a feeling of well-being. One feels something of humanity in this and similar spheres of the eternal cycle of all existence.

That is what I miss with English composers: the reflection which can only emanate from such studies and is mirrored in a *unified* series of thoughts (it does not necessarily always have to be a theme built into a canon or a fugue or an imitation thereof). Good, solid counterpoint, as not even the most brilliant instrumentation can cover up such defects. It would be like an arithmetician with good voice quality at his disposal but whose ideas are short and disjointed and not sufficiently logically linked. The continuous unrest of arbitrary or coincidental counterpoint is of no benefit. It leaves one empty; one admires it perhaps, but soon tires of it. *Belshazzar's Feast* by Walton last Wednesday left a deep, lasting impression on me: an outstanding, enthralling work. Reveals a great passionate imagination and great ability. True creative force and originality.

Nowadays many compose without a framework, and that is just what it sounds like: it looks like a picture without form, neither square nor round. It is supposed to be a picture, but it isn't one – it looks merely like an attempt. 'Well, you see', said Schubert once, 'the most important thing is "how", not so much "what".'[106]

A further occasion of melancholy was approaching. Christmas had always been a time of intense emotional significance for Fleischmann, a depth of feeling which, in his youth, was transposed into his nativity plays, and which recurred in joyful form when Aloys Óg was growing up in Cork. Those Christmases spent in the internment camps brought on acute distress. He was probably reminded of that pain as he contemplated the coming festive season without his son. It was a dark, wild night, 'the rain beating on the window panes' as he sat 'staring into the embers, into the hot, bright dying', writing his Christmas letter:

> The dismal dark days before the solstice, which depress the spirit, are moving towards their end. As you will see from the newspaper cuttings, storms have been howling through them and their legendary nights. The ships are seeking help and protection in the nearest harbours. A number have been destroyed and last night it seemed as though the earth were being blown out of its moorings. The struggle of the gods over the old laws. Conflict – light. The sacred nights of Christmas are at hand! Memory is sitting next to me. . . . Now at this time you are back home where the wonders of this world first became apparent to me and began to affect me. Longing and tears which have been buried for so long overpower me in the loneliness of the night before the fire.[107]

On the part of the letter in which he imagines his son in the presence of his ancestors, the ink has smudged, perhaps from a tear which fell on the page:

> . . . our thoughts will be around you and with you in the old home where our ancestors once went to Midnight Mass carrying lanterns in their hands. Maybe they will be near you in the cathedral at Midnight Mass, invisible like our thoughts, looking to see what the grandson and great-grandson from far away is like who is of their blood! The grandson whose father left the soil. Perhaps you will hear a gentle question: 'How are you faring?' Or you might be asked: 'Are you not pursued by the curse of homelessness?' A soft voice: 'Would you not like to remain with us?' As the Credo rings out through the wide halls, there resounds through the swelling tones in the midst of the Latin words – as once happened to me (have you ever heard the words?): 'Bind yourself to your dear fatherland, hold fast to it with all your heart; here grew the roots of your strength: there in the alien world you will be alone, a weak reed that will be broken by the first storm.'
>
> Christmas Eve at home! Near those who conceived us, who began there, lived their lives and came to their end. Some poor, others rich. The reports are dark and do not go back far. The annals are silent with regard to plebeians. The earth carried them for a while and then swallowed them up again at the same place, like shadows

and sagas. Here and there in the baptismal church records there are
a few yellowed entries of their names with donations noted for
masses for the repose of their souls. Here and there worn names
can still be read on gravestones: that is all that has remained of
them together with the few ounces of blood that still flow in our
veins. May the lights on the heavenly Christmas tree shine for
them, and may they harbour no ill-feelings towards us who still
wander on this earth. When the tower music scatters the simple
melodies over the dark gabled roofs of my youth and when later the
cathedral bells resound with their solemn tones – ACDEFGC E-flat
minor – think of us and join in our wish that we three may sit
happily again at the Christmas table and reunited celebrate
Christmas Eve once again as in the past.[108]

He copied out and enclosed the nativity story from the *Missale
Romanum* 'so that you won't forget your Latin!' Aloys Óg had often
expressed his deep gratitude to his parents for giving him the opportunity of experiencing the magnificent cultural life of the great city.
Perhaps Fleischmann felt haunted by his ancestors because he feared his
son might remain in Munich and abandon him in Ireland as he had
deserted his parents to follow his wife.

In his New Year letter, Fleischmann sums up what benefits 1932 had
brought them and faces the future with muted optimism:

> The old year did not bear us ill-will. We can be satisfied and thank
> God for the mercy shown to us. First of all, we were granted good
> health! It brought you success at the university and the valuable
> stay in one of the foremost artistic cities of the world. Mama was
> successful in her way and I in my sphere of activity. It brought us a
> radio, a car[109]; summer holidays in Dublin, Mount Trenchard [Lord
> Monteagle's home], Oysterhaven; furthermore electrical heating in
> all rooms, a new handsome leather armchair next to your desk, a
> big old Indian bronze vase and other smaller things. If the New Year,
> in the midst of adverse times, continues to show us as much favour
> as the old year, we will continue to be very fortunate and happy.[110]

But the serenity evident here is based on resignation, on acceptance
of bitter adversity. He sees himself as a failure, an uprooted outsider, his
hard work and his composing as mere attempts to keep the pain of his
exile from destroying him, his only protection being his small family:

> I have come to terms with my fate, with my squandered life, and
> drug myself with work. I fill what little free time I have with the
> opium of old-fashioned composing. My small, confined home is
> your love: it has become the foreign roof over my head. Everything
> else was merely the dream of a different existence and life. 'The
> years pass like the clouds and leave me standing here alone.' As long

as nothing breaks down inside, and we three are united and support each other, the heavens will protect us.[111]

He then gives an account of their lonely un-celebrated Christmas at home and of midnight mass at the Cathedral:

> Mama will have written to you about our modest Christmas cele-bration here at home. The most costly present of the evening was – Mama's tears! They shone in her eyes like jewels for the far-off son. Silence and loneliness competed and became more noticeable with every hour. The crib, shimmering faintly, stood alone in the big room. The festive joys usually marked by incense and myrrh wafting through the house were missing. Only Margret was pleased with her presents and went away at 8 o'clock. We two remained alone until the eleventh hour summoned us to leave. We returned at 2.30 a.m. in the car which Dr Cohalan [the bishop] put at our disposal. Over two thousand people went to Communion! My performances, including the pontifical vespers, were good. The old motets fresh and effective – with the Adeste and Cecilian Choir on high – splendid. Performed Pembauer's mass (I missed you very much during it); Missa Dies, Borgia and Palestrina's five-voice Exultate Deo Jacob were unusually good.
>
> . . . The classic Bax sent us the score of his fourth symphony with a delightful, warm-hearted letter. Show it to [Professors] Berberich, Haas and Dr Knappe; am curious to know what they think of this work. He seems in it to be more serene, simpler, to have left the technical behind him.[112]

The new year was to bring Germany the beginning of a dictatorship which was to last twelve years, organise brutality with an efficiency unique in the history of the world, to take the lives of perhaps eighty million people, to leave large tracts of Europe devastated and Germany in every respect in ruin. The Fleischmanns had received some enthusiastic accounts of the Nazis from German acquaintances: the Celtic scholar Ludwig Mühlhausen for one, who maintained that the reports in the foreign press about the Nazis' violence towards opponents and their per-secution of Jews were malicious Bolshevist inventions. Their son's accounts of Nazi student violence in the university, of the boycotting of Jewish businesses by storm troops and the removal of Jews from the uni-versity staff by the government testified to the accuracy of those press reports. Dachau had not voted in its majority for the Nazi party in January 1933; in March 1933 the first German concentration camp was built some miles outside the town in an old munitions factory. At first political oppo-nents of the new regime – communists, social democrats, trade union leaders, and those clergymen who had spoken out against the Nazis – were incarcerated there. The camp was run by the SS and not staffed by local people, so news of what was going on only gradually emerged. Many inmates were released in the course of 1934, and forbidden under pain of re-arrest to speak about their time there. Aloys Óg does not mention it in his letters of 1933 (none have survived of 1934), and may not have heard about the camp which was to make the name of Dachau synonymous with Nazi terror and infamous throughout the world.

The last letter to Aloys Óg in Munich was written in 1934 after Fleischmann's fifty-fourth birthday: it is profoundly melancholic. He knew that his son was returning to Cork that summer, but there had been complicated negotiations in the university over his appointment as deputy professor, and some irritation when Aloys Óg decided to finish the year in Munich before accepting the post. His father had suffered great agitation and indecision as to whether he should order him to return, as he had been advised to do; there had been controversy with his wife, who wanted her son given the freedom to decide. He may have been worried lest something should go wrong before the contract at the university was signed. The prospect of old age appears grim and his birthday brings painful reflection on the lost hopes of his life:

> When the cycle of life gradually begins to close and the number of years, counted backwards, becomes ever smaller, then the joyful thoughts become more sober and more muted with every ring in the tree. On such days one's thoughts wander around, herded together like sheep frightened by oncoming darkness, sensing that they are heading for an unknown and steep incline.
>
> . . . Such occasions, my dear son, no longer afford me much pleasure. Not because I have become old and have buried so many hopes in the course of my uprooted, squandered life, but probably because I was forced to look too deeply into the cruelty of human existence, and such days rouse all that which would better lie undisturbed forever within me. You are the only hope of my life. Not that I have great, lunatic expectations of you, or make demands of you. No – may my common sense preserve me from that. What I request of heaven is another ten years of work in order to provide a secure, worthwhile existence for you. Then darkness may descend. That is the birthday wish I have for myself.[113]

That wish was granted: he had indeed provided his son with a solid foundation on which he was able to build a secure, worthwhile existence. That same year, Aloys Óg returned to Cork, and was appointed acting professor of music at the university. He was twenty-four. Fleischmann was to live for another thirty years and to see his son follow in his footsteps in giving new life to that cultural manifesto of the Munster Society of Arts: succeeding in 'hewing in our own quarries' in a variety of creative fields and providing opportunities to see and hear in

Cork some of the best artists and ensembles of Europe. But the period during which Aloys Óg lived in Munich marked a turning point in the elder Fleischmann's life. From that time on there is a recurring leitmotif in the letters: the 'curse of homelessness', and the image of his life projected is that of shipwreck, of himself stranded on an alien shore with no prospect of return, the bright hopes of his youth turned to dust.

Tilly, Aloys Jun. and Aloys Fleischmann
after his return to Cork, September 1920

The funeral procession of Terence MacSwiney
passing through Patrick Street, Cork,
October 1920

Terence MacSwiney's
widow, Muriel

Carl Hardebeck

Aloys Fleischmann and Arnold
Bax in west Cork

The cathedral choir's Feis certificate of
1929 awarded by Arnold Bax

Tilly Fleischmann (*right*) in Gráig, Dingle
Peninsula, during a visit to the MacSwineys

Left: Hannah Hurley of Ovens,
County Cork, the Fleischmann's
housekeeper from 1943 to 1960

Right: Tilly Fleischmann 1931

Tilly Fleischmann, her son,
Aloys Fleischmann, Tilly's sister
Elsa O'Malley-Williams

At Stockleys *l. to r.*: Kate Curling of the Abbey Theatre,
Sean O'Faolain, Sophia Stockley (on the ground),
Germaine Stockley, Professor Stockley,
Father Pat MacSwiney, Aloys and Tilly Fleischmann

Harry Clarke Christmas
cards sent to the
Fleischmanns

Dora Ziegler of
Dachau

Ludwig Berberich,
professor of
church music at
Munich university,
and cathedral
choirmaster

Aloys Fleischmann and son on
the eve of the latter's departure
for Germany September 1932

Tilly Fleischmann and her
housekeeper Madge (*left*)
bidding farewell to Aloys
Jun. as he set sail
for Munich

Self portrait by Harry
Clarke, given to the
Fleischmanns by the artist

5. Handing on the Torch
1934–64

Aloys Fleischmann 1934

*Father and son co-operation in music
education*

In June 1934, twenty-eight years after
Fleischmann had come to Cork to
take up his post at the Catholic cathedral, his son returned from two years
of postgraduate studies in Munich to
take up the temporary post of acting
professor of music at the university.
Like his father, Aloys Óg was facing
many tests and ordeals, but he was
not venturing into a strange country:
he was coming home. So it was not
Mozart's *Magic Flute* that rang in the
young man's ears as he stood on deck
while the liner sailed up the estuary of
the River Lee, but the passage from
Wagner's *Tristan*: 'The Irish Queen' – and the idea of founding a symphony orchestra formed in his mind.[1]

It was put into practice later that year. The orchestra was founded to
provide advanced students, amateur and professional musicians with
an opportunity to perform music from the standard repertoire as well
as works by living Irish composers, and to give Cork audiences a
chance to hear such music in the days when gramophone records were
an expensive rarity. Four years after his appointment, he founded the
Cork Orchestral Society to promote the concerts of the Cork
Symphony Orchestra and to organise an annual series of recitals in the
city. Having composed two works in Munich, both of which were performed there,[2] he now adopted an Irish pseudonym, presenting his *Trí
hAmhráin* [Three Songs] under the name Muiris Ó Ronáin,

198

underlining his commitment to a specifically Irish form of art music.

His post was made permanent in March 1936, whereupon his mother received a letter from a stranger congratulating her and out-lining what the writer expected of the young professor:

> I wonder, if he later tries composition, could he produce a blend of the spirit of the ancient Irish Airs with modern music. Probably there is some form of music in which that could be attempted. I don't mean the Airs themselves, but their spirit: sad and melancholy, sometimes merry, sometimes breathing the indignation and hatred of a hunted race. Fitzgerald's poem of 'Omar Khayyam' was not a translation of a Persian poem as was once thought, but a beautiful vehicle in which the whole spirit of Persian poetry was conveyed. He first drank it in, loved it, made it his own, became a Persian, and then poured it out. If some one could do this for us – we can't do it ourselves as we are only emerging from the Penal Days – he would live.[3]

This interesting perception of how an outsider can become so immersed in a different culture that he can create in its spirit applied also to Ireland's Anglo-Irish poets and dramatists. But Aloys Óg had been drawn to the Gaelic legacy since his boyhood, and had by now already begun his quest to create conditions conducive to the composition and performance of new Irish music inspired by the nation's heritage.

He had learnt from his father, and from Daniel Corkery, that for the arts to flourish they must become part of the lives of people of all classes, which can only happen if there is a nationwide infrastructure to support them. On his appointment to the chair of music, the young academic drew up a plan of campaign which he pursued throughout his life. The calamitous state of music education was his first concern. Singing was obligatory in primary schools, but was rarely taught by qualified teachers; the arts were optional non-examination subjects on the curriculum of most secondary schools, few schools offered tuition in music and those that did were not obliged to employ qualified music teachers. The great majority of people teaching music in Ireland had no qualifications whatsoever, the great majority of pupils left secondary school without having had any experience of the arts.[4] Aloys Óg founded the Music Teachers' Association in Cork. Together with col-leagues in Dublin, he began petitioning the Department of Education to have music established in schools, to have it taught by competent teachers trained in recognised institutions and to have the teaching of music supervised by qualified inspectors. Negotiations went on for years with no tangible result. The Cork university music department, founded in 1906, had only produced two graduates up to 1931 since there was scant prospect of work. To break the vicious circle, Aloys Óg now campaigned at the local level, and succeeded in persuading some of the heads of religious teaching orders to allow members to study music. The work on both fronts gradually led to an increase in the number of students willing and able to study music at University College Cork.

Aloys Óg's efforts in this regard were supported by his father, who gave private organ and music theory classes to a number of young people who were to become teachers of music. Among the students were nuns and brothers from the Ursuline and Presentation teaching orders in Cork. Sister Marie Collins, then a novice in the South Presentation Convent of Cork, was among a small group selected by her order to study music. To help the three young nuns reach the necessary standard, it was decided that they should be given special instruction by the cathedral organist. Sister Marie remembers her first organ class and how Fleischmann's tuition qualified her for senior organ classes and examinations once she moved for the final phase of her training to the Dublin college:

> It was late August 1938 as we paced the terrace one evening after tea when the Mistress of Novices announced that three of us would be taking organ lessons from none other than Herr Fleischmann, famed in Cork. The lessons were to begin on the following Saturday. Saturday came and with bated breath we awaited his arrival at 2.30 p.m. in the organ gallery. A bicycle being his mode of transport, he arrived puffing and panting, looking like the real old German master-composers we see in pictures or stone carvings: hair shoulder length and receding from the forehead, bowing low and greeting us with his ever impeccable manners: 'Good evening, very reverend Sisters! We'll start, very reverend Sisters' etc. We began to assume that we were all Reverend Mothers in his sight.
>
> Being the junior I watched my two seniors take their turn on the stool, and begin the five finger exercises at his direction. Next he placed Bach's Voluntaries on the stand, instructing his student to begin with the pedals as a practice, proceeding to the left hand and finally to the right, building up the chord. After some time we graduated to Bach's Preludes and Fugues. Great scope here for pedal work! Soon I became his 'little Paderewski' as I seemed to be good at the pedalling.[5]

The nuns of this enclosed order were not allowed to leave the convent, could therefore not attend the cathedral services nor recitals or concerts: any music they heard was of their own making. So, on occasion, Fleischmann brought his music to them and had the cathedral choir give recitals in their chapel. Whereas the boys in Farranferris did not find a concert of sacred music good compensation for a cancelled cowboy film, the sisters did enjoy the performances, as Sister Marie reports:

Two or three times, while tutoring in South Presentation Convent, Herr Fleischmann brought his North Cathedral Choir to our chapel where they sang their motets for our delectation and appreciation. Being in an enclosed congregation, it was a great treat for us to hear choral music at its best. Once, to give his choristers a break, he decided to give us an organ recital; ... we just marvelled that anybody could produce such heavenly melodies on our very modest instrument. We recognised the touch of the master's hand.

Two years of one-hour Saturday lessons from this famous man gained for me admission to senior organ lessons and examination when I went to Carysfort Teacher Training College in Dublin. There my examination pieces had octave pedals a-plenty to negotiate, which kept me fit for four-hand and six-hand reels which were part of our teacher-training course!

Going to Carysfort broke my link with him. At the time of his demise we were still an enclosed congregation so I was unable to attend his funeral. I was so sad to hear he had passed away. Since our liberation after the last Council, I have had the opportunity to visit his grave and that of his esteemed family as a small sign of my admiration and appreciation of this great German who lived in our midst for so long and from whose love of polyphonic music we benefited so immensely. Ar dheis Dé go raibh a anam! [May his soul be given a place of honour at the right hand of God]

Sister Marie was to become a most active and successful music teacher; after the 'liberation' of the enclosed religious orders, she was able to bring her choirs to perform in the Cork International Choral Festival schools' competition, which they much enjoyed and where they did extremely well.

The state of music education in boys' schools was particularly dismal. Fleischmann gave organ and harmonium lessons to Presentation brothers in Coláiste Mhuire in Cork, but it was not until 1960 that the order sent a young man to study music.[6] A private pupil of Fleischmann's unconnected with religious teaching orders was Michael Weedle. He began to study the piano with Tilly Fleischmann while still at school, then took up the organ with her husband. After three years in a surveyor's office, he decided to give up his job and enroll for a degree in music. He described his work with Fleischmann as follows:[7]

'The old man', as everybody affectionately called him, was a very gentle person. Very early on in our relationship he began to teach me harmony. One evening he took out his pocket watch, used it to draw a circle on my book, marked the sequence of twelve major keys instead of hours and said: 'These are your pillars – build your house around them.' Minor keys came the next week. I had done some harmony in school and found it extremely difficult but now the old man quickly stripped away all the mystery (and this without any textbook) and it never bothered me again. This led on to improvisation and every lesson ended with: 'Now you make an improvisation.' On one occasion he said: 'You're playing in your darling key!' and I realised that I tended to play in F major always so I had to go out and take a few risks.

His English took a little bit of getting used to: 'When you play on der organ', 'You come until here', 'When somebody cross the church and he not genuflect, you know he's either a atheist or a organist.'

He was an ardent admirer of Bach so one was introduced to the great master very early on and nearly always had something of his on one's plate. He used to say: 'The great masters always sign their names with big letters', which (to me at any rate) was much more suggestive than: 'Play the cadence such and such a way.'

But he had one blind spot about his beloved Bach; he never put his pupils on to the Chorale Preludes because he considered them colourless. His own teacher, Josef Rheinberger, is referred to sometimes as a great Catholic musician and I wonder if he kept his students away from settings of Lutheran chorales, thus leaving a great treasure untapped.

Some years after my graduation I began to give organ recitals. The very first was broadcast by Radio Éireann from the Church of Christ the King in Dublin and the old man sent me a card with the picture of the North Cathedral. It is one of my treasured possessions.

The card of 14 April 1958 read: 'Congratulations! Your organ recital excellent. *Sic itur ad astra* [thus is the way to the stars]. Kind regards Aloys Fleischmann'. Michael Weedle was appointed music teacher in Clongowes Wood College in Naas, County Kildare, the Jesuit boarding school for boys. He founded and conducted a choir in the school, Cór Choill Buana [Clongowes Wood Choir], and one in the town, Nás na Rí Singers, the latter taking part in the Cork International Choral Festival for many years. He was one of the adjudicators for the schools competitions at the Choral Festival of 1987.

Both Fleischmann and his wife were involved in summer schools for music teachers organised at the university by their son in 1938 and 1939. Guest lecturers were the professor of music in University College Dublin, John Larchet, François Lefèvre, former director of the Schola of Lille University, and Seán Neeson, lecturer in Irish music at University College Cork. Recitals and concerts formed part of the programme. The cathedral choir gave performances of polyphonic music in the university's Honan Chapel; Fleischmann supervised organ classes in the cathedral; Tilly Fleischmann gave recitals of piano music, which were introduced by her son. Two members of the cathedral choir participated in the section on Irish music: Seán Neeson and Seán Óg Ó Tuama, both of whom performed traditional songs.[8]

Fleischmann also assisted his son by helping to arrange an Art Society painting exhibition in the university in 1939. Not long after his appointment to the chair of music, Aloys Óg had organised an Art Society exhibition of sculpture, with works by the Cork artists, Séamus Murphy, Marshall Hutson and Micheal O'Sullivan. It was the first exhibition of its kind in Cork, was introduced by Daniel Corkery, and 'made a profound impression'.[9] The sequel was to exhibit works by Paul Henry, Seán Keating, Harry Kernoff, Charles Lamb, Maurice McGonigal and J.B. Yeats. Fleischmann undertook a rare visit to Dublin towards the end of July 1939 to discuss the matter with Seán Keating and with the director of the National Museum. He was also acting as emissary for Father Pat MacSwiney on a somewhat more difficult issue, seeking not loans, but donations of artifacts for the planned museum in Kinsale. He knew the director of the Museum, the Austrian archaeologist, Dr Adolf Mahr, but had to negotiate with Mahr's deputy as Mahr had been 'summoned' to Vienna:

> Mahr waited until Tuesday.[10] But I saw his secretary and the vice-director, who was very cool at first, then thawed and at the end had become so warm that he offered a guided tour of the museum. When we got to Terence MacSwiney's death mask and I told him that I knew all the relatives who were depicted on the photograph personally, his helpfulness knew no bounds. (Father Pat can rest assured that he will be given everything he wants.) He follows Aloys's enterprises with great interest, he told me. Knows his portrait, his articles. He spoke with enthusiasm about the O`Neill lament and is full of admiration for the young man who has achieved so much.

The lament by Aloys Óg which the deputy-director mentioned was one of the *Trí hAmhráin,* the orchestral version of which had been given its first performance in Dublin's Gaiety Theatre in April 1938. It was written under the Irish pseudonym Muiris Ó Ronáin, but Aloys Óg's articles were published under his own name, and the portrait exhibited by Gabriel Hayes at the Royal Irish Academy that year also bore his name. So the deputy-director must have known from the outset that Fleischmann was the father of the young composer whose work he admired. It is striking that the coolness only vanished when it became evident that Fleischmann himself moved in nationalist circles.

Fleischmann had also been charged by the family with the exploration of all the churches 'which might be suitable for the plan we are quietly contemplating': no further information has come to light about this. In his letter home, he makes some harsh comments about a Dublin organist's 'deplorable tremolo organ playing' endured during his investigations. He had a full programme. He called on Stockley's daughter Sophia, who had moved to the capital having married Séamus Mallin, son of the executed 1916 insurgent. Fleischmann had meetings in Dublin with the bursar of UCC, Joseph Downey, as well as two former choir members, and visited his sister-in-law Rosa's grave and roamed around her old home. The two musicians he saw, Carl Hardebeck and Frederick May, clearly valued his company:

> On Monday morning I have to go to the museum again and then it's Keating. [the painter Seán Keating]. Hardebeck, to whom I brought [*in English:*] a bottle wisky, was most touching. He spent half the night playing to me and asked hundreds of questions. When I was leaving he said my visit had done more for his health than all 'the damn medicine he had to swallow'. He sends his warmest greetings to the Empress and to the young genius who is so good at working such beautiful Irish melodies into his compositions. I almost came home on Friday, but Fred insisted I postpone my departure and threatened that he would have nothing more to do with us if I disappointed him.[11]

He took the opportunity to see the Ballet Rambert at the Gaiety Theatre, which was presenting eleven ballets during this first visit to Ireland. *The Irish Times* critic's scathing comments on the dance had led to spirited defence from members of the public; in his letter home, Fleischmann deplored the lack of an orchestra. The vivid memory, which he had preserved for over thirty years, of a ballet by Otto Julius Bierbaum and Felix Mottl had been sustained by the splendour of the orchestral sound:

> Saw the Ballet Rambert which did not impress me deeply with their two – pianists. Such a contrast between the colours of the stage, with the variety of movement and colourful gestures of the dancers, and the lifeless tinkling in the orchestral pit, which has no warmth and sounds like a rehearsal. Such performances require a big full orchestra to flood through the hall like a sea of sound. When I think back on Mottl's 'Pan im Busch' [Pan and his Pipes] in the National Theatre in Munich! I can still hear it today. The Gaiety Theatre was half full and no wonder. That talkative man K sat near me, the promoter and composer of the 'Irish ballet', trying to think up witty comments for those in the vicinity and at the same time zealously recording his impressions with his pencil, while the two grand pianos marked time out of their black coffins for the artificial life on the stage.[12]

Within ten years, his son was to ensure with the Cork Symphony Orchestra that dance in Cork did not have to make do with pianos.

Resignation from the staff of the School of Music

The year after Aloys Óg's temporary professorship at the university had become permanent, his father gave up his professorship at the School of Music. Fleischmann resigned out of solidarity with his wife, who had endured several years of unpleasant conflict with the administrators of the institution: they both left the school in November 1937.

Little archival documentation concerning officials' policies of this period has survived: conclusions must be drawn from the executives' activities. They must have decided in the early 1930s to try to increase school enrolment numbers by modifying the curriculum. Up to that time students studied standard works of the literature for the various instruments as well as pieces based on Irish music. Now this programme was to be diluted with light music and the Irish component abandoned. The officials did not consult the head of piano about these plans, no doubt knowing that she would not give approval and believing that school policy was not a matter for staff but for government servants to decide.

In 1933 she sought the advice of Daniel Corkery, who advised her to complain to the Minister of Education and to ask Carl Hardebeck for support. Corkery suggested that in her letter she should 'sketch the great downfall that has taken place in the school since the years of the troubles when Terence MacSwiney took such interest in it. Believe me I feel for any artist who is struggling with people like [those officials] and with committees in general.'[13] She acted on his advice. Her intervention did not improve relations with the administration and was ultimately unsuccessful: half of the classical music taught under the previous syllabus was eliminated and replaced by light pieces; Irish music was no longer compulsory, the music of John Field and Carl Hardebeck was removed from the programme. Four years later, the conflict escalated and Tilly resigned. Seán Neeson offered to bring the matter before the Music Teachers' Association, as he believed the issues in question should be investigated.[14] There is no record that such an inquiry was requested: Tilly probably did not wish to return. Of her forty pupils at the school, thirty-nine left with her and continued their tuition on a private basis.

Her husband's position was very different. He did not have individual students who had selected him as their teacher: he did not teach an instrument but gave theory classes which students of all instruments attended in groups. As he was not their main teacher, there was no question of their leaving the school and taking private tuition with him. His financial loss was therefore considerable. However, his son no longer needed support: the post of acting professor had brought him an annual salary of £75; the permanent chair gave him an income of £200 per annum. Aloys Óg was not in a position to contribute much to the household finances, nonetheless, as most of his salary went towards defraying the costs of his orchestra's concerts, for which he was personally liable until 1938, when they were run under the auspices of the Cork Orchestral Society. Before the 1950s no documentation of Fleischmann's income from the cathedral has survived, but he mentioned in a letter to the cathedral administrator in 1945 that he received less than the lowest paid schoolteachers of the diocese.[15] However, he still had money from his mother's legacy in Germany, his wife was a careful and skilful manager of the domestic finances and so they were reasonably comfortable. It must have been a relief to them both that she was now free to determine the curriculum for her pupils as she saw fit without risk of conflict, as the strain had begun to prey on her health. But her attempts to establish the principle of consultation between officials and heads of department in matters of teaching had not succeeded, nor had she managed to prevent the introduction of light music to the school curriculum. But the Fleischmanns' departure from the School of Music did not lessen their influence on the musical life of the city: they both continued to teach and perform, and from 1934, through the manifold activities of their son, the family's impact as a whole was greatly strengthened.

Work with the cathedral choir

Training the boys and men of the North Parish to be choristers continued to be Fleischmann's principal teaching role; his ability as a pedagogue was evinced in the quality of music they produced, a singular achievement recognised by choir and public alike. Fleischmann did not leave any writings on his teaching methods; insight into how the excellence of the singing was attained, the nature of the choristers' commitment to the choir and their respect for their choirmaster derive from their accounts of their time with him.

Membership of the choir was, of course, voluntary; tuition was given free of charge. That it enriched the choristers' often none-too-easy lives is documented in letters they wrote to their choirmaster, and in accounts of their time in the choir written by former choristers. The choristers' sense of pride in being members of the choir is one leitmotif. William Martin joined as a boy, and sang for five years until he had to go to work at the age of fourteen – he served his apprenticeship for seven years, and then went on to night work from 5.00 p.m. until 5.00 a.m. As a child, he appreciated the recognition that came with choir membership, for instance during the public church ceremonies in the city on the feast of Corpus Christi:

> To see the choir walking in the Eucharistic procession with their soutanes and their surplices fired me. At that time it was only men who walked in the Corpus Christi procession: the women, the

families stood and watched them pass through the streets. Everybody was there: we saw huge crowds at either side of us and you'd hear people say: 'That's Willie Martin!' It was an honour to be there and you'd feel very proud. When the choir got down to Daunt Square, we went up on to the platform where the altar was: the only other people up there were the bishop and the priests – and we were there too.[16]

Public recitals were also proud occasions. In June 1934 the choir gave a concert under the auspices of the University Art Society: it was one of the many contributions of the cathedral choir to the cultural life of the university and, as it was broadcast, to that of the country. The programme included Palestrina's mass, *Missa Papae Marcelli*, its first performance in the Free State. Peter F. Lenihan sang at the concert; in a letter to Fleischmann written the following day, he describes with pride the distinguished audience's appreciation of the music:

To you yourself Sir, I offer my heartiest congratulations for the very wonderful performance of last night. I am afraid I have not sufficient language at my command to put in writing what I think, but I can, and will say this, Sir. There were some very noble words spoken afterwards by the gentlemen who came to congratulate us, and I feel very deeply honoured in being a member of a choir whose efforts at the recital caused such fine language to be spoken.[17]

The discipline expected and achieved is another leitmotif in almost all the accounts of the choir training. J.P. Cronin sang with the choir until he joined the Christian Brothers; he believed that the choirmaster's success in achieving discipline with a group of eighty small boys lay in his appreciation of their ability and effort:

From the very moment that we entered the choir he had a tremendous grip on us. He was always very strict during rehearsals and we had a 'holy' fear of him, but as the years passed we realised that he had to be so. At all times we had the greatest confidence in him, and our respect grew more and more as the years passed.

. . . He never let the opportunity pass when praise could be given to either men or boys. I am sure many an alto in particular will remember the patience and encouragement he gave to this section of the choir.[18]

William Martin also remembers the discipline, how it arose from the solemn nature of their work for the church services, and how it was tempered by praise:

You'd have to be in the cathedral for Sunday twelve o'clock mass at 11.40, and from 11.55 on no one spoke at all: it was sign language only. We couldn't be seen by the congregation as we were hidden behind a wooden partition covered with magnificent carvings. He'd come in then, and you could hear a pin drop. We were performing God's music in God's church. He had a great sense of that and made us realise it too. Even in the simple step of standing up, all together, no sound: we sat on benches, not chairs, not only because that meant you sat up straight, but because it was easier to stand up noiselessly. If there was a little movement – he had marvellous ears – his head would turn, and that was the end of that.

We used often think we were finished and were ready to go when he'd say: 'One more!' That might mean going through four or five hymns from start to finish. Then he'd tap, and clap. You knew by the way he tapped whether he was pleased or not. His face showed his feelings and everybody knew at once. If he put on a cross face when we were in the middle of singing, the seniors would stop because they'd know he wasn't satisfied with something. The next time you'd sing it would be different. All he had to do was to look and everyone listened. He always looked at you straight in the face. A powerful man, a powerful voice, yet his look was enough. He was severe, but when you got things right he beamed. He beamed all over, he lit up all over and said 'Gut, gut!'

To me actually he was the choir; it was built around him. He was the core, and his word was law. I'd love to be in the choir today and to have him there.

Fleischmann had allies in many of the mothers of his choristers, who insisted on regular attendance and whose word was law in the families. Canon James Bastible joined the choir as a small boy in 1908, not long after Fleischmann came to Cork. His mother tolerated no dissent: 'I recall a "strike" which my mother ended promptly when she ordered the ring-leader, my brother, back to his post.'[19] William Martin describes his mother's reaction to his announcement that he did not feel like attending choir practice: 'I remember one Friday night I said to my mam: "I don't think I'll go to choir at all tonight." "Get up!" was the reply. You just had to go. But once you got in you were alright, because it was only for an hour or an hour and a quarter.' The choirmaster's discipline was tempered with kindness, as Bob Barry points out:

> On important feasts in the church, the choir members wore purple soutanes and white surplices. I recall one occasion when a little boy who had only joined the choir, and had not yet been issued with a soutane but was determined to dress like the rest of the choir, decided to borrow a soutane from an altar server. This was fine, except that it was bright scarlet red. Now the choir was situated near

the sanctuary so we were in full view of the priests from the altar, and here was this little chap in the front row in his bright red soutane against a background of purple. He shone like a beacon! Herr Fleischmann looked at him and smiled, then patting him on the head he said to us: 'Gentlemen, you will notice that today we have a cardinal in our midst!' I am sure that somebody else might have moved that little boy to one side, or made him stand at the back behind others, but not our Herr Fleischmann. He saw the humorous side of things, and above all, he would not hurt or offend that little boy.[20]

Many former choristers marvel at the progress made with children the majority of whom had no previous knowledge of music. Brother J.P. Cronin:

The results he got from us boys who did not even know the elements of music, much less of sight reading, still amaze me. They could only have come from two characteristics of the man himself: his own high standards and tremendous hard work. Modern pedagogues might say his methods were old fashioned, but looking back I cannot imagine any other person teaching us so much and so thoroughly in such a short time.

One of the elements of the learning process identified is that the boys were taught to learn through listening to each other. William Martin, one of the few boys who had had music classes before joining the choir,[21] remembers this:

When we went in first we listened and that was how we learned. I had also sung before and I had played the piano so I had a good idea of music but you had to listen and learn and you were taught. Everybody would be singing and he'd say 'shhh' and you carried on – solo – then after maybe two or three notes everybody joined in again. That kept you on your toes. As the years went you kept listening to the others singing, and then you began to sing a little bit louder yourself.

Dom Clancy of Limerick, a former choir member who wrote having heard a broadcast, was struck by a reflective element in the choir's performance, which he perhaps recognised because of the way he had been taught to listen and to focus on the texts:

Regarding the performance of the choir, one could not, I suppose, say enough in praise. . . . If one might pick out some small thing to mention, it would be the beautiful pauses, during which one always felt the choir was still there, though no sound betrayed it. One might even say the choir meditated on the text. It was an inspiring performance.[22]

The fascination which the choristers found in the sacred music they sang was no doubt another factor leading to the remarkable discipline obtained by the choirmaster, whose only available sanction was dismissal from the choir. William Martin:

> I found great satisfaction in singing. I particularly loved Christmas and Holy Week. My first experience of the choir, as a new youngster, was during the Tenebrae services of Holy Week. It was an unforgettable moment when all the lights went out one by one in the church. Those ceremonies linger on in your mind. Even to this day if anyone starts to sing in Latin I still know the words: the music never leaves you. There was something unique about it: it was holy music.

The broadcasts brought the cathedral choir to many former members. Some of the writers expressly state that listening to this polyphonic music was an experience of an intense emotional quality; this is probably true for all those who went to the trouble to express their appreciation of the recitals in writing. Seán Óg Ó Tuama wrote of his nostalgia for his time in the choir, since the opportunity to hear such music was so limited for those living far from the cathedral. At the end of a series of choir broadcasts he wrote: 'I hear the Choir ends tonight, and felt a kind of sad exaltation: sad because such treats are so rare – and anyway that wonderful music does make one rather wistful – and with exaltation because those masters do raise one's emotions to the highest levels.'[23] The broadcast also brought much joy to Sister M. Dympna, a member of an enclosed religious order in Kinsale, followed not just by the nostalgia Ó Tuama wrote of, but by extreme frustration, as she reported to Tilly Fleischmann:

> At Reverend Mother's request I come to offer to the dear Professor, to you and to your gifted son our mite of congratulations on the wonderful broadcast of last night! It was truly 'a big bit of Heaven'! We 'listened in' in breathless rapture and delight, but I am sorry to have to record that our radio was 'shut off' just as Palestrina's Mass *started*! We left the Community Room with anguished souls and deep regrets! Alas! 'the 9-o'clock Bell' called us and we *had* to go – 'nolens-volens'! Personally, I remembered what Fr Charlie O'Connor said to us a few days ago, viz: 'that nuns go straight to Heaven when they die'! Why not? when they have to make *sacrifices* such as we made last night!! Oh! it was *cruel*, humanly speaking, but 'it is the law'.[24]

One can understand why the relaxation of the rules governing life in religious orders introduced by the second Vatican Council in the early 1960s was regarded by many as a liberation.

Irish radio could be heard in Britain, though the reception was often poor, as indeed it frequently was in Ireland. But emigrants who read

Irish newspapers and owned a radio were able to hear the broadcasts, however disturbed. Many members of the choir had to leave Ireland to find work: some of those in Britain occasionally 'listened in' to performances of their former companions and a number wrote to congratulate them. From one such letter the organisational skills needed to master the complications of life on a small budget become evident: the writer, Daniel Eaton, now in Edinburgh, rented a room in a boarding house, did not own a radio, and had to work until late in the evenings – but managed to hear the Cork recital:

> It was a fluke that I got yesterday's *Irish Press* here at 5 o'clock to-day. And a greater fluke that my fellow boarder here was at home to oblige me. Then I was again lucky in 'shaking' my manager off at 8.30 pm and rushing home to arrange that it was possible for me to intrude on my neighbour for thirty minutes.[25]

He was pleased and proud to note his neighbour's surprise on hearing the quality of the music. For another exiled chorister, Patrick Jeffery in London, the recital heightened his nostalgia for home and his dissatisfaction with his host country:

> I suppose you are indeed greatly surprised to hear from me after such a long time, first of all I suppose you remember me: I am Patrick Jeffery, who used be a privileged member of your choir some time ago and who still is in spirit. I am indeed ashamed of myself to admit that I did not write to you before now. You see, I was for a long time both homesick and disgusted with this country and could not put my mind to write to anybody, but after the Choir's broadcast on Sunday night I felt I had to write to you. Indeed I was very fortunate to have heard you at all. I was out on that Sunday evening and I came in about twenty past eight and something possessed me to look at the programme from Cork and there I saw to my delight that the Cathedral Choir were broadcasting from the Honan Chapel and you may be certain that I had my ears glued to that blessed contraption of a wireless! But alas, as you know, the reception here is very bad and the best I could hear was the mass, Gloria et Honora, and one or two motets, and they were very, very good indeed. The Choir seemed to have power and yet they were evenly balanced, but the best of all were the boys. Oh, how I wish the Choir were over here to show some of the so-called choirs over here in England how to sing. It is indeed very sad to go into a church here to listen to very painful choirs: indeed they are composers in themselves [since what they sing bears no resemblance to the original composition].
>
> Well, Mr Fleischmann, I want to congratulate you and your Choir and remember me to all your members, especially Thomas O'Reilly if he is still a member, and I pray with all my heart that some day I

will take my usual seat in your Choir once more and you may be sure
if such a thing happens it will indeed be a happy day for me.[26]

There is part of a letter among the Fleischmann papers written by a
chorister to his brother on the subject of a choir broadcast. It is of
special interest in that it shows, not only these men's knowledge of the
music and of the art of choral singing, but the degree of their involvement which brings them to communicate on the subject with each
other in such a manner. One of the Whyte brothers was in Dublin and
on the radio heard the cathedral choir in which his brother was singing:

> The broadcast was the best thing I ever heard; ye should be really
> proud of yourselves. As you know, I knew most of the pieces pretty
> well, and was listening for faults, but divil a one I could find.
>
> The sound in the empty church was wonderful, and the perfect
> blending of the parts was a thing no other choir could achieve. I'd
> love to be able to pick one piece out and say it was the best, but it
> really is impossible to do that. The only thing I'd like to say is that the
> O Quam Gloriosum is a beautiful motet. I always thought the
> singing of this (especially the tenor line) was too strenuous to be
> capable of producing sweet sounds, but indeed it was beautiful the
> way it ran so freely like harmonized Gregorian Chant. The Hosanna
> of the Sanctus was so pianissimo it was like a sound wafted on a
> gentle breeze that you'd have to strain your ears to catch it. The
> whole show was simply wonderful, and I couldn't say enough to
> praise it sufficiently. The Benedictus and Ave Maria were also
> striking. But I just couldn't say words enough to praise the whole
> performance. I suppose Herr F. is like a peacock over it. I'm drop-
> ping him a note congratulating him and the choir. Give all the boys
> my regards and congrats for such an excellent performance and a
> heavenly broadcast. I only hope I'll be with the choir again soon.[27]

The BBC set up its world service in 1934; two years later the first
Irish choir to be recorded by the station was Cork's cathedral choir: the
head of the team seeking material for the BBC's programmes told the
press he had been 'deeply impressed' by the choir's performance 'and
expressed his surprise at finding a choir of this calibre in Ireland'.[28] The
World Service broadcast extended the circle of listeners to musicians in
Bavaria. Fleischmann's colleague in Dachau, the organist Alois
Ritthaler, wrote to express his appreciation, although the reception had
been rather disturbed and, having no English, he had been unable to
follow the introductory explanations given by Aloys Óg:

> The boys' voices sounded splendid. It was a joy to hear those pure,
> bell-like sounds; these rich, full and yet so metallic sounding tones
> of a boy's voice would be ideal for the sound of a mixed choir. A pity
> that in this regard so little can be done here at home. Allow me to

congratulate you and the singers involved in this beautiful and excellent performance.

The veiled reference is to the Nazis' discouragement of church activities. Colleagues in Ireland also 'listened in': the Belgian organist, Ernest de Regge of Ennis cathedral in County Clare, wrote to say that their bishop, Dr Fogarty, had invited 'ten members of the cathedral' to his palace to hear the concert together and thanked Fleischmann for 'a first-class treat'.[29] The German organist, Joseph Koss, of St Mary's Cathedral Kilkenny, who had been interned with Fleischmann during the first world war:

> My dear Friend and Colleague,
>
> Hearty congratulations. Your broadcast from Cork Cathedral was magnificent, superb! Indeed I may tell you frankly you have no rival here in Ireland and few outside if any that could surpass your excellent performance of last night.
>
> Who was the announcer, may I ask, who gave with such fine diction and accent the useful historical assessments and translations?

The impact of that broadcast on non-enthusiasts of sacred music was attested by Professor T.C. Smiddy, family friend, pupil of Tilly Fleischmann, former professor of economics in Cork, in 1936 economic advisor to the Irish government:

> My dear Tilly,
>
> I cannot adequately find words to express how much I appreciated the excellence of the singing and its calm and harmonious restraint and 'uplift'. My family, who usually listen to the lighter type of music and to operas over the wireless, and who associate choir singing with monotony, were quite entranced, and thought the hour too short. Such artistic rendering of church music will set an inspiring standard in this country, and even in Great Britain. I, personally, doubt if such music is produced outside the best continental cities.
>
> Whilst the singing was excellent, the preface to each selection was most interesting, giving such a lucid description of the characteristics and line of development of each composer. Let me also congratulate Aloys on his clear enunciation. No announcer over the Athlone Radio has been comparable to his elocution – and this view is shared by my family: he may as well have been in the room talking *naturally* to us.[30]

His wife Lelian wrote separately to say how even she, a philistine, loved the performance.

Complete strangers were on occasion so pleased to hear such music that they wrote to thank the provider:

> I have just been listening with joy and delight to your beautiful choir
> from Cork. After 40 years of inferior church music in this small town
> you cannot realise the extraordinary pleasure you all gave me in
> hearing such an exquisite rendering of such lovely music. It was a
> revelation to me that such church music could be done in Ireland.
> The reception too was perfect here, indeed it was the most satisfac-
> tory broadcast from Athlone I have heard except their records.
>
> I hope you will forgive a perfect stranger writing to you, but I felt I
> must let you know the delight your choir gave me and my husband
> by our fireside.[31]

Praise of the cathedral choir was also heard from the boards of
Dublin's Abbey Theatre. On 31 July 1939, a play by the Cork dramatist,
T.C. Murray, was given its first performance there; the *Cork Examiner*
reported:

> A new play named *Illuminations*, by the well-known Irish dramatist,
> Mr T.C. Murray, received its first performance at the Abbey Theatre
> on Monday night. Of particular interest to Cork people is an allusion
> which occurs in the course of the play, spoken by the chief character,
> Brian Egan, a young solicitor, who decides to renounce the world
> and enter Mount Melleray. At one of the most tense moments in the
> play he refers to a wonderful experience in his life, hearing Palestrina
> sung by the Cork Cathedral Choir, under the conductor, Herr
> Fleischmann.

In the passage of the play mentioned in the newspaper, the young
solicitor wants to listen to a radio broadcast of the cathedral choir and
describes his reaction when he first heard it:

> I've heard it only once just by accident. I will never forget it. Oh the
> beauty of it, the purity of tone, I felt myself transferred to another
> world. Yes, to another world. I never felt anything like it before. I
> wish I could make you understand but I can't explain it. Nobody
> could. I was in ecstasy, something so divine, so wonderful. (*He
> switches on the radio but a shrill dance band is heard and he feverishly
> switches it off. Looking at the paper again*) Would you believe it, I was
> looking at yesterday's programme. What a shame to have missed it!

The dramatist wrote to Fleischmann on 21 May 1940

> My grateful thanks for your thoughtful kindness in sending word of
> the broadcast by the Cathedral Choir. To one listener at least the
> Choir's interpretation of di Lasso's work was a profoundly moving
> experience. From the simple invocation that formed the prelude to
> the Benedictus we had the breath of the human spirit in its highest
> moods. That so fine a thing should come to us from Cork made one
> not a little proud of one's city. It seemed a pity that no records were

made. One feels it a loss that so rare a piece of musical interpretation should perish.

My cordial congratulations – and again my thanks.

Musician visitors

The Fleischmanns enjoyed a brief friendship with Herbert Hughes, the distinguished collector of Irish folk music, one of the founders of the Irish Folk Song Society, composer and music critic.[32] The year they met him, he had just published the fourth volume of his *Irish Country Songs.* He had collected perhaps 1,000 folk tunes, mainly in Ulster, and was a friend of Padraic Colum and of W.B. Yeats. In 1936 he came with his wife and children to live for a year in Cahirciveen, County Kerry, in order to continue his studies of folk song in a different part of the country. There on 27 February he heard a broadcast given by the Cork cathedral choir; *The Irish Press* reported him as saying that he had heard the finest choirs in the world, but never anything more beautiful than this choir.[33] The two families visited each other during the summer, the Fleischmanns bringing Arnold Bax with them to Cahirciveen. In September Hughes wrote to Fleischmann:

> That was a very kindly thought to send me such a charming budget of songs, and I feel honoured indeed to possess them. How rare it is in these days to find work so sincere and so uncompromising as yours! Romance has been under a cloud for a long time now, chiefly through a reign of false values and interpretations, and it does me good to peruse these good things and realise that art, at least, has no boundaries and that Music and Poetry survive all the iniquities of mammon and mammon-worship.
>
> We look forward to meeting you again in the near future and hearing all your news.

It was he who suggested that Tilly Fleischmann should write a book on the tradition of piano playing in which she had been trained in Munich. She followed his advice, but he did not live to see her begin the work, let alone complete it. To the great sorrow of the Fleischmanns, Hughes died of pneumonia in May 1937, aged fifty-five.

In 1936 Aloys Óg invited Sir Richard Terry,[34] former music director at Westminster Cathedral in London, to act as external examiner to the music department of the university. A convert to Catholicism, Terry had begun his career as organist, choirmaster and scholar with a post as music teacher in the Benedictine school of Downside Abbey. There he embarked on studies of plainchant and Tudor liturgical music, on which he became the foremost authority, editing, publishing and performing these works in Westminster Cathedral with a choir which he brought to world standing. During his visit to Cork, he stayed with the Fleischmanns and attended a performance of the cathedral choir in the Honan Chapel of the university. That the two church musicians had a good rapport with one another can be seen from his letter of thanks:

> As you will see from this notepaper, I have not even yet got settled down at home. But I must send you just a preliminary line to say how I enjoyed my visit to Cork and to thank you for the *very* happy time you gave me.
>
> 'Rheinberger' now occupies an honoured position on my mantelshelf and looks very distinguished amongst the 'smaller fry' there. When I get back to London tomorrow, I shall send you my book on *The Music of the Roman Rite* in the hope that it may interest you.
>
> I shall long remember that glorious singing in the College Chapel. I think it is marvellous what you have managed to do with a purely voluntary organisation.
>
> Next time you broadcast I hope you will let me know so that I can listen in – I found my new radio-gramophone awaiting me when I got back. It is a 'superset' and therefore much more selective than my old one. But the curious thing is that when I switch on to Athlone I always get *Moscow*! Is there any other Irish station that would answer my purpose? The whole thing is very curious, as I used often get Athlone on my old set.
>
> All good wishes, and renewed thanks for a very delightful time.[35]

Fleischmann's response indicates how encouraged he felt that such an authority on church music should have been impressed by the performance of his choir.

> Dear Sir Richard,
>
> Please forgive the long delay in replying to your very kind letter. It gave me great joy to hear you enjoyed your stay in Cork and in our humble Musikantenheim [minstrel abode], and I hope it will not be the last time we shall have the honour of offering you hospitality.
>
> I am proud to hear that you have put my master Joseph von Rheinberger on your mantelshelf. Amongst his contemporaries he was noble in every sense of the word. His unassuming nature & keen catholic mind made him loveable, no matter how much his star may be clouded now with the rest of that romantic group.
>
> I am so thankful for the encouraging words you so kindly spoke to the choir. It warmed their hearts & made them very enthusiastic for further work. It was for the cathedral choir a historical event which will live on. It also made a deep impression on the Bishop and

amongst the clergy & stirred them up to take more interest in our efforts.[36]

The implication is that the quality of the cathedral music tended to be taken for granted by a somewhat indifferent administration, and that effort was required on the part of choristers and choirmaster to prevent disheartenment setting in. No doubt the choirmaster's gratitude and admiration for the distinguished guest were evident to his singers. Fleischmann continues in his letter:

> Perhaps I might tell you a little incident of which I heard and which occurred as you left the chapel after the recital, and came out into the dark. Two very small boys followed you on tip-toe for some time and then plucking up courage, crept up and touched your coat-tails, unseen and unheard. They dashed back in triumph to the others and told them that they had touched Sir Richard Terry!

> . . . I cannot end this letter without thanking you especially for your generous kindness towards my struggling son. His future, it seems to me, will be a thorny one.

> With all good wishes & respectful greetings from my wife and son

> I remain dear Sir Richard – Yours sincerely

The following summer, in June 1937, the choir gave a special recital for Terry. In a press interview, he said of the choir:

> I never imagined that there was in Ireland a choir capable of so beautiful a performance of music, representing the greatest period of art in the Church's history. It is remarkable to find such a large voluntary choir in a time of such world-wide turmoil, and I feel like a brother to the singers, who expressed the spirit to be found in the works of these old masters with such skill and such real musician-ship.[37]

That was to be his last visit to Ireland: he died the following April.

In 1936 Arnold Bax brought another English composer to the Fleischmanns who, like himself, felt very much at home in Ireland: E.J. (Jack) Moeran.[38] He was born in Norfolk, studied at the Royal College of Music in London with Charles Villiers Stanford and John Ireland, and developed an interest in the folk songs of his county. From the mid 1930s he often stayed in Kenmare, and frequently stopped off in Cork on his way.

Throughout the 1930s Bax returned regularly to Cork as a welcome guest of the Fleischmanns. After his marriage broke up, he never again had a home of his own, but lived mainly in Storrington, Sussex, in The White Horse inn, a place frequented by miners, whose company Bax

much enjoyed. Being a man of considerable private means, he did not
have to work for a living. Though extremely shy, he enjoyed his stays with
the Fleischmanns, as Aloys Óg reported on a BBC radio programme:[39]

> We brought him right around West Cork. Every year he came we
> brought him on picnics and he enjoyed these immensely. Especially
> the Irish place-names used to intrigue him because he had quite a
> good knowledge of Irish and he used to go round and produce very
> fanciful notions as to how these words were derived and sometimes
> a motif arising from one of these place names would crop up right
> through the day like a fugal motif. He was very witty and a marvel-
> lous companion.

The originality of Bax's thinking is reflected in his writing and allows
one to imagine his powers as a conversationalist. His description of the
splendours of Irish folk music is typical. He gently chides the nineteenth-century arrangers for having clothed 'their native melodies in all
too conventional dress' and then continues:

> of all countries in the world Ireland possesses the most varied and
> beautiful folk music, though even now it cannot be fully appreciated
> in its strange and startling richness until the great collection of
> gramophone records enshrined in the Library of the Irish Folklore
> Commission is made accessible to the general public. Here is folk
> music in splendid barbaric nudity . . . and despite more decent
> 'arrangements' by Stanford, Harty, Hughes, and others 'there's more
> enterprise in walking naked.' This music derives from the heart and
> core of Ireland.[40]

The outings with Bax were not only memorable for the entertaining
quality of the conversations, but occasionally took a dramatic turn, as
Tilly Fleischmann recounted in her Bax reminiscences.[41] Once, during an
unusually dry spell of weather, they visited the beautiful gardens of
Illaunacullin or Garnish Island near Glengariff. Bax inadvertently started
a fire, and had to face the incensed owner of the estate in front of fourteen charred fir trees. The incident reached the British press, Arnold's
brother Clifford being named as the perpetrator. Another time Bax had
failed to tell his hosts before setting out on a trip to west Cork that his
fourth symphony was being performed in London by Sir Henry Wood,
who expected him to 'listen in'. By the time they found out, it was too
late to return home. As they drove through the village of Ahakista,
Father Pat MacSwiney remembered he had a colleague there who
owned a radio. The house was deserted, but Father Pat climbed in
through an open window, and found the radio just in time for the beginning of the work, to which they listened in rapt silence in the gathering
dusk. As soon as they began to discuss it, the lights were switched on

and a frightened housekeeper appeared with tea and scones, to test whether the intruders were merely unmannerly mortals or spectral visitors from another world. Bax told the story to Sir Henry, who professed surprise that his friend should resort to burglary to hear his music.

Bax was knighted in 1937. Fleischmann had met Bax's mother, having visited her in London on his way to Germany the previous year, so he wrote to congratulate her. He adds a drop of irony regarding the significance of the honour with an anecdote about an Irish fiddler to whom Bax had awarded a prize at a Feis. The fiddler had complimented the adjudicators on the wisdom of their ruling, hinting that any other decision would have damaged their reputation:

> We were overjoyed to hear the good news of the Knighthood bestowed on your great son. 'It's well for them,' said once a Fiddler to Sir Arnold when a prize was given him in the Feis. Indeed, 'it's well for them' and it is an honour for the court and the nation, to have such an eminent, outstanding Artist. Virgil wrote somewhere: 'What I am from birth, that I am. Nor emperor, nor king can make me more or less.' – Knighthood was bestowed on your son long ago, by the king of kings, as you held him first in your arms, and offered him up to the Highest. Let me, with my small family, congratulate you dear Madam, profoundly and sincerely, with an 'Ad multos annos' for the Mother as well as for our beloved friend. [42]

Contact with Germany up to 1939

Fleischmann visited Germany for the last time in the summer of 1936. Only one postcard has survived; it is stamped with a swastika and the slogan: 'Munich – capital city of the Movement'. The card depicts the famous Bad Tölz Boys' Choir, whose concert in Munich he had attended:

> Have just heard this choir sing in the Odeon. The voices sounded beautiful and fresh, 8-part motets, folksongs. The enthusiasm was colossal. 6 encores. Our choir is much fuller and richer and my paintbrush [his interpretation?] certainly much more colourful and differentiated. Talked to one of the choirboys who gave me a lot of interesting information.
>
> Berberich will have the choir sing the 20-part work by Richard Strauss for me at a rehearsal. He sends his kindest regards.

It must have been a source of pride to Fleischmann to know that his Cork choir could stand comparison with the best in Germany. On the other hand, he may have seen with some bitterness how restricted his field of activity was compared to that of his colleagues, who travelled all over Germany giving concerts, acclaimed wherever they went.

By the summer of 1936, the National Socialists had been in power for over three years. They were carried by a wave of enthusiasm emanating from large sections of the population and were actively supported by a majority of young people, who hoped to help the country rise up after the humiliation of the peace treaty that followed defeat in the First World War, the ensuing hyper-inflation which destroyed the savings of ordinary people and brought them close to starvation, and the terrible poverty, unemployment and despair after the international financial crash of 1929. Jobs were being created, provision was made for the poor and the administration modernised. A sense of purpose and community was fostered through a network of organisations providing amenities and control at all levels and through very skilful deployment of mass rallies and spectacles. It was not then evident that this was being financed by huge loans which ultimately made wars of conquest and plunder inevitable.[43] From the outset, loyalty of party members was rewarded with jobs, housing and goods seized from the country's 100,000 Jews. That was how Ludwig Mühlhausen, for instance, was appointed director of the Commerce Library in Hamburg, and later to the chair of Celtic Studies in Berlin.[44] Dissent was not tolerated: it entailed loss of position or imprisonment: within three months of the party's election victory, 25,000 dissidents had been taken into custody. The double strategy of sweetmeat and whip (*Zuckerbrot und Peitsche*) was most effective. As the Protestant parson, Martin Niemöller, was to put it afterwards:

> When they came for the communists, I didn't protest, as I wasn't a communist.
>
> When they came for the trade unionists, I didn't protest, as I wasn't a trade unionist.
>
> When they came for the Jews, I didn't protest, as I wasn't a Jew.
>
> When they came for me, there was nobody left who could have protested.[45]

In September 1935 the Nuremberg Race Laws were announced at the annual party rally. These penal laws stripped German Jews of their civil rights, disbarred them from the civil service, from the professions, from the economic life of the country, forbad intermarriage between Jews and non-Jews and made sexual intercourse between them a criminal offence. The process of systematic expropriation of property and assets had been undertaken from January 1933: it was now given a legislative framework.

Fleischmann stayed in Munich with Berberich and in Dachau with the Rösslers. He must have heard from Dora Ziegler that, after the passing of the Nuremberg laws, her brother divorced his Jewish wife, whom he sent to America. The camp was now known all over Germany, news of it spread by those political prisoners who had been released after a year, forbidden to speak of what they had endured. This had given rise to ominous rumours and the sort of fear the National Socialists needed. Fleischmann's daughter-in-law remembered him saying that people were afraid to talk to him. He may have heard of the fate of the Jewish writer, Georg Hirschfeld, with whom in his youth he had regularly attended the Dachau painters' *Stammtisch,* or weekly inn session, and who had been a founding member of the Dachau Music and Drama Society. Hirschfeld's dramas of social realism were among the books burnt by Nazi students in Munich in 1933; he was forbidden to publish, could find no work and was to take his own life in 1942.

Fleischmann's friend, the poet and local historian Franz Schaehle, had been dismissed from his post as secondary school teacher as he had refused to join the NSDAP.[46] He was now living with his wife and child in very straitened circumstances, avoided by colleagues and most friends and, as all publishing was now under party control, with no chance of seeing any work in print. The two men had planned to meet during Fleischmann's stay, but the visitor failed to make contact. It is possible that he was afraid of compromising Schaehle. Fleischmann's son had been the first to sign a note of protest against the dismissal of Jewish academics from German universities under the Nuremberg Race Laws, which was drawn up by members of Cork university staff and handed in to the German Embassy in Dublin.[47] Germaine Stockley's sister, Annette Kolb, had had to leave Munich and emigrate to Paris in 1933. She had already been exiled during the First World War – her spirited denunciation in 1915 of the militarism and war propaganda of all combatant nations had led to a riot during a lecture in Dresden;[48] the following year the Bavarian War Ministry denounced her for 'subversive pacifist activities' and forbade her to write and to travel. Her subsequent publications did nothing to alter her reputation. Ludwig Mühlhausen knew of these links from his time teaching in the Irish department of Cork university; Fleischmann knew from the Celtic scholar's letters extolling the NSDAP that he was now a member of the SA.[49]

Fleischmann was involved in his son's summer schools for teachers at the university during his holidays in 1938 and 1939, so he did not visit Germany. With the beginning of the war in August 1939 all links with the country were severed. For a full decade, he was to be without news of his friends, without letters, newspapers, books and music. He stood in no danger of being interned, as the Irish government adopted a policy of neutrality. However, during the course of the war, the Allies briefly contemplated an invasion of Ireland to be able to use the ports as military bases; had that happened, he might once again have been deprived of his freedom. During the First World War, before his

internment in 1916, he had avoided all public appearances with his
choirs. This time there was no need for such caution: the cathedral choir
continued to give recitals and to broadcast. But he lost one of his most
talented choir members, Seán Óg Ó Tuama, who was interned in the
Curragh camp for the duration of the war. Seán Óg had a beautiful
voice, was deeply committed to the Irish language and culture, and had
his own choir, An Claisceadail, which gave many broadcasts on the
radio singing his arrangements of Irish music. He came from a family of
'a very strong Republican tradition', as Máire MacSwiney Brugha puts
it. When the emergency legislation directed against the IRA came into
force in 1939, 600 men suspected of IRA membership and involvement
in its bombing campaigns in Britain were imprisoned, and 500 more
interned without charge. Among the latter was Seán Óg Ó Tuama, who
had never been involved in political activities but who was taken into
custody just in case.[50]

As the war years brought severe restrictions for civilian travel, the
Cork Orchestral Society could no longer bring foreign artists to the city.
Bax did not visit Ireland again until 1946. The war put an end to Aloys
Óg's plans to establish a Festival of Cork similar to that of Salzburg, as
it would have involved foreign orchestras and soloists on a large scale.
But the musical life of the city continued, fed from its own resources.
The Cork Symphony Orchestra continued to perform, both
Fleischmanns to compose, and Aloys Óg was a frequent guest con-
ductor with the Radio Éireann Symphony Orchestra.

Fleischmann no longer had immediate family in Germany, but it
was a cause of intense distress to him that another conflagration should
have been unleashed over the peoples of the world. He must have been
haunted by his memories of the previous one. During those years he
lost two of his oldest friends. Father Pat MacSwiney died, after much
ill-health, in November 1940 at the age of fifty-five. They had been
close friends for nearly thirty years, the priest almost being part of the
family. John J. Horgan concluded his obituary in the *Cork Historical and
Archaeological Society Journal* of that month:

> Those who were privileged to witness his last silent homecoming,
> when the men of Kinsale carried his remains through the twilight
> streets amidst a reverent and stricken people to the old Church
> where he had ministered so long, knew that this saintly cultured
> priest and true patriot had not worked in vain.

The other friend was William P. Stockley, whom Fleischmann had
known from the beginning of his time in Cork. He died in 1943, after
which his widow went to live with her daughter in Dublin. Though she
continued to correspond and visit until her death in 1949, the closing of
the beautiful, hospitable home and the departure of the gifted singer,

vivacious, witty and beloved friend must have brought great sadness. From Dublin in 1944 she wrote to him, in German as always:

> Last Easter the Professor was still so well that he sent me off to the Cathedral. I still hear his farewell words when he said to me: 'I'm alright – don't hurry' as he opened his Tenebrae book. Oh Aloys, it often hurts so much that I have to creep away. But they are all good to me.
>
> In deep affection, as of old,
>
> Germaine[51]

1941–47: THE WAR YEARS

The enlarged family

Aloys Óg became engaged to Anne Madden in 1940. Her people were Cork merchants: her father had been director of a wine and grocery store, who had died when she and her sister were children. She was related to many of the other Cork business families. Among her ancestors was a member of the United Irishmen who fled the country with Napper Tandy after the defeat of the rising, was imprisoned in Hamburg, and ended up a general in France. Her great-aunt was a friend of the Fenian, John Mitchel and several of her mother's relatives had been Lord Mayors of Cork. She was not a musician; but had become involved in the University Art Society during her medical studies, as well as being captain of the university hockey team. After her graduation she worked for a year in England, returning home once travelling to Ireland had become difficult and war censorship of letters irksome. When it had become clear that her friendship with Aloys Óg could bring her into the family, Fleischmann took her for a five-mile walk along the Lee fields. She found approval: unlike his father and his grandfather, Aloys Óg did not have to face opposition to his marriage, even if his parents might have preferred a daughter-in-law who could have sung in his choir, played in his orchestra, helped with rehearsals and the copying of music. The young wife faced a considerable challenge in taking up residence with a bi-lingual closely-bonded family of three musicians of very different cultural background.

The wedding took place on 4 June 1941; having spent their honeymoon on the Blasket Islands, the couple moved into Oileán Ruadh (Red Island), about seven miles from Cork city. The spacious Georgian house, situated on five acres of land, had a splendid view over Lough Mahon. On one side terraced lawns stretched down to the stony shore, on which there was a small ruined watch-tower built during the Napoleonic wars. The house stood on an elevation of about thirty feet above the estuary, the high bank reinforced by a wall. Tall old trees provided shade in summer, a large walled orchard protection from the winds. Aloys Óg's study gave on to a little walled and paved rose-garden with fountain. In the eighteenth century the house had also belonged to an immigrant musician: to the first Huguenot to settle in Cork, a French composer and dancing master by the name of Laurence de la Main,[52] whose son, Henry, became organist in St Fin Barre's Cathedral. During the war of independence, a major of the British army lived there, who was shot in the house by republicans and was said to haunt the place. That may have helped the family acquire the property for the price of £700.

The inconveniences of such a house became apparent during the family's first autumn on the island. There was no central heating; coal could no longer be imported and turf was found to be a poor substitute. Fleischmann had a paraffin stove made for his study, which was placed in the middle of the room, a long pipe conveying (most of) the fumes to the chimney. A wind turbine was installed on the roof to provide electricity, but the force of an equinoctial gale was such that Aloys Óg had to climb up in the middle of the night to dismantle the contraption lest it should be ripped off and half the roof with it. The sea wall collapsed during another storm; a few weeks later the ceilings of two rooms capitulated to the force of gravity. Furthermore, as petrol shortages made public transport scarce and erratic, the three musicians had to bicycle the seven miles into the city and back every day to get to work. The older Fleischmanns, especially, must have been striking figures in inclement seasons: he enveloped in a voluminous waterproof cape which covered half the vehicle, she trailing long skirts in all weathers. All three generally enjoyed excellent health during those years, perhaps due to the rigorous regime of exercise.

Fleischmann, for the first time not living in town, loved the quiet of the island, the trees, the water and his rowing boat. Their friends called it 'the paradise'. E.J. Moeran frequently came, as did the pianist Charles Lynch, the singers Maura O'Connor and Rita Lynch, the dancer and piper Joan Denise Moriarty, the painters Pat Hennessy and James Craig, the sculptors Marshall Hutson and Séamus Murphy with families. Walburga Swertz, now in her late eighties, came once a week to do the sewing for her daughter. The gardens were looked after by Mr Geary, the housekeeping taken care of by Hannah Hurley of Ovens, County Cork.

Three grandchildren were born on the island; over each one their grandfather pronounced an ancient blessing: 'May you find ease on earth' [*Möge dir die Erde leicht sein*], adding: 'may you journey on it in safety and happiness and reach the end without calamity' [*und du sie ohne Unheil glücklich durchwandern*].[53] There are no accounts of the grandchildren in Fleischmann's correspondence with Schaehle, but he recorded a few scenes in his notebooks. One, written in June 1946, is entitled 'From the Land of Childhood'. The eldest was not quite four, Aloys Neil (called 'Buddy') two, and the baby three months old:

> The young people and the youngest have taken off for Ardmore. The house is really lonely without the little scamps we are used to: Ruth and Buddy. We also miss quiet Anne-Kathrine's blue bright eyes very much. Ruth explained to me as they were leaving why I couldn't come with them: [*in English*] 'because Holy God would cry if you not play the organ on Sunday in the church.' Their faces flushed with excitement, they got into the car that Mummy drove, waved their little hands vigorously, chorused 'Goodbye Ga-pa, goodbye Granny, goodbye Hannah' – and they were gone. Off to a wonderland to build sandcastles, go fishing, play around in the sand on the shore of the wide sea, cheering the ships that passed quietly and majestically in the far distance.
>
> It was reported to us that Buddy, equipped with new trousers, new shoes and socks, a brand new coat, and a hat complete with feather was allowed to attend Mass for the first time in Ardmore. He had of course been warned that he would have to be very quiet etc. And during the mass and sermon he was indeed as quiet as a mouse; but when the priest came back for Benediction vested in a cope, the altar boys appeared with lighted candles and thurible, and the organ unexpectedly pealed out, he turned around suddenly, looked up to the organ gallery and called out in a loud voice of pleased surprise: 'Ga-pa, Ga-pa playing organ!' Many heads turned in amusement towards the little disturber of the peace, and among the young people the lively shout aroused much hilarity, which certainly will not have heightened the solemnity of the occasion.
>
> Oh happy time of youth when miracles, dream and reality still intermingle blissfully!

In 'Reflections on Bran', written during Easter week of 1952 after the disappearance of his beloved collie, he describes what a delightful companion the dog had been to the grandchildren:

> On the small island he used to have great sport on the big fields which belonged to the property. He loved to play with the grandchildren and would jump up high in excitement and joy, roll in the grass like a boisterous small boy, his paws waving in the air, would let them tussle with him, and would roll with the children down the grassy slope of the lawn like a big hairy football, to the delighted shouts and laughter of his playmates.

To his wife's niece, Frieda Williams, he wrote on 14 November 1944 (in English):

As I was in bed ill, my baby granddaughter visited me one day. Bran was lying on the floor stretched out. She bending down gave Bran a most affectionate salutation, laying her little head on his. After a while she looked round the room, pointing up at Christ's picture: 'Wha i tha?' (What is that?) 'Who do you think?' She looked at me, and up again, pointing her tiny finger at Christ's face and said without hesitation: 'Ga-pa!' (Her own invented expression for Grandpapa). You see I am not an ordinary man any longer. I am exalted to a great, pardon me, to a God! Remember that when talking to me in future!

In 1947 the communal life with the grandchildren came to an end. To Fleischmann's intense sorrow, the island house had to be given up: the family moved back into the city, into two separate houses. The grand-children were due to begin school, and could not travel such distances twice a day by bus nor cross the city alone. The family did not have a car. The rise in wages that came after the war brought an increase in the cost of domestic staff, without which such a house could hardly be main-tained, and which proved to be beyond the reach of the family's modest income. Strained relations between the two women of the house, both strong personalities, led to the decision to separate. Anne and Aloys Óg moved into an old converted flax mill, with stream and pond, just outside the city, twenty minutes on foot from the large Victorian terraced house into which the parents moved, a few doors down from where they had lived before going to Oileán Ruadh. For the next twenty years, Aloys Óg called every evening to their home unless he was away.

Activities of the cathedral and Cecilian choirs during the war years

In the 1940s the cathedral choir was involved in much music in the city. The boys' choir performed in Humperdinck's opera *Hänsel und Gretel*, and in the Dublin Grand Opera Cork productions of *La Bohème* and *Martha*. Fleischmann founded a new secular choir, the Cork Cecilian Choir, to give recitals in the city. Both this new choir and the cathedral choir took part in a production of the Cork Little Theatre Society in March 1943 of *Cradle Song* by Gregorio Martinez Sierra, providing inci-dental music. The Cork actor, Dan Donovan, was a member of the Society:

> The Little Theatre Society was founded in the mid thirties by some of the best known amateur actors and groups to present local work and quality plays and, by using the Opera House as a venue, perhaps to accumulate some cash with the intention of obtaining or building a small uncommercial 'art' theatre. There was quite a strong move-ment throughout these islands fired by the same ambitions. Some of the best known people in the Cork theatrical circle helped to found it. These included Sean and Geraldine Neeson, Jim Stack and Eddie

Golden, who had recently left The Loft after a dispute with Fr
O'Flynn. The Society played a significant role in establishing a local
voice for drama in the old Opera House, where there was a long
musical tradition.

Sierra (1881–1947) was a dramatist, novelist, poet and a key figure
in pre-war Spanish drama; his *Cancion de Cuna* (*Cradle Song*) is a
nativity play, rooted in Spanish life and culture and colour – a lovely
piece of theatre, involving all the theatrical arts.[54]

The play was produced by the former cathedral choir member, James
Stack. The two choirs performed music by Suriano, the Spanish composer Vittoria, and carols. Fleischmann received a letter of thanks from
the Society on 8 March 1943:

Dear Herr Fleischmann,

It is extremely difficult to express to you, personally, our gratitude for
all you have done for us in connection with the production of *The
Cradle Song*.

The offer of help in providing a musical setting was in keeping with
the keen interest you have always shown in our activities, but the
generous extent to which this assistance was carried was quite
beyond our reckoning.

The perfect choice of the music, the beauty of its rendering, and your
extraordinary personal interest and care that every note and bar
should be completely in the spirit of the play and its atmosphere, is
something for which we can never adequately thank you. It transformed our venture and lifted it to a height we did not hope
otherwise to attain.

The cathedral choir supported all Aloys Óg's enterprises requiring
choral singing. It was invited to augment the University Choral Society,
and took part in the Handel oratorios *Saul* and *Judas Maccabaeus* as
well as the Serenata *Acis and Galatea*, which were performed in the
university. During Cork's Kermesse of 1944, sponsored by William
Dwyer of Sunbeam, the Cork Symphony Orchestra and cathedral choir
gave an open-air performance of *A Midsummer Night's Dream* with
Mendelssohn's complete incidental music.[55]

The elder Fleischmann's recitals were always written up in the Cork
press and favourably reviewed. The critics, however, were generally not
musicians and comments on the quality of the performance were therefore rare. During the 1940s, Dublin's *Standard* newspaper engaged a
music critic who had studied the subject and graduated from UCC in
1939: the Christian Brother, Joseph Reade. He strove to make the cathedral choir's achievement known and appreciated nationally, in
particular in Dublin, where he now lived. He pursued a long-term

educational strategy with his music criticism in *The Standard*; the advocacy of sacred music of the kind fostered in Cork was part of this.

On 20 July 1943, he wrote to congratulate Fleischmann for having
established the Cork Cecilian Choir and on its performance at a
madrigal recital he had attended:

> After years of labour and perseverance you have succeeded in
> bringing about a revival of the great art of Sacred Polyphony. It is to
> be hoped that you will be equally successful in your efforts to revive
> an art which is almost extinct, namely, that of the Madrigal, which
> one might also speak of as the art of Secular Polyphony. Please
> accept my sincerest congratulations, and my heartiest wishes for the
> prosperity of your new venture.

> I very much regret to say that I was not able to write a proper criticism
> of the broadcast for *The Standard*. Mr O'Curry, the editor, recently
> expressed his dislike of too much criticism in my column, and asked
> me to devote more attention to articles of a more general nature,
> which would be helpful and informative for the average reader of the
> paper, especially for those in the country districts. His belief is that a
> criticism appearing almost a week after a concert or a recital cannot
> possibly interest the average reader. I have written a sort of general
> article on the Madrigal, and have made particular mention of the
> broadcast. Actually I had to interrupt my new series of articles to get
> it in; (a series on 'Church Music' which the editor is very keen on). I
> do hope the article will do some good, and that you will approve of it.
> Please write to me and give me your opinion; also, I would be very
> grateful if you would read my series on Church Music and furnish me
> with a criticism. You know how much I value your opinion, and to
> have it would be both helpful and gratifying to me.

> I was very sorry to miss seeing you when I was in Cork recently. On
> my way back to town the evening I spent at Oilean Ruadh, you actu-
> ally passed me on the road. I called you but you did not recognise
> me. I enjoyed a delightful chat with Frau Fleischmann and Prof.
> Fleischmann; it was almost like old times. I hope it will not be long
> before I go to Cork again and then I shall certainly see you.

On 4 April 1944, during the week before Easter, the cathedral choir
gave a recital of sacred music in the Honan Chapel of the university,
which was broadcast by Radio Éireann. The music critic of *The Standard*
reviewed the performance with enthusiasm, on 7 April declaring the
choir to demonstrate a degree of excellence unequalled in Ireland, a
claim which was to lead to controversy in the paper:

> We still fondly cling to our sterile cult, the semi-theatrical and super-
> ficial in regard to music for the church, and so on Good Friday in
> some churches . . . we are condemned to listen to music of the most

sentimental type, utterly divorced from the spirit and character of Gregorian chant, with organ accompaniment, and a profusion of solos when at the same time the seven last words of Christ on the cross are being preached. . . .

Under those circumstances then it is with the utmost pride and enthusiasm that one has occasion to speak of the unique work being done by the Cork Cathedral Choir under its distinguished director Aloys Fleischmann. On Monday last we were again given the price-less opportunity of hearing this unique, remarkable choir in a recital of polyphonic music for Holy Week. One was uplifted to an unusual degree by the extraordinary tonal beauty and contrasts, and the burning intensity of devotional expression. The boy sopranos and altos achieved an almost ethereal quality of tone.

The technical attainments of this choir particularly in regard to quality, balance, rhythmic control and strength of attack are quite without parallel in this country, and one might rank them without hesitation with the great church choirs of the world. In Aloys Fleischmann the choir has an inspired director and artist of the most sensitive order, who possesses an immense understanding and highly specialised experience of sacred polyphony through years of unceasing study of its many intricacies and unselfish labour for its welfare. His work is of immense importance to the church and to the country, and it is to be hoped that it will not go unrewarded. The very least one might expect is that this wonderful choir should be heard more often than once or twice a year from Radio Éireann as is the case at present.[56]

In response to this report, a letter to the editor appeared on 21 April 1944 from a Mr J. Clery of Dublin. He listed a number of Dublin church choirs whom he considered excellent, and wrote that 'the claims of your critic for the Cork choir' seemed 'a trifle exaggerated': that no Irish choir could be said to have the same quality as that of Westminster Cathedral. The music critic of *The Standard*, writing on the same day, upheld his praise of the Cork cathedral choir:

I am acquainted with the work of the Dublin choirs he [Mr Clery] mentions and with many more throughout the country that I have heard from time to time through Radio Éireann and in no case have I experienced that magnificent breadth of tone, unblemished quality, rhythmic balance, lofty dignity and intensity of expression always attained by the Cork Cathedral Choir in its treatment of sacred polyphony. I acknowledge with alacrity the competence of the Dublin choirs cited by Mr Clery . . . but competence hardly mirrors greatness, and on that supposition I stake my claim for the Cork choir. . . .

Mr Clery's choice of Westminster Cathedral Choir as a superior example to any in Ireland is, as it happens, rather unfortunate since the testimony of the late Sir Richard Terry, its most distinguished choirmaster, disclaims its superiority to the Cork choir. In 1936, while Sir Richard was in Cork as External Examiner at the University, a performance of sacred polyphony was staged for him by the Cork choir, after which he spoke in the highest possible terms of what he had heard, expressing his surprise that the work of the choir had achieved but local approbation as distinct from international, and ranked it unhesitantly with the great church choirs of the world. This was the sincere testimony of a distinguished musician, acknowledged throughout the world as an impeccable authority on Catholic Church music. His testimony has been wholly confirmed by such reliable critics as Sir Arnold Bax and Sir Granville Bantock.[57]

The discussion in *The Standard* closed on 5 May 1944 with a letter to the editor from James Delany, organist and choirmaster at St Joseph's, Berkley Street, Dublin:

The notes of your critic and the letter of Mr J. Clery on music in our churches are most interesting and deserve the attention of all interested in the noble art that has been fostered by the church. After many years of experience I thoroughly agree with the views of your critic regarding the amount of unfitting music heard in our churches, and the excellent work of the Cathedral Choir Cork. While I agree in the main with Mr Clery's statement regarding good work done by some Dublin choirs, I am of the opinion that none of these reach the high level attained by the Cork choir.

An undated letter from Joseph Reade describes what he considered a breakthrough with regard to the cathedral choir's reputation in Dublin. He writes that the admiration generated by a recent choir broadcast was such that it had led a number of people to consider setting up a *schola cantorum,* a training college for church music, with Fleischmann as director:

Quite candidly, I find it impossible to express in words the feelings of joy, of satisfaction, and of pride awakened in me as a result of the recital on Monday week last. I want you to know that I have not been so profoundly moved by any musical experience for a very long time. For me the recital has been an occasion of personal triumph, for it has more than amply vindicated the proud boasts I have been making to so many people here in Dublin concerning the Cork Cathedral Choir. . . . I have already heard the suggestion being made many times in the last week, as a result of the broadcast, that a National Schola of Church Music should be founded and that you should be called upon to direct its destinies. . . . Another suggestion envisaged the idea of your Choir being used as an instrument for the propagation of liturgical music, by means of widespread recitals through the country at the expense of the Church, the government, or some private body with sufficient interest and money to sponsor such a venture. . . .

> Please convey to the Choir my sincerest congratulations and grati-
> tude for the really excellent performance; I am proud beyond
> expression to be a Corkman, and to have been associated with you
> and them, in a very little way, in the magnificent work you are doing.

Reade wrote that he was aware Fleischmann would react with scepticism to his report, but considered the ideas put forward to be a
development of significance in their work for church music in Ireland.

After the war, Joseph Reade was sent by his order to the United
States. No school of church music was founded, no scheme for the
propagation of liturgical music instituted – and the work of the cathedral choir ceased to be reviewed in the national press. During the 1940s
Fleischmann's son established his reputation as a composer and conductor in the capital, but he was not active in the field of sacred music.

During the dark times towards the end of the war, the recitals and
broadcasts of the cathedral choir provided moments of solace and
peace to many, some of whom took the trouble to write to the conductor. Moirin Chavasse, biographer of Terence MacSwiney, wrote in
1944 from her home in Galway:

> We were listening to your choir a few days ago and I must send you
> a line to thank you from my heart for your gift. These days, listening
> to the Radio could almost make one think one was tuning-in to the
> infernal regions, and in at this welter of hate and destruction and
> misery your music came through like a breath from Paradise. One
> may hear beautiful music still, but it is seldom indeed that it is
> expressed with that exquisite and lovely perfection that can only be
> brought into being by genius. I think when interpretation reaches a
> certain level it not only sets free something nearly inexpressible that
> yet is trying, as it were, to break through the score, but it becomes
> also in a sense creative.[58]

Patrick Hennessy was present at a recital in the Honan Chapel
during that same time of the world's 'unbearable agony':

> Dear Alois,
>
> I have just returned from the recital in the Honan Chapel, and before
> I go to bed, feel that I must thank you for what has been one of the
> happiest evenings I have spent in Ireland. I cannot put into words
> the joy I felt on hearing your choir sing that superb music, particu-
> larly the 'Caligaverunt Oculi Mei', which through the medium of
> those innocent voices sounded like the cry of all mankind in its
> unbearable agony. Only once before do I remember being so pro-
> foundly moved, when I heard – was it Furtwängler? – conducting
> *Fidelio* in Paris.
>
> Please excuse this hurried note. I felt that I must let you know how
> deeply I appreciated the concert tonight, and can only marvel at the

wonderful instrument you have created to express such incomparable music.

I most earnestly hope that we may have the opportunity of hearing many more such recitals in the near future.[59]

Many Irishmen fought in the war with the British army, among them a number of Fleischmann's former choristers. One of these, Michael Drinan a corporal stationed in Ceylon with the Royal Army Pay Corps, wrote to the choirmaster in June 1942. It was a bird singing which reminded him of the choir, and the memory of the serenity and peace brought to him by its music which prompted him to write. The letter card bears a Ceylonese postage stamp, and both a British and an Irish censorship stamp; it was written on 3 June 1942:

> You will, I am sure, be somewhat surprised on receipt of these few lines. It is even probable that you will have to don your 'thinking hat' to recollect the name of Drinan. But I don't think you forget your boys, no more than they forget you.
>
> Well, Sir, much water has 'passed beneath the bridge' since I left Corcaigh and your 'super-choir' far, far behind. I've travelled many thousands of miles and seen many weird and wonderful sights, believe me, Sir. I cannot give you a pen-picture (even if I could) of the various places I've been to, due to the very irksome censorship rules. They are so strict. Well, I'm wondering if our thoughts will come 'under the hammer' next.
>
> But one thing I cannot and will not forget, and that is the heavenly time I had whilst a member of your 'songster band', both as boy (glorious days) and man. How I wish I were once more in your grand company, where I was wont to sing with my other 'warbling companions' (God bless them) 'Ecce Sacerdos' or the 'Tenebrae' or some beautiful motet. Then again, how I long to recapture that indescribable feeling of contentment and peace of mind with nothing to pervade my soul but beautiful thoughts when you played solo on that magnificent organ of St Mary's North. If God so wills, I will once again, I hope, be permitted to rejoin your Choir, Sir. Please remember me to those members of the Choir who were there, and I hope still are, when I was a member. I think they should be real 'senior boys' now.
>
> In Ceylon many varieties of birds there are, all chirping and singing. My abode at present happens to be set in a clump of trees from whence some beautiful plumed songster is giving vent to his feelings. But I'm sure those little 'Cork Cherubs' at present under your care, would probably drive that poor bird to suicide were he to hear them sing.

Well, Sir, I know that my Motherland, Éire, is not having a very happy time just now but, being Éire, my dear country, it can withstand any amount of buffeting and still smile through the storm. Everything will turn out right yet, Sir, so *keep smiling* and if you would, say a little prayer for me. Thank you.

Best regards to ALL. Erin go brágh.

Anguish at the outcome of the war

Fleischmann composed a long birthday letter to his son in 1945, a month before the end of the war in Europe. He speaks of birthdays as 'Janus days', which invite reflection on past and coming years, as symbolised in the double-headed Roman god protecting beginnings and ends, gates and doorways. Fleischmann accordingly reviews Aloys Óg's life. He describes his emotions on hearing of the child's birth, the pleasure of watching the child grow in the early years, the torment of separation during the First World War, and how he found the boy on his return. He formulates his wishes for his son:

> Providence has endowed you with a bright intellect and laid the most splendid of all gifts in your cradle: in compensation, as it were, for the grief of losing our home, you were granted the language of the heavens – music. The most sacred and most beautiful of all the arts. May it provide you with support and succour against the disappointments and trials of this world during your pilgrimage through it.
>
> You are a child of spring. The earth rejuvenated and decked herself out when you opened your little eyes for the first time and looked into the world. She put on a new gown to greet you! We three were all born in April. As the celestial chart shows, under the triple-star constellation of Cassiopeia. So these three stars met and illuminated us three newly-born. Let us hope that the same constellation will one day also lead us three, with all our loved ones, happily united to the heavenly town of Bethlehem. . . .
>
> This letter has become far too long. But when one wants to say a great deal at one time, one can get distracted and wander off, especially when deeper questions arise and one is without a friend with whom to discuss them from time to time. Old age also makes the blood warmer and the thoughts more garrulous, in particular when one feels lonely. Don't forget that thirty additional years press on my back than on yours, including eleven years of war. All that wears one down and perhaps also makes one sentimental. (In 30 years you too will see the world with different eyes!)[60]

He then discloses the grim prospects confronting himself and his wife: that he has no provision for his old age, as the war has annihilated his savings. The money he had inherited from his mother and his uncle had been deposited in the bank in Dachau; there it was frozen with the beginning of hostilities. To finance the war, the German Ministry of Finance used savings of citizens – as well as the assets robbed from German Jews and from the occupied countries. The war bonds were now worthless:

> Furthermore there is the loss of the remains of my fortune, which I had hoped would bring relief to your dear mother and to me in our old age. That has now been lost. The projects I had thought up for those 33 000 marks! An extension with four rooms, a little kitchen and a separate entrance. The publication of your best works, together with some of my songs, choral and organ works, as well as a really good Blüthner grand piano at last for Mama. Now it has all melted away like froth and – like my destroyed, ruined home – is henceforth but a dream.

> And so I look back on a squandered life without roots, without security for my old age. On a life which began so full of hope. 'I came here a stranger; as a stranger do I depart.'

The quotation is from Schubert's *Winterreise*. His sixty-fifth birthday was approaching, normally retirement age, but neither he nor his wife had pensionable posts. Ten years before, in his birthday letter to Aloys Óg in Munich, he had hoped to be granted a further decade of working life to facilitate his son's career. He now realised that both he and his wife would have to work until the end, and would become a burden to their son once their strength failed them:

> I hope to God that those milestones (now easily counted) which your mother and I have still to pass by will see us both able to work. This great worry often torments me at night. I hope I never have to experience a birthday when I am unable to work or have become a burden to you.

By April 1945 most large German cities had been targeted by Allied bombers. Ninety per cent of the centre of Munich was destroyed in October 1943; accounts and pictures of the destruction of Dresden in February 1945 had appeared in all the newspapers. Fleischmann's affliction over the fate of his 'destroyed, ruined home' represses his knowledge of the relentless German bombing of Britain from 1940 to 1941. He may not at that time have been aware of the slaughter of civilians in Guernica by German bombers in 1937, in Warsaw in 1939, in Rotterdam in 1940, and the policy of scorched earth and massacres of civilians perpetrated by the German army in the Soviet Union. His focus is purely on the fate of civilians in Germany; abhorrence is expressed for the Allied leaders responsible for their destruction:

> Those benefactors of the peoples, 'the Big Three', whose godfather
> was no other than Lucifer, the prince of hell, have brought this
> about. Attila, Nero, Ivan the Terrible were humanists with limited
> means compared to these heartless barbaric monsters in human
> form which the earth has spewn out in our time.[61]

The 'Big Three' – Churchill, Roosevelt, Stalin. It is striking that the man
bearing the main responsibility for the apocalyptic havoc is not mentioned.

This letter was written three weeks before the end of the war in
Europe. The previous day the concentration camp of Buchenwald near
Weimar had been liberated, shortly afterwards Bergen-Belsen. A fortnight later, on 29 April, 30,000 prisoners in the camp near Dachau were
liberated by American troops.[62] The Soviet army had reached Auschwitz
on 27 January, but as fighting still raged, it took many weeks before
English-speaking war correspondents arrived there. After the capitula-
tion of Germany on 8 May, victims' accounts of life in the camps, reports
by Allied soldiers and photographs of what the troops had found began
to appear in the newspapers in America and Britain, providing
irrefutable evidence of the scale and horrific nature of the crimes committed in the name of one of the most cultured peoples of Europe.
Many in Ireland had not believed Allied reports about the criminal terrorism of the Nazis. After the First World War, many of the stories about
German atrocities had turned out to be fabrications; it was widely
assumed that in the Second World War, too, the first victim of hostilities had been Truth.[63] Fleischmann now suffered the anguish of seeing
his beloved country a pariah among the nations of the world, and the
name of his home town a synonym for the systematic savagery of the
infamous regime.

1947–64: THE LAST YEARS – AFFLICTIONS AND CONSOLATIONS

Contact with Germany re-established after ten years

In April 1949 Fleischmann received a letter from Franz Schaehle, the first
communication from Germany for ten years. He wrote back to give
warning that letters were still unreliable messengers, and that all pictures,
books, newpapers and music were still being 'put to death as heretics at
the border' – censorship was still very much in place in both countries.
Schaehle painted a grim picture of the desolation of the country:

> Half of Munich is a desolate landscape of rubble and wreckage; our
> whole beloved and once so proud fatherland lies in absurd chaos;
> we ourselves have become worn-out and exhausted and are
> without purpose in life and devoid of hope. There is hardly anything
> that has not been fundamentally ruined in Germany, whether it be
> the school system, the law, honesty in trade, ownership of works of

art, academic institutions, housing and so on and so forth. The sole
and single refuge for those of sensitive frame of mind are quiet
corners of the countryside, in the forests and on the moors, which
have not yet been reached by the madness of these times. No
description can convey to those who did not themselves experience
the hair-raising decades of our downfall even an idea of what we
had to endure during the period of the criminal Nazi terrorism,
helpless and defenceless as we were, and what we, completely
innocent victims of this era, furthermore continue to endure, as if
we bore any responsibility, with no prospect of peace and a return
to the order we knew in our youth and which could help us to bear
sad old age.[64]

In June 1949 he describes what has become of the Munich he knew as
a young man:

> We two, my daughter and I, feel we are an island in the ocean of an
> alien, cold world, the foundations of which are crumbling and disin-
> tegrating in a manner not even the darkest imagination could have
> anticipated.
>
> To touch on that closest to us: you know what has happened to our
> beloved old Munich. But unless one has seen the atrocity, one's
> image of it falls far short of the devastating reality. Though the very
> worst of the rubble has been removed, even now, after five years, the
> sight tears at one's heart at every visit. Only a few weeks ago I stood
> on the site of the Ludwig Grammar School, with which nine years of
> school memories bond me. Not a single stone remains of the enor-
> mous building: only a completely flattened waste of broken tiles and
> weeds. It is as though at night the spirits of our old teachers were
> condemned to haunt the place, lamenting and accusing. A lost
> world, once so proud and prosperous. The Church of the Holy Spirit,
> where I was married in 1925, the registry office, the hotel where we
> held the wedding reception, the house of my parents-in-law, our
> first apartment – all smashed and pulverised. The Pinakothek [Art
> Gallery], the old Academy, the State Library, University, the Gate of
> Victory, the Isar Gate – ruins, wreckage. The Church of St Peter a
> doomed, hopeless ruin. The Church of St Michael – most likely
> irreparable, gone for ever; the Church of St Boniface – disappeared
> off the face of the earth. Things are not much better in Augsburg.
> Donauwörth no longer exists; the degree of radical destruction to be
> seen in Würzburg is said to surpass all else.[65]

Schaehle writes of his daughter's distaste for everything German,
which has led her to study foreign languages with a view to emigrating
at the first opportunity. Fleischmann strenuously advises against this,
adamant that Germany will recover its integrity and economy and urges
his friend to warn his daughter against 'the curse of homelessness',

against the bitter fate of being 'stranded on an alien shore' from which all too often, as in his case, there can be no return.

A further source of pain is the fact that the town he left has changed beyond recognition. From 1950 he took the Munich newspaper, *Münchner Merkur*,[66] and the Dachau paper *Dachauer Nachrichten*. From these he learnt how much his old home had changed. Much of the moorland had been drained and used for agriculture or building; the storks, cranes and eagles of his youth had disappeared, the weir in which he had swum as a boy given way to electricity works. The town had grown from the 5,000 souls in his youth to 25,000 with the thousands of war refugees now housed on the site of the concentration camp. As he put it to Schaehle in the summer of 1950: 'After decades in foreign parts, the torn and anguished soul finds itself not only an alien abroad but now a stranger at home.' In the summer of 1951, his wife's niece invited him to take a continental holiday with her family, in the course of which she planned to visit Munich and Dachau. Fleischmann declined, finding himself, as he wrote to Schaehle, unable to face the sight of the ruins 'of his devastated, broken home', and the many tombstones bearing names of friends whom he had hoped to see again after the war.

In December 1949, the choirmaster of Dachau, Alois Ritthaler, wrote to tell his colleague that his tower music had once again been performed on Christmas Eve from the steeple of the church of St Jakob's, as it had been since his departure in 1906, with the exception of the two world wars, when Fleischmann could no longer arrange for the four musicians to be paid. He was overjoyed at the news and astounded that in times of such hardship the custom should have been revived without his having commissioned it.[67] He was much comforted by the renewal of contact with his home town and with Schaehle, a man of immense integrity, sensitivity and melancholy disposition who, like himself, sought solace in creative work. They were never to meet again, but corresponded for the next twelve years until Fleischmann's last illness. Fleischmann also derived consolation from the friendship of three German aristocrats who found themselves in Cork after extraordinary odysseys, having been expelled from their lands in the former Austro-Hungarian empire and in eastern Germany once these areas had been liberated from the National Socialists by the Soviet army. They were among the millions of German refugees who wandered the roads around 1945: the number of displaced persons who survived the slaughter of the war with their lives and little else came to an estimated twelve million – the most terrible exodus in the history of the world. A young baroness managed to reach Cork; she and the elderly Vera Countess of Zedtwitz[68] were looked after by the nuns in the convent in Clifton for some years before they departed for Canada in 1950. Fleischmann much admired the stoicism of the stranded nobility, as he wrote to Schaehle after their departure:

I miss these refined, cultured, warm-hearted people, the direct recent news about Germany, and our German conversations spiced with their wit and humour. Their sad fate they bear without a word of bitterness or complaint, indeed almost with cheerfulness. Their destiny is reminiscent of that of the 'wild geese', the aristocratic Irish families driven out by Cromwell into the four corners of the world, leaving nothing behind but the ruins of their castles on the hilltops and some descendents eking out a living as itinerants walking the roads of the land. They share the *fata hominem*.[69]

Post-war work with the cathedral choir

After the war, the cathedral choir continued to support Aloys Óg's work. He started out on a new venture in the field of dance, collaborating with Joan Denise Moriarty's ballet group in its first performance at the Opera House. From then on, for the next forty-five years, his Cork Symphony Orchestra was to play during the annual Ballet Week, and he to compose five ballets for Moriarty's companies.[70] In 1948, the cathedral choir performed in Borodin's *Prince Igor* dances, and for Aloys Óg's ballet, *The Golden Bell of Ko* at the Opera House. The nightly direction of the choir for the ballet performances was undertaken by Fleischmann's student, Michael Weedle, as the circumstances might have proved somewhat difficult for the elderly choirmaster – the choir sang from the wings, in the dark, the choral director standing on a box, his score illuminated by torchlight.[71] Where the performances did not involve such perilous balancing acts, the choirmaster himself officiated. Fleischmann also helped to organise the centenary celebration of the Ursuline Convent of Blackrock in Cork in September 1955. Sister M. Peter wrote to thank him after the performance:

> What can we say to you for the superb music you gave us yesterday – to us that we might offer it to the Lord of Beauty as if it were ours? And not the music alone but all the care and thought and attention you spent on us in the preparation of the Festival.
>
> The whole function was a great experience for us, and deeply enjoyed by each one of us. You will have your little boys for a practice tonight – I send up a few sweet things for them. And will you tell them again what we thought of their singing? – the men too.
>
> You were so kind and encouraging about our little choir – thank you a thousand times over for everything.[72]

The loyal, unpaid labours of the cathedral choir had to be rewarded, especially those of the boys. The choirmaster occasionally handed out sweets after choir practice; once a week, free access was granted to the cinema in the local parish hall: the number seeking entrance usually exceeded the number of boys in the choir. Choir benefactors sometimes treated the boys by sending cakes after a particularly good recital. A garden party was once given by Professor Stockley and his wife, who never failed to support the choir and attended all public performances. The choirmaster, unable to be there, had delegated an adult choir-member to supervise the guests. The behaviour of the boys did not turn out to be in keeping with the angelic sounds they produced: their exu-berance proved beyond the control of their minder and hosts. They were deemed to have disgraced themselves and the ensuing choir prac-tice proved stormy. There was no danger of such lapses during the annual party given by the cathedral administrator in the oratory of St Vincent's Convent, as the bishop was often present. Once their hunger had been stilled – with cream cakes, sticky currant buns, sandwiches and lemonade – the boys were invited to perform. This provided Fleischmann with an opportunity to assess their interests and talent so that he could offer help where it might be needed. It may often have been something of an ordeal for the young choristers, who risked being made fun of by their peers or failing to meet the choirmaster's stan-dards. Seán Barrett remembers him reproving boys who sang popular songs: '"Why do you sing these music-hall songs? Have you not got your own great Irish music? Why do you not sing your Irish songs?" If you knew a Gaelic song learned at school, or if you could step-dance, you were lauded.'[73] J.P. Cronin, a former choirboy who joined the Christian Brothers:

> At the annual Christmas party at the oratory Herr Fleischmann would pick out a few boys to sing for the bishop. They would be rewarded by receiving a banana or orange from the bishop's table. The procedure was similar at the annual outing to Rochestown. I was picked to sing on every one of these occasions, but never was I prouder than at the 1952 outing.

> During the practice the previous day, he asked if any boys played instruments. Mine was a lonely hand that emerged above the eighty heads or so in the room, and I said I played the violin. When practice finished he asked me to bring the violin along to the outing. I was abashed and said I had only been learning for nine months. He assured me that did not matter. So on the feast of Sts. Peter and Paul June 1952 I played the few tunes I knew and the boys sang. After the meal he sent for me and flattered me with congratulations, after some conversation dismissing me with the advice that when again playing for singers to make sure my key was within their range.

> That week we had one more choir practice for a mass in U.C.C. After the rehearsal he called me aside and told me that if I wanted tickets for musical concerts or financial support for my music lessons he would be only too glad to help. I was astonished at this generous

offer, but did not have the heart to tell him I was entering a Juniorate at the Christian Brothers in a little over a month. Two years later I met him again and he had not forgotten me.[74]

Evidence of interest in music could lead to the boy being offered organ lessons, as happened with Joe Cunningham, with John Reidy (as Seán Ó Riada was then called) and with James Blanc, who eventually gave up his work as a carpenter to become organist in a Dublin church. David MacInerny sang in the choir for twelve years; he too was offered special tuition:

> In the mid 1950s I took singing seriously enough to take lessons, which rewarded me with some success at Feis Maitiú. I also began a singing career with operatic, Gilbert and Sullivan and operetta companies, playing minor parts and graduating to principal parts. During this time Aloys took a personal interest in my singing and gave me singing lessons, including some at his home at Wellington Road. He also attended a number of my performances. I deeply appreciated his help and encouragement.[75]

Such tuition was given free of charge to those whose parents could not have afforded fees. Jack O'Donovan reports that Fleischmann stopped giving private tuition once he noticed that it usually led to those gifted singers being offered concerts in the city paishes, whereupon they often abandoned the cathedral choir.[76]

The summer choir excursions with the men gave Fleischmann the opportunity to get to know them better, to find out about their work and families in a relaxed and pleasant context. He clearly enjoyed those outings himself. There was singing in the bus on the way down and back. After high tea in the hotel, there was an impromptu concert, the men singing their madrigals, interspersed with solos items, to the delight of the hotel guests. The choir had quite a large repertoire of glees and madrigals, some of which were Fleischmann's compositions. Many German folk tunes and about twenty-five Irish folk songs were arranged by him for these social occasions. One chorus of his that was particularly popular with the boys was 'The Poor Little Donkey', dedicated 'To all the suffering donkeys of Ireland'. This outing marked the end of the choir year, work not resuming until the first Sunday in September. Fleischmann always seemed delighted to see the choir again: it was as if he had missed them over the holiday months.

He had a special theory or 'dogma' about the rewards in store for church choir singers. He expounded it in a letter (written in English) to Terence O'Connor on his retirement from the choir in 1947:

> Thank you for your letter, the surplice and soutane. Your resignation, and so with your departure from the Cathedral choir after 34 years

faithful service, hurts my old heart. To see members leaving their post, with whom I was so many hundreds of times united in worship and praise of the Almighty is saddening. No, we shall not forget your appreciated great help, neither your loyalty especially during the troublesome dark years. May you be rewarded for your long, voluntary membership, later on when I am no more.

It is my firm belief that those whom God gave the precious gift of a voice, and this gift is used here on earth for His honour and glory, that their souls have a better chance to reach the dimension of the singing angels, and will find a reserved corner there. Indeed, it is a pity that this, my dogma, is not the general Credo of the clergy, nor the official dogma of the Church. If that would be the case, there would not be in Éire any organ gallery large enough to hold the numerous members.

Please accept my heartfelt thanks for your faith and services, and don't forget your membership in the Cathedral choir, which embraced your boyhood as well as the half of your life.

With all good wishes to you and your family

Your old Regens chori[77]

The struggle with the cathedral administration for repairs to the damaged Walcker organ

The state of the cathedral's Walcker organ became a source of much grief to Fleischmann after the war. During the 1930s and 1940s, it suffered serious damage due to the negligence of the cathedral administration. Four administrators came and went, each having been in office for at least six years. The choirmaster requested, petitioned, implored them to have the splendid instrument properly repaired. In vain.

The heating system of the building operated through a coal furnace. When the danger of war became evident and, with it, that of interrupted coal imports, large quantities were purchased to have supplies for bad times. Great piles of coal dust were left lying around in the yard in dangerous proximity to the organ motor house. This had disastrous consequences for the instrument, as Fleischmann described in an undated draft letter (written in English) to Canon Ahern, cathedral administrator between 1949 and 1956:

> Sitting at the organ, I feel like a priest must feel who suffers from a grievous stutter and has to avoid a great number of indispensable words, thereby is continually handicapped in the delivery of his sermon. Similarly, I cannot touch whole sections of the essential notes and chords on any of the manuals otherwise they howl and scream out like tortured living beings, and the loud shrieking dissonances would painfully disturb the priest and the entire

congregation in every church service. Under such a handicap I have
to accompany Gregorian chant, which requires the most delicate
support, with swiftness and flexibility. Since years, I have managed
to cover the deplorable defects of the Cathedral organ through the
never failing choir, otherwise every sacred service would be gravely
interrupted by howling, ciphering pipes, bustling and noises.

The deplorable calamity goes back to Very Rev. Canon Cohalan's
time [1929–37]. It arose through sheer carelessness and stubborn-
ness of the immovable, most omnipotent sacristan. In spite of my
appeals and warnings, a heap of coal dust and filth was accumulated
before the badly fitted door of the motor house, and remained there.
Several times I removed it as well as I could, but in vain. It always
appeared anew. It must be remembered that dust, especially coal
dust, is for organs, what poison is to the bowels of a human being.
As I could not succeed to have the place cleaned and kept free from
dust and rubbish, in my despair, I asked the Canon to engage a
handy man to build a little wall between the lower frame of the door
(one foot high by two and a half feet wide, approximately two hours'
work). Magnanimous and well-meaning as Dr Cohalan always was
towards the Cathedral choir and to me personally, instead of
engaging a simple handy man, he engaged an architect who wrote
an official report, dismissing my proposal as a whim. The beetles and
spiders that crept in under the door, the dust and filth blown into
the corners of the little motor room did not make him wonder (igno-
rant in organ concerns) how they could have got there. The architect
obviously took his engagement in this matter as a joke, a mere trifle.
He had the last word. His word was law, the matter dropped.

Very Rev. Canon Cullinane [1937–43] succeeded Canon Cohalan. In
the meanwhile the air-sucker attached to the motor wheel had
carried day by day loads of coal dust into all the airways, channels,
and into the 5,000 pipes, which devoured the most delicate fine
leather of the mobile air-pockets fixed under each pipe. Canon
Cullinane had it in his mind to engage the original firm, E.F. Walcker
in Ludwigsburg, to repair the damage; but there were many difficulties in the way of getting a permit for foreign tradesmen! The
restoration remained a dream.

When discussing the matter with the next administrator, Canon
O'Keeffe [1943–9], Fleischmann was greatly pained, and incensed, to
hear him describe the cathedral choir as a burden to the diocese.
Fleischmann wrote at length to remonstrate and make practical suggestions for the raising of the necessary funds – estimated by him to
come to about £200. The undated draft was written (in English) in
Oileán Ruadh between 1945 and 1947:

I hope this long letter is not as painful to read, as it was to write. But
your statement about the 'enormous and colossal' outlay for the

Cathedral Choir was indeed embarrassing and new to me, since not one of your five predecessors ever mentioned it during the long years I served them. In fact, their opinion was contrary to yours. This is not surprising, since any fully paid schoolmaster under your jurisdiction draws at present – not to speak of the near future – a higher salary annually than the whole Cathedral Choir, including the organist. I would like to remind you that some of your predecessors also went through a trying time. As one, not many years ago, pointed out, he lay sometimes sleepless in his Procrustean bed, and added smilingly, but not caused by the choir 'which is always a source of satisfaction to me and to us all'. Small wonder, after nearly life-long work, and economy to the last degree, that I was spellbound to hear for the first time your repeated remarks that you find the choir an enormous burden on the Administration. I can only remind you of the indefatigable, faithful and unpaid labour of the members, young and old. 'Commovent homines non res, sed de rebus opiniones.' [Epictetus: 'It is not things that disturb men, but opinions about things.']

Canon O'Keeffe did allow repairs to be undertaken, but only on the most damaged sections of the instrument. So, as Fleischmann wrote to the canon's successor: 'as it was only a patched up job, the cure of the great, long neglected patient did not last long. My fears proved right: Canon O'Keeffe's good intention and cheque went almost for nothing.'

Canon Ahern was the seventh cathedral administrator Fleischmann had worked under. He had ample opportunity to study how they operated. He became good friends with several, and knew them from their long association with the cathedral before they were appointed to this post of highest responsibility. He had hoped that Canon Ahern would be sympathetic to his cause:

In my long association, I noticed that every Administrator is anxious to come though his period safely, as if through a tunnel. He sees to it that he does not overstep the financial outlays of his predecessor, so as to successfully reach the exit. Consequently the costly dilemma of the restoration of the organ was continually postponed and delicately laid from one shoulder to the next.

My hopes were boundless as you, dear Canon, came down from the lofty heights of Cloheen endowed with the Administratorship of the Cathedral Parish. At the first opportunity I lamented about the destruction of our great organ. Alas! soon I realised to my dismay that you have the heaviest burden to carry, heavier than all those six predecessors whom I had the honour to serve.

Fleischmann outlined how the money could be raised – the sum needed is now estimated to be £500 – citing examples of previous efforts made in the diocese and proposing that each parish organisation be asked to sponsor one aspect of the repairs or one part of the organ and to organise collections both in the parish and in the city. He was confident that the money could be found with relative ease, as the choir enjoyed wide support in the city and had 'a host of friends all over Ireland, as well as across the channel', attested, he wrote, by 'hundreds of letters in my possession, received after our broadcast performances'. In a long letter to Canon Ahern of 8 September 1952, urgently requesting small repairs in the church space in which the choir sang and in the library, he once again deplores the state of the organ. He ends with an appeal:

> Many years ago, dear Canon, you came down from the heights of Cloheen to sing with gusto the Lamentation of Jeremiah! Now, as you are high on top of us, Vah, I have to sing the Jeremiad, the woeful tale of the Cathedral choir, and lament, to soften your kind fatherly, but – administrative heart!
>
> I appeal to you to be charitable towards an old, (via radio over whole Eire) well known institution, which is upheld with much love and labour under difficult circumstances. I beg [you] to be sympathetic, and help to solve its dilemmas, so that the members feel, that the Administration does not neglect their necessary wants, and is not indifferent towards their efforts.
>
> If I had not completely lost as a result of the two wars my parents' and uncle's legacies, I would certainly not hesitate to bear the costs of repair myself, to save this worthy instrument from ruin as well as the faithful choir's hard work from being spoiled by the distorted intonation; and at last to get rid of the torture of playing on this destroyed organ which shadows and saddens the last years of my life.

No reply to any of Fleischmann's earlier letters to the administration is to be found among his papers. Dr Cornelius Lucey succeeded his 96-year-old predecessor in 1952; he responded courteously, assuring Fleischmann of the administration's appreciation of his work and that the matters he had raised would be looked into. Repairs were not undertaken on the organ until after Fleischmann's death in 1964.

Illness and a papal honour

Fleischmann had, on the whole, enjoyed robust health for most of his life, once he had recovered from the after-effects of the injury sustained while a prisoner of war. But the 1950s brought some hospital sojourns. A few months after his seventieth birthday, he had an accident at home, which he described to Schaehle:

> My accident came about through impatience. I was having the bathroom renovated. The house painter, a man of much courtesy, but more partial to his whiskey than to me, let me down, which is why I

decided to apply the splendid colours myself to the last unpainted corner. Proudly revelling in my achievement with the yellow and dark-green, I made to execute the final masterly strokes, reached out with zest, when there was a crash and I found myself on the floor like an old tree struck down by lightning – a victim of the fine arts.[78]

His Christmas letter to his friend in 1951, however, was less entertaining. He had spent seven weeks in hospital on the flat of his back in serious pain with acute sciatica. The first attack, suffered ten years previously, had been cured through cauterisation of the nerve with a hot iron. This was done three times, involving severe burning of the skin, and was extremely painful, but effective. However, the doctors now declared that method to be 'outdated' and gave him pain medication which he found ineffective and damaging to his powers of concentration. In May 1953 his wife nearly died of jaundice after surgery for gallstones. It was her first and only stay in hospital. The following March he was again hospitalised with acute sciatica and double pneumonia. He wrote to Schaehle that the doctors had given him up. But he recovered in time to conduct the Easter ceremonies. On Easter Sunday after the mass, the bishop summoned him to the high altar and, in the presence of the congregation, awarded him a papal gold medal for his forty-eight years of service to the diocese. They had probably planned this for the fiftieth anniversary of his arrival in Cork, but brought it forward because of his serious illness. He wrote to Schaehle on 17 May 1954:

> It would have been quite a pleasant affair, had it been done quietly without such a fuss being made. That sort of thing does not appeal to me. Having to stand there listening to the excessive praises and torrents of words, I didn't know whether to laugh or weep. My fingers were hurting when I got home from all the hand-shaking.

> This unexpected business cost me 163 letters of thanks (including one from the German Embassy),[79] which I could not just acknowledge with a printed card. It reminded me of my boyhood when one day the great army (consisting of fifteen boys equipped with wooden swords) appointed me their 'general' to be addressed as 'Your Excellency' and adorned my proud chest with a shiny brass cross! I was proud then of the glittering ornament. But times have changed.

On the creative urge

Schaehle had lost his much-loved wife during the war: she had died of cancer after long illness and great suffering. After the war he was not reinstated in his school, despite the acute shortage of teachers, but merely allowed to teach on a part-time basis until the staff had returned from the prisoner-of-war camps, whereupon his services were dispensed with. Instead of being honoured and welcomed back into the school as a man of integrity who had accepted serious hardship rather than join an iniquitous political party, his dismissal by the Nazis was allowed to stand. His former colleagues probably felt uncomfortable in his presence: not only the many party activists, but also those who had joined unwillingly, since he was living proof that they had had a choice, albeit a very hard one. During the first years of their renewed correspondence, Schaehle frequently wrote of his disheartenment, anger and disgust at developments in Germany, and reported that he had ceased to write or paint. Fleischmann remonstrated energetically with him, insisting that anyone endowed with such gifts must continue to be creatively active until the end. He argued repeatedly that Schaehle was blessed with his intelligent and caring daughter and that alone for her sake, he had a duty to resist depression. The encouragement given to his friend provides interesting insight into his own creative work, and his perception of it. On 1 January 1950 he wrote:

> Of course, at our age we only slowly come to terms with loss. The darkness can but with difficulty be removed from the wounds – beloved faces and forms do not pale. Untouched by transience, they live in our hearts; a tired sense of pessimism, as dangerous as disease, seeks to establish itself. But this must be fought at all costs. We must remain active, though the field of activity is not decisive: otherwise brooding idleness brings a gradual decline, often accompanied by sickness, before we take leave of this planet. And that is not a pleasant or desirable ending. 'The mind forms the body' – it also preserves the body! Let us take those blessed by God, the great ones, as our example. With few exceptions, none of them put the pen away. None laid down the brush, the chisel until it fell out of their hands. Most of the joys which our lives brought us in our youth and early manhood belong to the past. One becomes modest, indeed very modest, with the years and what remains to us is just this: – continuing to work in the customary manner within the limitations of our talent, of which we are now acutely aware. 'Genius is sufficient unto itself.' But not only genius, talent too brings, with the joy of creating, oblivion of the world. That can bring happiness, sometimes great happiness, and make what remains of our lives worth living. Let us take for ourselves Lord Byron's epitaph: 'Her talents were of the more silent class.'

In reply, Schaehle wrote that he could see no point in continuing to write given that there was no interest in his work and no chance of publication, that his painting and writing was a pure pastime, if not a waste of time. On 17 February 1950 Fleischmann urges him to continue working for his own sake and to realise how valuable his gift is.:

> If I were you I would not term your artistic activities insubstantial playing around [*wesenslose Spielerei*]. Of course, if you think about it,

that is what every form of artistic creativity is, as existence is half dream and has to do with fantasy, visions and shadows – a play into the non-existent. . . .

Just imagine your life deprived of all that: how impoverished it would have been and how barren the path we still have to take if we did not have this palliative, the intoxication of creating or whatever you want to call it. A farmer from the village of Webling I once met as he staggered home, merry due to the drink he had taken, said to me: 'Let me tell you, me dear fella, it's great to be a bit drunk now and again. It gives you new courage. After all, you have to get something out of life, don't you?'[80]

He regards drunken intoxication as the most sublime – and we the intoxication of a vision as the highest. Look back with pride on your artistic work. Compare your life with that of your colleagues who were not endowed with this gift. And you fortunate man, you have 'a little flower in your garden' which you must look after and care for! So nothing for it but continue to work, and look forward to the future with hope and trust!

There is no condescension in the account given of the small farmer from the neighbouring hamlet whose life of unremitting toil is temporarily transformed through an occasional visit to the inn: Fleischmann recognises himself in him and sees the similarity of their needs. In a second example of the need to escape limitations, he underlines the differences between himself and his renowned composer friend Bax:

I have for many years had a faithful, devoted friend. A writer of symphonies. Arnold Bax is his name. Lives in London, is knighted, celebrated, Elgar's successor as 'Master of the King's Musick' etc. Yet not happy. I have spent many summer months in his company. He has often told how much he – envies me! For a long time I could not understand it. One can probably sum it up like this: he seeks in greatness what he cannot reach, while I in my limitations reach in small things what I am not looking for. He drinks from the ocean and becomes thirstier since his instinct – he calls it his disease – compels him to. I drink out of my tiny spring in which the little herb contentment grows. He will live; I shall not. His works (among which are great and splendid ones) will be preserved as treasures and enrichment of musical literature. I have already in my will bequeathed my paltry bundles to the kitchen to be used as kindling for the fire. So what? I found in them my lonely exhilarations of the imagination – and they were beautiful, 'me dear fella'! What more can one want?

Six years later, he paints a picture of himself lost in the world of sounds, fascinated by their relationships and constantly experimenting with composition:

I have been too long silent. Forgive me: it was not due to lack of feeling for you, my esteemed friend. Time runs through my fingers like water. 'The disease', as Arnold Bax called composing, absorbs all the hours, days and weeks and prevents me from coming to my senses and being reasonable. Then come the duties of my two posts and many others. They say that as you get older, you become wiser. My personal experience has been that one becomes more foolish and enmeshed in one's customary vices. I am addicted, not to drink, but to music. A disease almost as bad as alcoholic stupefaction. I often feel like a lonely chess player brooding endlessly over the figures, interested in problems bordering on infinity, just as acoustic mathematics and their enigmatic relationships fascinate me. I cannot account for this aimless day-dreaming and wasting of time. 'It is a disease.' If I am not checkmated and if, due to simple-mindedness, the result turns out to be tolerable, I am pleased for a day or two, lay the piece aside on the pile of music with the other silent ones and take no further notice of it. One thing is certain: I am not plagued by ambition! My philosophy of life resembles that of the sparrow outside the window: it is not pessimistic. I remember pleasant things, forget the unpleasant. For me the world is not a vale of tears. Existence is no tragedy, aberration, guilt. I know no moods in which things and events only appear negative or evil. Am no gloomy pessimist – though no Elysian either, or trusting heir to heaven – i.e. am a pro forma Catholic although baptised, brought up in the shadow of the church and *my* holiness even honoured in the most distant corner of Europe by *his* Holiness for virtues unknown to me. 'The world is queer' – our old housekeeper's favourite saying.[81]

Friends and family

A German visitor

The recluse was sometimes persuaded to leave his study for outings with his grandchildren. One memorable occasion was his seventieth birthday, when he ascended Mount Brandon, the second highest mountain of Ireland, on a very chilly 24 April 1950 with his son and three grandchildren. Sometimes his work at home was interrupted by visitors. In October of that year he had an unannounced guest from Germany: Schaehle's daughter Hildegard. She had made her way to Scotland to see a friend, took the ferry to Belfast, and hitch-hiked down to Cork. She had not given notice of her plans, as Fleischmann had advised her father against permitting such a journey in what he considered perilous times. It so happened that the student was given lifts by two former choir members, so she was delivered right to the front door. However, the Fleischmanns were not at home; the housekeeper did not allow her to come in and wait, obviously not giving much credence to her story. Hildegard found a bed in a Protestant hostel until she found her father's friend at home the following morning. In a letter to Hildegard's father, Fleischmann explained why the housekeeper had been so suspicious:

> Shortly before your daughter arrived, a policeman called to the house and asked to speak to Prince Georg of Saxony (grandson of the last king), who was allegedly living with us. He said the poor young man had come to Cork a beggar and had been admitted to a hospital. Countess Vera von Zedtwitz, likewise a homeless refugee, had called in great haste just before her departure to America to tell us about him, and said he had come to Cork to continue his medical studies. She asked us to look after the unfortunate youth. That is why the poor man gave our address to the police. My wife instructed our housekeeper, Hannah, that if a beggar called, he was to be treated with kindness, invited in and she was to be immediately informed of his arrival. And sure enough, next morning the bell rang, and there was a beggar on the doorstep. Hannah bowed to him, and brought him into the drawing room. My wife appeared and greeted the ragged pauper with much deference, as she believed those impoverished through no fault of their own deserved particular sympathy and more respect than those with wealth and royal splendour. It gradually became clear that the man she had taken to be His Royal Highness was in fact a poor sick beggar, who was surprised and astounded at the courtly welcome. The astonishment was mutual! (It occurred to me later that the courteous welcome was probably quite appropriate for it is well known that the beggars and travelling people here are mostly descendants of the nobility driven from their lands and castles by Cromwell and who have since then had to survive by begging for bread and alms and eking out a miserable existence travelling the roads of Ireland.) And your little daughter arrived the very next evening after this incident. We trust that Fräulein Hildegard has forgiven us.[82]

Hildegard Schaehle recorded her impressions of the family in her diary. Fleischmann cancelled as many of his classes as possible to have time for her; he took her to see the university, and gave her a special performance on the harmonium in the Honan Chapel, which moved her greatly. During a trip to Blarney, he talked about his youth; at home, he played his settings of her father's poems and was gratified by her interest. To her surprise, she was taken to the cinema by Tilly, who told her how they loved the art cinema club recently founded, where they were at last able to see good continental films. She was amused at Fleischmann's typical 'Munich grumbling' over Irish casual ways, and at his derisive comments on his wife's habit of breakfasting in bed – she had not had breakfast with him more than a dozen times during their long married life. Hildegard found in Tilly a lady from a world long gone rather like that of the *Forsythe Saga*, an excellent conversationalist, her artist's sense of theatre now second nature, with every coming into a room a stage entrance.

Fleischmann accompanied his guest to Dublin – it was his first visit to the capital since 1939. The reason for the visit was a Bax concert on 17 October 1950 given in the Phoenix Hall by Aloys Óg with the Radio Éireann Symphony Orchestra. They played Bax's *Concertante for Orchestra and Piano Left Hand,* with Harriet Cohen as soloist, and his Third Symphony. Hildegard noted that at the concert Fleischmann was greeted by large numbers of people, all obviously delighted to see him.

She had grown up in an anti-fascist family, and fully accepted the view of the Allied forces now presented everywhere in Germany: that they had come at great sacrifice to liberate a misguided, guilty, captive people. She was astonished that nobody she spoke to in Ireland had any respect for the American or British armies and their role in the war, though they were all appalled by the reports of the crimes of the Nazis – they told her that during the war they had taken such accounts to be British propaganda. She was utterly astounded that neither Fleischmann nor his daughter-in-law approved of the Nuremberg trials, that they thought it shameful that the Germans had been deprived of the opportunity to try the Nazi leaders themselves. She had understood from the German newspapers that foreigners were shocked by reports that the Germans were not particularly interested in the trials and not over-concerned to see justice done – this was quite a new perspective. She defended the Allies, describing the terrible state Germany was in and explaining that people in such despair might not have taken action against their former leaders, being too concerned with mere survival. She did not convince them, and concluded that Fleischmann's views on Germany and Allied policy were too coloured by Irish nationalist perspectives, that he seemed to see Germany as being colonised by the victorious Allies.

Some time after Hildegard's departure, the Fleischmanns finally met the royal refugee:[83]

> For a while we heard nothing more. After a symphony concert in the university an enthusiastic member of the audience came up to congratulate my son. He introduced himself to us – it was the 'beggar' we had been expecting, now most elegantly attired. As he told us later on, his aunt, the Archduchess of L[uxembourg], had sent him the clothes. From then on he often came to the house to play chess with me. A distinguished, most cultured young man, who wanted to finish his studies in medicine here. His experiences, adventures and tribulations, he said, would fill a book. In comparison to such fates, our circumstances are comfortable. But we can learn a great deal from these harassed, impoverished people. Used to luxury, they must now lead lives of humiliating penury. They accept this with patience, with humility, without a word of complaint. Admirable, too, is their sensitivity and tact, which allows them to adapt to every situation,

and furthermore an innate, natural modesty in their dealings with others. He would not allow his title to be used and asked me after a short time to address him by his first name. But I could not do that. I live in the past, and respect for the ancient dynasty is second nature to me, even if the crown at present lies in the dust.

Now the Christmas holidays are long over and he whose distinguished character and physiognomy are so striking has not returned. Nobody has had news of him. Strange! Before his departure, he told me that since his flight a stranger has been following him everywhere, who appears again and again, but disappears whenever he tries to speak to him. I do hope that nothing has happened to the good-natured man. These days all sorts of things are possible, here on these islands, too.

No further mention of him was found among the Fleischmann papers: it would seem that he was never heard of again.

A piece of satire on five-fold grandfatherhood

Fleischmann's last grandchild was born on 23 June 1952. A letter to Schaehle written three weeks later is exceptional in that he not only writes about personal family matters, but is quite scathing about his daughter-in-law and about Irish notions of their gentility in general. The baby was christened James Alan, the first name being that of his maternal grandfather:

I have been a five-fold grandpapa for the past few weeks! Pentatonality now pervades my son's 'Glen House'. I pitied the helpless creature when it was shown to me. Now this little stranger must, like us, journey through the world of light and shadow towards an unknown goal. At his mother's suggestion, the boy was given a considerable number of names, I suspect in order to underline her ancient lineage. I cannot remember them all, but they include: James, Rathagar, Vocht, Benjamin, Melchisadech, Caspar, Melchior and Baltasar, Buxtehude, Theodorus, Carolus, Gregorii, Henrici, Hyronymi, Petritici, Caesari, Leoni, Peter and Paul, Philippi, Rochi, Wenzel, Isidori, Hilarii, Isaac etc. as well as many others to be found in the druidic and Jewish calendars. As I am sure you know, every old Irish family likes to imagine it belongs to the nobility and claims to be directly descended from the heroic king, Brian Boru. This is quite possible, as the said gentleman had over three hundred women and thousands of children. Which proves that he was not only brave in battle, but also a hero in bed. Even a daughter of Pharaoh married one of these courageous kings so experienced with women. Colourful as a butterfly is the history of this country, for shipping connects. At my request the announcing of the birth with twenty-one canon salutes was dispensed with, as I loathe shooting.

This cascade of scorn is reminiscent of some of the diatribes in old Irish literature, in which the poet's anger is dissipated by the virtuosity of the abuse. The first son had been called Aloys Neil, and was the fourth in succession of the family to carry the name Aloys. It was surely fitting that the second son should be named after his mother's family. Perhaps the real cause of this epistolary volley was displeasure at the number of children Aloys Óg was producing – both Fleischmann's father and he himself had made do with one. The account of the christening celebration is pure fiction:

> Mother and child are well, which is the best part of the whole event. That and the fact that the champagne was excellent reconciled me with the celebrations. I delivered the speech and included a few comments, for instance that from the pulpit the cuckoo cries encouragingly: 'Increase and multiply!' Very easy to do. However, not quite such a simple matter for the breadwinner, etc. My speech did not meet with general approval among the many relatives – 'who can count the numbers, or name the names of those who came'! But that was of no concern to me. Only a few cousins, overburdened fathers of large families, slapped me on the back, praised my speech and shared my view.

He had some reason to be disgruntled, as the growth of his son's family was to bring him considerable inconvenience during his summer break:

> In August I shall be buried alive in Kerry. I am not looking forward to it. What can I do but try to grin and bear the ordeal. The new baby and its mother will not be coming, but my wife and Aloys (who wants to finish his piano concerto there) will be going with four children, 3, 6, 8 and 10 years old. The exodus out of Egypt will be like a tinker's caravan travelling around the country with all belonging to them. Only the tinker's caravan will be missing on the journey (eight hours by car) and the donkey – though not the latter, for that is us! A place by the sea less far away would have been a much wiser choice on account of the small children – in case of illness and so on – than such a remote primitive fishing village in the most westerly corner of Europe. But what can you do if you are a five-fold grandfather! You think you're driving, but you're being driven!

A great deal was indeed being asked of the seventy-two-year-old grandfather. The family was to stay in the MacSwiney cottage near Dunquin on the Dingle peninsula. The Ford Model T car, which Aloys Óg had borrowed from his kind uncle-in-law, could not make great speed on the narrow, bumpy roads of Kerry of those days, in particular given the load it had to transport: three adult and four half-size passengers plus luggage for a month. Fleischmann was going to have to act as nursemaid to four lively small children in a cottage which, though charming and surrounded by the most glorious scenery, had none of the comforts of city life such as running water, inside lavatory and electricity. He will, perhaps, have found some compensation in the good company of the neighbours: both the residents, whom the family had known for decades, and the scholarly visitors staying in the area.

The death of Arnold Bax

In 1953, Fleischmann lost his friend of twenty-five years' standing, Arnold Bax. Bax died in Aloys Óg's house during a visit to Cork as external examiner to the music department of the university. His unexpected death left Fleischmann in 'emotional turmoil', as Franz Schaehle interpreted the account he was given of the sad event. But once Fleischmann had recovered from the shock, he and his wife may have found comfort in the knowledge that the circumstances of their friend's death corresponded to an astonishing degree with his own wishes.

Bax died one month before his seventieth birthday. The foreword to his autobiography *Farewell, My Youth* is introduced by Yeats' lines:

> 'What shall I do with this absurdity –
> O heart, O troubled heart – this caricature,
> Decrepit age that has been tied to me
> As to a dog's tail?'

The foreword is entitled 'My hard curse upon increasing age', and begins: 'If I live to be seventy I shall celebrate that birthday by abusing old age with a malevolence even more savage than that evinced by Yeats in the bitter and splendid poem I have quoted.' There was no malevolence or bitterness in the end. A few days before his death he heard his music played by the Radio Éireann Symphony Orchestra, conducted by Aloys Óg. That Bax evening in the Phoenix Hall in Dublin began with the *Overture to Adventure*; the *Concertante for Orchestra and Piano Left Hand* was performed by his friend Harriet Cohen, for whom the piece was written; the last work was *The Garden of Fand*, inspired by the Irish legend of the sea-goddess, whose garden was a place of eternal youth and bliss. This orchestral poem was one of the many Irish pieces Bax wrote. He said of this phase of his life:

> I think I may claim, in all modesty, that I was the first to translate the hidden Ireland into musical terms and all this I owed in the first place to Yeats. His was the key that opened the gate of the Celtic wonderland and his the finger that pointed to the Magic Mountain whence I was to dig nearly all that may be of value in my own art. Neither does my debt to that great man end there: for his poetry has always meant more to me than all the music of the centuries. All the days of my life I bless his name.[84]

Bax's love of the sea had been heightened during the decade in which he stayed in Glencolumcille in Donegal for long periods, summer and winter, where the people accepted the fluent speaker of Irish as one of themselves:

> I like to fancy that on my deathbed my last vision in this life will be the scene from my window on the upper floor at Glencolumcille, of the still, brooding, dove-grey mystery of the Atlantic at twilight; the last glow of sunset behind Glen Head in the north, with its ruined watch-tower built in 1812 at the time of the scare of a Napoleonic invasion; and east of it the calm slope of Scraig Beefna, its glittering many-coloured surface of rock, bracken, and heather, now one uniform purple glow.

His wish to die in Ireland came true, that country which he 'loved better than any land"beneath the visiting moon"'.[85] His last view of the sea off the southern coast was very similar to the vision described above, as Aloys Óg recounted in a BBC interview:

> What happened was that he was a visiting examiner to our College and when the examinations were finished he was taken by a friend of his to the old Head of Kinsale. It was in the evening, there was a marvellous sunset and he stood at the very tip of the old Head looking out into the west. Now he says in his autobiography that he would like to think that upon his death-bed his last vision would be the deep, brooding, dove-grey mysterious Atlantic. I cannot but think that while he was standing there he must have remembered the performance of *The Garden of Fand* which we had just had in Dublin a few days previously – which I actually conducted with the Radio Éireann Symphony Orchestra – and I do feel that when he looked out into the Atlantic there the whole background of *Fand* must have been in his mind because he was lost in thought and finally had to be aroused from his reveries and brought home. Within a couple of hours he was dead: heart failure.[86]

Bax was buried in Cork in St Finbarr's cemetery. He lies in the 'musicians' corner', next to the Fleischmanns, the Neesons, Charles Lynch and Joan Denise Moriarty; his headstone was made by his friend Séamus Murphy. A commemorative service was held for Bax in St Martin-in-the-Fields on 20 October 1953 at which Anne Fleischmann represented the family.[87] In 1956, the Bax family and Harriet Cohen donated Bax scores, books and personal effects, including his piano, to the music department of the university, on condition that a Bax Room be established in which they were to be exhibited. The composer, Ralph Vaughan Williams, Bax's sister, Evelyn, and Harriet Cohen were present at the opening. (Vaughan Williams delivering the first Bax Memorial Lecture.)

Worries and consolations in the family

Another old friend died in May 1955 under tragic circumstances: J.B. Horgan, brother of the solicitor and husband of Rita Wallace. Fleischmann had known him for over thirty years, was very fond of him, a regular visitor in his beautiful house, and conversed with him in German. He composed a special wedding piece for the marriage of Horgan's daughter. Horgan fell while fishing in a flooded river and was swept away: his body was not found for a week. In a letter to Schaehle Fleischmann wrote: 'He was a highly respected eye, ear and throat specialist who studied in Vienna and Munich. He was a good and kindly friend. Many of the poor will mourn his passing.'[88]

In June 1956, Aloys Óg went to London to be treated for chronic headaches by the American osteopath who had cured his wife's back trouble, from which she had suffered for years. He had begun to suffer from headaches as a student in Cork; the pain level increased during his studies in Munich, possibly because of the strain imposed by the rigorous courses. There he had first informed his parents of the problem, as he had to ask them to pay the cost of consulting a specialist. He was not cured and the knowledge of the condition caused his parents much distress: his father asked two professors whom he knew well (Berberich and Ursprung) to watch over his son, which the young man may have found embarrassing. It would seem that the elder Fleischmanns only realised when Aloys Óg took off for London that the problem had persisted for twenty years. They had frequently admonished him for overworking: during the summer of 1949 Aloys Óg received a letter from his father warning against the perils thereof, but the letter was jocular and witty, though real concern is evident that damage can arise:

> through incessant overwork, too much cycling, incessant rushing around, too little rest and not enough moderation, too little sleep and too much gulping down of meals, through endless letter-writing which produces gases in the brain and throws the writer's mental capacity into the letter-box from whence it will not re-emerge. Furthermore ... through long conversations held after rehearsals and performances while the talker, dripping with perspiration, stands in draughty doors or near open windows, making pretty compliments and saying all sorts of nice things. Finally the exhausted, selfless 'dasher' cycles off heavily burdened into the cold air of a rainy night, because the bus is too slow for him and he still has to write and post important letters to all parts of Ireland.[89]

But in the mid 1950s, the tone changes. The osteopath had discovered from her patient that he had had a motor-bike accident as a student, and had not had the injury treated to avoid upsetting his parents. The damage was no longer reparable. The patient's father wrote of his worries to Schaehle:

My peace of mind is constantly disrupted by my son's mad, feverish
pace, his risky ventures, efforts, agitations which undermine his
health. He is perpetually tormented by new plans that increase his
workload still further and overstretch and overtax his nerves and his
strength. One ordeal is scarcely over when the next arrives, robbing
him of his sleep.[90]

In the summer of 1957, Fleischmann wrote a lengthy epistle to his
son, who was on holiday in Kerry with the family, imploring him to
reduce his workload. It ends:

I have to laugh – the 'moderation' I set out to practise has already
brought me to page 14 of this letter! Forgive me. But as we never talk
things out honestly, openly and in friendship – and never have done
so in all your life – love takes the place of friendship, and love knows
no bounds! I know full well that this letter will not give you pleasure,
as nobody likes to look at a distorted image of themselves in a mirror
or to be shown such an image, even if it is well meant. You might
perhaps take it from your mother, but not from the Boss, who is
always growling and who would be better off looking after himself.
['*The boss*' *was the term used by Hannah Hurley when speaking of
Fleischmann; it was jocularly used by the family, too.*][91]

Needless to say, such exhortations proved fruitless: Aloys Óg did not
abandon any of his causes and campaigns and could not, therefore,
reduce the burden of his work. However, the elder Fleischmann on
occasion urged his son to further activity, namely to more composition.
Aloys Óg's *Clare's Dragoons* was performed by the London Symphony
Orchestra, conducted by Maurice Myles with the BBC Singers and
broadcast on the BBC on 16 June 1957:[92]

Dear Son, Your work is a fiery affair which sweeps non-patriots as
well. A sure hand leads to a magnificent climax and fills one with
enthusiasm to the end. It is a most successful piece which will not
fade quickly and which raises the patriotic text shining like a
burning torch to the skies. It reminded me of the Dublin performance at which K. van Hock (who was sitting behind me) at the end
shouted so loudly with enthusiasm that he put the heart across me.
Hearty congratulations. May this success stimulate you to new
work. There can be no doubt that your composition was the best
structured, most interesting opus of the evening of Irish composers.
Good luck for the future.[93]

The last surviving letter to Tilly shows that, however difficult
Fleischmann may have found his life as an exile, his relationship with
his wife provided him in his old age with riches of an indestructible
nature:

2.IV.1956

My beloved Tilly –

My heartiest congratulations on your 74th birthday

May the preserver of all life, the almighty God, bless you with good health for all your devoted love and goodness on our long journey through this world of dreams, light and shadow which is drifting towards eternity. You are surrounded by my love, that of our son, and by the love of the grandchildren. We are all linked in a bond of harmony and an indestructible sense of belonging together – a happy family. You are our constant focal point with your tireless kindliness and your zeal in seeking to perfect your art. In good times and bad we look up to you whilst the children grow and the years pass. We all have the feeling that as long as you are with us, no harm can come to us. For you are a child of spring: the source of happiness for us all, and like spring, the bringer of ever renewed warmth and growth. Capricious fate, beloved Tilly, has made us rich in our old age, has endowed our modest lives with pleasures which make life worth living and the 74th anniversary of your birth radiates bright sunshine. May the Heavens continue to be merciful to you and to us all.

In veneration and love

Your Aloys

A last collaboration and a flowering of choral music

For a decade after the beginning of the cold war, Europeans lived in fear of a nuclear holocaust. The annihilation of the cities of Hiroshima and Nagasaki in 1945 had demonstrated the capability of mass destruction now in the hands of the American government, which was soon to come into the possession of that of the Soviet Union, of Britain and France. A series of crises seemed to be keeping the world poised on the brink of a third global war: the Soviet blockade of Berlin in 1948, the Korean War of 1950–53, the Soviet suppression of the Hungarian rising in 1956, the American-Soviet confrontation over nuclear missiles on Cuba in 1962. The testing of nuclear bombs continued. The unusually bad weather, even by Irish standards, during the post-war decade led to widespread fears concerning the impact of these tests on climate and health. Fleischmann wrote to Schaehle of the ice-cold May of 1955, telling him that Irish coastal dwellers were convinced that atomic testing had changed the direction of the Gulf Stream, causing abnormal cold, occasional unnatural heat, drought and storms of terrifying violence. The high unemployment and poverty of the country led to the emigration of 30,000 young people every year during that decade. Like so many others, Fleischmann was deeply pessimistic about the *condition humaine* and sought solace by submerging himself in the past, as he wrote at Easter 1952:

> Our dismal present brings one to sing tenfold the praises of the past and to cherish and retain its memory. For this miserable world seems

to be the gravedigger of the beautiful and sublime, to feed on cruelties, vileness and brutality, to foster in word and image pleasure in
killing and in viciousness, to sustain the cults of war and hatred –
thus preparing the ground once again for the another slaughtering
of millions, as if this were perfectly normal.[94]

He was profoundly disturbed by the popular culture of the 1950s –
mystified by accounts of German *'Halbstarken'* or English teddy boys
tearing the cinemas apart during rock'n'roll films and appalled by
cinema newsreels showing girls screaming in hysterical frenzy during
pop-star shows. Yet the decade was to bring an unexpected flowering of
Irish traditional music, partly initiated by one of his students, and of
secular choral music, bringing a last period of collaboration with his son.

In 1952 a national festival, or Tóstal, was inaugurated by the Minister of Industry and Commerce, Seán Lemass, as part of an effort to
end economic depression, to stimulate innovation and build a tourist
industry. It opened up the country to European cultural influences,
anticipating the economic ties to come twenty years later with Ireland's
accession to the European Community. Under the auspices of Cork's
city council, the business community, sports organisations and arts
groups participated in the city's first three-week festival in 1953. A performance of Handel's *Messiah* in Cork by Sir John Barbirolli's Hallé
Orchestra and Our Lady's Choral Society of Dublin was organised by
the Cork Orchestral Society. The cathedral choir took part in the festival
with a recital in the Honan Chapel on 24 April 1953, Fleischmann's
seventy-third birthday. The Tóstal was to continue until 1960. Whereas
the University Art Society had brought small ensembles from the continent to Cork in the 1920s and 1930s, the city's Tóstal committee (with
government funding and generous private sponsorship)[95] brought
some of the world's greatest orchestras and soloists. Fleischmann was
particularly delighted by the visit of the Bavarian Bamberg Symphony
Orchestra, as he wrote to Schaehle in April 1957:

> We had never before heard of the Bamberg Symphony Orchestra
> (the city of Amadeus Hoffmann) when it arrived to give a concert.
> We were surprised by its outstanding achievements. The Vienna
> Philharmonic and the London, Boston and Hallé Orchestras who
> were heard here were impressive, but did not make as lasting an
> impression as this splendid provincial orchestra. Every Bavarian
> should be proud to have such an outstanding cultural institution. We
> were all astounded and delighted. Keilberth, the conductor, told us
> how badly they had been treated in England. Their passports were
> taken away from them as in times of war. They had great difficulty in
> getting to Scotland. Their performances were merely given a few
> lines in the press.[96]

The visits of such orchestras could not continue indefinitely, the costs being too high. But cultural contact with the European continent was created on a permanent basis with the founding of Cork International Choral and Folk Dance Festival in 1954 and the Cork Film Festival two years later, both of which are still flourishing today.

Such festivals were not creations of the moment: the foundations had been built during decades of dedicated work, especially in the case of the Choral Festival. The Department of Education appointed the first inspector of music in independent Ireland, Donnchadh Ua Braoin, in 1932. He managed against enormous odds to establish choral singing in the primary schools, despite having only three assistants to work with 5,400 schools and half a million pupils.[97] In 1932 the former cathedral choir member, Pilib Ó Laoghaire,[98] began his indefatigable work to promote choral singing in the small towns and villages of Munster, where it was virtually unknown. As county music organiser of the Cork Vocational Education Committee, he travelled 250 miles per week to work with the twenty-three choirs he founded – during the war years the mode of transport was the bicycle. He started a choral festival in Coachford in 1946, which was attended by up to 400 choristers annually in the early 1950s; the setting up of a schools' choir festival, Cór Fhéile na Scol, was a further major achievement. When the Cork International Choral Festival began in 1954, Pilib's choirs constituted the basis. In the first international competition, his Cork Leeside Choir, Cór Cois Laoí, tied for second place with the Italian Puccini Choir, coming just behind the German winner. Fleischmann reported to Schaehle:

> We had an international choral week here – most interesting. Large numbers of choirs – the Italians were very good. But the Dortmund choir won to wild tumultuous applause. Its young conductor came to me and wept for joy. The next morning they wended their way to the boat, singing and carrying the well-deserved trophy – a large shield – together with a hundred pounds sterling in their pockets.[99]

He served on the festival's artistic advisory board for ten years; his son was festival chairman from 1953 until 1967, and then director for twenty years.

The Choral Festival had a significant impact on the members of the cathedral choir. The great masterpieces of church music had been their daily fare. They had never heard these sung anywhere else: the radio broadcasts of such music were generally their own, and very few members had gramophone records in those days. Now, during the festival, some of the outstanding continental choirs performed the music with which the Cork cathedral choristers had been familiar since childhood. In this new encounter, the beauty of the music struck them forcibly; they also realised that their interpretation and performance could well stand comparison with those of the visiting choirs. The cathedral choir could not participate in the festival, as the competition for church choirs was not introduced until 1977. However, some choir members felt sufficiently encouraged to found secular choirs of their own or to join such choirs. The cathedral choir augmented the Ursuline Past Pupils' Choir, conducted by Geraldine Neeson, at the first performance of Fleischmann Junior's choral dance suite, *Bata na bPlanndála* [The Planting Stick] at the Festival of 1957.

Local choirs, national choirs competed, compared standards, formed friendships. One of the festival's aims was to foster small choirs, particularly in rural areas and in small towns, by establishing special competitions for them. Adjudicators were briefed to encourage by providing detailed written comments with constructive criticism. The festival encouraged choirs to study the folk song heritage, and created incentives for Irish composers to write for choirs. Fleischmann was party to discussions about an important innovation: the establishment of a seminar on contemporary choral music to be hosted by the university. Distinguished foreign and Irish composers were to be commissioned, their works analysed and performed at the seminar and then presented to the public at the festival. He was too ill to attend the first seminar in 1962 at which *Ceathramhaintí Éagsúla* by Seán Ó Riada was given its first performance by Pilib Ó Laoghaire's Cór Cois Laoí, together with compositions by Henk Badings, Darius Milhaud and Edmund Rubbra.

The Cork International Choral Festival realised the aims of the Munster Society of Arts in a manner no doubt far exceeding the expectations of its founders in 1924. Despite Fleischmann's worries about the added burden which the festival placed on his son's shoulders, it must have been a cause of much pride during his final years to see what his son had helped to achieve and to know that his own work had not been without influence in this regard. He also lived to see the beginning of the great revival of Irish traditional music, brought about in no small measure by his former student, Seán Ó Riada. Fleischmann knew of the success of the Claddagh record company, established in 1959, of Ó Riada's group, Ceoltóiri Cualann, founded in 1961, and of the Chieftains, formed in 1962. As Bax had so ardently desired, Irish music, of the traditional field, was beginning its journey to the countries of the world which Irish literature had undertaken with such success forty years previously.

During his last years of service at the cathedral, when his strength was beginning to fail him, Fleischmann was given much assistance by two members of the choir and by one of his students. Edward Evans, the leading tenor, who had sung in the choir for thirty-five years, often took practices. The organist of Blackpool parish church, Margaret Hickey, frequently deputised at the cathedral: she had been a pupil of Fleischmann's, for many years acted as his copyist and had an almost filial devotion to him. Fleischmann's other organ assistant often drove him to the cathedral for services and from 1960 also helped by taking choir practices. The long walk to the cathedral had become taxing for the eighty-year-old. Jerome O'Callaghan, who had joined the choir as a boy in the 1940s, was listening to music in the front room of his house near the cathedral one Sunday morning in the early 1960s when he saw somebody sit down on his window-sill. To his astonishment, he realised it was Fleischmann. He opened the window quietly, and turned up the volume of the Schubert Impromptu No. 3. It may have been the last time the choirmaster walked to work, having found the exertion of climbing the hill too much for him.

The letters to Franz Schaehle written between 1957 and 1961 document increasing ill-health, and a growing sense of alienation from the world. Yet there is also evidence of Fleischmann's continued interest in the development of ideas and the discoveries being made by scientists in a wide range of fields.

In October 1957 he wrote that he had been ill for six weeks, not with Asian flu, but with a version which an international medical conference at Stuttgart had dubbed 'atomic flu', which brought him utter weakness. He wrote of the alarmingly bad weather, of masses of dead fish being washed up on shores, which the fishermen attributed to atomic testing. In December of the following year, he described the terrible summer of 1958, that he had caught Asian flu and suffered from depression. However, in July 1959 he was thankful to be so well compared to many others of his age, and described his fascination at the astounding images being discovered in the 'book of nature':

> At the moment I am reading about 'The Immensity of the Universe'. About stars, planets, illuminated heavenly bodies, 'Theories of Origin', 'Living Molecules. Fundamental Biological Mechanisms', incredible infinities with flaming life. Billions of shining, glowing, enormously large globes, which like coloured soap bubbles, seem to be a bright game of the creator, and with their splendid, overwhelming variety and mathematically limited freedom, numb our limited senses. (Too much of this could throw one off one's balance!) And yet stupid humans shout for yet more miracles and travel to – Lourdes!!

In December 1959 he announced to his friend that old age had really settled in: he had given up smoking. He did so in the vain hope of persuading his wife to follow suit after the discovery of a link between tobacco consumption and lung cancer. That month another bond with Dachau was severed: Dora Ziegler died, the singer who had performed so many of his lieder, the daughter of the brewer who had sponsored his nativity plays. In May 1960, he sketched his condition:

As a grievous sinner goes to his Easter duty, so do I come to you, to thank you for your fidelity and your kind letter. As it is at our age and this stage of our journey through life: one is always a bit tired. The energy is lacking, the receptiveness of our younger days, the buoyancy of a strong sense of joy in life. On the present monotonous, lonely road, Lady Melancholy often takes my arm, accompanying me for long stretches. Last month I crossed over stealthily into my eightieth year! With so many years on one's back one becomes worn out and strangely modest – without grumbling. One friend after the other disappears. One is already used to disappointments, abandons hope and reads Schopenhauer.[100]

He mourned the abandoning of the old liturgy: 'Easter is over, thank God. Those new ceremonies come nowhere near the traditional accustomed ones (with the splendid Lamentations of the prophets, the 'Tenebrae' which encompassed a number of old masterpieces of the art) with regard to sublime solemnity and emotional depth.' In November 1960 he wrote of his declining energy and disillusionment with the road taken by the arts:

One just dies like a leaf on the tree: slowly but inexorably and one actually becomes used to it! Even to this constant tiredness – which seems to be in the air. Pleasures which gave zest to life have gradually disappeared; loneliness has moved in and envelopes one. One allows oneself to drift without reflection on the waves of time – into eternity.

The art is gone which all my life long sustained and strengthened me. Networks of wire have taken the place of painting and are given mystical interpretations! Electrical noise they call 'music'. The best thing to do is to make off and close the door behind one.[101]

The only glimmer of hope was the outcome of the American election: he reported that the Irish entertained great hopes of the new president, 'who is deft, intelligent and cunning, as they [the politicians] all are here. We shall soon see what he is capable of.' But at Easter 1961 he wrote that he was reading Goethe's *Faust* and the romantic German writer Chamisso, was disgusted by the politics of the time and glad he would not live to see the new period.

The last broadcast of his music he heard on 12 January 1960, when the Radio Éireann Singers under Hans W. Rosen performed his *Vier Geistliche Gesänge*.[102] On Whit Sunday 1961 he conducted the choir at the cathedral for the last time;[103] during the summer, he was too ill to leave the house. The diagnosis was cancer. In August he sent Schaehle a postcard, writing that he was feeling somewhat better but that the terrible weakness remained – the shaky handwriting is evidence of this.

His bed was brought down to the dining room on the ground floor; he could no longer climb the stairs to his study in the attic and had difficulty in making his way up one flight of stairs to the bathroom. Once he had become an invalid, his wife could no longer cope and, on 7 January 1962, he had to be moved to the Incurable Hospital run by the Sisters of Charity. He spent the first weeks in a public ward before a tiny private room became free. He had many visitors. Tilly came every day, as did Aloys Óg; the family, members of the choir and friends called regularly. For a while, Aloys Óg was able to take him out in a wheelchair, and he was able to get from the wheelchair into his assistant-organist's car for a drive – at the end of which a glass of whisky strengthened him for the return to the hospice. For over a year before his death he was unable to leave his bed. He could not attend any of the lunchtime concerts given during the summer of 1963 in the School of Art, which were dedicated to him and Tilly by their founder and sponsor, Gerald Y. Goldberg.[104] He did not suffer physical pain, but some six months before his death he wrote that he had prayed to God that it would not come to this, that he was enduring 'grief for which there are no words'. He was deprived of music, except for the occasional concert on the radio. Books and his thoughts were what remained to him. He continued to read, and during the last six months of his life filled forty-five pages of an exercise book with notes – comments on his reading and general observations on life. He recorded his dreams occasionally: once of terrible storms, once of the sea, the splendour of which consoled him, and carried before his mind's eye the dearly-loved images of his native place.

His strength ebbed away gradually, to his wife's intense distress. His son remembered his eyes taking on an extraordinary brightness towards the end. He died on 3 January 1964, aged eighty-three, and was buried the following day after a requiem mass at the cathedral, sung by the choir in the presence of the bishop. The choir sang at the graveside:

> 'At his requiem mass, many past members of the choir turned up to join us in the singing. Then at the graveside we sang a final farewell to our beloved choirmaster. It was his *Canticum Zachariae*, one of the choir's favourite pieces:
>
> > Requiem aeternam dona eis Domine
> > Et lux perpetua luceat eis.[105]

Tilly received over a hundred letters of sympathy (each of which she replied to personally) and twice that number of mass-cards. Some weeks later, Seán Ó Riada sent her the manuscript of his *Four Hölderlin Songs*:

Dear Frau Tilly,

I had intended writing to you at the time of your husband's death,
but, in view of my friendship with you both, and the regard which I
felt, it seemed to me that any ordinary letter of sympathy would have
been totally inadequate to express my feelings.

I had already, in 1956, sketched a song-cycle on poems by Hölderlin
which I intended dedicating to him, but it failed to progress. When I
heard of his death, I revised the idea of the song-cycle, which now
includes only one (Hälfte des Lebens) poem from the original cycle.

I hope you will accept it as a token of my sympathy, and also that it
may be of some little comfort for your great loss, and as a sign of
regard for his memory.

I think he might have liked it.

The songs were included in a memorial concert given in June by the
Radio Éireann Singers under Hans Waldemar Rosen, sung by Cáit
Lannigan; the broadcast included Fleischmann's *Vier Geistliche Gesänge*
[Four Sacred Songs]. At the Choral Festival of 1964 the Sunbeam Male
Voice Choir performed four Fleischmann works as a tribute to the con-
ductor's teacher.[106]
Letters sent to Tilly from two former choir members and a student of
hers sum up what Fleischmann meant to them. One was Jim Blanc,
now an organist in Dublin:

Madame et chère amie,

Hearing from you brought back many memories of one who had the
greatest influence on my life. . . . I feel very lonely for your dear
husband's counsel, advice and above all, his friendship. Your letter is
a great consolation for one who now travels a lonely road not
knowing where it leads.

My church and all my organ music were destroyed by fire last July.
Although I still retain my post there is no adequate means, at the
moment, of expressing my service to God through the talents which
he has given me.

I had a dream of your husband about ten days ago and still ponder its
meaning. The dream placed me in St. Mary's Cathedral where, alas,
all was debris. The organ was gone but the wooden structure which
enclosed the choir still remained. All the joys of former days, the High
Masses and the beautiful music, which seemed to draw aside the curtains of eternity for a brief moment – all were remembered. In my
dream I wept that for me it is no more. How I longed to return to
Cork just to sing again in the choir under Herr Fleischmann's direction – if only he were still on earth. Then I saw your husband standing
in a corner of the choir and he had a very benign expression. He wore
a black soutane of very fine material and there was a black sash
around his waist similar to that worn by bishops with the exception

of the colour. He seemed to know I was anxious about the organ and told me not to worry. 'The pipes are stored and will be used again.' This consoled me and I departed by the Sacristy.

Such was the dream. Whatever the road ahead is to be, one thing is certain: your dear husband's example of total dedication to that which pertains to God, will always be my inspiration.[107]

While reading for his BMus degree in University College Cork, Donal Twomey had studied the piano with Tilly Fleischmann. In a letter to him about her husband, she had used the word 'poor' as an epithet, which both she and her son regularly employed as a euphemism for 'dead'. Twomey couldn't have known that and, having complimented her on the rest of the letter, objected to the description:

I am sure you will forgive me if I offer one little criticism. I find your use of the word 'poor' in describing your husband a complete misfit. He wasn't poor, he was very rich in all that matters. His humanity was rich, his spirit was rich and his marvellous sense of humour was rich. His artistic integrity was so rich that I shall never forget some of the values he gave me up in that wonderful attic, where we discussed everything from the cat to the clergy. The next time you write about him don't call him 'poor': it does not fit. He had a difficult life being a 'fish out of water' and never having the proper outlet for his talents but his brave and rich spirit never once gave in. He composed, taught and performed and I for one shall always feel richer for having known him.[108]

Brother Cronin read of Fleischmann's death in Gibraltar, where he was teaching. He wrote a long letter of sympathy to the widow, describing in detail what he valued about his time in the choir and expressing his esteem for the choirmaster, whom he had visited in the hospice during his holiday the previous summer. His letter ends:

Herr Fleischmann has made a tremendous impact on my life, and I look back with pride on my time as one of his choir boys. His example, patience, hard work, and devotedness have been a guiding light to me. In particular his disinterestedness in any honour or publicity. I hope the beautiful compositions I know him to have written will not die with him.

May the thousands of voices that came under his influence; the thousands and thousands of notes resulting from his fingers; the hundreds of motets and masses that he taught and conducted; the energy that he lost in the cause of his sacred task; and even the perspiration and vapour that poured forth from his brow while conducting broadcasts, joined with the humble prayers he was saying on his beads as I entered his room last August; and the prayers of all those who loved and admired him all cry to God for the speedy reward due to this faithful servant. May he rest in peace, amen.[109]

Aloys Fleischmann Jun.
1935

Herbert Hughes, Aloys
Fleischmann, Susanne
Hughes, Arnold Bax 1936

Séamus Murphy at work
on a sculpture of Pádraic
Pearse

Arnold Bax and E.J. Moeran
visiting the Fleischmanns

Aloys Fleischmann, 1936,
by Franz Berberich
(*Photo: Julian Dodd*)

Franz Schaehle with his wife
and daughter Hildegard

Anne Fleischmann
née Madden and Aloys ,
Honan Chapel, 4 June 1941

Ernest Lyons, the bride's
uncle, and Aloys
Fleischmann at his son's
wedding, 4 June 1941

Walburga Swertz in
her late eighties

With the painters Craig *(left)* and Hennessy *(middle)* in Oileán Ruadh

The Aeolian and cathedral choirs 1941

Fleischmann with John O'Riordan *(left)*, and Father Seán Daly on a choir outing

Tilly Fleischmann in Gráig with four of the five grandchildren 1952

Aloys Fleischmann in Gráig 1952

Rita Horgan *née* Wallace and her husband

Pilib Ó Laoghaire

Seán Ó Riada

The cathedral choir: Joe Cunningham *(front row first left)*; Ned Evans *(front row first right)*

Tilly and Aloys Fleischmann

The Music of
Aloys Georg Fleischmann

SÉAMAS DE BARRA

THE DACHAU NATIVITY PLAYS

As is evident from the few pieces of juvenilia that have survived, Aloys
Fleischmann showed considerable creative talent as a boy. When he
was only fifteen years old his competence was acknowledged by a commission from the Dachau Journeymen's Association and the following
year, 1896 – the year he was admitted to the preliminary course at the
Royal Academy of Music in Munich – he composed an *Ave Maria* for
female-voice choir of remarkable technical and stylistic sophistication.
Nothing else survives that can with certainty be ascribed to his years as
a student, however, and it is not known how much music he may have
composed during this period. But it seems likely that his time in the
Academy was principally occupied with his studies and that he temporarily subordinated his creative impulse to the disciplined acquisition
of technical skill.

It is only after his graduation in 1901 and his return to Dachau to
take up his appointment as organist and choirmaster at St Jakob's
Church that his urge to compose appears to have reasserted itself.
Between 1902 and 1906, when he left Germany to work in Ireland, he
wrote a great deal of music, including sacred music, choral works and
songs. His reputation, however, was principally founded on a highly
successful series of musical nativity plays, which brought his name to
wider national attention. The first of these was staged in January 1903
as a showcase for the pupils of the Choir School he had established. On
this occasion he performed an already existing piece by Michael Haller
entitled *Sonnenwende* [Solstice] and his creative contribution was confined to making an arrangement of the score for string orchestra. This
initial venture was so well received that he felt encouraged to attempt
something more ambitious, and the following year he composed an
elaborate work for children's voices, mixed-voice choir and full
orchestra based on a modern adaptation of a sixteenth-century play.
The new work was staged under the title *Ein altes Weihnachtsspiel* [An
Old Christmas Play] in January 1904 to even greater acclaim.

269

The introductory movement with which *Ein altes Weihnachtsspiel* commences is based on a chorale prelude for organ by Brahms (Op. 122, No. 8), which employs the fifteenth-century melody 'Es ist ein Ros' entsprungen' [There is a Rose that Bloometh]. Fleischmann's adaptation culminates in a statement of the tune by the choir which, in its suggestion of angelic voices, anticipates events in the first act of the play. The drama begins on a bitterly cold night with three shepherd boys watching their flocks. They see strange lights in the sky and one of the youths says he hears mysterious singing. There is a sudden surge of excitement in the orchestra and the Choir of Angels enters singing 'Glory to God in the highest'. After this jubilant proclamation, the peacefulness of Christmas is simply and effectively conveyed by the ensuing setting of 'Stille Nacht! Heilige Nacht!' [Silent night! Holy night!]. But the atmosphere of tranquil serenity is soon dispelled. The music becomes darkly ominous as a Choir of Prophetic Spirits foretells the bitter death that will come to the newborn child. The shepherds' fear on hearing the disturbing prophecy is vividly depicted in the orchestra, as is the sudden appearance of the Archangel Gabriel who announces the birth of Jesus and urges the boys to go to Bethlehem and see the marvellous event for themselves. One of them worries about wolves preying on his sheep, but the others declare their willingness to trust in God and Act I concludes with their departure for Bethlehem.

Act II introduces the three kings, who are presented by the narrator after a brief orchestral introduction. They explain why they set out on their lengthy quest and that they have lost their way. As they seek directions from the shepherd boys, the Archangel Gabriel reappears. He informs them of the miraculous birth of the Son of God in a stable and invites them to see the child. Although not explicitly stated either in the score or in the printed libretto, the shepherds and the kings now presumably appear in a final tableau depicting the child Jesus with Mary and Joseph. The Choir of Angels re-enters exhorting all Christians to be joyful and the mixed-voice choir responds with a splendid fugue on a theme by Rheinberger, 'Lob, Ehr und Preis dem Vater werd' [Praise and Honour to the Father], which marks the climax of the piece. There is a pause after the fugue to allow for a short spoken epilogue and the work concludes with a recapitulation of the chorale melody 'Es ist ein Ros' entsprungen'.

Although *Ein altes Weihnachtsspiel* is straightforward in its general conception, it is nonetheless subtly realised. Formally, the work occupies a middle ground between a play with incidental music and an oratorio. The principal characters – the shepherd boys, the kings and the Archangel – do not sing, and Fleischmann's score consists predominantly of an accompaniment to the spoken dialogue that reflects the changing situations and depicts the thoughts and feelings of the protagonists. His handling of the continuous orchestral commentary is imaginative and colourful and he shows a flair for devising musical gestures that are appropriate to the unaffected simplicity of the story. But the music is by no means confined to this subordinate background function: as in oratorio, the two choirs also contribute to the unfolding of the action, heightening the emotional impact at crucial junctures in the drama. On one level, the success of the work is due to Fleischmann's delicate management of this shifting emphasis between music and the spoken word until, ultimately, the drama is subsumed into a purely musical culmination with the final fugue.

Ein altes Weihnachtsspiel was by far the longest and most complex work Fleischmann had composed up to that time. How much he learned from the experience of writing it can be judged from the extent to which the score he produced for the 1905 play surpasses it in quality. *Die Nacht der Wunder* [The Night of Wonders] is a more ambitious and sophisticated achievement in every respect. The literary style of Franz Langheinrich's libretto – which is based on a tale by the Swedish writer Selma Lagerlöf – may be somewhat affected, but, in contrast to the artlessness of *Ein altes Weihnachtsspiel*, it has a cast of sharply defined characters and presents a vividly imagined series of events. The transference of the action to the town of Dachau and the surrounding countryside is an inspiration – a device that serves not only to emphasise the universal relevance of the Christmas story, but one that also affords opportunities for charming local colour.

Fleischmann's score is again written for children's choir, mixed-voice choir and orchestra and, as before, the work combines the characteristics both of a play and an oratorio. The Prologue does not contribute to the dramatic action, but consists of an extended choral meditation on the significance of the Nativity. It opens with mysterious murmuring figurations in the orchestra evocative of nocturnal darkness. This darkness is clearly intended to be understood in a psychological as well as a literal sense: the Chorus of the People enters, reflecting on the uncertainty and misery of human existence. Suddenly, the voice of Joseph (who is described merely as the Stranger in the *dramatis personae*) is heard off-stage, as he wanders through the town searching desperately for lodgings. A quartet of Voices from on High comments on the stranger's request and asks if love can ignore his plea for compassion. In reply, the townspeople ask to be taught what love and compassion are, as they know only pain and toil in their daily lives. The principal theme of the piece is thus announced and a connection is effectively established between the Prologue and the ensuing action.

The first act is preceded by a delicately scored prelude in which the sound of shepherds' flutes establishes an appropriately pastoral mood. The curtain rises on the countryside at night. A landowner lies sleeping by a campfire. Three young shepherds while away the time posing each other riddles until they are interrupted by a boy who runs onstage with news of a stranger who has been refused lodgings in the town. He is coming across the fields, the boy says, walking over the backs of the sleeping sheep without disturbing them and paralysing the dogs with fright. At this, the landowner wakes, none too pleased at having been disturbed. He repulses the stranger rudely and hurls his spear at him, but it merely rebounds harmlessly from the man's body. The stranger then asks for fire to warm his wife and newborn child and there is general astonishment when he picks up the live coals in his bare hands without being burnt. As the mysterious figure departs the landowner cries, 'Up, let us follow him and see if we can find the meaning of these wonders.'

The atmospheric orchestral prelude to Act II is a finely wrought miniature tone poem that depicts the lonely beauty and mystery of a winter's night on the Dachau moors. This act features the three pagan princes who describe their journey in search of the child-king: 'Indeed I see the splendour of the star' one of them says. 'But where is the great palace?' They meet the stranger who asks them to follow him. When they arrive at the stable the scene is immediately flooded with heavenly light as angels surround the manger. The repentant landowner falls on his knees. The work ends in a similar manner to the opening with the Chorus of the People asking if the hard struggles of their daily lives are now at an end. Heavenly Voices answer:

> Without love there is no meaning
> To this world that we call home.

As in *Ein altes Weihnachtsspiel*, the principal characters in *Die Nacht der Wunder* do not sing, and apart from the Prologue and the closing pages of the work, which are choral, Fleischmann's score again largely consists of an orchestral background to the spoken dialogue. Although it shows all the qualities of imagination and invention that characterise the earlier work, the piece evinces a much greater degree of technical assurance, especially in creating long spans of music – such as the Prologue – which have a symphonic breadth and sweep. With *Die Nacht der Wunder* Fleischmann produced an accomplished and genuinely affecting score, which was justly praised at the time of its performance as marking the high point of his early creative achievements. Before he left Dachau in 1906, he was involved with one final Christmas production, which was based on readings from the bible with music by Michael Pretorius (1571–1621). This was a far more modest affair and Fleischmann's creative contribution to it was minimal, although it was preceded by performances of the Prologue and final chorus of *Die Nacht der Wunder*, which he specially adapted for the occasion.

VOCAL MUSIC AND CHORAL MUSIC

A large portion of Fleischmann's output consists of vocal music. There are over eighty songs with piano, and several with orchestral accompaniment. Most of these are settings of German texts. Throughout his life, Fleischmann turned almost exclusively to German poets when seeking suitable words for music, but after the First World War when it became apparent that he was likely to remain in Cork, he was diligent in supplying both his songs and his choral works with serviceable English singing translations. These were made for him by various friends such as Fr Pat MacSwiney, Mary Lucy, her son Seán (later a well-known poet and Professor of Modern English in University College, Cork) and Walter Henley.

Some of the finest of these songs date from the Dachau period, and together with the nativity plays they rank as the most impressive creative achievements of his early years. They are excellent examples of the German lieder tradition as it had developed up to the end of the nineteenth century, especially in its manifestation as unpretentious *Hausmusik*. The subject matter of most of the texts that Fleischmann chose to set draws on the great themes of the Romantics – unrequited love and spiritual loneliness. Theodor Storm's 'Schliesse mir die Augen beide' [Close my eyes], a poem that inspired many composers, clearly had a personal resonance for Fleischmann. His manuscript is inscribed 'Meiner Lieben Tilly' [To My Dear Tilly] and dates from 1904, the year before he and his future wife got engaged. A set of *Vier Gesänge* [Four Songs] dates from around the same time. This group of fine songs comprises two setting of poems by Franz Evers, 'Stille Stunde' [Quiet Hour] and 'In sommertiefen Nächten' [In High Summer Nights], and one each by Storm and Peter Cornelius, 'Der Abend' [The Evening] and 'Einsamkeit' [Loneliness] respectively. Although they cannot be assigned to a specific year, *Nachtlied* [Night Song] and *Nicht daheim* [Not at Home], settings of poems by Karl Stieler, almost certainly belong to the Dachau period too, as does *Zur Nacht* [To the Night] for voice and orchestra which, again, is to words by Storm.

While rewarding for the professional singer, all of these pieces remain within the capacity of the talented amateur. Their graceful and melodically distinguished vocal lines skilfully exploit the full compass of the voice and the characteristic colours of the different vocal registers. The accompaniments are for the most part straightforward, and are generally conceived as supporting the voice rather than as an equal focus of attention. Fleischmann tends to rely on standard accompaniment patterns such as arpeggio figurations and repeated or syncopated chords: even at its most elaborate, the keyboard writing lies gratefully under the hands and eschews virtuosic passagework. Although the textures of these songs are not especially notable for their originality, the accompaniments are unfailingly apt for the subject matter of the song and well-suited to the character of the vocal line.

Fleischmann shows a resourceful handling of the late-Romantic harmonic vocabulary that was still a lingua franca for composers at the turn of the twentieth century, particularly for those working in the Austro-German tradition. In all of his early work, he confines himself to this triadically based idiom, heightened by standard chromatic inflections and third-related progressions and occasionally enriched with more unusual chordal juxtapositions. If he refrains from venturing into the borderlands of indeterminate tonality, as does, say, Hugo Wolf, his manipulation of this common harmonic language is by no means routine. In fact, given the generalised nature of his accompaniments, which rarely seek to depict specific imagery, the persuasiveness of his settings lies to no small extent in his ability to reflect the fluctuating emotional content of the words in sensitively nuanced harmonic progressions.

It is in his handling of form, however, that Fleischmann displays the precise control of detail that distinguishes the accomplished miniaturist. Although many of these early pieces have a through-composed vocal line, this is never allowed to deteriorate into amorphous arioso. While the melodic curve as it unfolds appears to respond spontaneously to the changing moods of the text, Fleischmann ensures coherence by means of unobtrusive rhythmic and intervallic correspondences, and a skilful handling of tessitura. This vocal freedom is normally contained within a clearly defined overall structure, which is principally articulated in the accompaniment. The demarcations of internal formal divisions by the introduction of contrasting patterns are generally well judged, as are the restatements of earlier material, which are rarely literal but carefully refashioned and redirected to move naturally to a close. Fleischmann's craftsmanship as a composer is perhaps nowhere more in evidence than in his ability to subordinate his melodic and harmonic invention to the requirements of the structure. It is this natural and unforced co-ordination of technique and imagination that places these songs on a level of distinction above the ordinary.

Although not the most ambitious or necessarily even the finest of the early songs, the 1904 setting of *Schliesse mir die Augen beide* is nonetheless sufficiently representative as well as being short enough – a mere twenty-two bars – to discuss in some detail as an illustration of Fleischmann's early manner. The basic piece comprises four four-bar phrases for the voice: a pair of thematically parallel, diatonic phrases neatly balanced by a pair of chromatically inflected, contrasting phrases. The problem for the composer is how to circumvent the restrictions imposed by this four-square ground plan without at the same time compromising its essential simplicity: in other words, how to reconcile sophistication of technique with uncomplicated directness of utterance.

Fleischmann achieves this balance with great skill. The two-four bar at the end of the second phrase is crucial as, in effect, it displaces the phrase accent by half a bar. This asymmetry produces a subtle sense of phrase syncopation and a concomitant underlying sense of unrest that is maintained until the second last bar of the vocal line. Here the introduction of a second two-four bar ingeniously re-aligns the phrase and bar accents to coincide with harmonic resolution when, for the first time in the piece, the vocal line cadences onto the tonic note. The two-bar interlude for the piano is now balanced by a postlude which rounds off the song by recalling the opening melody, and the final half bar balances the two beat anacrusis of the beginning.

Harmonically, although the first half of the song is diatonic, Fleischmann is careful to avoid tonic closure: the limpid G major tonality is coloured only by the supertonic chromatic chord to effect the cadence on to the dominant at the end of the first phrase, and by the mediant chromatic chord to effect the cadence onto the relative minor at the end of the second. The harmonic content of the second pair of phrases is more chromatic and dissonant, producing a sense of urgency that is reinforced by the repeated notes in the right hand of the accompaniment and by the syncopated bass line. This urgency makes explicit on the surface of the music the underlying tension engendered by the disjunction of the phrase and bar accents. Unlike the first two phrases, which are cadentially defined, the third and fourth phrases flow seamlessly together carrying the music forward towards a culmination. The effect of this climactic moment is so well judged that Fleischmann does not need to raise the dynamic level above *mezzo forte*. Instead, the additional two-four bar creates a perfectly placed expansion of the final vocal phrase that effortlessly accommodates both the heightened emotion and the remoter harmonies that express it. The double function of this second two-four bar – to re-establish phrase symmetry and at the same time to provide space for the climax – is expertly realised. The harmonies are also tellingly chosen: the flat submediant and tonic minor chords followed by the beautifully unexpected B major chord convey the depth of feeling with an economical precision possible only for a composer in complete control of his materials. The ensuing A minor chord leads inevitably to a cadence on the tonic and a return to the diatonic radiance of G major. After a momentary clouding over of the harmony, this simple but perfectly realised miniature comes to a serene close.

Fleischmann's move to Cork in 1906 had no immediate effect on to the style of his music, which seems to have remained virtually unchanged at least until the end of the First World War. The musical language of lieder such as *Oft denk mit Wehmut ich zurück* [The hours I spend with Thee] or *Unter den Linden* [Under the Linden], both of which were composed in the prisoner-of-war camp in 1918, differs little

Ex. 1: *Schliesse mir die Augen beide*

from those of the Dachau period. But if works like these show that he was still content to mine the same vein, they also demonstrate that this entailed no falling off either in imagination or craftsmanship. *Unter den Linden*, a setting of a poem by Walter von der Vogelweide, is a particularly engaging piece with a memorable piquancy of melodic invention. The apparent simplicity of the opening belies the skill with which he uses the minimum of notes to establish an atmosphere that is at once warmly lyrical yet tinged with sadness. The handling of dissonance is very subtle and the easy rise and fall in harmonic tension is so smoothly achieved as to seem completely artless.

Ex. 2: *Unter den Linden,* opening

The ensuing refrain makes a delightful contrast to the opening. The change of time signature combined with the new, lightly flowing melody in the piano aptly express the lovers' carefree happiness as symbolised by the 'Tan-da-ra-dei' of the nightingale singing in the branches overhead. At every point, Fleischmann contrives to make the right gesture. He gives the diatonic texture only the lightest of chromatic colouring, for example. In the verse this is confined to mediant chromatic and supertonic chromatic discords. Consequently, when in the refrain the subdominant chord (A flat) is highlighted with its own flat mediant (C flat) and minor subdominant (D flat minor) the effect, although momentary, is sufficiently rich to suffuse the entire passage with a warm radiance. At the conclusion of the refrain, he gently dispels

Ex. 3: *Unter den Linden*, bars 21–36

Ex. 4: *Heimat, liebe Heimat!* opening

the blithe mood by alternating the dominant note with the darker flat submediant as in the introduction (bar 6), and thus effectively prepares for the return of the more measured lyricism of the verse.

Occasionally, Fleischmann abandoned the chaste model of the lied and essayed a style that approximates more to the popular parlour song, one of a number of different song types he explored at various stages during his career. Of pieces in this manner *Heimat, liebe Heimat!* [Home, Beloved Homeland!], a setting of words by Adolf von Stern that also dates from 1918, is a particularly good example. Here sentiment has been replaced by something closer to sentimentality. But within the conventions of the type the song has genuine charm, and while the lush harmonies recall the easy emotion of operetta, its memorable, if ingratiating vocal lines evince a finely polished technique.

Fleischmann also composed a considerable number of lieder suggestive of stylised folk songs, a genre in which his immediate model was almost certainly Brahms. Amongst his compositions in this vein, one might mention *Altdeutsches Minnelied* [An Old German Minnesong], *Im Volkston – Von alten Liebesliedern* [In the Folk Style – From Olden Lovesongs], the set of five *Kleine Romanzen und Lieder im Volkston* [Little Romances and Songs in the Folk Style] and also, perhaps, the slightly

Ex. 5: 'Die Liebenden', (ii) from *Kleine Romanzen und Lieder im Volkston*, opening

more elaborate *Das Rosenblatt* [The Roseleaf]. Some of these are cast in simple strophic form, while in others the principal melodic material is offset by contrasting ideas. In all of them, however, he manages success-fully to recreate the frank naivety and spontaneous tunefulness of Austro-German folk music, while at the same time unobtrusively deep-ening the emotional resonance by pointing the words with a discreet but telling use of chromatically inflected harmony.

Although there is a change in Fleischmann's compositional style from 1920 or thereabouts, it is difficult to make any but the most general observations about this development. Firstly, very few of his manuscripts are dated and it is not possible to say exactly when most of the music was written. Secondly, significant differences between his pre-war and post-war idioms notwithstanding, much of what was composed after 1920 maintains a recognisable stylistic continuity with his earlier work. Even if he never again reverted to the late-Romantic idiom of the Dachau years, neither did he relinquish all the traits of his earlier manner and it is possible that some pieces may be of a later date than their style might suggest. Furthermore, once fixed, the resources of his post-1920 compositional idiom seem to have altered very little in the remaining forty years or so of his life. In consequence, it is not possible to establish even an approximate chronology for his output as a whole, let alone date particular works, on the basis of internal stylistic evidence.

It is principally in his harmonic idiom that the most striking stylistic development occurred, which had a corresponding effect on melodic invention and, to a lesser extent, on texture and form. The harmonic vocabulary of Fleischmann's later music is notable for its greater tonal elusiveness and a freer treatment of dissonance often involving a heightened chromaticism – which brought about an accompanying expansion of expressive range. It also frequently features strong modal inflections, an aspect of his style that may well have been influenced by his intimate knowledge of Gregorian chant and sixteenth-century polyphony. In some works, however, the employment of these disparate harmonic and tonal resources produces an impression of incongruity. In many of the sacred pieces in particular, there are moments when the introduction of chromatic elements into a fundamentally diatonic or modal idiom seems ill-judged. In other works, however, he managed to bring these elements into a satisfactory relationship with one another, with results that are far more persuasive.

Amongst the most interesting of the post-war vocal works is a group of songs to poems by Rabindranath Tagore and three songs pub-lished as Op. 26 in 1929 by the London firm of Augener. Three of the six Tagore settings also exist in a version with orchestra and were undoubt-edly designed to be performed as a set. With the exception of the third song, 'Do not go my love', which is perhaps the finest of them, the colourful and idiomatic orchestral versions are more successful than the versions with piano.[1] All six songs, however, demonstrate clearly some of the salient characteristics of Fleischmann's later approach in their blend of diatonic modality and dissonant chromaticism creating, in this case, an appropriately exotic atmosphere. The result here is only partially convincing, however, and the Tagore settings are an uneven achievement. The three songs that comprise Op. 26 are harmonically less adventurous. The middle song, *Awakening,* is somewhat unfocused, but the first, *Night,* and the third, *The Fool,* are strong pieces, the latter in particular, in a driving six-eight time, is one of Fleischmann's most effective fast songs.

Far more successful in its exploitation of modal colouring is *Abendfrieden* [Evening Peace], a setting of a short poem by Gerda von Robertus. Formally, this song is a model of conciseness, as it lasts a mere twenty-five bars: each of the outer two of its three seven-bar phrases has a one-bar prefix and the song as a whole is brought to a conclusion with a two-bar suffix. Ostensibly in the key of A minor, there is only one perfect cadence in the piece. Otherwise the tonality is ambiguous throughout. The opening two bars comprise an elaboration of pre-dominant harmony (essentially a prolonged decoration of the subdominant D minor chord). This eventually moves to a dominant seventh in bar 3, but the tonic is evaded and the harmony returns to D minor. The pitch G sharp is also heard in bar 5, but the augmented sixth chord of which it is a component is still oriented towards D minor. Finally, the leading note occurs again at the end of bar 6 as part of a dominant diminished seventh chord that seems to have clear tonal implications. But these are once again avoided and, surprisingly, the tonality shifts instead to a bright F major.

The song's initial sombre evocation of the setting sun and the fading strokes of the Angelus bell gives way to a lighter atmosphere with this move to F major. The poet now looks up from the darkening earth – so aptly depicted by the tenebrous progressions of the opening – and sees the high clouds forming processions in the sky, which rise 'like incense from the twilight hills'. Fleischmann vividly suggests these images by the simplest of means. Firstly, he replaces the low-lying harmonies with a higher floating figure in thirds (bar 9); and, secondly, he sets this in an open harmonic space defined by the juxtaposition of unresolved and tonally indeterminate discords – essentially, an A minor seventh chord prolonged for three bars followed by a G minor seventh. This progression produces a sense of appropriately nebulous modality – an Aeolian (or perhaps, Dorian) A minor, succeeded by a Dorian G minor which remains ambiguous enough to accommodate simultaneously a strong suggestion of Phrygian A minor. This leads to a return of the opening material, which is now remodelled to move to a brief but intense climax before cadencing for the first

Ex. 6: *Abendfrieden,* opening

time onto a tonic chord. A two-bar suffix makes a final allusion to the Phrygian A minor as the piece ends in a subdued mood with an interesting variant of the plagal cadence. Although hardly more substantial than a fragment, this song is a highly finished piece and its dexterous manipulation of tonal ambiguity demonstrates *in nuce* the technical adroitness and expressive subtlety of which Fleischmann was capable in his later music.

The *Drei Gedichte von Ludwig Finkl* [Three Poems by Ludwig Finkl] is arguably not only the most integrated and internally balanced set of

Ex. 7: 'Viel zu viel', (ii) from *Drei Gedichte von Ludwig Finkl*, ending

songs that Fleischmann produced, but is also a work that demonstrates, perhaps, the furthest reach of his post-1920 style. The set opens
with a tempestuous setting of 'Das heimliche Ständchen', which was
entitled 'Lady Mine' by Walter Henley, who provided an English
singing translation. Although there are strong background tonal references (D minor), the dissonant harmonies are often strikingly
unpredictable and are matched by a corresponding angularity in the
melodic line that is unusual in Fleischmann's vocal writing. 'What shall
we have left when roses fade in our heart?', the poet asks in the second
song, 'Viel zu viel' [Too Many]. Fleischmann's setting juxtaposes plan-
gent chromatic dissonances and a limpid diatonicism in a remarkable
evocation of the dread for the future, on the one hand, which is implied
by the poet's question, and his unswerving declaration of constancy on
the other. The piece ends with an original and highly effective cadence
that manages to condense into three chords the entire emotional spec-
trum of the song.

The final song of the set, 'Die schönste Rose' [The Sweetest Rose], is
in the manner of a stylised folk song with a cheerfully insouciant diatonic tune and the lightest of arpeggio accompaniments. Initially, this
seems to have little in common with the preceding songs. But the
giojoso opening gives way to a slower contrasting strain, the unconventional chromatic progressions of which establish a clear stylistic
connection with them. This subsidiary idea is cleverly contrived to
suggest a moment of pensive absorption that is psychologically plau-
sible, yet does not compromise the overall carefree mood.

Unfortunately the scope of this brief survey imposes severe limits on
the number of individual works that can be singled out for detailed
comment. One final song that deserves to be mentioned, however, is a
setting of *Drei Rosen* [Three Roses] by H. Pankow. In each of the poem's
three stanzas a mother tells of picking three roses for her son at different stages of his life. In the first stanza, two red roses and one white
rose decorate his cradle as a child. The same in the second stanza decorate his helmet as a young soldier going to war. In the third stanza the
boy is dead – presumably killed in battle – and the sorrowing mother
brings three white roses as a memorial garland for his picture.
Fleischmann responds with a deeply felt and moving setting that
conveys the successive emotions of tenderness, pride and grief with an
impressive sureness of touch. Each stanza of the poem commences
with the same line – 'Drei Rosen hab' ich im Garten gepflückt' [Three
roses from the garden have I brought]. These words are always set to
the same music, but with three different continuations. Initially, it yields
to a strain that appropriately suggests a cradlesong. It is then transformed into an assertive quasi-military passage that brings the second
stanza to a bravely confident climax. The poem concludes with a varied

repetition of the final line of the opening stanza – 'Schlafe mein Sohn, schlafe' [Sleep, my son, sleep] – but now, of course, having a tragically different import. With a simple but superbly judged shift to the tonic minor on the word 'Schlafe', Fleischmann contrives to unite this reference to the cradlesong with a heartbroken recollection of the

Ex. 8: *Drei Rosen,* opening

2

sang_____ be - glückt: "Schla - fe mein Söhn - chen, schla - fe,
joy___ else have sought: "Sleep___ my ba - by boy, sleep on,

schla - fe mein Söhn - chen schla - - fe!"
sleep___ my ba - by boy, sleep_____ on!"

march-like variant, and thus find exactly the right means of sounding the deep note of anguished loss and dignified resignation that makes this one of his finest songs.

Throughout his life Fleischmann continued to devote much of his creative energy to the composition of vocal music, and the most ambitious project of his later years was a series of *Balladen und Legenden* [Ballads and Legends] for solo male voice and orchestra. He appears to have started to plan these at the beginning of the 1930s. Initially, he envisaged composing four such pieces but he later expanded this to six and, ultimately, to seven. He also broadened the scope of his original idea by re-conceiving two of them as choral works. As was his custom, he chose his texts from the German poets, but the fact that he took the trouble to provide English singing translations (not all the translators, incidentally, are credited in the manuscripts) suggests that he hoped they would be performed in Ireland, or at any rate in Cork. He did not bring the project as a whole to completion, however, and there is no evidence that any of the individual pieces were heard in public. Of his projected setting of Schiller's *Die Teilung der Erde* [The Division of the Earth] no trace has been found amongst his papers, which suggests that it was never written. Two other settings – one of Otto Ernst's *Nis Randers*, the other of *Der seltsame Gast* [The Ominous Guest] by Josef Eichendorf – exist only in vocal score and were probably never orchestrated, while the existing full score of his setting of Theodor Fontane's *Swend Gabelbart und St Edmund* [Swend Gabelbart and St Edmund] is unfinished, although incomplete by only a few bars. The one orchestral score he brought to a fully edited final state is *Der Schelm von Bergen* [The Scamp of Bergen], a setting of a poem by Heine. Of the remaining two works, the score of *Darthula* seems somewhat sketchy in places while there are two draft orchestrations, each for slightly different forces, of *Milisint*.

These last mentioned pieces – *Darthula* and *Milisint* – are the two choral works and they are of particular interest in that their Irish subject matter shows a conscious attempt on Fleischmann's part to explore links between the German literature that fuelled his imagination and the legendary lore of his adopted country. *Milisint*, possibly the first work in the series to be completed (the vocal score is dated 1932), is a setting of a poem by Eduard Mörike which is based on an ancient Irish story about the Milesians. The Irish connection with *Darthula* is perhaps a little more oblique. The text is Herder's translation of a passage from the eighteenth-century *Ossian*, James Macpherson's putative translations from the Scots Gaelic of poems attributed to the legendary Ossian or, in Irish, Oisín. Macpherson's work is loosely and creatively based on tales from the Irish Red Branch cycle and the lays of Fionn mac Cumhaill (whom he names Fingal) that had long been current in the oral traditions of Scotland. The Dar-thula of Macpherson's poem is the Deirdre of Irish legend. Interestingly, although Herder is credited in Fleischmann's manuscripts, there is no allusion to Macpherson: it is the

Irish connection that is emphasised and the text is carefully attributed to 'Ossian (3. Cent.) Gaelic Poet, eldest son of Fin-Mac Coul [*sic*]'.

The various texts of the *Balladen und Legenden* are highly picturesque and they afforded the composer excellent opportunities both for the delineation of character and the depiction of vividly narrated incidents and situations, some of which tend towards the macabre and involve supernatural occurrences. Fleischmann clearly relished these opportunities, and enjoyed finding the most suitable musical means to convey the individual atmosphere of each poem. With the exception of *Darthula*, all of them narrate a story of sorts and thus pose the compositional problem of imparting a convincing musical unity to what is essentially a linear narrative structure. In order to have the necessary freedom to respond to the import of the text as it unfolds, the vocal part needs to be cast in an arioso or recitative style. The kind of phrase repetition and formal expansion demanded by full-blown lyrical melody would merely retard the recounting of the tale, and a succession of separate song-like sections would frustrate any sense of narrative progress. The task of achieving musical coherence, therefore, is relegated to the accompaniment, where tightly controlled motivic organisation allows for a correspondingly flexible vocal line. Fleischmann is fully alert to this compositional problem, and perhaps his most conspicuously successful solution is to be found in his setting of Heine's *Der Schelm von Bergen*.

At the beginning of the poem a ball is in progress. The host is a nobleman whose wife dances with a masked stranger. When she insists on unmasking him he is revealed to be the common hangman of Bergen and she is appalled at having been deceived into familiarity with a man of such low social rank. To alleviate her humiliation her husband ennobles the stranger on the spot, granting him the title of Schelm von Bergen or Knave of Bergen. (In Fleischmann's manuscripts this is misleadingly translated as Scamp of Bergen.) Structurally, the work falls into two principal sections: the opening ball scene followed by the scene of the unmasking and subsequent ennoblement. Fleischmann's handling of the first part is very skilful. He sets up a buoyantly lilting dance strain in the orchestra, which introduces a number of important ideas that are subsequently developed to provide a varied but coherent background for the soloist's narration. Although the actual material of the second part is also good, the conclusion is fragmentary and the music does not attain sufficient momentum to complement satisfactorily the continuous sweep of the opening. That Fleischmann seems to have been aware of this flaw may be deduced from the prolonged fanfare-like passage marking the ennoblement with which he brings the scene to a close. But because it is not well integrated into the musical fabric, this strikes the listener as a perfunctory afterthought added on to remedy an obvious structural deficiency, and in spite of much imaginative writing, one is left with an overriding impression of formal imbalance.

A similar dance-like background unifies the textures in his setting of Eichendorf's parable *Der seltsame Gast* in which Death, the ominous guest of the title, casts his grim shadow over a wedding party. Fleischmann's depiction of the storm at sea described in *Nis Randers* unfortunately does not eschew obvious onomatopoeic devices such as *tremolandi* and chromatic scales, a recourse to cliché that also mars to some extent his treatment of *Milisint*. This particular ballad concerns a usurping monarch, Milisint, who has murdered his brother's son in order to gain the throne. On the night of his coronation, after his attendants have gone and he is alone, he yearns to feast his eyes once again on his crown and commands it to be brought to him. To his horror, it is brought to him not by his son but by the bloody ghost of his nephew. The night passes and the terrifying apparition vanishes, but the following morning Milisint is discovered to be dead. Fleischmann attempts to establish an eerie atmosphere and a growing sense of dread as the supernatural manifestation gradually approaches the king, but the diminished seventh harmonies on which he relies are too hackneyed a device and the result is unconvincingly theatrical. Supernatural events also furnish the basis for *Swend Gabelbart und St Edmund*, which recounts how the statue of the martyred St Edmund stepped down from its pedestal to confront and slay the Viking invader Swend Gabelbart. As in the companion pieces, the contours of Fleischmann's flexible vocal line are well adapted to the text, but in spite of some effectively dramatic moments the thematic material is on the whole less memorable in this work and it is perhaps the least distinguished of the set.

Darthula, a late addition to the *Balladen und Legenden,* is also arguably the finest of them. Scored for mixed-voice choir, it is the only one not to feature a solo voice. The text is a lament on the death of the tragic heroine Darthula and is lyrical rather than narrative in style. In its wild expression of grief and its resigned acceptance of death, it demands a very different treatment to that of other poems and Fleischmann responds with some of the most eloquent music he composed for this entire group of works. The thematic invention is distinguished and the richly resourceful harmonic idiom articulates a well thought-out tonal design and a convincing structure. The result is a composition that traverses with assurance a wide emotional range, moving naturally and inevitably from climaxes of radiant intensity to moments of poignant tenderness.

Of the few other works for chorus and orchestra in Fleischmann's output, the most distinguished are the *Zwei Gesänge* [Two Songs] which were performed in Dachau in May 1906. These settings of Goethe's 'Wanderers Nachtlied' [The Wanderer's Night Song] and 'Über ein Stündlein' [On a Little Hour] by Paul Heyse are substantial scores. Not

Ex. 9: *Darthula*, opening

only do they confirm Fleischmann's complete command of the resources of the Romantic style, but in the quality and fluency of their invention, the richness of their harmonies and their well-proportioned structures they are also amongst the most attractive of his early compositions. The writing for orchestra is very accomplished and together with the scores of the two nativity plays they show this aspect of Fleischmann's art at its best. *Gotenzug* [The Last Goths], a setting of a poem by Felix Dahn, was also performed in Germany 1906. This powerful march-like movement for male voices and orchestra is a dark and unusually compelling work, and like the *Zwei Gesänge* is superbly orchestrated. Fleischmann clearly liked the piece as he conducted it again in Cork in April 1909 in a concert that also included a performance of the second of the *Zwei Gesänge* which was sung to English words by Terence MacSwiney under the title 'Wait, O Be Patient Awhile'.

The same 1909 concert featured the first performance of *A Festive Ode*. This new work also had a text by Terence MacSwiney which was based on a German original of Fleischmann's own devising. *A Festive Ode* is a hymn to Ireland and is of considerable interest in showing Fleischmann's desire to identify himself with his new surroundings in the years immediately following his move to Cork. Scored for mixed-voice choir, children's choir and an orchestra of woodwind and brass and timpani, it opens in stirring style –

> Swept by the sea, by rocks girt round,
> See from the surging waves arise
> A lonely land in peace profound
> Whose stretching shores and open skies
> Give greeting to the mariner's eyes.

– and it concludes with the choir declaiming 'Hail, Eire, hail' in an ardent patriotic climax. This piece successfully combines technical brilliance with dignity of utterance and, as befits the theme, is more popular in its appeal than many of the preceding works. It seems unlikely that *A Festive Ode* was ever heard in the orchestral version – all the Fleischmann works in the 1909 concert were probably performed with the orchestral scores arranged for piano and harmonium. The full score of the work is dated 1910, and it is likely to have been made with a view to a second performance that never took place.

Although most of the other secular choral works are *a cappella* a few have instrumental accompaniment. Amongst the most interesting of these is a short cantata for solo baritone (or tenor), female-voice choir and organ, *Wunden hast du, Geliebter* [Wounds thou hast, beloved], to words from an old German Passion play. In its chromatic, appoggiatura-laden harmonic idiom, this piece recalls Bach's more mystical moods. The two later works that comprise Op. 47 are pervaded by a similar emotional intensity. These pieces which, again, are for female-voice choir and organ but this time with soprano soloist, also have religious themes: the first is a setting of *Das Hochzeitfest zu Kana* [The Marriage Feast at Cana] by Clemens Brentano, and the second a setting of *Cor Jesu* [Heart of Jesus] by Carl Ludwig Schleich.

Ex. 10: *A Festive Ode,* opening

2

A substantial amount of the unaccompanied choral music is for male-voice choir. Almost all of these pieces are short and straightforward as the low pitch of the medium inhibits the textural and harmonic complexity necessary to sustain extended forms. To write well for male chorus, the composer is largely reliant on his ability to invent good melodic material with clear rhythmic outlines in order to vitalise what will necessarily be a plain harmonic idiom and predominantly homophonic textures. In general, the genre is not perhaps a very rewarding one as it requires a considerable degree of compositional restraint. But Fleischmann negotiates the problems skilfully and his works for male voices demonstrate his sound professional understanding of what is required.

The best of these pieces are undoubtedly the *Acht Lieder für Männerchor* [Eight Songs for Male-Voice Choir], which were published

Ex. 11: 'Liebesahnung', (v) from *Acht Lieder für Männerchor*, opening

in Munich in two sets of four. The published scores are undated but the designation Op. 3 suggests that they are early works. Fleischmann clearly wrote them with accomplished choirs in mind as they make considerable demands on the singers – the upward vocal range of the first tenor, for example, extends to the note B on several occasions. The resources of a conventional late nineteenth-century harmonic idiom are deployed with maximum effectiveness and the basic progressions are spiced with a telling use of contrapuntally derived discords. Well-chosen appoggiaturas and suspensions offset the chordal texture by lending an occasional quasi-polyphonic independence to the parts and the resultant inner movement is just enough to ensure sufficient textural variety. Fleischmann is resourceful in inventing attractive material within very circumscribed limits and he shows much ingenuity and imagination in imbuing each of the eight short pieces with a distinct character of its own.

Few of the later works for male voices are quite as technically demanding as the *Acht Lieder*. In general, they tend to adhere to a more diatonic idiom and avoid extremes of vocal register. Nor on the whole do they show comparable textural sophistication. Occasionally, he employs canonic devices to provide interest: the complex six-part writing, for example, at the opening of 'Trink ich Wein' [If I Drink Wine] – the first of the *Studentenlieder aus dem 16. Jahrhundert* [Student Songs from the Sixteenth Century] – turns out to be merely a short, easily manageable canon at the unison. But more often he relies on techniques of obvious effectiveness such as the juxtaposition of unharmonised melodic phrases and answering chordal passages. This no doubt reflects a practical response to the standard of the choirs for which, presumably, he wrote many of these works. Still, he frequently contrives to compose charming music. A touching piece entitled *Eine Hand voll Erde* [Earth, a Little Handful] and a witty setting of Longfellow's 'Beware' stand out as being particularly memorable. The latter (the second of *Three Male Choruses*) shows to good effect the distinction with which he can handle the simplest of procedures as well as his flair for inventing piquant harmonic progressions.

Surprisingly, given a lifetime's experience of training and conducting choirs, the music for unaccompanied mixed-voice chorus cannot be ranked amongst Fleischmann's most distinguished work. The number of very simple homophonic settings – including arrangements of songs from the *Kleine Romanzen und Lieder im Volkston* (which also exist in versions for male voices) as well as other pieces in a similar style such as *Rosenzeit* [Rose of June] – suggests that, again, this may be due to the variable quality of the choirs with which he worked.

That said, his two most ambitious works in this medium, the *Vier Geistliche Gesänge* [Four Sacred Songs] to words by Mörike and the *Drei*

Ex. 12: 'Beware', (ii) from *Three Male Choruses*, opening

Gedichte von Freiherr von Eichendorf [Three Poems by Freiherr von Eichendorf], are on the whole disappointing. Despite some effective moments, the tortuous harmonic progressions and the strained climaxes of the Mörike settings create the impression that he was striving after a profundity of expression which eluded him. The second of the Eichendorf songs, 'Windsgleich kommt der wilde Krieg geritten' [Tempest the Steed of Wild War Clatters] with its onomatopoeic *portamenti* suggesting the storm of the title, presents difficulties of pitching that would undoubtedly deter most conductors from attempting it. Apart from this, although the harmonic idiom is in general more transparent, all three Eichendorf pieces suffer from a similar sense of strain at the climaxes. The third song of the set, 'Schon Kehren die Vögel Wieder ein' [Now Hither the Swallows Wing their Way], is perhaps the most fully achieved.

Ex. 13: *Rieden*, bars 1-12

Einfach und schlicht

Fleischmann's skill as a choral composer is demonstrated to far better advantage in a small handful of unpretentious part songs that include an amusingly skittish piece entitled *Das Geheimnis* [The Secret] – or, on some manuscripts, *Mein Schatz* [My Love] after the first line of the poem, 'Mein Schatz hat mich geküsst' [My love has kissed me] – and a wistful song about forsaken love, *Wegenwart* [Erica, the Enchanted Flower]. To these can be added *Rieden*, a polished and mellifluous setting of a poem by Franz Schaele inspired by the grave of the poetess Princess Marie Gabriele of Bavaria at Rieden near Dachau.

If none of these pieces merit comparison with the best of the songs for voice and piano, their colourful harmonies and graceful melodic invention lend them an appealing charm of their own.

MUSIC FOR THE CHURCH

On his appointment as Regens Chori to the Cathedral of St Mary and St Anne in 1906, Fleischmann was expected to put the directives of Pius X's *Motu proprio* into practice. Apart from its negative legislation on the participation of women in church choirs, this document specified Gregorian chant and the sacred polyphony of the sixteenth century as the most appropriate music for use in the liturgy. At this period, of course, the Catholic liturgy was still in Latin. Modern composers who wished to write new works for the church not only had to set Latin texts, which may not in itself have been an impediment, but they were also constrained to emulate the spirit and, in some respects, the techniques of the officially approved music, which may have been creatively more inhibiting. Fleischmann was conscientious in implementing the Papal directives and his choir acquired a reputation, not only in Cork but nationally and even internationally, for the quality of its performances of sixteenth-century polyphony. There can be little doubt that his genuine desire to work within the terms of the *Moto proprio* also largely determined the nature of his own sacred compositions

Only about half of his church music appears to have been composed for the cathedral choir. Some liturgical works date from his early years in Dachau. Many others are known to have been occasioned by circumstances that were not related to his official duties and these include a substantial number of pieces composed for various convent choirs in County Cork, which is the likely provenance of most if not all of the sacred music for female voices. Even if this cannot be verified in every instance, it is reasonable to assume that the remaining music for mixed-voice and male-voice choirs was written for the cathedral, and it is interesting to note how little of it was composed for general everyday use. Fleischmann made only two settings of the Ordinary of the Mass, for example. One of these was written in 1948 for the boys of St Finbarr's College, Farranferris. It is possible that the other, a very simple homophonic setting in four parts, may have been written for the cathedral choir, although the present writer is inclined to think otherwise. (As it survives, this work is incomplete: the single existing copy – which is not in Fleischmann's hand – consists of the choral part with occasional empty bars indicating a missing accompaniment.) But even if this is so, a solitary setting of the Ordinary suggests that as a composer Fleischmann was content to remain in the background and select most of the cathedral choir's regular repertoire from the music approved by the Vatican. This is further borne out by the fact that he composed so few motets. Apart from settings of the *Ave Maria*, *Ave Maris Stella*, *Dextera Domini*, *Haec Dies* and one or two other familiar texts, he made no consistent attempt to provide music for the Proper of the Mass either. The exception, for some reason, is the rite of Benediction of the Blessed Sacrament, for which he composed several versions of the *Tantum ergo* and the *O Salutaris hostia*, both as complementary pairs of pieces and as separate works.

Most of his cathedral music, therefore, was written either for specific events or to meet particular requirements of a practical nature. The first category includes the various settings of the *Ecce Sacerdos Magnus*, which is customarily sung at the ceremonial entrance of the bishop into the cathedral. As one might expect, these settings aim at a certain splendour of sonority appropriate to the pomp of the occasion, one of them being elaborately scored for choir and organ with additional brass ensemble. There is also a setting of *Terra tremuit* for similar forces which bears a fulsome dedication in Latin to Canon Michael O'Sullivan, who personally financed the purchase of a new organ for the cathedral in 1924. It was probably written for performance at a special ceremony to inaugurate the new instrument, as was the simple *Organ Blessing* for unaccompanied voices. Other works that are likely to have had merely an occasional performance are the *Requiem* (which may have been written in 1920 for the funeral of Terence MacSwiney) and the *Roman Te Deum*, which, like the *Ecce Sacerdos Magnus*, would only have been heard at ceremonies of unusual magnificence.

The second category includes pieces like the *Canticum Zachariae* (or Benedictus) for the service of Tenebrae and the choral responses (*Responsoria Chori*) for the St John Passion, both of which may have been heard annually at Passiontide. Fleischmann is likely to have composed works of this kind either because he was unable to find anything suitable or simply because he was not in a position to purchase the music he required. Remarkably, the cathedral authorities appear to have made no effort to build up a library of sacred music during the fifty-five years of Fleischmann's tenure. Fleischmann was consequently obliged to spend an inordinate amount of time that might have been put to better and more creative use in the unrewarding drudgery of copying such music as he needed, much of which, one imagines, could easily have been bought. His papers include a substantial number of transcriptions and adaptations of standard sacred works which testify to this industry. It was not merely a matter of copying the scores: the choral parts also had to be copied in a form that would allow them to be mechanically reproduced. And when these sets of choral parts eventually became worn out, new sets would have to be prepared. If Fleischmann found he did not have the kind of piece he required for a particular ceremony to hand, therefore, he seems to have had little choice but to compose it himself. No doubt he took a justifiable pride in exercising his skills as a fully equipped Kapellmeister and enjoyed being able to provide suitable music as occasion demanded. Nonetheless, one suspects that much of what he wrote for the cathedral choir owes its existence to these necessitous circumstances rather to any urgent creative impulse.

A considerable number of the liturgical works are closely connected with plainchant. The practice of combining plainsong with original material represents a venerable tradition in the composition of sacred music, and Fleischmann's interest in it is likely to have been stimulated by the *Motu proprio*'s emphasis on the fundamental importance of Gregorian chant in the celebration of the liturgy. Amongst works of this kind are various plainsong melodies for the Credo into which he introduced fully harmonised passages to replace sections of the original, the length of the text justifying the transition from monophony to polyphony to highlight important moments such as the central 'Et incarnatus est' and the concluding 'Et vitam venturi'. Other such works include the *Roman Te Deum* mentioned above. Here plainchant alternates with original material throughout, as it does in the *Vexilla Regis* where the odd numbered verses of the hymn are sung to the Gregorian melody and the even numbered to Fleischmann's own music. The short *Ave Maria* for male voices in Ex. 14 provides a good illustration of the style: the unadorned plainchant of the first part is complemented by the expressive harmony of the second, which, although appropriately restrained, permits a more affective response to the words. In its careful avoidance of any undue obtrusion of the composer's personality this piece also typifies the creative discretion that informs most of Fleischmann's church music.

Perhaps the subtlest example of Fleischmann's handling of plainsong is to be found in the *Three Motets based on Gregorian Themes* for male-voice choir (the third of which also exists in a version for mixed-voice choir). All three are settings of Marian texts – *Ave Maria, Recordare, Virgo Mater* and *Assumpta est Maria*. According to a note in the composer's handwriting which is included with the manuscripts, they were inspired by a visit to 'a remote monastery church, where the monks, with candles at their side, sing their nightly Nocturnes and psalms'. Fleischmann's unusually free treatment of the plainchant is handled with considerable compositional tact: new ideas seem to grow spontaneously from fragments of the Gregorian melodies and both are seamlessly grafted onto a harmonic and tonal background that attempts to evoke in purely musical terms the devotional atmosphere he describes.

Ex. 14: *Ave Maria* (simplex)

All of Fleischmann's sacred music was designed to be performed as an integral part of the liturgy. The external form of that liturgy is not the same today as it was when he was active as a composer, however. Latin has been abandoned, and there is little place in the contemporary Church for sacred music that is not sung in the vernacular languages. This situation has led to the neglect of far greater figures than Fleischmann, of course. But while the music of Palestrina and the other polyphonic masters will continue to be heard – even if rarely in the circumstances for which it was written – the music of minor figures like Fleischmann, which might otherwise have retained an honoured place in the repertoire of their local churches, seems largely destined for oblivion. Unfortunately, if the Church for which it was composed has no use for it now, this music has little viability outside the context of religious services. Because its effectiveness and to some extent its structural validity are largely dependent on its liturgical function, it would not survive translation to the concert hall. Furthermore, while Fleischmann's tendency to stylistic self-effacement may be praiseworthy in a composer committed to enhancing the ceremonies of the church in the spirit of the *Motu proprio*, it robs his sacred music of the vivid and attractive personality that makes the best of the secular music interesting. It is usually expertly tailored to its purpose, of course, and at its finest is well-turned, but it would not necessarily make for rewarding listening under other circumstances.

Among the few viable pieces that might be considered exceptions are the *Zwei Ave Maria* [Two Ave Marias], which do not appear to have been composed for the cathedral choir in Cork. They are dedicated to his friend Monsignor Ludwig Berberich, Kapellmeister at the cathedral in Munich, who performed either one or both of them with his choir there in 1930. Both settings are in eight parts (the first of them is laid out for double chorus) and they show to good effect Fleischmann's ability to handle the massed effects and textural complexities this kind of *a cappella* choral writing normally entails. *Sacris solemniis,* a similar piece in seven parts, has the same opulently full choral writing and Romantic harmonic idiom as the *Zwei Ave Maria,* characteristics that set all three pieces somewhat apart from most of the other church music. Arguably one of his finest sacred works, *Sacris solemniis* is fluent, shapely and expertly laid out for large choir. After an antiphonal opening where the soprano and alto voices in four-part harmony are answered by the tenors and basses also in four parts, the re-entry of the upper voices (now in three parts) quickly brings the music to a sonorous climax from which there is a gradual descent to a tranquil close on the tonic C minor. The only shortcoming from the point of view of concert performance (but not necessarily liturgical performance) is that the second verse of the hymn is set to the same music as the first and the repeat of the

Ex. 15: *Sacris solemniis,* opening

climax requires careful handling in order to achieve a satisfactory sense
of overall structure. The work ends with an ordinary plagal cadence and
tierce de Picardie, to which, however, Fleischmann manages to impart a
fresh turn by a simple build up of vocal entries.

ARRANGEMENTS AND INSTRUMENTAL MUSIC

Like the greater part of the sacred music, Fleischmann's many arrangements are for the most part also functional in nature. They can be
divided into two categories: arrangements of Irish folk music, and what
for convenience might be described as miscellaneous arrangements.
The latter group chiefly comprises settings of various carols, hymn
tunes and plainchant melodies for use in church services and they
range from straightforward *a cappella* harmonisations to elaborate versions with organ accompaniment. Few of these pieces are in any way
remarkable, although Fleischmann's professionalism is always in evidence. Some of them could still be heard with pleasure, however,
particularly the settings of the carols, which, unlike the sacred music,
have not been made redundant by changes in the liturgy. The small
handful of arrangements not written for voices includes the *Turmmusik
in der Christnacht* [Tower Music for Christmas Night], and the story is
told elsewhere in this book of how, just before he came to Cork in 1906,
Fleischmann arranged several well-known carol tunes for brass
ensemble which he organised to be performed every Christmas Eve
from the steeple of St Jakob's church in Dachau as an exile's greeting to
his native place. Also worth mentioning here is a version for harmonium and piano of the Organ Concerto in F, Op. 137, by Rheinberger.
This was made during 1917 and 1918 while he was in the prisoner-of-
war camp in Oldcastle, County Meath. It is possible that he had an
opportunity to play through the concerto in this form with a fellow
prisoner, or perhaps he intended to study it with a view to future public
performance and wished to make a rehearsal score. If this is so, it was
not until March 1930 that he was eventually in a position to play the
concerto publicly (with orchestra) when he took part in a broadcast
concert from the Cathedral of St Mary and St Anne which was organised by the Cork radio station.[2]

Given Fleischmann's general lack of familiarity with Irish folk music,
it is not surprising that his arrangements are largely of well-known
tunes such as popular Thomas Davis ballads, songs from the *Irish
Melodies* of Thomas Moore and airs from the Bunting collections. Most
of these settings are choral and consist of homophonic *a cappella* harmonisations of the simplest kind without any attempt at textural
diversity or polyphonic elaboration. Clearly designed to lie well within
the modest capacity of the amateur choirs for which they are most
likely to have been composed, there is little to distinguish them from

numerous similar folk song arrangements by figures like Carl Hardebeck or Éamonn Ó Gallchobhair.

Fleischmann composed comparatively little instrumental music, most of which is for the organ. Around the time of his marriage, however, he wrote a piano work for his wife, *Rhapsodie über eine irischer Weise* [Rhapsody on an Irish Air], which she performed at a concert in Dachau in 1906 shortly before the couple left Germany for Cork. Based on the well-known jig tune 'The Irish Washerwoman', this is a substantial showpiece of considerable difficulty and it exploits a wide variety of pianistic devices to brilliant effect. Although structurally diffuse, it shows an impressive understanding of virtuoso keyboard writing and is a telling tribute to Tilly Swertz's technical accomplishments as a pianist. Feeling, perhaps, that the piece lacked cogency, he produced a shorter version of the work in 1921, and Tilly included it in a programme of modern piano music she gave in 1926 under the title *Nachklänge aus einem irischer Musikfest* [Memories of an Irish Music Festival]. Fleischmann subsequently made a third, very condensed and much simpler version of the piece for flute and piano, although it is not known what circumstances occasioned this or even if it was ever performed. Only one other complete piano work has survived, *Has Sorrow thy Young Days Shaded*, which is based on the song of the same name from Moore's *Irish Melodies*. Written in 1913, this short lyrical albumleaf is technically undemanding and the original melody is tastefully provided with contrasting material designed to amplify, but not disturb the prevailing atmosphere of tranquil melancholy. As the manuscript is annotated with Tilly's fingerings, it may well have been composed for one of her recitals, perhaps as an encore.

Fleischmann's organ music falls into three principal categories. The first comprises music of a purely functional nature for use by a professional church organist: it includes sets of introductions, modulations and interludes designed to enhance the liturgical performance of various Gregorian chants, as well as a fairly comprehensive set of accompaniments and cadence formulae to support and embellish reciting tones of different pitches. As is the case with the sacred music, however, the practical utility of these pieces is unfortunately bound up with liturgical conditions that no longer obtain. The second group encompasses various short works such as preludes and several sets of character pieces (the *Three Lyrical Tone Sketches, Three Pieces* and the *Three Improvisations on Gregorian Themes*). In general, it is probably true to say that the characteristic weaknesses in Fleischmann's compositional armoury are more exposed in the medium of purely instrumental music than anywhere else. That he was probably aware of this may partly account for the small number of such works in his output and explain why he composed comparatively little music even for the organ, his own instrument.

Technically, his most compromising limitation is a dual tendency to routine textural organisation and rhythmic flaccidity, with the inevitable consequence that his melodic invention often falls short of memorability. This shortcoming affects his work to varying degrees and even his better music is not always free of it. In his finest pieces, however, Fleischmann turned these technical shortcomings to positive account and circumvented their negative effects, at times being able to transcend them altogether. Apart from the best of the works with orchestral accompaniment such as *Die Nacht der Wunder* and the *Zwei Gesänge*, such weaknesses are perhaps least in evidence in the music for voices, particularly in the songs with piano. Here he displays a sure instinct in choosing texts that permit him a convincing compositional response within the natural compass of his artistic range. His exploitation of the tension between verbal and musical rhythm usually results in a distinguished vocal line, or at least in a melodic contour that is well suited to the declamation of the words. His handling of standard accompaniment patterns is also sufficiently deft to ensure ongoing rhythmic interest. As far as the sacred music is concerned, absence of rhythmic energy is not always a fault – in some instances it may even be appropriate – and liturgical effectiveness can often compensate for thematic invention that is less than compellingly vivid. But in writing for instruments such defects become all too apparent and a fluent command of harmonic technique is not alone enough to make up for lack of vital interest elsewhere. Ultimately, although they have an easy, unforced sense of continuity and a formal neatness, these organ pieces fail to attain genuine distinction.

The harmonic idiom of the various preludes suggests that they date from before 1920. The various short character pieces were probably written later, although he seems to have conceived the *Three Lyrical Tone Sketches* during the period of his internment in 1917 and 1918. In some respects, the character pieces are the more imaginative works and the *Three Improvisations on Gregorian Themes*, while also vulnerable to the charge of rhythmic and textural monotony, are unusually adventurous harmonically and formally. The second piece, 'Vor einem Madonnenbild Andrea del Sartos" [Before a picture of the Madonna by Andrea del Sarto] – which is based on the Gregorian *Ave Maria* – is undoubtedly the finest of the set. A curiously intense evocation that recalls the music of Herbert Howells, there is nothing else quite like it in Fleischmann's output and one wonders if it was merely an isolated experiment or if it might represent a vein of creativity, deeper and more subtle that that from which he drew most of his later music and which for some reason he left largely unexplored.

Apart from the third of the *Three Pieces* mentioned above which is a fugue 'über ein jonisches Thema' [on an Ionian Theme], Fleischmann also composed a number of independent fugal works, which comprise

Ex. 16: 'Vor einem Madonnenbild Andrea del Sartos", (ii) from
        Three Improvisations on Gregorian Themes, opening

the final category of organ music. The *Introduction and Fugue on the theme of the Magnificat (Tonus VIII)* and the *Fuga Impromptu on the Easter Alleluia* both date from 1918, and as they were originally composed either for organ or for orchestra they also represent his only purely orchestral works. Later revised versions of these pieces also exist, which in some respects show marked differences to the originals. Although based on the same plainchant motif, the fugue entitled *Das österliche Alleluja* [The Easter Alleluia] bears no relation to the above *Fuga Impromptu* and is a completely different working of the theme. While an untitled fugue in C major seems little more than an exercise, the *Fantasie-Prelude and Fugue on the Gaelic Hymn to St Patrick* is undoubtedly the most ambitious as well as the most technically demanding work in this category.

Although Fleischmann was a skilled contrapuntist, these pieces are perhaps too reminiscent of the academic approach to fugal composition to rank highly as original creations. They unfold according to fairly predictable quasi-Baroque procedures, and while they possess greater rhythmic interest than the short pieces, this is largely due to the self-generating momentum of the counterpoint. Formally, however, they are less predictable than the academic model and the strict contrapuntal working out of the material is occasionally suspended to allow for the introduction of radically contrasting passages. But these episodes are not always equally successful, and while they undoubtedly provide variety they can have the effect of dissipating the energy that has been generated. They also suggest that Fleischmann's view of the fugue is essentially a Romantic one, something that is further borne out by his readiness to bring the works to a conclusion with an imposing peroration rather than with a genuinely polyphonic culmination. *Das österliche Alleluja* ends with a full chordal version of the theme above a running bass in the manner of Mendelssohn, for example. But this is relatively modest compared with the grandiose alternative ending for additional brass instruments, timpani and mixed-voice choir which he supplies for the *Fantasie-Prelude and Fugue on the Gaelic Hymn to St Patrick*, and the setting of the complete canticle he provides as an optional choral finale for the earlier version of the *Fugue on the theme of the Magnificat*.

That two very different versions exist of the *Fugue on the theme of the Magnificat* and the *Fuga Impromptu* has already been mentioned, and this touches on a very unusual feature of Fleischmann's output: not only did he make alternative versions of a surprising number of works, but he often seemed unable to bring a piece into a definitive final form. Some works survive in three or four separate manuscripts each of which diverges to a greater or lesser extent from the others. In some cases the differences may be slight, consisting of little more than the re-composition of the final cadence; in others they may amount to extensive revisions. Even where a manuscript is described as the 'final version', it will not necessarily be free from subsequent pencilled annotations, which obviously makes any question of a possible performance somewhat problematic. One of the most extreme instances of this is the *Fantasie-Prelude and Fugue on the Gaelic Hymn to St Patrick.* No complete continuous score of the work exists. The six different manuscripts of the Fantasie-Prelude correspond to six distinct versions of the movement, although all are based on the same material and some are quite closely related. There is no indication, however, as to which of them might embody the composer's final thoughts. There are four different versions of the Fugue. Three of these – for organ alone, for organ with additional brass instruments, and for organ, brass and choir – are fairly similar in content and, apart from the different forces, diverge principally in the way the concluding bars are handled. The fourth version, on the other hand, has a much longer choral finale in which the original fourteen concluding bars have been extended to fifty-one. The complete work was apparently conceived in three sections: the Fantasie-Prelude (in C major), followed by a four-part harmonisation of the hymn tune sung *a cappella* by the choir, or alternatively played *pianissimo* on the organ (in A flat major), and finally the Fugue (in C major). The surviving choral and instrumental parts suggest that it was performed in the shorter version for organ, brass ensemble and chorus according to this scheme. It is not known, however, which version of the Fantasie-Prelude was used. Although such a bewildering abundance of alternative versions is exceptional, Fleischmann's habitual second and third thoughts, sometimes made years after a work was written, throw an interesting light on his creative personality even if one is not always convinced that his revisions constitute unqualified improvements.

The shape of Fleischmann's compositional career and the nature of the work he produced at the various stages of his life prompt a number of speculations. As a young man in his twenties he impressed his contemporaries as having exceptional promise. His earliest boyish efforts gave a clear indication of unusual talent and this was confirmed by the steady stream of accomplished works he produced after he left the Royal Academy of Music in 1901. His music not only showed a command of the basic disciplines of his art – harmony, counterpoint, orchestration and form – but, more importantly, it demonstrated an ability to deploy these techniques in the service of a unified style. To be sure, his early work reflected the current idiom of late Romanticism, but the angle of that reflection suggests that a distinct creative personality had already begun to emerge.

There can be no doubt that Fleischmann found it very difficult on a personal level to leave Germany. It also seems clear that being uprooted from his native country had a negative impact on his art. To be removed from the spiritual environment that sustained his imaginative life and to be transplanted into an alien culture was disruptive enough in itself; but from a purely practical point of view, Ireland in 1906 was not in any way comparable to Germany either in the opportunities it afforded composers for the performance and publication of their work or in the sophistication of its audiences. It must have been a source of bitter regret that just as his name was beginning to come before a larger public and his abilities to be acknowledged by influential musicians such as Richard Strauss, who commented favourably on *Die Nacht der Wunder*, he had to abandon his hard-won advantages and begin again in almost wholly unpropitious circumstances.

During his first years in Cork he endeavoured to relate artistically to his new situation as the patriotic hymn *A Festive Ode* shows. Nonetheless, he continued to cherish the hope of return to Germany until the First World War made this impossible. When he was eventually allowed back to Cork in 1920 after his five-year internment he had to reconcile himself to the fact that his future now lay in the city. It is from this period onwards that circumstances seem to have seriously impinged on his creativity. Undoubtedly, he felt isolated. Cork did not offer much by way of active musical life, and it afforded little congenial artistic society and virtually none of the intelligent professional or critical response to his work that an artist needs in order to develop. The dearth of professional music-making discouraged the production of orchestral works and made the revival of existing works requiring orchestral forces unfeasible except in the unsatisfactory compromise of a piano reduction. If it seems somewhat surprising that he wrote so little music for the organ, one must ask what public there would have been for organ recitals in Cork in 1920, at a time when audiences for concerts of any kind were so sparse. Although some of his songs received occasional concert performances, others were never heard publicly. He was even hampered to some extent in composing the music for which there was an evident demand: his cautious approach in many of the choral works and arrangements undoubtedly reflects the modest abilities of the choirs with which he worked, and while his own cathedral choir attained a high standard of performance, the nature and scope of his sacred music was largely determined by the routine demands of his official post.

The incomplete state in which he left the series of *Balladen und Legenden* strongly suggests frustrated creative ambition. This large undertaking, to which he devoted an enormous amount of time and energy over the best part of a decade, clearly indicates a desire to extend his range beyond the composition of miniatures and short pieces of sacred music. But he must have realised that the chances of having any of these works performed in Cork were virtually non-existent. Obviously, one cannot be certain that his talent would have fulfilled its bright promise had he been able to remain in Germany, but it is equally true that the conditions in which he now found himself were not conducive to its full realisation. There is little in his later work that seems to be on the same trajectory as the music he composed before he left Dachau. It is not that his creative spark was extinguished: in spite of circumstances, he continued to produce some fine pieces even if his scope was restricted. But his frequent inability to arrive at a definitive version of a piece seems to indicate that discouragement prompted at least a partial retreat into a private world where the exacting business of bringing a work to a final performable state could be postponed indefinitely. If on one level, however, composition seemed to become something of a solipsistic activity, on another level, he contentiously expended his gifts as fully and as practically as circumstances would allow and, in the last analysis, the extensive catalogue of his works must qualify any sense of unrealised potential. The fact remains that few if any composers working in Ireland in the early decades of the twentieth century were as consistently productive.

Aloys Georg Fleischmann:
An Annotated Catalogue of Compositions

SÉAMAS DE BARRA

INTRODUCTION

The catalogue is divided into the following categories: Stage Works; Orchestral Works (subdivided into music for Orchestra, Chorus and Orchestra and Solo Voice and Orchestra); Choral Music: Accompanied; Choral Music: Unaccompanied (subdivided into music for Mixed Voices and Male Voices); Sacred Music; Vocal Music (subdivided into Lieder, Other Songs and works for Narrator and Piano); Instrumental Music (subdivided into music for Organ and Miscellaneous Instrumental); Arrangements (subdivided into Arrangements of Irish Folk Music and Other Arrangements). As most of Fleischmann's MSS are undated, it has not been possible to establish a chronology for his work: the entries are therefore arranged in alphabetical order within each division and subdivision of the catalogue. Where there is more than one setting of the same text, the order in which these settings have been listed does not necessarily imply chronological order, although the listing does take into account the evident age of the MSS as well as the dates of composition where these are known.

Certain features of this arrangement require, perhaps, a few words of explanation. The division of Vocal Music into the separate categories of Lieder and Other Songs highlights the uninterrupted importance of the German tradition in Fleischmann's imaginative life after he moved to Cork in 1906 and his continued recourse to German texts for his work. Although the three pieces comprising Op. 26, for example, were published as songs in English by Augener in 1929, and are for that reason listed under Other Songs, they were all originally conceived as settings of German words. Similarly, the division of Fleischmann's Arrangements into two categories serves to highlight his creative engagement with Irish folk music. A different problem was encountered in categorising the church music. The fine distinction between original work based on plainchant and arrangements of plainchant melodies can occasionally become blurred, and it is not always easy to determine where one ends and another begins. It was decided to list any work containing original material, however minimal, under Sacred

Music, and relegate the rest (usually straightforward harmonisations) to Other Arrangements. In a few doubtful cases, however, the allocation remains tentative. Works with religious texts that are not liturgical are not listed in Sacred Music.

The information for each entry is given in the following order:

1. Title: The title of a work is given either as it appears on the MS or on the existing copy of the music where the MS is lost. German (or occasionally Irish) titles are followed by English translations in square brackets. Where a German (or Irish) text has been provided with an English translation, the English title is as it appears on the MS; otherwise the translations of the titles are editorial. Titles of works in Latin are generally not translated as they refer to standard liturgical texts. Titles in square brackets are editorial. In the case of an arrangement of a work by a known composer, the composer's name follows the title. Where a work comprises more than one separate movement, individual titles and, where relevant, their translations are similarly listed.

2. Text: Except where it is included in the title of a work, the name of the author is listed first. Doubtful attributions are indicated by a question mark, and unknown authorship (except in Sacred Music) is indicated by 'Words?'. In the case of Arrangements, the source of both the musical material and the text (whether traditional or credited to a composer/author) is given where this is known; otherwise unknown or anonymous authorship is not generally specified. The original language of the text is given next, followed by language(s) of translation, with the name of the translator(s), where known, in brackets. Where a work comprises more than one separate movement and there is more than one author/translator, the relevant information is given after each individual item. In some cases, all or part of the above information may be given in the form of direct quotations from a programme note, a libretto or MS where this is of particular interest. The sources of all quotations are indicated.

3. Forces: Details of orchestral forces are given in the standard abbreviations. In Vocal Music, all works listed are for solo voice and piano unless otherwise specified.

4. General notes: In some cases, brief descriptions of the extant MSS are given where these are of particular interest or relevance. All annotations and markings relating to the date and place of compositions have been reproduced. Although they are neither consistently nor systematically employed, some works bear opus numbers and these are also listed where known. Where a work exists in more than one version for different forces these are listed in the appropriate category and are fully cross-referenced. Details of performances are given where known. Additional relevant information is included where appropriate.

STAGE WORKS

Die Nacht der Wunder [The Night of Wonders]
'Dachauer Krippenspiel 1905/Die Nacht der Wunder/nach einer Christuslegende von Selma Lagerlöf/von/Franz Langheinrich./Musik von A. Fleischmann./Mit Zeichnungen von H. Stockmann.' [Dachau Nativity Play 1905/The Night of Wonders/after a Christian Legend by Selma Lagerlöf/by/Franz Langheinrich./Music by A. Fleischmann./With set designs by K. Stockmann.] (title page of printed libretto). German. Mixed-voice choir, children's choir and orchestra [3222.4030.timp.perc.hp.str]. Full score, vocal score (of prologue only) and set of orchestral and choral parts extant. First performed in Dachau in 1905 (probably on 3 and 4 January). The prologue and final chorus of *Die Nacht der Wunder* were subsequently adapted by the composer to precede *Krippenbilder*, the Dachau Kinderfestspiel [Children's Festival Play] of 1906, which was based on words from the Bible with music by Michael Pretorius (1571–1621). Performed in Dachau on 6 and 7 January 1906.

Ein altes Weihnachtsspiel [An Old Christmas Play]
'[I]n zwei Aufzügen/Text aus dem 16. Jahrhundert/Dichtung nach Josef Beer' [In two Acts/16th century text/ adapted by Josef Beer] (from printed libretto). '[C]omponiert für Kinderstimmen, Harfe, Chor und grosses Orchester/Miss Tilly Swertz in Freundschaft zugeeignet' [Composed for children's voices, harp, choir and large orchestra/Dedicated in friendship to Miss Tilly Swertz] (cover of MS full score). German. Mixed-voice choir, children's choir and orchestra: [2222.2230.timp.perc.hp.str]. 1904. Full score and set of orchestral and choral parts extant. Josef Beer (1851-1908), an Austrian composer principally of opera, had himself written music for his adaptation of the play. According to Ursula Nauderer in her article on Fleischmann's nativity plays in the exhibition catalogue *Auf Weihnachten zu: Altdachauer Weihnachtszeit*, (Dachau 2003), p. 76, the Dachau publisher Franz Mondrion adapted Beer's text for Fleischmann. First performed in Dachau in 1904 (probably on 3 and 4 January).

Sonnenwende [Solstice]
'(Kinderfestspiel der Singschule Dachau)/Dramatische Weihnachtsmärchen in 4 Aufzügen/Dichtung von Anton Kohl/Für dreistimmigen Frauenchor komponiert von Michael Haller/Op. 51/Für Streichorchester instrumentiert von Alois Fleischmann' [(Children's Festival Play of the Dachau Choir School)/Dramatic Christmas Tale in 4 Acts/Poem by Anton Kohl/Composed for three-part female choir by Michael Haller/Op. 51/Arranged for string orchestra by Alois Fleischmann] (title page of printed libretto). German. 1902. No score extant, but there is a complete set of strings parts and an additional part for harmonium amongst Fleischmann's papers. See Other Arrangements below. This first Dachau Kinderfestspiel [Children's Festival Play] was performed on 1 January 1903.

Sweet Miracle
'A Drama adapted from the Portuguese of Eça de Queiroz with a translation into Irish by Rev. G.M. Cussen O.P.' (MS). Irish. Female-voice choir and piano. Incidental music. 'Xmas 1929' (MS).

The Magic Pool
'To the 12 year old poetess/with best wishes for the future./Dedicated in true friendship to Mary & John Horgan [,] Lacaduv/The Magic Pool/Poem by Joan

Horgan. Music by Aloys Fleischmann/A play for the stage/with Fairies' and Dwarfs' Dance/Female Chorus (Soprano I, II and Alto)/and/Small Orchestra' (title page of MS full score). English. Orchestra: 1111.1000.str. Incidental music. Piano/vocal score extant; complete pencil sketch of full score extant. There is no copy of the play amongst Fleischmann's papers.

ORCHESTRAL WORKS

Orchestra

Alleluja für Orchester oder Orgel [Alleluia for Orchestra or Organ]

Orchestra [2222.22cnt031.str] or organ. Based on a plainchant melody. Two MSS are extant. The first, bearing the above title, is dated 'Douglas Camp 1918' and contains the organ version written out below the orchestra. The second, which comprises the orchestral score only, is in a copyist's hand and is entitled simply *Easter Alleluja* (in a different hand to that of the copyist) and is stamped 'Prisoners of War Camp/Oldcastle/23 Mar 1918'. The *Fuga Impromptu on the Easter Alleluia* for organ listed below is a later (?) version of the work from which it differs in several important respects. Except for the fact that it is based on the same plainchant theme, *Das österliche Alleluja* [The Easter Alleluia], also for organ and listed below, is a completely unrelated piece. See Instrumental Music/Organ below.

Präludium und Fuge für Orgel oder Orchester über dem Magnificat im VIII Kirchenton [Prelude and Fugue for Organ or Orchestra on the Magnificat Tonus VIII].

Orchestra [2222.22cnt021.str] or organ, with an alternative ending for additional SATB choir. Based on a plainchant melody. Three MSS are extant: the first bears the above title, and contains the organ version written out below the orchestra; the second, which is laid out in the same way, comprises the alternative choral ending only; the third, in a copyist's hand, is for orchestra only and is stamped 'Prisoners of War Camp/Oldcastle/8 April 1918'. The *Introduction and Fugue on the theme of the Magnificat (Tonus VIII)* for organ listed below is a later (?) version of the work from which it differs in several important respects. See Orchestral Works/Chorus and Orchestra and Instrumental Music/Organ below.

Chorus and Orchestra

Abendfeier in Venedig [Sunset in Venice (Ave Maria!)]

E. Geibel. German. Mixed-voice choir, with distant voices (children's or female voices) and orchestra [2222.0000.str] or organ. Two MSS are extant: one, in a copyist's hand, is stamped 'Prisoners of War Camp/Oldcastle/22 Aug 1917' and consists of the orchestral part only; the other is a full score in the composer's hand, laid out for orchestra and choir (with the organ version included at the bottom of the page) of which the final page is missing. A later, revised version of this work with the accompaniment reworked for organ only also exists. For a fuller account of the work see Choral Music: Accompanied below.

A Festive Ode

Terence MacSwiney. English. Mixed-voice choir, children's choir, orchestra [2(picc)131.3332.timp (no str)]. The several MSS of this work are variously entitled *Festode, Festgesang, Festive Hymn* and *A Festive Ode*. Full score and vocal score extant. The printed choral part, bearing the title *A Festive Ode*, has a dedicatory inscription to the Cork Choral Union and attributes the words to Aloys Fleischmann ('(a German text by the composer may have furnished the basis for MacSwiney's words). First performed 28 April 1909 by Cork Choral Union, augmented by children's voices from the choirs of the Cathedral of St Mary and St Anne and St Vincent's Convent School, conducted by Fleischmann. For this performance, the accompaniment was probably performed on piano and harmonium. The full score of the work is dated 1910 and may have been completed with a view to a second performance that never took place.

Darthula

'Ossian (3. Cent.) Gaelic Poet, eldest son of Fin-Mac Coul' (MS); 'The words from Ossian (aus *Stimmen der Völker* von Herder)' (another MS). English and German. Mixed-voice choir and orchestra [22(ca)22.2020.hp.str]. Pencil sketch of full score extant, which, although incompletely edited, appears to be in a fairly final form. Vocal score also extant. This work seems to have been conceived as a late addition to the series of *Balladen und Legenden* [Ballads and Legends]: see notes to *Der Schelm von Bergen* [The Scamp of Bergen] listed in Orchestral Works/Solo Voice and Orchestra below.

Flötenlied [Flute Song]

Clemens Brentano. German. Female-voice choir, flute solo and small orchestra [2clars, 2ca (=2hn), pf. str]. Five MSS are extant: the first is a full score in the composer's hand (with the orchestral part arranged for piano at the bottom of the page); the second is also a full score in the composer's hand stamped 'Prisoners of War Camp/Oldcastle/8 Oct 1917'; the third is a vocal score in the composer's hand stamped 'Prisoners of War Camp/Oldcastle/8 Oct 1917'; the fourth, in a copyist's hand, is stamped 'Prisoners of War Camp/Oldcastle/8 April 1918' and consists of the orchestral part only. On the fifth (later?) MS, a vocal score, the work is entitled *Abendständchen* [Serenade] and is described as being for female-voice choir, flute solo and small string orchestra. No full score of this version is extant.

Gotenzug [The Last Goths]

H. Felix Dahn. German and English. Male-voice choir and orchestra [3(picc)222. 4231.timp.perc.str]. Full score and vocal score extant. Performed in Dachau in 1906, and in Cork on 28 April 1909 by the Cork Choral Union, conducted by Fleischmann (probably with piano accompaniment).

Grabgesang [Song of the Grave]

Words? (Über den Hügel hin ziehen die Wolken [Over the Hills the Clouds Pass By]). German. Mixed-voice choir and wind orchestra. Sketch only extant. There is also a separate MS of the choral part, slightly shorter than the present sketch and apparently complete in itself. See *Über den Hügel* listed in Choral Music: Unaccompanied/Mixed-Voices below.

Milisint or *Die traurige Krönung* [Milisint or The Sorrowful Crowning]

Eduard Mörike, 'nach einer irische Sage' [after an Irish Legend] (MS). German and English. Baritone solo, mixed-voice choir and orchestra. While a complete vocal score of this work exists, the orchestral score never seems to have been finalised. Two pencil drafts for a full score survive amongst the composer's papers, each for slightly different forces: the first for an orchestra of 1222.2320.timp.perc.hp.str; the second for an orchestra of 0220.2200.timp.perc.str. The complete sketch of the vocal score is dated 'VIII.32.' Although the work is entitled *Milisint* on some MSS and *Die traurige Krönung* on others, with both occasionally used as title and subtitle, Fleischmann appears to have settled finally on the former. The work was conceived as one of a series of *Balladen und Legenden* [Ballads and Legends]: see notes to *Der Schelm von Bergen* [The Scamp of Bergen] listed in Orchestral Works/Solo Voice and Orchestra below.

Präludium und Fuge für Orgel oder Orchester über dem Magnificat im VIII Kirchenton [Prelude and Fugue for Organ or Orchestra on the Magnificat Tonus VIII].

This work has an *ad libitum* choral finale. See Orchestral Works/Orchestra above.

Zwei Gesänge [Two Songs]

(i) 'Wanderers Nachtlied' [The Wanderer's Night Song], Johann Wolfgang von Goethe; (ii) 'Über ein Stündlein' [On a Little Hour], Paul Heyse, 'für Solostimmen, gemischten Chor u. kleines Orchester' [for solo voices, mixed choir and small orchestra] (MS). Orchestra: 2fl.4hn.str. Full score, vocal score and set of orchestral parts extant. This work was performed in Dachau on 17 May 1906 by the Choir and Orchestra of the Musikalisch-dramatischer Verein [Dachau] conducted by Fleischmann. There was a performance of (ii) 'Über ein Stündlein' under the title 'Wait, O Be Patient Awhile' (with English words by Terence MacSwiney) in Cork on 28 April 1909 by the Cork Choral Union, conducted by Fleischmann (probably with the accompaniment adapted for piano and harmonium).

Solo Voice and Orchestra

Abend im Moor [Evening on the Moor]

Franz Schaehle. German. This is an unedited and incomplete sketch (four introductory bars missing) for high voice and string orchestra (?) of a song for voice and piano [= harmonium]. See Vocal Music/Lieder below.

Ave Maria

High voice and string orchestra. Latin. 'Motette für eine hohe Singstimme und Streichorchester/komponiert/von/Alois Fleischmann/In Verehrung und Dankbarkeit/der hochwohlgeborenen/Frau Dora Ziegler/gewidmet/Partitur/Dachau im Mai 1904' [Motet for high voice and string orchestra/composed/by/Alois Fleischmann/In admiration and gratitude/dedicated to/the most nobly born/Frau Dora Ziegler/Score/Dachau in May 1904] (MS). On the first page of the score in pencil: 'Prachtvoll gesungen von Frau Dora Ziegler' [Splendidly sung by Frau Dora Ziegler]. This work also exists in a version with accompaniment for organ. See *Ave Maria* [second setting] listed in Sacred Music below.

Der Schelm von Bergen [The Scamp of Bergen]

Heinrich Heine. German and English. Tenor and orchestra [2222.2220.timp.str] or piano. A full score and vocal scores of *Der Schelm von Bergen* are extant. One MS of the vocal score is dated 'Cork im Mai 1938'. Fleischmann appears to have planned a series of *Balladen und Legenden* [Ballads and Legends] in the early 1930s for solo male voice and orchestra. From lists included with the various MSS it seems that the initial conception was for four such works, and that this was later expanded to six: (i) *Swend Gabelbart und St Edmund* [Swend Gabelbart and St Edmund], Theodor Fontane; (ii) *Der Schelm von*

Bergen [The Scamp of Bergen], Heinrich Heine; (iii) *Der seltsame Gast* [The Ominous Guest], Josef Eichendorf; (iv) *Nis Randers*, Otto Ernst; (v) *Die Teilung der Erde* [The Division of the Earth], Friedrich Schiller; (vi) *Die traurige Krönung* [The Sorrowful Crowning] (also entitled *Milisint*), Eduard Mörike. This set was subsequently augmented by yet a further work, *Darthula*, a setting of an extract from *Ossian* (James Macpherson) in a translation by Gottfried Herder. The original conception of *Die traurige Krönung* (or *Milisint*) was subsequently modified to include chorus, while *Darthula*, it seems, was conceived from the outset for chorus and orchestra (see Orchestral Works/Chorus and Orchestra above). Of these seven works, only the full scores of *Der Schelm von Bergen* and *Darthula* were completed. Fleischmann appears to have commenced but never completed the orchestration of *Swend Gabelbart und St. Edmund* and while there are drafts for two different orchestrations of *Milisint* among his papers, neither of them was brought to a finished state. *Der seltsame Gast* and *Nis Randers* exist only in vocal score. No trace of *Die Teilung der Erde* has come to light, which suggests that it may never have been written. Schelm von Bergen is the name of a German noble family. According to a legend, the executioner of Bergen took part in a masquerade and danced with the Queen. As executioners were considered ignoble in those days – 'Schelm' is the German for 'knave' – the King ennobled him to avert disgrace from his wife. Misleadingly, the MSS translate 'Schelm' as 'scamp'.

Der seltsame Gast [The Ominous Guest]

Josef Eichendorf. German and English. Baritone and orchestra. Vocal score (containing many pencilled alterations) extant; no full score survives amongst Fleischmann's papers and it seems unlikely that the work was ever orchestrated. *Der seltsame Gast* was conceived as one of a series of *Balladen und Legenden* [Ballads and Legends]: see notes to *Der Schelm von Bergen* [The Scamp of Bergen] listed above.

Des Sängers Fluch [The Singer's Curse]

Ludwig Uhland. Speaking voice and orchestra. German and English. Vocal score only extant. See Vocal Music/Narrator and Piano below.

Einsamkeit [Loneliness]

Peter Cornelius. German. High voice and orchestra [2222.4000.str]. This is a version of No. (ii) of *Vier Gesänge* [Four Songs]. The MS is untitled. See Vocal Music/Lieder below.

Heimat, liebe Heimat! [Home, Beloved Homeland!]

Adolf von Stern. German. High voice and orchestra [1121.22010.str]. Orchestral version of *Heimat, liebe Heimat!* for voice and piano (see Vocal Music/Lieder below). A second (copyist's) MS, specifies 2 cornets rather than 2 trumpets, and is stamped 'Prisoner of War Camp/Oldcastle/28 Mar 1918'.

Hochzeitliches Lied [A Wedding Song]

Words? German. High voice and orchestra [2222.2210.str]. This song also exists in a version with piano accompaniment. See Vocal Music/Lieder below.

Nis Randers

Otto Ernst. German and English (P. [*recte* W.?] Henley). Vocal score only extant. Although described on the existing score as being for high voice and piano, *Nis Randers* was originally conceived as one of a series of *Balladen und*

Legenden [Ballads and Legends] for voice and orchestra: see notes to *Der Schelm von Bergen* [The Scamp of Bergen] listed above.

Oft denk mit Wehmut ich zurück [The hours I spent with Thee]

Words? German and English. Voice and orchestra [1122.4000.str]. This work also exists in a version for voice and piano. See Vocal Music/Lieder below.

Swend Gabelbart und St Edmund [Swend Gabelbart and St Edmund]

Theodor Fontane. German and English (Mary Lucy). Baritone and orchestra [2222.2220.timp.perc.org.str] or piano. The vocal score is extant, but there is only an incomplete pencil sketch of the full score amongst Fleischmann's papers and it seems unlikely that the orchestral version was ever completed. *Swend Gabelbart und St Edmund* was conceived as one of a series of *Balladen und Legenden* [Ballads and Legends]: see notes to *Der Schelm von Bergen* [The Scamp of Bergen] listed above.

Three Songs with Orchestra

(i) 'Pluck this little flower' [Pflück die kleine Blume], (ii) 'He came and sat by my side' [Er kam und sass neben mir], (iii) 'Do not go my love' [Geh nicht Geliebte von mir]. Rabindranath Tagore. English and German. High voice and orchestra [2222.2000.pf.hp.str]. See also Six Songs to Poems by Rabindranath Tagore listed in Vocal Music/Other Songs below.

Unter den Linden [Under the Linden]

Walter von der Vogelweide. German. Voice and Orchestra [1122.1000.str]. MS stamped 'Prisoners of War Camp/Oldcastle/7 Jan 1918'. This work also exists in a version for voice and piano with a slightly less elaborate introduction. Fleischmann later reworked this 1918 setting as (ii) of *Zwei Gedichte von Walter von der Vogelweide* [Two Poems by Walter von der Vogelweide], for voice and piano. See Vocal Music/Lieder below.

Zur Nacht [To the Night]

Theodor Storm. German. High voice and orchestra [2222.4200.tomp.hp.str]. Full score and set of orchestral parts extant.

CHORAL MUSIC: ACCOMPANIED

Abendfeier in Venedig [Sunset in Venice (Ave Maria!)]

E. Geibel. German and English. Mixed-voice choir with distant voices (children's or female voices) and organ. 'Abendfeier in Venedig' by E. Geibel was set to music by Wilhelm Koehler-Wümbach for soprano and alto voices, solo violin and piano [= harmonium]. This setting was published in Hamburg by L. Hoffmann and reprinted as a supplement to *Beilage zum Kunstwart* (Munich), n.d. There is a copy of this supplement amongst Fleischmann's papers, together with two separate MSS of Koehler-Wümbach's composition in a copyist's hand. Fleischmann's is a completely new and original setting of the poem. The work also exists in a version with orchestra, one MS of which is stamped 'Prisoners of War Camp/Oldcastle/22 Aug 1917'. See Orchestral Works/Chorus and Orchestra above. This later revised version diverges from the 1917 score in a number of respects and the accompaniment is reworked for organ alone. It bears the inscription: 'Dedicated to the memory of His Holiness St. Pius X one-time Patriarch of Venice and restorer of the Musica Divina, in humble veneration.' (MS). On another MS, which also bears the dedication to Pius X (in German), it is described as 'Zwei geistliche Gesänge I' [Two Sacred Songs I], the second being *Exaudi nos* (see below).

Biblical Scene: Das Hochzeitfest zu Kana/The Marriage Feast of Cana
Clemens Brentano. German, English (Seán Lucy) and Latin. Soprano solo, female-voice choir and harmonium [= organ]. Op. 47, No. 1.

Choreinlage [Choral Interlude]
'Selig sind die Verfolgung leiden/"Beati qui persecutionem"/für/Kinder = Frauen = Männerstimmen u. Blasorchester/zur/Orgelsonate Op. 98/über dem gten. Psalmton/von/Josef Rheinberger' [Choral Interlude/'Blessed are those who are persecuted'/for/Children's, Female and Male Voices and Wind Orchestra/on/Organ Sonata Op. 98/on the Tonus Peregrinus/by/Josef Rheinberger] (MS). Orchestra: 4 trumpets, 2 tenor horns, euphonium, tuba.

Cor Jesu [Heart of Jesus]
Carl Ludwig Schleich. German and English (Seán Lucy). Soprano solo, female-voice choir and harmonium [= organ]. Op. 47, No. 2.

Das Kätzchen [The Kitten]
Words anon. German and English (Walter Henley). Female-voice choir and piano. This work also exists in a version for female-voice choir and string quartet.

Das Mädchen und der Kuckuck. [The Maiden and the Cuckoo]
Joh. W.L. Gleim. German. Female-voice choir and piano. There is also a version of this work for male-voice choir. See (iii) of *Three Male Choruses* listed in Choral Music: Unaccompanied/Male Voices below.

Der Versammlung zu Ehren [In Honour of the Gathering]
'[A]uf Wunsch für den Gesellenverein/geschrieben/1895' [Written at the request of the Journeymen's Association, 1895] (MS title page). Unison voices and piano. (i) [No title]: 'Wo unsre Schar beisammen ist . . .' [Wherever we flock together . . .] (first line); (ii) [No title]: 'Wo unsre Schar beisammen ist . . .' [Wherever we flock together . . .] (second setting of the same text; first line); (iii) Verwahrung: od. der bereiste Bayer [Protest, or the Travelled Bavarian]: 'Sieht man ein' Bayern gezeichnet so ist ein Maßkrug dabei . . .' [When you see a Bavarian depicted it is with a tankard . . .] (first line); (iv) Rodensteins Auszug [Rodenstein's Departure]: 'Es sagt sich was im Odenwald . . .' [A saying goes in the Odenwald. . .] (first line), 'Preis-komposition von C. Hering' [Prizewining composition by C. Hering]; (v) Meinwirths Reclame [Innkeeper's Advertisement]: 'Je röther Meinwirths Nase ist je besser ist sein Wein . . .' [The redder my innkeeper's nose the better his wine . . .] (first line); (vi) Beim Wein am schönen Rhein [Drinking on the Banks of the Lovely Rhine]: 'O edler Herr von Rodenstein . . .' [O noble Baron von Rodenstein. . .] (first line), 'Musik v. Brunner' [Music by Brunner]; (vii) [No title]: 'Frisch auf erhebt euch vom Sitze . . .' [Arise from your seats . . .] (first line). Of these seven pieces two, (iv) and (vi), are not by Fleischmann; Fleischmann is credited as the author of the words as well as the music of (v).

Donkey Ballad
'Poem by Mary Deegan (aged 12 years)' (MS). English. Unison children's choir and piano. 'Dedicated to all suffering donkeys in Ireland'; 'Cork VII 1950' (MS).

Exaudi nos
Guido Maria Dreves. German and English. Solo voice [= semi-chorus],

mixed-voice choir and organ. Described on both surviving MSS as 'Zwei geistliche Gesänge II' [Two Sacred Songs II], the first being *Abendfeier in Venedig* [Sunset in Venice] (see above). Dedication: 'Msgr. Lorenzo Perosi Maestro di Capella Sistina Roma zugeeignet' (MS). Op. 40. On the older of the two surviving MSS as well as on a surviving set of choral and organ parts, the work is entitled *Salva fac nos.*

Fantasie-Prelude and Fugue on the Gaelic Hymn to St Patrick
This work has an *ad libitum* choral finale. See Instrumental Music/Organ below.

Präludium und Fuge für Orgel oder Orchester über dem Magnificat im VIII Kirchenton [Prelude and Fugue for Organ or Orchestra on the Magnificat Tonus VIII].
This work has an *ad libitum* choral finale. See Orchestral Works/Orchestra above and Instrumental Music/Organ below.

Two Christmas Songs
Female-voice choir and organ [=piano]. German and English. The various MSS of this work comprise in fact three different songs: (i) 'An der Krippe sass Maria' [By the manger sat Maria], Carl Ludwig Schleich; (ii) 'Über die Hütte weht der Wind: A Sacred Lullaby' [Over the stall the winds away (on some MSS entitled simply Christmas Night)], '(Aus *Des Knaben Wunderhorn*)' (MS); (iii) Christkindleins Wiegenlied, [no English text], '(Aus *Des Knaben Wunderhorn*)' (MS). Fleischmann never appears to have made a final decision which two songs should be paired: on some MSS he lists (i) and (ii), and on others he lists (i) and (iii). There are also versions for solo voice and organ [= piano] of (i) and (iii) amongst the MSS. A title page for (ii) is extant on which the work is described as for 'Soprano and Organ (or Harmonium)' but the score is missing. See Vocal Music/Lieder below.

Wunden hast du, Geliebter [Wounds thou hast, beloved]
'Worte aus einer alten Passion' [Words from an old Passion Play] (MS). German. Baritone [= tenor] solo, female-voice choir and organ [= harmonium].

CHORAL MUSIC: UNACCOMPANIED

Mixed Voices

Als ich dich kaum gesehen [Scarcely Had I Seen You]
Theodor Storm. German.

[Choral Greetings]
(i) Choral Union Greeting: 'Pure and true forth our clear song starts', 'Cork, Spring 1908' (MS); (ii) (a) Choral Greeting I: 'Age knows no sorrow youth ne'er grows old', (b) Choral Greeting II: 'We rise to sing a song'; (iii) Choral Greeting: 'Now let the voices resounding' [first setting]; (iv) Choral Greeting: 'Now let the voices resounding' [second setting]. Words? Although only one MS is dated, all of these short pieces were probably composed for Cork Choral Union between 1908 and 1909 when Fleischmann was conductor of the choir.

Das Alte Lied [The Old Song]
Heinrich Heine. German and English (Walter Henley). This work also exists in a version for solo voice and piano (see Vocal Music/Lieder below). One MS is dated 'Herbst 1918 Knockaloe, Isle of Man'.

Das Geheimnis [The Secret]
Words? German and English. On one of the copies of this piece the title is

given as *Mein Schatz* [My Love] after the opening line of the poem (see below).

Die Liebenden [The Lovers]

Klaus Groth. German and English. This work also exists in a version for voice and piano. See (ii) of *Kleine Romanzen und Lieder im Volkston* [Little Romances and Songs in the Folk Style] listed in Vocal Music/Lieder below.

Die Müllerin [The Miller Lass]

Heinrich Seidel. German and English (Walter Henley). This work also exists in a version for solo voice and piano under the title *Die Bachstelze* [The Wagtail]. See Vocal Music/Lieder below.

Die Soldatenbraut [The Soldier's Bride]

Eduard Mörike. German and English (Revd. P. MacSwiney). This work also exists in a version for male-voice choir (see below), and in a version for voice and piano. See (iii) of *Kleine Romanzen und Lieder im Volkston* [Little Romances and Songs in the Folk Style] listed in Vocal Music/Lieder below.

Drei Gedichte von Freiherr von Eichendorf [Three Poems by Freiherr von Eichendorf]

(i) 'Aus der Heimat' [From My Homeland], (ii) 'Windsgleich kommt der wilde Krieg geritten' [Tempest the Steed of Wild War Clatters], (iii) 'Schon Kehren die Vögel Wieder ein' [Now Hither the Swallows Wing their Way]. German and English.

Es fiel ein Reif [There Fell a Frost]

Heinrich Heine. German and English. This work also exists in a version for male-voice choir (see below).

Es steht eine Linde [There Stands a Lime]

L. Pfau. German and English (Walter Henley). This work also exists in a version for solo voice and piano. See (i) of *Kleine Romanzen und Lieder im Volkston* [Little Romances and Songs in the Folk Style] listed in Vocal Music/Lieder below.

Friedensgebet [Prayer for Peace]

Emil Hadina. German. One MS is stamped 'Prisoners of War Camp/Oldcastle/16 Nov. 1917'.

Mein Schatz [My Love]

See *Das Geheimnis* [The Secret] above.

Rieden

Franz Schaehle. German and English. Rieden is a place near Dachau: 'Riden bei Leutstetten/Am Grab einer Geistesfürstin/Prinzessin Maria Gabriela von Bayern.' [Rieden near Leutstetten/at the grave of a poetess/Princess Marie Gabriele of Bavaria] (MS). Fleischmann seems to have intended this work to be part of a set entitled *Aus Fernen Tagen* of which it was to be No. 4. No trace of the complete set has been found amongst his papers, however, nor any indication of what the other pieces may have been.

Rosenzeit [The Rose of June]

Eduard Mörike. German and English.

Über den Hügel hin [Over the Hills the Clouds Pass By]

Words? German. This is a slightly shorter version, apparently complete in itself, of the choral part of *Grabgesang* [Song of the Grave] for mixed-voice choir and wind orchestra. See Orchestral Works/Chorus and Orchestra above.

Vier Geistliche Gesänge [Four Sacred Songs]
> Eduard Mörike. German and English. (i) 'Zum Neuen Jahr' [The New Year], (ii) 'Gebet' [Prayer], (iii) 'Altes Verslein' [An Old Verse], (iv) 'Denk' es, O Seele!' [Know This, My Soul]. Op. 35. Two different copies are in the hand of Franz Berberich (nephew of Monsignor Ludwig Berberich) and are dated 1928 and 1929 respectively. First performed by the Choir of Munich Cathedral, conducted by Ludwig Berberich, in 1929(?). No. (i) broadcast on Radio Éireann (by Radio Éireann Singers?), 12 January 1960.

Wegenwart [Erica, the Enchanted Flower]
> [First (earlier?) setting (A major)] Julius Wolff. German.

Wegenwart [Erica, the Enchanted Flower]
> [Second setting (G major)] Julius Wolff. German and English. Although the copyist's score of this later setting has both German and English words, the song is simply entitled *Erica/The Enchanted Flower* with an explanation that 'Erica' means 'heather'.

Male Voices

Acht Lieder für Männerchor [Eight Songs for Male-Voice Choir]
> Vol. 1: (i) 'Aufblick' [Glance], Eichendorff; (ii) 'Im Herbst' [In Autumn], Adolf Grimminger; (iii) 'Zutrunk' [Toast], Börries von Münchhausen; (iv) 'Trost' [Consolation], J. Stinde. Vol. 2: (v) 'Liebesahnung' [Presentiment of Love], Karl Stieler; (vi) 'Meersabend' [Evening at Sea], Strachwitz; (vii) 'Unterm Fenster' [Under the Window], Adolf Grimminger; (viii) 'Schutzengel' [Guardian Angel], Fr Von Kobell. German. Published by Verlag von Jos. Aibl Sortiment, Munich n.d., as Op. 3.

Ave Musica Sacra! (Canon)
> Words? Boys' voices [= female-voice choir]. Latin. On another MS this piece is entitled 'Viva O Musica!'

Come Follow Follow Me! (Canon)
> Words? Boys' voices [= female-voice choir]. English.

Der verlorne Schatz [Lost Love]
> Karl von Lemcke. German and English

Die Soldatenbraut [The Soldier's Bride]
> Eduard Mörike. German and English (Revd. P. MacSwiney). This work also exists in a version for mixed-voice choir (see above), and in a version for voice and piano. See (iii) of *Kleine Romanzen und Lieder im Volkston* [Little Romances and Songs in the Folk Style] listed in Vocal Music/Lieder below.

Ding-tang! O Joyful Feast (Canon)
> Words? Boys' voices [= female-voice choir]. English. MS entitled merely 'Xmas', followed by the word 'canons' in pencil.

Drei steyerische Lieder im Volkston [Three Songs from Styria in the Folk Style]
> Words anon. German. (i) 'Darf s' Diendl liabn?' [May I woo the Maid?], (ii) 'Dienderl tief drunt im Thal' [The Maid in the Valley Below], (iii) 'Mein Schatzerl ist wandern' [My Treasure has Departed].

Eine Hand voll Erde [Earth, a Little Handful]
> Words? German and English.

Ein Musicus wolt fröhlich sein [A Musician Wished to be Merry]
> Words from *Des Knaben Wunderhorn*. German.

Es fiel ein Reif [There Fell a Frost]
> Heinrich Heine. German and English. This work also exists in a version for mixed-voice choir (see above).

Fünf Gedichte von Theodor Körner [Five Poems by Theodor Körner]
> (i) 'Die drei Sterne' [The Three Stars], (ii) 'Kommt, Brüder' [Come, Brothers], (iii) 'Das Volk steht au' [The People Rise Up], (iv) 'Trinklied vor der Schlacht' [Drinking Song Before the Battle], (v) 'Gute Nacht' [Good Night]. German. There is an MS of (v) 'Gute Nacht' dated '18.I.1920', and inscribed 'Meinem lieben verehrten Onkel/Herrn Thomas Deger/fürstliche Verwalter/in Dankbarkeit gewidmet/zur Erinnerung/an die frohen Tage des Widerschauen/nach lange, harte Trennung/1914---1920/Schloss Kreuth/im Winter 1920' [To my dear revered uncle/Thomas Deger/administrator of the princely estate/dedicated in gratitude/in memory/on the happy day of meeting again/after a long hard separation/1914–1920/Schloss Kreuth/Winter 1920] (MS).

Gut Singer und ein Organist [Good Songsters and an Organist]
> Words? German.

Interval Canon
> Words? Boys' voices [= female-voice choir]. English and German. 'Cathedral Choir 1947' (MS). A teaching canon, the melody of which is constructed from the successive rising intervals of the diatonic scale as indicated by the words: 'The first, the second, the third, the fourth, the fifth, the sixth, the seventh, the octave: learn the intervals with care, sing like birdies in the air. For God's praise and for his glory, every note must clear and round in the musica sacra sound.'

I see his blood upon the rose
> Joseph M. Plunkett. English. Pencil sketch (complete) extant.

Lasst uns singen [Let Us Sing]
> Words? German.

Lieder der Landsknechte [Soldiers' Songs]
> (i) 'Got Gnad' [God's Grace], 'Fliegendes Blatt 1550' (MS); (ii) 'Wir zogen in das Feld' [We Went to the Battlefield], 'Aus dem 16. Jahrh.' (MS); (iii) 'Frisch auf zum Streit' [Let Us Up and Off to Battle], 'Altes Kriegslied' (MS); (iv) 'Unsere liebe Frau' [Our Dear Lady], 'Melodie um 1550' (MS); (v) 'Ei du feiner Reiter' [Oh, You Handsome Rider], 'Weise von Samuel Schmidt 1624' (MS); (vi) 'Schlafen wöllen wir gehen?' [Do We Wish to Go to Sleep?], 'Anon. 1603' (MS). German.

May I Love the Lassie?
> Words? English.

Musicaklang [The Sound of Music]
> 'Anon. 1596' (MS). German.

Nachtwächters Stundenruf [Night Watchman's Call]
> 'XVII Cent.' (MS). German and English. Bass voice, male-voice choir and horn *obbligato*.

Noel, Now Sing a Saviour's Birth
> Words anon. English.

Star of the East!
> Reginald Herber (1811). English.

Studentenlieder aus dem 16. Jahrhundert [Student Songs from the Sixteenth Century]

Words? German. (i) 'Trink ich Wein' [If I Drink Wine], (ii) 'Trink und singt' [Drink and Sing], (iii) 'Wolauf ir brüder' [Courage, You Brothers]. The first song listed here is not explicitly identified on the MS, but the subject matter suggests that it was intended to be part of this set. As the other two songs are numbered (ii) and (iii), it can plausibly be placed first.

Three Male Choruses

(i) 'Tanzlied' [Dancesong], Words?; (ii) 'Beware!', H.W. Longfellow; (iii) 'Die Schäferin und die Kuckuck' [A Shepherd Maiden Watched her Lambs], Joh. W.L. Gleim. German and English. There is also a version of (iii) 'Die Schäferin und die Kuckuck' for female-voice choir and piano. See *Das Mädchen und der Kuckuck.* [The Maiden and the Cuckoo] listed in Choral Music: Accompanied above.

Vom Untergang der 'Grossen Armee': Fluchtlied 1812 [Of the Downfall of the 'Grande Armée': Song of Flight 1812].

Words anon. (German folksong).

SACRED MUSIC

Ad Completorium [The Office of Compline]

See Other Arrangements below.

Adoremus

[First setting]. Latin. Male-voice [= female-voice] choir and organ. The words 'St. Finbarr's' written in pencil over the title acknowledge that the piece is based on St Finbarr's Hymn, like the first and third settings of *Ecce Sacerdos Magnus* and the setting of *O Salutaris* from the *Hibernian Benediction* [I] listed below, which are also based on the same tune.

Adoremus

[Second setting]. Latin. Female-voice choir and organ. Although the organ part appears to consist solely of a three-bar introduction, the voices were probably accompanied throughout.

Adoremus et Postludium super 'Puer natus in Bethlehem' (cantus liturgici) [Adoremus and Postlude on 'A boy is born in Bethlehem' (a liturgical melody)]

[Third setting]. Latin. Female-voice choir and organ. Latin. 'A.F. 1937' (MS).

Adoremus

[Fourth setting]. Latin. See *Irish Adoremus* listed below.

Ad tuum Nomen

Latin. Female-voice choir [with tenor and bass voices *ad libitum*] and organ.

Angelis suis

Latin. Unison children's choir [= soprano solo], mixed-voice choir and organ. 'Very Reverend Martin, Canon Murphy P.P.V.F./Bandon/gratissimo animo dedicatum' [Dedicated with deepest gratitude to the Very Reverend Martin Murphy, Bandon] (MS). On some copies of the score the dedication reads: 'Revmo. Martin Canonico Murphy/Precentori, Diocesis Corcagiae [sic]/etc.' [Precentor of the Diocese of Cork]. These copies are dated 1935.

Anima Christi

Latin. Unison voices and organ. 'A.F. 1930' (MS).

Assumpta est Maria

Latin. Mixed-voice choir [six parts]. Version of *Assumpta est Maria*, (iii) of *Three Motets based on Gregorian Themes* listed below.

Ave Maria

[First setting]. Latin. Female-voice choir. '1896' (MS).

Ave Maria

[Second setting]. Latin. High voice and organ. 'Dachau im Mai 1904' (MS). This work also exists in a version with accompaniment for string orchestra. See Orchestral Works/Solo Voice and Orchestra above.

Ave Maria

[Third setting]. Latin. See *Zwei Ave Maria* listed below.

Ave Maria

[Fourth setting]. Latin. See *Zwei Ave Maria* listed below.

Ave Maria

[Fifth setting]. Latin. Mixed-voice choir. 'Style Ancien' [Ancient Style] (MS).

Ave Maria

[Sixth setting.] Latin. See *Three Motets based on Gregorian Themes* listed below.

Ave Maria

[Seventh setting]. Latin. 'in Dorian Mode' (MS). Mixed-voice choir. '1.V.1948' (MS).

Ave Maria

[Eighth setting]. Latin. High voice and organ [with female-voice choir *ad libitum*]. 'To Reverend Mother and Community Drishane Convent Christmas 1959' (In Fleischmann's hand on reproduction of copyist's score).

Ave Maria

[Ninth setting]. Latin. Male-voice choir [and organ]. The first half of the text is sung to Gregorian chant; the second half is set for three-part male-voice choir. There also exists a pencil sketch of an (organ?) accompaniment for the chant, suggesting that instrumental support may have been envisaged throughout.

Ave Maria

[Tenth setting]. Latin. Solo voice (?), mixed-voice choir and organ. Incomplete (setting extends to the words 'fructus ventris tui' only).

Ave Maria

[Eleventh setting]. Latin. Solo voice (?), male-voice choir and organ. Incomplete: sketch only extant.

Ave Maria

[Twelfth setting]. Latin. Fragment consisting of complete text (somewhat unusually treated) for soprano and alto voices. Two bars' rest at the beginning indicate either a missing accompaniment or missing parts for lower voices.

Ave Maris Stella

[First setting]. Latin. Soprano solo [with female-voice choir *ad libitum*] and harmonium [= organ]. 'To Rev. Sister M. Berchmans Convent of Mercy Charleville '(MS).

Ave Maris Stella

[Second setting]. Latin. Male-voice choir and organ. 'Cathedral Cork 1929' (MS).

Ave Maris Stella

[Third setting]. Latin. Male-voice [= female-voice] choir. There are two versions of this piece: (i) *a cappella*, (ii) with organ accompaniment. One of the MSS is dated 'A.F. 31', and on two of the MSS the work is described as 'No.

I', which suggests that it was designed as a companion piece to *Concordia laetitia* (described as 'No. II' and bearing the same date), listed below.

Ave Maris Stella

[Fourth setting]. Latin. Mixed-voice choir.

Ave Musica Sacra! (Canon)

Latin. Boys' voices [= female-voice choir (SSA)]. On another MS this piece is entitled *Viva O Musica!* Not a liturgical text. See Choral Music: Unaccompanied/Male Voices above.

Beata es, Virgo Maria

Latin. Soprano solo, female-voice choir and harmonium [= organ]. 'To the members of the Convent Choir [Drishane]/Gaudeamus omnes in Mariae' (MS).

Beati sunt

'Geistlicher Gesang (Aria di chiesa)' [Sacred Song (Church Aria)] (MS). Words from the Bible: Sermon on the Mount. Latin. Tenor solo and harmonium [= organ].

Benedictio Hibernica [Hibernian Benediction]

On two MSS this work is entitled *St. Finbarr's Benediction*. Two movements: (i) *O Salutaris hostia* [eighth setting listed below], (ii) *Tantum ergo* [I], 'X Cent, St Gall MS' (referring to the melody?) (MS) [fourth setting listed below]; *Tantum ergo* [II], a second (alternative?) setting [fifth setting listed below]. Latin. Female-voice choir and organ (tenor and bass voices appear to have been added later to the *O Salutaris* and *Tantum ergo* [II]). Despite the similar title and the same texts, this work bears no relation to either of the two works listed below as *Hibernian Benediction*. One of the MSS is dated 'Cathedral Cork 1938'. On another MS the composer's name is given as 'Patrick Eire', apparently a pseudonym which, for some reason, Fleischmann adopted in this instance.

Canon: Let us sing and praise the Lord

English. Four [treble = soprano] voices.

Canticum Zachariae (Benedictus)

Latin. Male-voice choir.

Concordia laetitia

Latin. Female-voice choir [sopranos 1 and 2, with alto voices *ad libitum*] and organ. One MS is dated 'A.F. 31', and on it the work is described as 'No. II', suggesting it was designed as a companion piece to the *Ave Maris Stella* [third setting] (described as 'No. I' and bearing the same date) listed above.

Credo from *Missa Regia, Primi Toni* by Henry Du Mont (1610–84)

Latin. Mixed-voice choir. Replacement settings for choir of three portions of the text – 'Et incarnatus' (to 'sepultus est'), 'Et in Spiritum Sanctum' (to 'procedit') and 'Et vitam venturi' (to the end) – which Fleischmann made for a Credo in plainchant style by Henry Du Mont. There are two different versions of 'Et in Spiritum Sanctum'. Unlike *Credo IV* listed below, this MS does not include a harmonic support for the complete original which is not transcribed, but there also exists amongst Fleischmann's papers a separate harmonisation for mixed-voice choir of the entire *Credo* from this Mass (see Other Arrangements below). The *Missa Regia* is one the *Cinq messes en plainchant* which Du Mont published 1669. Better known as the *Messes Royales*, these settings remained popular in many provincial churches up to the twentieth century. There also exists an MS organ accompaniment for another complete mass from the *Cinq messes*, the 'Messe du 2 me. ton' (MS), amongst the composer's papers, which may also be by Fleischmann (see Other Arrangements below).

Credo I
[First version]. Latin. Mixed-voice choir. Replacement choral setting of the words 'Et incarnatus' (to 'homo factus est') for Credo I from the *Liber Usualis*.

Credo I
[Second version]. Latin. Mixed-voice choir. Replacement choral settings for the words 'Deum de Deo' (to 'Deum verum'), 'Et incarnatus' (to 'sepultus est'), 'Et in spiritum sanctum' (to 'qui prophetas') and 'Et vitam venturi' (to the end) for the plainchant Credo I from the *Liber Usualis*. A pencil sketch only extant.

Credo IV: quod juxta editionem Vaticanum/Harmonice ornavit/cum/'Et incarnates'/et/'Et vitam'
Latin. Mixed-voice choir and organ. The plainchant Credo IV from the *Liber Usualis* supplied with a harmonic support on the organ, as well as replacement choral settings for the words 'Et incarnatus' (to 'sepultus est'), and 'Et vitam venturi' (to the end). 'Cork I. MCMXXXVIII' (MS). There are two other replacement settings of the 'Incarnatus est' for unspecified Credo chants amongst Fleischmann's papers: (a) 'Incarnatus est' (to 'factus est'); (b) 'Et incarnatus est' (to 'factus est'), marked 'In Nativitate Domini'.

De Profundis
Latin. Female-voice choir [with tenor and bass voices *ad libitum*] and organ. 'Parish Church Choir, Kinsale 1942' (MS).

Dextera Domini
[First setting]. Latin. Treble voices [= male voices] and organ. 'A.F. Bantry X 35' (MS).

Dextera Domini
[Second setting]. Latin. Male-voice choir.

Diligis Justitiam
Latin. Mixed-voice choir. This work has been provided with alternative endings.

Domine non sum dignus
Latin. Mixed-voice choir. '1918' (MS).

Ecce Sacerdos Magnus
[First setting]. Latin. Mixed-voice choir, brass ensemble and organ. There are two versions of this work amongst the MSS, and the composition of the brass ensemble is different for each: for what appears to be the earlier version it is 2 trumpets, soprano cornet, 2 horns, 3 trombones and tuba; and for the second version (although no instruments are named on the score), 2 trumpets, 2 horns, 3 trombones and tuba. The work is based on *St Finbarr's Hymn*, and included with the MSS on separate sheets are draft dedications to two successive bishops of Cork, Daniel Coholan and Cornelius Lucey. It is not clear, however, if these dedications apply to this particular work, although in view of its greater elaboration than the other settings listed below, this would seem to be likely. It is possible that this setting was re-dedicated to Cornelius Lucy when he succeeded Bishop Coholan, or alternatively that one of the dedications applies to one of the other settings of text. Neither version exists in a final, fair copy.

Ecce Sacerdos Magnus
   [Second setting]. Latin. Mixed-voice choir and organ.
Ecce Sacerdos Magnus
   [Third setting]. Latin. Male-voice choir and organ. 'On the theme of St
   Finbarr's Hymn' (MS). This setting also exists in a version for female-voice
   choir and organ that was included in the *Sacred Music for the Ceremony of
   Reception and Profession* (see below).
Ecce Sacerdos Magnus
   [Fourth setting]. Latin. Mixed-voice choir [with organ *ad libitum*].
Ecce Sacerdos Magnus
   [Fifth setting]. Latin. Male-voice choir and organ.
Ecce Sacerdos Magnus
   [Sixth setting]. Latin. Female-voice choir and organ. 'A.F. III 32' (MS).
Ecce Sacerdos
   [Seventh setting]. Latin. Male-voice choir [with organ *ad libitum*]. 'Facilis'
   [Easy] (MS).
Four Old Tunes for Eastertide and Ascension Day
   See Other Arrangements below.
Grosser Gott wir loben dich [Te Deum laudamus]
   German. Children's voices, organ, 2 trumpets [= 2 flugelhorns], tenor trom-
   bone and bass trombone. This piece is an Appendix [*Anhang*] to the
   Kommunionlieder listed below.
Haec dies
   Latin. Male-voice choir.
Hibernian Benediction [I]
   (i) *O Salutaris hostia*, on the theme of St Finbarr's Hymn [sixth setting listed
   below]; (ii) *Tantum ergo*, on the theme of St Patrick's Hymn [sixth setting
   listed below]. Latin. Mixed-voice choir.
Hibernian Benediction II
   (i) *O Salutaris hostia* [seventh setting listed below], (ii) *Tantum ergo* [seventh
   setting listed below]. Latin. Mixed-voice choir.
[Hymns]
   This set of MSS consists of seven pieces, numbered II to VIII (the first piece
   appears to be missing), each simply entitled 'Hymn', without any further
   details given. The pieces are obviously unfinished: the layout of the MSS
   includes a stave for what is apparently intended to be a vocal line, although
   it is blank virtually throughout; underneath this is a fully worked-out accompaniment on two staves for a keyboard instrument (harmonium, possibly, or
   organ).
In Festo Corporis Christi [For the Feast of Corpus Christi]
   This miscellaneous collection of pieces consists of music for the ceremonies of
   the Feast of Corpus Christi. In Cork, these ceremonies involved a procession
   through the city streets from the Cathedral of St Mary and St Anne to a
   central outdoor location where Benediction of the Blessed Sacrament was celebrated. Fleischmann provided a series of preludes for brass ensemble [2
   cornets, 2 trumpets, 3 horns, 2 baritones, euphonium, 3 trombones, 3 bass
   tubas and timpani] as well as arrangements of various hymns (for various
   brass ensembles) to be performed at these events. An original set of four preludes was later expanded to seven, and the hymn tunes (which presumably

accompanied congregational singing) include 'Hail, Queen of Heaven', 'To Jesus Heart All Burning', 'I'll Sing a Hymn to Mary', etc. There are a number of additional items such as a Portal Fanfare (for brass) to be sounded as the procession left the cathedral, and various Signals (also for brass), which were to be played, presumably, to mark the Elevation of the Sacred Host at the Benediction.

Invocation (Laudate Dominum)
>   Latin. Female-voice choir.

Irish Adoremus (cum laudate)
>   Latin. Unison voices [solo voice?] and organ. Based on a plainchant melody. [*Adoremus*, fourth setting].

Jesu dulcis memoria
>   Latin. Mixed-voice choir and organ.

Kommunionlieder [Communion Songs]
>   (i) 'Herr, ich bin nicht würdig' [Lord, I am not worthy], (ii) 'Lasst die kleinen zu mir kommen' [Suffer the little ones to come unto me], (iii) 'Jesus, dir leb' ich' [Jesus, I live for thee]. German. Mixed-voice choir. Of a (projected?) set of seven songs only the three listed above have come to light. A setting of *Das deutsche Te Deum laudamus: Grosser Gott wir loben dich* for children's voices, organ and brass instruments follows in the MS as an Appendix [Anhang] (see *Grosser Gott wir loben dich* listed above). 'Den Erstkommunikanten in der Heimat gewidmet' [Dedicated to the first-communicants of my native place] (MS).

Laudate Dominum de coelis
>   Latin. Mixed-voice choir [seven parts].

Litany B.M.V. [Beatae Mariae Virginis]
>   Latin. Male-voice choir and congregation.

[Mass]
>   (i) Kyrie, (ii) Gloria, (iii) Sanctus, (iv) Benedictus, (v) Agnus Dei. Latin. Mixed-voice choir. Written in very simple homophonic style. The only existing photocopy of the untitled MS (not in Fleischmann's hand) is laid out in close score throughout and consists of the choral part only with occasional blank bars indicating a missing accompaniment (for organ?).

Mass in Honour of St Finbarr
>   (i) Kyrie, (ii) Gloria, (iii) Credo [Credo III from the *Liber Usualis* with replacement settings for 'Et incarnatus' (to 'factus est'), 'Et iterum' (to 'non erit finis'), 'Et unam sanctam' (to 'Ecclesiam') and 'Et vitam venturi' (to the end)], (iv) Sanctus, (v) Benedictus, (vi) Agnus Dei. Latin. Male-voice choir and organ. 'Dedicated to the students at St. Finbarr's College, Farranferris [Cork] 1948.' (MS). 'The thematic material of this mass is taken from the old Irish tune, now sung as the Hymn of St. Finbarr, and from the Missa Magne Deus (Solesmes Ed.). The polyphonic writing is exceedingly simple and the range limited to suit that of young students' voices . . .' (MS).

[Music for the Benediction of the Blessed Sacrament]
>   (i) *Cor Jesu sacratissimum*, (ii) *Adoremus*, (iii) *Laudate Dominum*, (vi) *Parce Domine*. Latin. Mixed-voice choir. Pencil sketch (complete?) extant.

O esca viatorum
>   Latin. Female-voice choir and organ, with alternative version for mixed-voice choir [tenor voices *ad libitum*] and organ.

Oremus pro Pontifice [Let us pray for the Pope]

Latin. Male-voice [= female-voice] choir and organ.

Organ Blessing

Latin. Mixed-voice choir. 'Cathedral Choir Cork 22 VI 1924' (MS). Written for the inauguration of the new organ in the Cathedral of St Mary and St Anne, Cork.

O Sacrum convivium

Latin. Two-part choir [male or female voices] and organ.

O Salutaris hostia

[First setting]. Latin. Male-voice choir [with alternative setting of second verse for six-part mixed-voice choir].

O Salutaris hostia

[Second setting]. Latin. Female-voice choir and organ [soprano 1 and alto, with soprano 2 *ad libitum*].

O Salutaris hostia

[Third setting]. Latin. Female-voice choir [sopranos 1 and 2, with alto voices *ad libitum*] and organ.

O Salutaris hostia

[Fourth setting]. Latin. Two-part [female-voice] choir and organ [= harmonium]. 'Ad duas voces' (MS). '19 VI MCMXXXX' (MS). Paired with *Tantum ergo* [eighth setting], see below. Another MS is dated 1937.

O Salutaris hostia

[Fifth setting]. Latin. Two variants of the same (original?) melody: (a) for unison voices with (organ?) accompaniment: (b) for mixed-voice choir.

O Salutaris hostia

[Sixth setting]. Latin. See *Hibernian Benediction* [I] above.

O Salutaris hostia

[Seventh setting]. Latin. See *Hibernian Benediction* II above.

O Salutaris hostia

[Eighth setting]. Latin. See *Benedictio Hibernica* above.

Pange lingua

[First setting]. Latin. Mixed-voice choir. Original material alternating with plainchant.

Pange lingua

[Second setting]. Latin. Mixed-voice choir. Original material alternating with plainchant.

Pange lingua

[Third setting]. Latin. Mixed-voice choir. This setting opens with a variant of a plainchant melody for Cantor, and continues in (harmonised) plainchant style for choir.

Pange lingua

[Fourth setting]. Latin. Mixed-voice choir. See note to *Pange lingua* [fifth setting] below.

Pange lingua

[Fifth setting]. Latin. Mixed-voice choir. A copyist's score of these two simple settings of the *Pange lingua* (the fourth and fifth) also includes a setting of the *Benedictus* attributed to Guiseppi Ercole Bernabei (1620–87). Three separate copies of this *Benedictus* in Fleischmann's hand survive.

Pange lingua

[Sixth setting]. Latin. Mixed-voice choir. Sketch only extant.

Pange lingua

[Seventh setting]. Latin. Mixed-voice choir. Sketch only extant.

Requiem

This work consists partly of original music and partly of harmonised plain-chant melodies from the *Missa pro defunctis.* (i) Kyrie [four-part choir; original]; (ii) Graduale (Requiem aeternam) [text sung on a monotone, with free organ accompaniment]; (iii) Tractus [accompanied plainchant]; (iv) Dies Irae [accompanied plainchant alternating with original setting of verses 4, 6, 8, 10, 12, 14, and 16; accompanied plainchant from the 'Lacrimosa' to the end, with free four-part cadence]; (v) Offertorium [1] [the text recited on a mono-tone with free organ accompaniment]; (vi) Offertorium [2] [alternative version: accompanied plainchant]. Latin. Mixed-voice choir and organ.

Responsoria Chori [Turba] ad Cantum Passionis Domini nostri Jesu Christi secundum Ioannem.

Choral responses [the people] for the St John Passion. Latin. Mixed-voice choir.

Roman–Irish Te Deum

[*Te Deum*, first setting]. Latin. Also entitled *The Irish 'Roman Te Deum'*, this is (xvii) of *Sacred Music for the Ceremonies of Reception and Profession* listed below. Female-voice choir and organ [= harmonium]. The title, *The Irish 'Roman Te Deum'*, refers to the fact the setting employs motifs taken from St Patrick's Hymn as well as from plainchant.

Roman Te Deum

[*Te Deum*, second setting]. Latin. Mixed-voice choir and organ. An MS page amongst Fleischmann's papers bears the title: 'The "Roman Te Deum"/auctore ignoto [author unknown]/(circa 1600)/arranged for/Congregational singing, mixed voices (auxiliary choir ad lib) and organ/by/Aloys G. Fleischmann/Regens Chori Cork Cathedral/1937/All rights reserved'. Although described as an arrangement, the plainchant melody is very freely treated and the work also includes original material. There also exists a less elaborate (earlier?) version of this work.

Sacerdos et Pontifex

[First setting]. Latin. Mixed-voice choir.

Sacerdos et Pontifex

[Second setting]. Latin. Male-voice choir [treble voices – 'pueri' (MS) – tenor and bass voices] and organ.

Sacred Music for the Ceremony of Reception and Profession

Ceremony of Reception: (i) *Ecce Sacerdos Magnus*, see *Ecce Sacerdos Magnus* [third setting] listed above' (ii) *O gloriosa Virginum*, (iii) *In excitu Israel*, (iv) *Quae est ista*, (v) *Regnum mundi*, (vi) *Veni Creator Spiritus*, (vii) *Ecce quam bonum*, (viii) *Deus misereatur nostri*, (ix) Postludium I and II; Ceremony of Profession: (x) *Immola Deo*, (xi) *Veni Sancte Spiritus*, (xii) *Tenuiste manum*, (xiii) *Anno Christum*, (xiv) *Veni sponsa Christi*, (xv) *Suscipe me Domine*, (xvi) *Posuit signum*, (xvii) *Te Deum* ['The Irish "Roman Te Deum"' (MS)] see *Roman-Irish Te Deum* [*Te Deum*, first setting] listed above, (xvii) Postludium III: Fugue for organ on an Ionian (Gregorian) theme. Latin. Female-voice choir and organ [= harmonium]. 'Preface: During a visit to a convent I was requested to make a polyphonic setting for the Ceremonies of Reception and Profession. I built these settings on Gregorian motifs for three voices:

Soprano I and II and Alto (*ad lib.*) with organ or harmonium accompaniment [. .] Cathedral Cork Febr. 1945.'There are two different settings of (xii)
Tenuiste manum amongst the MSS. The MS of (xiv) *Veni sponsa Christi* bears
the designation Op. 52. No. (xvii), Postludium III, is a version of Fuga (über
ein jonisches Thema) [Fugue (on an Ionian Theme)], (iii) of *Three Pieces* for
organ (see Instrumental Music/Organ below).

Sacris solemniis

Latin. Mixed-voice choir [seven parts]. This work appears to be one of a
(projected?) set of *Hymni Eucharistici,* but none of the other pieces listed on
the cover page has come to light.

Salve Mater

Latin. Female-voice choir [alto voices *ad libitum*] and organ.

Sub panis alma specie

Latin. Mixed-voice choir and organ.

Super Flumina Babylonis: Psalm CXXXVI

[First setting]. Latin and English (Marie Lucy). Baritone solo, mixed-voice
choir. 'Componiert im Kriegsgefangenlager [Composed in the Prisoner of
War Camp] Isle of Man im November 1918' (MS).

Super Flumina Babylonis

[Second setting]. Latin. Mixed-voice choir [tenor voices *ad libitum*] and organ.

Tantum ergo

[First setting]. Latin. Female-voice choir [sopranos 1 and 2, alto voices *ad
libitum*] and organ. 'Ad duas voces' (MS).

Tantum ergo

[Second setting]. Latin. Female-voice choir [sopranos 1 and 2, alto voices *ad
libitum*] and organ. This setting is based on a plainchant melody, phrases of
which alternate with original material.

Tantum ergo

[Third setting]. Latin. Female-voice choir.

Tantum ergo

[Fourth setting]. Latin. Female-voice choir and organ. This is the first of two
(alternative?) settings in the *Benedictio Hiberniae* listed above. 'X Cent, St
Gall MS' [melody?] (MS).

Tantum ergo

[Fifth setting]. Latin. Female-voice choir and organ (tenor and bass voices
appear to have been added later). This is the second of two (alternative?) settings in the *Benedictio Hibernica* listed above.

Tantum ergo

[Sixth setting]. Latin. Mixed-voice choir. See *Hibernian Benediction* [I] listed
above.

Tantum ergo

[Seventh setting]. Latin. Mixed-voice choir. See *Hibernian Benediction* II listed
above.

Tantum ergo

[Eighth setting]. Latin. Two-part [female-voice] choir and organ [= harmo-
nium]. 'Ad duas voces' (MS). '19 VI MCMXXXX' (MS). Paired with *O Salutaris
hostia* [fourth setting], see above. Another MS is dated 1937.

Terra tremuit

Latin. Mixed-voice choir, 2 cornets, 2 horns, 2 trombones [+ tuba *ad libitum*] and organ. The choral parts are supplied with a printed cover which bears the inscription: 'Promotori Illustri Fautorique Celebri Musicae Divinae/hoc in insula/Reverendissimo Domino Michael O'Sullivan/Canonico Cathedrali Corcagensi/hoc opusculum/animo devoto gratissimoque dedicat' [This little work is dedicated with devotion and deepest gratitude to the Very Reverend Michael O'Sullivan, Canon of the Cathedral of Cork, Illustrious Promoter and Celebrated Patron of Sacred Music in this island].

The Nativity (Gloria in excelsis Deo) (Canon)

Latin. Four [treble = soprano] voices.

Three Motets based on Gregorian Themes

(i) *Ave Maria* [fifth setting listed above], (ii) *Recordare, Virgo Mater*, (iii) *Assumpta est Maria*. Latin. Male-voice choir. No. (iii) also exists in a version for six-part mixed-voice choir; see *Assumpta est Maria* listed above.

Tota pulchra es Maria

Latin. Female-voice choir and organ (?). On the surviving reproductions of the MS the work is described as 'motet for two-part chorus'. The fact that the piece commences with a seven-bar introduction and is in four parts (close score) throughout suggests the composer also envisaged an accompaniment, although no instrument is specified.

Ut queant laxis

Latin. Male-voice choir [= mixed-voice choir]. Plainchant melody with a free cadence in four parts. Fleischmann's choir in the Cathedral of St Mary and St Anne commenced all practices, performances, recitals, and broadcasts by singing an Invocation or Invocare, presumably as a warm-up exercise. This was the famous hymn to St John, *Ut queant laxis*, which Guido d'Arezzo used in developing his method of sight singing around the beginning of the eleventh century. The initial pitch of each successive phrase of the tune (which Guido himself may have written) forms a series of ascending steps, and the syllables sung to these pitches – Ut, Re, Mi, Fa, Sol, La – became the basis of a system of mnemonics for the notes of the scale. Appropriately, *Ut queant laxis*, the origin of this fundamental teaching device, became the choir's signature tune. 'A.F. 24 June 32' (MS).

Vexilla Regis

Latin. Mixed-voice choir. Verses 1, 3, 5 and 7 are sung to the plainsong melody, and these alternate with a setting for four voices of verses 2, 4 and 6: the piece concludes with a simple four-part cadence.

Zwei Ave Maria [Two *Ave Marias*]

(i) for double four-part choir [*Ave Maria*, third setting listed above], (ii) for four-part choir with divisions [*Ave Maria*, fourth setting listed above]. Latin. Mixed-voice choir [eight parts]. 'Amico meo carissimo/Hochwürdigen Herrn Professor Ludwig Berberich/Kapellmeister/"Zu Unser Lieben Frauen"/am Dom in München' [To my dearest friend/the Reverend Professor Ludwig Berberich/Church musician/"To our dear ladies' (? – it is not clear what this refers to)/at the Cathedral in Munich] (MS). One (or perhaps both) of these pieces were performed in Munich Cathedral by the Munich Cathedral Choir, conducted by Ludwig Berberich on the Feast of the Assumption, 15 August 1930.

VOCAL MUSIC

Lieder

Abendfrieden [Evening Peace]
  Gerda von Robertus. German and English.
Abend im Moor [Evening on the Moor]
  Franz Schaehle. German. Voice and piano [= harmonium]. There is also a
  sketch of an arrangement of this song for voice and string orchestra (?). See
  Orchestral Works/Solo Voice and Orchestra above.
Altdeutsches Minnelied [An Old German Minnesong]
  Words anon. German and English.
Abschied [Departure]
  Words? German.
Abschied [Departure]
  Julius Rodenberg. German and English. 'Engl. trs. Mrs Brise/Copyright 1891'
  (MS).
An die Nacht [Night]
  Wilhelm Michel. See *Night* listed in Other Songs below.
Aufblink [Night and Shadows]
  Richard Dehmel. German and English. Performed by Mrs J.B. (Rita) Horgan
  (accompanied by Fleischmann himself or, perhaps, by Tilly Fleischmann) on
  30 April 1933 as part of a recital of Fleischmann's compositions held in
  Clanloughlin, the singer's house in Cork, and again by the same singer (and
  accompanist?) in the same venue on 7 June 1934.
Aus der Kinderwelt [From the World of Children]
  Zwei Lieder für Klavier und eine mittlere Singstimme [Two Songs for Piano
  and Medium Voice]/Two Musical Sketches: (i) 'Die Erste Klavierstunde' [The
  First Lesson], (ii) 'Der heimliche Klan' [Trudi]. Words? (Fleischmann?).
  German and English. Published: Verlag Wilhelm Berntheisel, Munich, 1931,
  as Op. 39.
Barbarazweige [On Barbara's Day]
  Clemens Brentano, 'Aus *Des Knaben Wunderhorn*' (MS). German and English.
  'Copyright 1933' (copyist's score). The title literally means 'St Barbara's
  Twigs'. This refers to the custom of cutting twigs from the cherry tree around
  mid-December (St Barbara's Day), which are then put into water so the buds
  will open and flower before Christmas.
Das Alte Lied [The Old Song/'There was an ancient King']
  Heinrich Heine. German and English (Walter Henley). This work also exists in
  a version for mixed-voice choir (see Choral Music: Unaccompanied above).
Der Phantast [The Fool]
  Franz Schaele. See *The Fool* listed in Other Songs below.
Der Kirschendieb [The Cherry Thief]
  Words? German and English.
Das Lied [The Song]
  Ludwig Finkl. German
Das Rosenblatt [The Roseleaf]
  Julius Bierbaum. German and English (Walter Henley).
Das Steckenpferd [The Hobby-horse]
  Friedrich Rückert. German and English.

Das Volkslied – Es war im Dorfe Hochzeit [The Folksong – At a Village Wedding]
    Franz von Bodenstedt. German and English.
Der Erbe [The Heir]
    Otto Ernst. German and English (Revd. P. MacSwiney). 'Meinem Sohne zu eigen' [Dedicated to my son] (MS).
Der Schelm von Bergen [The Scamp of Bergen]
    Heinrich Heine. German and English. Baritone and piano. This work also exists in a version with orchestral accompaniment, and was conceived as one of a projected series of *Balladen und Legenden* [Ballads and Legends]. See notes to *Der Schelm von Bergen* [The Scamp of Bergen] listed in Orchestral Works/Solo Voice and Orchestra above.
Der seltsame Gast [The Ominous Guest]
    Josef Eichendorf. German and English. Although only the vocal score of this work is extant, it is the only one of the *Balladen und Legenden* for solo male voice and orchestra not described on the MS as performable in an alternative version for voice and piano. See *Der seltsame Gast* and also the notes to *Der Schelm von Bergen* [The Scamp of Bergen] in Orchestral Works/Solo Voice and Orchestra above.
Der wehe Fuass [The Sore Foot]
    Words? German. 'A Schnaderhüpferl' (MS), a kind of witty satirical song popular in Alpine regions.
Die Amsel [The Blackbird]
    Rudolf Baumbach. German and English.
Die Bachstelze [The Wagtail]
    Heinrich Seidel. German and English (Walter Henley). This work also exists in a version for mixed-voice choir under the title *Die Müllerin* [The Miller Lass]. See Choral Music: Unaccompanied/Mixed Voices above. Performed by Mrs J.B. (Rita) Horgan (accompanied by Fleischmann himself or, perhaps, by Tilly Fleischmann) on 7 June 1934 as part of a recital of compositions by Fleischmann given in Clanloughlin, the singer's house in Cork.
Die Königskinder [The King's Children]
    Gertrud Freiin von le Fort ['Gertrud Freiin de la Fort' (MS)]. German.
Drei Gedichte von Ludwig Finkl [Three Poems by Ludwig Finkl]
    (i) 'Das heimliche Ständchen' [Lady Mine], (ii) 'Viel zu viel' [Too Many], (iii) 'Die schönste Rose' [The Sweetest Rose]. German and English (Walter Henley).
Drei Rosen [Three Roses]
    H. Pankow. German and English (Walter Henley). Performed by Mrs J.B. (Rita) Horgan (accompanied by Fleischmann himself or, perhaps, by Tilly Fleischmann) on 30 April 1933 as part of a recital of Fleischmann's compositions held in Clanloughlin, the singer's house in Cork, and again by the same singer (and accompanist?) in the same venue on 7 June 1934.
Du armer Wald! [You Poor Wood!]
    Oskar Freiherr von Redwitz. German, '4.IV.1901' (MS).
Ein kleines Lied [A Little Song]
    Marie von Ebner-Eschenbach. German.
Ein Vogel singt im Walde [A Songbird fills the Wood]
    Anna Ritter. German and English (Walter Henley).
Es geht ein Liedchen im Grunde [There Goes a Popular Ballad]
    Anna Ritter. German and English (Walter Henley). This is a transposed

version of (iv) Das Ringlein sprang entzwei [The Song of the Ring] from *Kleine Romanzen und Lieder im Volkston* [Little Romances and Songs in the Folk Style]. See below.

Flieder im Mondlicht [Lilac in Moonlight]

Franz Langheinrich. German and English. This song is described as No. 7 of a set entitled *Heimatlieder*, of which only one other, *Heimat, liebe Heimat!* listed below, appears to have survived.

Herbst [Autumn]

J.P. Jacobson. German and English.

Heimat, liebe Heimat! [Home, Beloved Homeland!]

Adolf von Stern. German and English. This song is described as No. 4 of a set entitled *Heimatlieder*, of which only one other, *Flieder im Mondlicht* listed above, appears to have survived. The song also exists in a version for voice and orchestra. See Orchestral Works/Solo Voice and Orchestra above.

Hochzeitliches Lied [A Wedding Song]

Words? 'nach Dante-Rossetti' (MS). German and English. This song also exists in a version with orchestral accompaniment (see Orchestral Works/Solo Voice and Orchestra above). Supplied with an English singing translation by M. Lucy, it is also entitled *Epithalamion/Liebesnacht*. Walter Henley subsequently wrote new words for the same music (which were in turn translated into German, possibly by the composer) and in this form it was published under the title *The Awakening* [Das Erwachen], Op. 26 No. 2, by Augener Ltd, London in 1929 (see Other Songs below).

Ich träumte [The Vision]

Paul Verlaine ['Mon rêve familier']. German (Herman Hesse) and English (M. Lucy). On another MS the title is given as 'Mein Traum' [My Dream]. The original French text is not set.

Im Volkston – Von alten Liebesliedern [In the Folk Style – From Olden Lovesongs] *Trab, Rösslein trab* [Trot along, little Horse]. 'Aus *Des Knaben Wunderhorn*' (MS) [From The Youth's Magic Horn]. German, with an English singing translation supplied on separate sheet.

In meiner Heimat [In My Dear Homeland]

Carl Busse. German and English (Revd. P. MacSwiney). Performed by Mrs J.B. (Rita) Horgan (accompanied by Fleischmann himself or, perhaps, by Tilly Fleischmann) on 30 April 1933 as part of a recital of Fleischmann's compositions held in Clanloughlin, the singer's house in Cork, and again by the same singer (and accompanist?) in the same venue on 7 June 1934.

Kleine Romanzen und Lieder im Volkston [Little Romances and Songs in the Folk Style]

(i) 'Es steht eine Lind' im tiefen Tal' [Beneath Yonder Lime], Ludwig Pfau; (ii) 'Die Liebenden' [The Lovers], Klaus Groth; (iii) 'Die Soldatenbraut' [The Soldier's Bride], Eduard Mörike; (iv) 'Des Ringlein sprang entzwei' [The Song of the Ring], Anna Ritter; (v) 'Liebesbrief' [Loveletter], 'Worte aus dem Kurländischen' (MS) [Words from the Kurländischen]. German and English (Walter Henley). The composer has not numbered the songs in this set: the above ordering is for convenience only. Nos. (i), (ii) and (iii) also exist in versions for mixed-voice choir, and (iii) in a version for male-voice choir. See also *Es geht ein Liedchen im Grunde* [There Goes a Popular Ballad] listed above.

Klein Suschens erster Kirchengang [Small Susan's First Visit to the Church]
Words? English and German. 'Mezzo-Soprano or Barytone [*sic*] and House-organ or Piano' (MS). 1933.

Leise kam sie [Tiptoe Love]
Gustav Falke. German and English (Walter Henley).

Lieder aus der Jugendmappe [Songs from the Album of Youth]
(i) 'Mai' [May], Reinhard Volker; (ii) 'Auf den Tod eines Vögleins' [On the Death of a Little Bird], Ludwig Bechstein; (iii) Das traurige Wiegenlied' [The Sad Lullaby], Words?; (iv) 'Der Brief' [The Letter], Theodor Storm; (v) 'Erste Liebe' [First Love], E. Grosse; (vi) 'Gottesdienst der Liebe' [The Service of God], Words?; (vii) 'Letzter Hauch' [The Last Breath], David Friedrich Strauss; (viii) 'Letzter Wunsch' [A Last Wish], Julius Sturm. Apart from *Mai*, described as No. 1, the composer has not numbered these songs. An English singing translation is provided only for (v) (Marie Lucy) and (Walter Henley). Two of the MSS are dated: (vi) 1998 [*recte* 1898], and (viii) 1897.

Meiner lieben Tilly! [To My Dear Tilly!]
See *Schliesse mir die Augen beide* [Close my eyes] below.

Mir träumte [I Dreamt]
Franz Evers. German and English. Performed by Mrs J.B. (Rita) Horgan (accompanied by Fleischmann himself or, perhaps, by Tilly Fleischmann) on 30 April 1933 as part of a recital of Fleischmann's compositions held in Clanloughlin, the singer's house in Cork, and again by the same singer (and accompanist?) in the same venue on 7 June 1934.

Nachtlied [Night Song]
K. Stieler. German. The MS is designated 'Op. 6, No. 6', but apart from *Nicht daheim* listed below no other songs from Op. 6 have come to light.

Nachtlied [Night and Stars]
Friedrich Hebbel. German and English (M. Lucy).

Nicht daheim [Not at Home]
K. Stieler. German. The MS is designated 'Op. 6, No. 4', but apart form *Nachtlied* [K. Stieler] listed above no other songs from Op. 6 have come to light.

Nis Randers
Otto Ernst. German and English (P. [*recte* W.?] Henley). Although described on the existing score as being for high voice and piano, *Nis Randers* was originally conceived as one of a projected series of *Balladen und Legenden* [Ballads and Legends] for voice and orchestra. See notes to *Der Schelm von Bergen* [The Scamp of Bergen] listed in Orchestral Works/Solo Voice and Orchestra above.

Oft denk mit Wehmut ich zurück [The hours I spent with Thee]
Words? German and Englis. MS stamped: 'Prisoners of War Camp/Oldcastle/1 Feb 1918'. This work also exists in a version for voice and orchestra. See Orchestral Works/Solo Voice and Orchestra above.

Pfingstblume [Peony]
Words? German and English.

Ricky
Julius Bierbaum. German and English (Seán Lucy).

Schliesse mir die Augen beide [Close my eyes]
Theodor Storm. German. '12.VIII.04' (MS). The MS is simply headed 'Meiner Lieben Tilly!' [To My Dear Tilly!]; the author of the words is not credited.

Performed in Dachau on 17 May 1906 by Josef Birchan (baritone) and Tilly Fleischmann (piano); also performed by Mrs J.B. (Rita) Horgan (accompanied by Fleischmann himself or, perhaps, by Tilly Fleischmann) on 30 April 1933 as part of a recital of Fleischmann's compositions held in Clanloughlin, the singer's house in Cork, and again by the same singer (and accompanist?) in the same venue on 7 June 1934.

Schlummerliedchen [Slumber Song]
Adolf Holst. German, with an English singing translation supplied on separate sheet. 'Dem lieben Märchen! 26.V.1915' (MS) [To dear little Mary (Mrs J.B. Horgan, née Windle)].

Serenade – Herziges Schätzle du! [Serenade – Sweetheart, thou jewel mine!]
'Poem in the Swabian idiom' (MS). German and English.

Sommerbild [Summer Picture]
Friedrich Hebbel. German and English (Marie Lucy).

Swend Gabelbart und St Edmund [Swend Gabelbart and St Edmund]
Theodor Fontane. German and English (Mary Lucy). Baritone and piano. This work also exists in a version with orchestral accompaniment (see Orchestral Works/Solo Voice and Orchestra above) and was conceived as one of a projected series of *Balladen und Legenden* [Ballads and Legends]. See notes to *Der Schelm von Bergen* [The Scamp of Bergen] listed in Orchestral Works/Solo Voice and Orchestra above.

Two Christmas Songs
The various MSS of this work comprise in fact three different songs which also exist in versions for female-voice choir and organ [=piano]: (i) 'An der Krippe sass Maria' [By the manger sat Maria], Carl Ludwig Schleich, German and English; (ii) 'Über die Hütte weht der Wind: A Sacred Lullaby', '(Aus Des Knaben Wunderhorn)' (MS) [Over the stall the winds away (on some MSS simply entitled 'Christmas Night')], German and English; (iii) 'Christkindleins Wiegenlied', '(Aus *Des Knaben Wunderhorn*)' (MS), German. A title page for (ii), describing it as for 'Soprano and Organ (or Harmonium)', exists but the score is missing. Fleischmann never appears to have made a final decision which two should be paired: on some MSS he lists (i) and (ii), and on others he lists (i) and (iii). See Choral Music: Accompanied above.

Unruhige Nacht [The Disturbed Night]
Conrad Ferdinand Meyer. German and English (Mary Lucy). One MS is dated 'V. IX. MCMXXXXIII'.

Unter den Linden [Under the Linden]
Walter von der Vogelweide. MS stamped: 'Prisoners of War Camp/Oldcastle/7 Jan 1918'. This is an earlier version of (ii) of *Zwei Gedichte von Walter von der Vogelweide* [Two Poems by Walter von der Vogelweide]. This song also exists in a version for voice and small orchestra (see Orchestral Works/Solo Voice and Orchestra above), which has a slightly more elaborate introduction.

Vier Gesänge [Four Songs]
(i) 'Der Abend' [The Evening], Theodor Storm; (ii) 'Einsamkeit' [Loneliness], Peter Cornelius; (iii) 'Stille Stunde' [Quiet Hour] Franz Evers; (iv) 'In sommertiefen Nächten' [In High Summer Nights], Franz Evers. German. One MS of Der Abend is dated 'Dachau im Herbst 1904'. There also exists a (later?) copy of (iii) with English words entitled 'A Dream in a Dream', as

well as a version of (ii) for voice and orchestra (see Orchestral Works/Solo Voice and Orchestra above). Nos. (i) and (ii) together with *Schliesse mir die Augen beide* were performed in Dachau on 17 May 1906, by Josef Birchan (baritone) and Tilly Fleischmann (piano).

Zwei ernste Gesänge [Two Serious Songs]

(i) 'Stimme in der Dämmerung' [A Voice in the Twilight], 'Altdeutscher Gebetspruch' [An Old German Prayer] (MS); (ii) 'Schnitter Tod' (1683) [Death the Reaper], words from *Des Knaben Wunderhorn*. German and English.

Zwei Gedichte von Walter von der Vogelweide [Two Poems by Walter von der Vogelweide]

(i) 'Das Helm-Messer' [The Blade-Oracle], (ii) 'Unter den Linden auf der Heide' [Under the Linden by the Heather]. German and English (Walter Henley). There is also a earlier version, dating from 1918, of *Unter den Linden* amongst Fleischmann's papers (see above), which exists in versions for voice and piano as well as for voice and small orchestra.

Other Songs

In Exile

Words? Medium voice and piano. 'A little song to a faithful ex-choir boy of the Cork Cathedral Choir in remembrance of the old times Cork in Summer 1955' (MS).

Late in the Night [Spät in der Nacht]

Oliver Linden. English and German (Aloys Fleischmann?). Fleischmann came across the poem in an issue of *The Humorist* (29 March 1930): his cutting from the magazine is attached to the MS.

Night [An die Nacht]

Wilhelm Michel. English (Walter Henley) and German. Published: Augener Ltd., London, 1929 as Op. 26 No. 1. Performed by Mrs J.B. (Rita) Horgan (accompanied by Fleischmann himself or, perhaps, by Tilly Fleischmann) on 30 April 1933 as part of a recital of Fleischmann's compositions held in Clanloughlin, the singer's house in Cork, and again by the same singer (and accompanist?) in the same venue on 7 June 1934.

Pangur Bán/Der Mönch und der weisse Kater [White Pangur/The Monk and the White Cat]

Robin Flower's translation into English of an eighth-century Irish poem, with free German translation by the composer. Medium voice, harpsichord [= piano = harmonium].

[Six Songs to Poems by Rabindranath Tagore]

(i) 'Pluck this little flower' [Pflück die kleine Blume]; (ii) 'He came and sat by my side' [Er kam und sass neben mir]; (iii) 'Do not go my love' [Geh nicht Geliebte von mir]; (iv) 'Trust love' [Traue der Liebe]; (v) 'It was in May" [Es war in Mai]; (vi) 'The Man and the Beast' [Das Tier und der Mensch]. English and German. High voice and piano. The first three songs listed here also exist in versions with orchestra: see *Three Songs with Orchestra* listed in Orchestral Works/Solo Voice and Orchestra above. It is not clear if all six songs were conceived as a set: Nos. (v) and (vi) are designated Op. 54, No. 9 and Op. 54, No. 10 respectively, but there is no evidence that the other four songs were designed as companion pieces, or that a complete cycle of songs to poems by Tagore was ever written. Some of these Tagore settings were performed by Dora Ziegler in Dachau in 1926, probably at a private recital held in the Ziegler villa. Mrs J.B. (Rita) Horgan sang Nos. (i), (ii) and (iii) (accompanied by Fleischmann himself or, perhaps, by Tilly Fleischmann) on 30 April 1933 as part a recital of Fleischmann's compositions held in Clanloughlin, the singer's house in Cork. Rita Horgan also sang (ii) and (iii), accompanied by Lord Monteagle, on 13 April 1934 in the Clarence Hall in Cork, and (accompanied either by Fleischmann or Tilly Fleischmann) she performed (i), (ii) and (iii) again in Clanloughlin on 7 June 1934 as part of another recital of Fleischmann's compositions. In 1954, Fleischmann submitted (ii), 'He came and sat by my side', for a competition that was organised by the Arts Council of Ireland and adjudicated by John F. Larchet. It was awarded it a prize of £15 (24 June 1954).

The Awakening [Das Erwachen]

Walter Henley. English and German. Published: Augener Ltd, London, 1929 as Op. 26, No. 2. See *Hochzeitliches Lied* [A Wedding Song] in Orchestral Works/Solo Voice and Orchestra and Vocal Music/Lieder above. Performed by Mrs J.B. (Rita) Horgan (accompanied by Fleischmann himself or, perhaps, by Tilly Fleischmann) on 30 April 1933 as part of a recital of Fleischmann's compositions held in Clanloughlin, the singer's house in Cork, and again by the same singer (and accompanist?) in the same venue on 7 June 1934.

The Fiddler of Dooney

W.B. Yeats. English. 'After an Old Irish Dance Tune' (MS). Medium voice and piano.

The Fool [Der Phantast]

Franz Schaele. German and English (Walter Henley). Published: Augener Ltd, London, 1929 as Op. 26, No. 3.

The Sandman (Lullaby)

Words? Medium voice and piano. English and German.

Narrator and Piano

Des Sängers Fluch [The Singer's Curse]

Ludwig Uhland. German and English. There are two MSS of this work. The first is laid out for piano, although the score has (later?) annotations in pencil indicating instrumentation. The piano part has also been annotated with fingering here and there, which suggests that the piece may have been performed, or at least rehearsed in this form. The text is in German. The second MS consists of a revised version of the work with the text in English (no translator is credited). This second MS also contains indications of instrumentation, which seem to confirm that the work was initially conceived for narrator and orchestra. No full score has been found, however, and it seems unlikely that the work was ever orchestrated.

Ein Schicksal [Fate]

Gottfried Kinkel. The handwriting on the MS suggests that this is a very early work.

INSTRUMENTAL MUSIC

Organ

Alleluja für Orchester oder Orgel [Alleluia for Orchestra or Organ]
    See Orchestral Works above. See also *Fuga Impromptu on the Easter Alleluia* below.
Das österliche Alleluja [The Easter Alleluia]. Fugue.
    Apart from utilising the same plainchant theme, this work bears no relation to the *Fuga Impromptu on the Easter Alleluia* listed below.
Deo Gratias (Recitations on G)
    This appears to be a voluntary designed, perhaps, to follow the intoning of the Deo Gratias (on the reciting tone G) at the conclusion of the mass.
God have Mercy: Postludium I, Postludium II
    The MS comprises a harmonisation (presumably for accompaniment purposes) of the hymn tune 'God have Mercy', followed by two organ postludes based on motifs taken from it. See Arrangements/Other Arrangements below.
Fantasie-Prelude and Fugue on the Gaelic Hymn to St. Patrick
    (with *ad libitum* parts for 2 cornets, soprano cornet, 2 horns, 2 tenor trombones, bass trombone, tuba, and mixed-voice choir). While there are several MSS of this work amongst Fleischmann's papers, none of them contains the complete work in a final form. The various MSS of the Fantasie-Prelude are separate to those of the Fugue. There are often major differences between the MSS and although the existence of a complete set of brass parts and some choral parts indicates that the work was performed, it is not clear from the surviving material what Fleischmann's final conception may have been. The work is also referred to as *Tulit Spem Patricius* on some of the MSS. On one MS the work is designated Op. 38, on another Op. 52.
Fuga Impromptu on the Easter Alleluia
    This is a (later?) version of the *Alleluja für Orchester oder Orgel* [Alleluia for Orchestra or Organ] listed above. See also Orchestral Works/Orchestra above.
Impromptu: From the sketch book for organ music
    Written on the reverse side of the MS sheet containing the *Postludium (Facile)*, listed below.
Introduction and Fugue on the theme of the Magnificat (Tonus VIII)
    Not only do the various MSS of this work bear slightly different titles – 'Fantasy, Prelude and Fugue on the theme of the Magnificat (Tonus VIII)'; 'Introduction and Fantasy-Fugue'; 'Fantasy and Fugue on the theme of the Magnificat (Tonus VIII)'; 'Magnificat with Fugue' – but they also contain compositional variants, particularly in the handling of the concluding bars. This is a later (?) version of the *Präludium und Fuge für Orgel oder Orchester über dem Magnificat im VIII Kirchenton* [Prelude and Fugue for Organ or Orchestra on the Magnificat Tonus VIII] listed below, from which it differs significantly. See also Orchestral Works/Orchestra and Orchestral Works/Chorus and Orchestra above.
Introductions, Modulations and Interludes in the Church Modes between the Antiphons of Vespers 'In Festis Beati Mariae Virgine'
    'A.F. 1935' (MS).
[Introductions, Modulations and Interludes in the Church Modes]
    For the plainchant *Missa fons bonitatis*.

Postludium (F major)

Postludium (*Facile*) (E flat major)

> Written on the reverse side of the MS sheet containing the *Impromptu: From the sketch book for organ music* listed above.

Praeludium (C major)

Praeludium (D flat major)

> The only MS of this work is to be found in a sketchbook which also contains early versions of the *Praeludium in E dur*, the *Präludium in A* (*No.4*) and 'In Memoriam: Joseph Rheinberger' from the *Three Lyrical Tone Sketches*, all of which are listed below.

Praeludium in E dur [Preludium in E major]

Praeludium in G

> Pencil sketch (complete) extant.

Präludium in A (No. 4)

> Pencil sketch (complete) extant. The 'No. 4' on the MS suggests that this work was planned as one of a set of organ preludes and it is possible that some of the other preludes listed above may have been conceived as companion pieces, although there is no direct evidence that this was the case. No MS of a complete set of organ preludes has been found amongst Fleischmann's papers.

Präludium und Fuge für Orgel oder Orchester über dem Magnificat im VIII Kirchenton [Prelude and Fugue for Organ or Orchestra on the Magnificat Tonus VIII]

> See *Introduction and Fugue on the theme of the Magnificat (Tonus VIII)* above. See also Orchestral Works/Orchestra above.

Recitationscadenzen, kleine Improvisionen und Präludien der Töne F (♯) G (♭) A (♭) B♭ [Recitations-Cadences and Versetten [*sic*] to be used as an accompaniment for intoning in the keys: F (♯) G (♭) A (♭) B♭]

> The MS is prefaced with a note on the correct method of singing a text on a reciting tone: 'The accompanying organ playing (which pays no attention to the pauses in the text) ought to be more freely [*sic*], unforced, and in the manner of an improvisation. It should be neither too loud or [*sic*] too soft, to support and embellish the singing part.' The accidentals in brackets after the keys in the title can be taken to indicate suitable alternative pitches where these might prove convenient.

Three Improvisations on Gregorian Themes

> (i) *Ave Maris Stella*, (ii) 'Vor einem Madonnenbild Andrea del Sartos'' [Before a picture of the Madonna by Andrea del Sarto], (iii) *Stabat Mater*.

Three Lyrical Tone Sketches

> (i) Prelude (C major), (ii) 'In Memoriam: Joseph Rheinberger' [E flat major]; (iii) 'To an Old Organ' [A major]. There is no title page on what appears to be the revised MS, and none of the pieces has either an individual heading or a tempo indication (with the exception of the direction Adagio for the middle section of the third piece). A second group of MSS, however, which consists of what are apparently earlier versions of (ii) and (iii) only, contains a title page for the whole set and bears the designation Op. 56. In a somewhat modified form, these pieces also exist in an arrangement for wind sextet (flute, oboe, 2 clarinets, bassoon and bass clarinet): in relation to the organ version, these wind versions are in the order (ii), (i) and (iii) – although (i) is incomplete – and are in the same keys. There is a second adaptation of the third piece for string

quartet under the title Postludium. This latter MS is stamped 'Prisoners of War Camp/Oldcastle/24 Nov. 1917', and it is likely that the wind version also dates from the same period. The present organ work appears to be a reworking of this earlier material. No. (i) Prelude is essentially a transposition of *Preludium* (D flat major) listed above. See also Miscellaneous Instrumental below.

Three Pieces

(i) Toccata, (ii) Pastorale-Serenade: 'Shepherds at the Crib' (after a picture by Antonio Allegri di Correggio, 1494–1534), (iii) Fuga (über ein jonisches Thema) [Fugue (on an Ionian Theme)]. No. (iii) is a version of (xvii) Postludium III of the *Sacred Music for the Ceremony of Reception and Profession*. See Sacred Music above.

[Untitled fugal piece in C major]

The style of this work suggests that it was conceived as an exercise in four-part polyphonic writing for the organ.

Miscellaneous Instrumental

Albumblatt für Violine und Klavier [Albumleaf for Violin and Piano]

This work is lost. A concert programme survives for a performance (the first?) in Dachau on 13 November 1904 which states: 'Seinem lieben ehemaligen Lehrer in Dankbarkeit und Verehrung' [Dedicated to his dear former teacher in gratitude and respect].

Has Sorrow thy Young Days Shaded (Album Leaf)

Piano. 'Cork im Frühling 1913' (MS). Based on an air from *Irish Melodies* by Thomas Moore. Performed by Tilly Fleischmann (under the title 'Album Leaf') on 7 June 1934 as part of a recital of compositions by Fleischmann held in Clanloughlin, the Cork home of singer Rita Horgan.

In Festo Corporis Christi [For the Feast of Corpus Christi]

Preludes for brass ensemble. See Sacred Music above.

Postludium

String Quartet. This is an earlier (?) version of (iii) 'To an Old Organ' from *Three Lyrical Tone Sketches* for organ listed above.

Recollection of an Irish Feis

Flute and piano. This work is an abbreviated and simplified version of *Rhapsodie über eine irischen Weise* [Rhapsody on an Irish Air] for piano listed below.

Rhapsodie über eine irischer Weise [Rhapsody on an Irish Air]

Piano. This work also exists in a revised and abbreviated version for piano entitled *Nachklänge aus einem irischer Musikfest/Cuimhní ar Fheischeoil* [Memories of an Irish Music Festival], the MS of which is dated 1921. The air on which the piece is based is the jig tune 'The Irish Washerwoman'. Original version performed by Tilly Fleischmann in Dachau, 17 May 1906 and again in Cork on 21 November 1906; revised version performed by Tilly Fleischmann in Cork in 10 March 1926; she performed it again on 7 June 1934 as part of a recital of compositions by Fleischmann held in Clanloughlin, the Cork home of singer Rita Horgan.

[Three Pieces for Wind Sextet]

Flute, oboe, 2 clarinets, bassoon and bass clarinet. Untitled version of *Three Lyrical Tone Sketches* for organ listed above. Of the second piece, (i) in the organ version, only the conclusion is extant. See Instrumental Music/Organ above.

[Untitled piece].

Piano. It is not clear if the extant MS comprises the complete work: the nature of the music suggests that these may be the concluding sections of a longer piece.

ARRANGEMENTS

Arrangements of Irish Folk Music

[Album of Six of Irish Melodies for Voice and Piano]

(i) 'Has Sorrow thy young days shaded' [Hat Gram deine Jugend empfangen] [first setting], from *Irish Melodies* by Thomas Moore; (ii) 'Eileen, Alannah'; (iii) 'She is far from the land' [Sie ist fern von dem Land], from *Irish Melodies* by Thomas Moore; (iv) 'I wish I were on yonder hill' [Ich woll ich wär auf jenem Berg], 'An old Irish Melody' (MS); (v)'The harp that once thro'Tara's halls' [Die Harfe von Tara], from *Irish Melodies* by Thomas Moore; (vi) 'Tho' the last glimpse of Erin' [Weit über dem Meere], from *Irish Melodies* by Thomas Moore. English and German. See below for second setting of (i) 'Has Sorrow thy young days shaded'.

[An] Crúiscín Lán [The Full Jug]

Words anon. English. Male-voice choir. 'Drinking Songs No. III' (MS): the whereabouts of the first two songs is unknown. Although the title on the MS is in (faulty) Irish, the words are in English.

Bán-Chnuic Éireann Ó [The White Hills of Erin O]

Donncha Rua Mac Conmara. Irish and English. Mixed-voice choir.

Clare's Dragoons

Thomas Davis. English. Male-voice choir. 'Air – "Viva la!"' (MS). There are two variants of this setting amongst Fleischmann's papers.

Come to the Hedgerows

English. Male-voice choir. 'Air and words from Dr. Joyce's collection' (MS). The attribution of the source is crossed through on the MS, and it is certainly somewhat misleading. The tune was collected by Patrick Joyce, and was published in Petrie's 1855 *Ancient Music of Ireland*. It appeared there under a different title, however 'As a Sailor and a Soldier were walking one day' and with different words. It is not known who re-named the tune or wrote the words that Fleischmann set.

Dán-Mholadh na Ghaedhilge [Poem in Praise of Gaelic]

Séaghan Ó Séaghdha. Irish and English. Mixed-voice choir.

Eibhlín, a Rúin [Eileen Aroon]

[First setting]. Words anon. English. Female-voice [= male-voice] choir. 'A.F. 1931' (MS).

Eibhlín, a Rúin [Eileen Aroon]

[Second setting]. Words anon. English. Mixed-voice choir. Curiously, the MS is entitled 'Éire, a Rúin' [Ireland, My Love], although both words and tune are those of 'Eibhlín, a Rúin'.

Erin! The tear and the smile

Air and words from *Irish Melodies* by Thomas Moore. Male-voice choir. This is the same melody as 'Eibhlín, a Rúin'. See above.

Has Sorrow thy Young Days Shaded

[First setting]. See (i) of Album of Six of Irish Melodies for Voice and Piano above.

Has Sorrow thy Young Days Shaded
[Second setting]. Air and words from *Irish Melodies* by Thomas Moore. English. Mixed-voice choir.
Hunting Song
Words anon. 'Aus Goodman Gesangbuch' [From the [James] Goodman Songbook] (MS). English. Two-part children's choir and piano. 'A.F. 31' (MS).
Ireland, Ireland, Over All! – A Patriotic Song
Words? English. Unison voices and piano. The unknown author appears to have fashioned his verses to fit a variant of the melody usually associated with Thomas Moore's 'Silent Oh Moyle!'.
Kathleen O'More
George Nugent Reynolds. English. Male-voice choir.
Let Erin Remember the Days of Old
Air and words from *Irish Melodies* by Thomas Moore. English. Male-voice choir. 'A.F. 1931' (MS).
My Bonny Cuckoo
Words anon. English. Mixed-voice choir. '(Bunting Air) 1793' (MS), from E. Bunting, *The Ancient Music of Ireland*, 1840.
Silent Oh Moyle!
[First setting]. Air and words from *Irish Melodies* by Thomas Moore. Mixed-voice choir [six parts].
Silent Oh Moyle!
[Second setting]. Air and words from *Irish Melodies* by Thomas Moore. Mixed-voice choir [four parts].
Silent, Oh Moyle!
[Third setting]. Air and words from *Irish Melodies* by Thomas Moore. Male-voice choir.
Silent, Oh Moyle!
[Fourth setting]. English. Air and words from *Irish Melodies* by Thomas Moore. Sketch of harmonisation in three parts (for keyboard?).
[Slán le Máighe] [Farewell to the River Maigue]
[Aindrias Mac Craith.] Female-voice choir. Incomplete sketch: the MS is entitled simply 'Irish Air', and has no text.
The Battle-Eve of the Brigade
Thomas Davis. English. Male-voice choir. 'Air "Contended I am"' (MS).
The Bells of Shandon
Sylvester O'Mahony (Father Prout). English. Female-voice choir and piano. 'A.F. 1931' (MS).
The Irish Raparees: A Peasant Ballad of 1691
Charles Gavin Duffy. English. 'Air –"Jack, the Joly [*sic.*] Ploughboy"' (MS)
The King of Ireland's Cairn
[First setting]. Ethna Carbery. English. Male-voice choir. Air 'The Maids of Mourn Shore' (Petrie, ed. Stanford), better known as 'Down by the Sally Gardens' with words by W.B. Yeats.
The King of Ireland's Cairn
[Second setting]. Ethna Carbery. English. Mixed-voice choir. See first setting above.
The Rakes of Mallow
Words anon. English. Male-voice choir.

There is a gentle gleam
> Samuel Lover. English. Male-voice choir.

The Shan Van Vocht
> [First setting]. Words anon. English. 'Street Ballad, Anno Dominis 1796' (MS). Male-voice choir. 'Air: "Sean Bhean Bhocht" [The Poor Old Woman]' (MS). Version of setting for Mixed-voice choir listed below.

The Shan Van Vocht
> [Second setting]. Words anon. English. 'Street Ballad, Anno Dominis 1796' (MS). Mixed-voice choir.

The Wild Geese
> William Drennan. English. Male-voice choir. 'Air "The Wild Geese" (Géadhna Fiadhaine)' (MS).

Three Old Irish Airs from Bunting
> (i) 'When filled with thoughts of life's young day' [tune: 'The Wheelwright'], Gerald Griffin; (ii) 'What! Passed away those happy hours' [tune: 'The Foggy Dew'], Gerald Griffin, 'Addressed to a Friend'; (iii) 'Sweet Portaferry' [tune: Sweet Portaferry], words anon. The three airs are taken from E. Bunting, *The Ancient Music of Ireland*, 1840. Male-voice choir.

Two Celtic Ancient Lullabys
> (i) 'Rocked in the Cradle of the Wind', ([James] Goodman); (ii) 'Suantree – Hush Song', (Edward Walsh). English and German (Fleischmann?). Medium voice and piano.

Other Arrangements

A Child is born in Bethlehem
> 'An Old Christmas Carol (Speyer Hymn Book)' (MS). Latin and English (Revd. P. Mac Swiney). Female-voice choir and organ. '1938' (MS). There is also a version of this setting for mixed-voice choir and organ. Broadcast performance on Radio Éireann (by Radio Éireann Singers?), 27 February 1967.

Ad Completorium [The Office of Compline]
> Latin. Mixed-voice choir, lector and organ. Arrangement of the plainchant for the Office of Compline.

Adeste Fideles
> [First setting]. Carol. Latin. Mixed-voice choir and organ. This setting has fairly elaborate introductory material and specifies the additional use of children's choir. 'Bandon Parish church choir (1929)' (MS).

Adeste Fideles
> [Second setting]. Carol. Latin. Female-voice choir and organ. 'A.F. XI. 30' (MS).

Ad Nativitatem [For the Nativity]
> (i) 'Quem pastores', (ii) 'De noctu sacra carmen (Ad Oves)'. Two carols. Latin. Male-voice choir and organ. One MS is stamped 'Prisoners of War Camp/Oldcastle/16 Nov 1917.' There is also a (later?) version of these settings for mixed-voice choir and organ.

Adoro te
> Latin. Male-voice choir. Plainchant melody.

Ancient Xmas Carol: In natali Domini
> Latin. Soprano solo, female-voice choir and organ. 'A.F. XI. 30.' (MS).

Angels We Have Heard/Angelos Audivium
    [First setting]. Carol. English and Latin. Mixed-voice choir and organ. [G major].

Angels We Have Heard/Angelos Audivium
    [Second setting]. Carol. English and Latin. Unison voices (?) and organ. [F major].

Attende Domine
    Latin. Mixed-voice choir. Plainchant melody.

Ave Maria
    Latin. Unison voices (?) and organ. Plainchant melody. On same MS sheet as *O Sanctissima* [third setting]. See below.

Ave Verum: Prosa antiqua usu recepta
    [First setting]. Latin. Male-voice choir [and organ]. Plainchant melody [A major]. One MS is stamped 'Prisoners of War Camp/Oldcastle/16 Nov. 1917'. On another MS, which also contains the *Rhythmus S. Thomae Aquinatis* (see below), the setting is supplied with a *Postludium* for organ. There also exists a (later?) slightly varied version of this setting.

Ave Verum
    [Second setting]. Latin. Female-voice choir. Plainchant melody [G major].

Creator summe rerum
    Hymn tune (?). Latin. Female-voice choir. Written on the upper half of the same page as the arrangement of *O Maria, Virgo pia*. See below.

Credo from *Missa Regia, Primi Toni* by Henry Du Mont (1610–84).
    Latin. Mixed-voice choir. See Sacred Music above.

Das Schifflein – Abschiedslied [The Little Ship – Song of Farewell]
    Ludwig Uhland. German. Arrangement of (folk?) melody (collected?) by Friedrich Silcher. 'Douglas/Isle of Man/16.I.1919' (MS). The reverse side of the MS sheet on which the music is written is signed by some of Fleischmann's fellow internees in the Douglas Prisoner of War Camp.

Die Ehre Gottes [The Glory of God] by L. van Beethoven, Op. 48, No. 4
    [First setting]. German. Male-voice choir. MS stamped 'Prisoners of War Camp/Oldcastle/6 Oct 1917'.

Die Ehre Gottes [The Glory of God] by L. van Beethoven, Op. 48, No. 4
    [Second setting]. German. Male-voice choir and orchestra [1120.2210.timp.str]. Set of choral and orchestral parts stamped 'Prisoners of War Camp/Oldcastle/6 Oct 1917'. MS not in Fleischmann's hand and the arrangement may not be his.

Ein Kind geborn in Bethlehem [A Child is born in Bethlehem]
    'Alte Weise aus dem Paderborngesangbuch [Old air from the Paderborn Songbook]/English version by Revd. P. Mac Swiney' (MS). German. Mixed-voice choir and organ. Described on the MS as the second of *Zwei Weihnachtsgesänge* [Two Christmas Eve Songs]. The first, *In Bethlehem geboren*, which is listed on the MS, has not come to light. The MS has no English text. Despite very similar titles, this piece bears no relation to *A Child is born in Bethlehem* listed above.

[Four Hymn Tunes]
    (i) 'Cúnamh chughainn O Phádraig' [= St. Patrick's Hymn/Tulit Spem Patricius]; (ii) 'Soul of my Saviour'; (iii) 'O Sanctissima' [fourth setting]; (iv) 'We stand for God'. Very simple four-part harmonisations in close score without text. The inscription 'Buttermarket [*recte*: Butter Exchange?] Band' in

pencil at the top of the first page of the MS suggests that these may be sketches of arrangements for the well-known Cork Butter Exchange Band.

Four Old Tunes for Eastertide and Ascension Day

(i) 'Laetare', (ii) 'Surrexit Christus', (iii) 'Maria Osterfreud', (iv) 'Ascendit Deus'. German and English (Seán Lucy). Female-voice choir and harmoniun [= organ]. Op. 48 (on another MS the work is designated Op. 49). See Sacred Music above.

From Heaven High

[First setting]. 'Old Christmas Carol' (MS). English. Female-voice choir and organ.

From Heaven High

[Second setting]. 'Old Christmas Carol' (MS). English. Mixed-voice choir. 'XI. 1948' (MS).

God have Mercy

Hymn tune. Four-part harmonisation in close score (no words), followed by two Postludes (for organ?). See Instrumental Music/Organ above.

In Festo Corporis Christi [For the Feast of Corpus Christi]

Various hymn tunes arranged for different brass ensembles. See Sacred Music above.

In Nativitate Domini. Hymnus II Vesper [*Jesu Redemptor*]

Latin. Mixed-voice choir. Plainchant melody.

In Vigilia Paschae [For the Easter Vigil]

Latin. The MS comprises various plainchant melodies for Holy Week ceremonies, unaccompanied until near the end when organ support is introduced.

Jesu dulcis memoria

Latin. Mixed-voice choir. Plainchant melody.

Jesu, Salvator mundi by Menegali (c. 1700)

Latin. Male-voice choir. 'Copyright by A.F. 1930' (MS).

John Peel

English folk song. English. Male-voice choir? One choral part (tenor or soprano) only extant.

Lauda Sion

Hymn tune. Latin. Male-voice choir. In the same MS as arrangement of *O esca viatorum* [second setting]. See below.

Little Jesus

'Irish Xmas Carol' (MS). English. Solo voice (unison voices?) and organ (piano?).

Messe de 2me. ton [Mass in the 2nd mode] by Henry du Mont

Latin. This is an arrangement for organ and voices of one the *Cinq messes en plain-chant,* known as the *Messes Royales,* published by Du Mont in 1669. There is no attribution of authorship, and it cannot be stated with any certainty that it is Fleischmann's own arrangement.

[Miscellaneous arrangements for brass ensembles]

Short arrangements, and sets of arrangements for various brass ensembles, some of which, to judge from the MSS, probably date from Fleischmann's Dachau years. Not all of the pieces are identified by name, but amongst them are arrangements of 'Aufblick', the first song from Fleischmann's own *Acht Lieder für Männerchor* [Eight Songs for Male-Voice Choir], Op. 3 (see Vocal Music: Unaccompanied/Male Voices above), and the hymn tune 'Grosser

Gott', known in English as 'Holy God, we praise thy name'. One curious item amongst these miscellaneous MSS is a sketch (in pencil) for a work for 2 cornets, 2 horns and 3 trombones, the title of each movement of which is taken from the ordinary of the Mass – Kyrie, Gloria, etc. Whether this is a sketch for a projected mass by Fleischmann himself, or a projected arrangement for brass of an unidentified original remains a matter for conjecture.

Missa in hon. S. Thomas de Aquino [Mass in honour of St Thomas Aquinas] by Josef Gruber, Op. 83.

Latin. Mixed-voice choir (seven parts), timpani and brass ensemble. The title page states that the score is arranged by Aloys Fleischmann, but does not specify for what forces the original was composed.

Motette [Omnium potens] (17 Century)

Latin. Male-voice choir and organ and (or?) brass ensemble [2 trumpets, bass trumpet or euphonium]. Unidentified motet. 'Prisoners of War Camp/Oldcastle/3 Nov. 1917' (MS). See *Rhythmus S. Thomae Aquinatis* below.

O esca viatorum

[First setting]. Latin. Female-voice choir. Plainchant melody. Written on the upper half of the same page as the arrangement of *O Sanctissima* [second setting]. See below.

O esca viatorum

[Second setting]. Latin. Male-voice choir. Plainchant melody. In the same MS as the arrangement of *Lauda Sion*. See above.

O Glorious Lady, throned on high

Hymn tune. English. Female-voice choir.

O Maria, Virgo pia

Hymn tune (?). Latin. Female-voice choir. Written on lower half of the same page as the arrangement of *Creator summe rerum*. See above.

O quam amabilis

'XVII cent. Melody (Antwerp 1609)' (MS). Latin. Female-voice choir [with tenor and bass parts *ad libitum*].

O quam glorifica

Latin. Unison voices [with four-part (SATB) cadence] and organ. Plainchant melody.

Organ Concerto in F, Op. 137, by Josef Rheinberger

Harmonium and piano. Various pages of the MS are stamped 'Prisoners of War Camp/Oldcastle/27 Oct. 1917', 'Prisoners of War Camp/Oldcastle/28 Jan. 1918', 'Prisoners of War Camp/Oldcastle/1 Feb. 1918'.

O Salutaris hostia

Hymn tune. Latin. Male-voice choir. Set of choral parts stamped 'Prisoners of War/P.C./Oldcastle' [n.d.].

[O Salutaris hostia etc.]

Harmonisations for organ (?) of various plainchant melodies for *O Salutaris hostia*, *Tantum ergo*, and *Cor Jesu*.

O Sanctissima

[First setting]. Hymn tune. Latin. Mixed-voice choir and organ.

O Sanctissima

[Second setting]. Hymn tune. Latin. Female-voice choir. Written on the lower half of the same page as the arrangement of *O esca viatorum* [first setting]. See above.

O Sanctissima

[Third setting]. Hymn tune. Four-part harmonisation without words. On the same MS as the harmonisation of the plainchant *Ave Maria*. See above.

O Sanctissima

[Fourth setting]. See *Four Hymn Tunes* listed above.

Puer natus in Bethlehem

Latin. Mixed-voice choir and organ. Plainchant melody. One MS indicates the use of a solo voice for specific passages.

Rhythmus S. Thomae Aquinatis

Latin. Male-voice choir. Harmonisation of plainchant melody with Interludium and Postludium for organ. One MS, which is stamped 'Prisoners of War Camp/Oldcastle/3 Nov. 1917', also contains an arrangement of 'Quem pastores' (see *Ad Nativitatem* above), and an arrangement of an unspecified seventeenth century motet for male-voice choir and organ and (or?) brass ensemble [2 trumpets, bass trumpet or euphonium]. See *Motette* [Omnium potens] above.

Rorate caeli desuper

Latin. Mixed-voice choir and organ. Plainchant melody.

Salve! Flos et décor Ecclesiae

'Piae Cantiones 1582' (MS). Latin. Female-voice choir and organ.

Silent night! Holy night! by F. Gruber

[First setting]. English. Mixed-voice choir. Carol. There is also a version of this setting for organ solo (which may have been used as a Prelude), to which is attached an Interludium based on the tune and a short coda marked *Fine*. Another MS of this organ solo (showing some differences with the above) is entitled *Stille Nacht, heilige Nacht!*, and described as 'Organ Praeludium . . ./für/Miss Margaret O'Hickey/Cathedral organist-assistant Cork/Xmas 1959'.

Silent night! Holy night! by F. Gruber

[Second setting]. English. Female-voice choir.

Sonnenwende [Solstice]

Dramatisches Weihnachtsmärchen in 4 Aufzügun [A Dramatic Christmas Tale in 4 Acts] by Michael Haller, Op. 51, arranged for string orchestra by Fleischmann. See Stage Works above.

The glad news on the hills (Shepherd song)

'Old Air from the Paderborner-Gesangsbuch 1609' (MS). English (alternative title on some MSS: 'Be ye glad and joyful sing'), Latin ('Jubilate omnis grex') and German ('Fröhlich seitt undt Jubilerdt'). Mixed-voice choir and organ. This arrangement appears to have been planned as one of a set: on one MS it is described as 'No. VI'. There are two variant settings: one for the forces described above, the other for unison voices (or solo voice?) and organ. The organ parts in the various MSS also differ significantly from one another. 'Cork Cathedral 1927' (One MS).

The King of Heaven

'A XVI Century Christmas Carol' (MS). English. Mixed-voice choir (six parts).

The Virgin Passed a Thorny Wood

'Circa 1600' (MS). Carol. English. Mixed-voice choir.

[Three Sequences]

(i) *Victimae paschali laudes*, (ii) *Veni Sancte Spiritus*, (iii) *Lauda Sion*. Latin.

Mixed-voice choir and organ. Plainchant melodies.

Tulit Spem Patricius [St Patrick's Hymn]

Hymn tune. Latin. Mixed voice choir, brass ensemble [2 cornets, 2 horns, 3 trombones] and (or?) organ.

Turmmusik in der Christnacht. [Tower Music for Christmas Night]

Two MSS are extant. The first, entitled as above, is described as 'Drei alte, geistliche Lieder/für/2 Trompeten in B und 2 Posaunen' [Three old, sacred songs/for/2 trumpets and 2 trombones] (MS), and contains: (i) 'In dulci jubilo'; (ii) 'Adeste Fideles'; (iii) 'Stille Nacht, heilige Nacht!'. The second MS, entitled *Turmmusik in der Christnacht in Dachau,* is described in similar terms except that '(od. Tuben)' [or tubas] is indicated as an alternative to the trombones. It contains the following arrangements: (i) 'Es ist ein Ros' entsprungen' [There is a Rose that Bloometh]; (ii) 'Stille Nacht! Heilige Nacht!' [Silent Night! Holy Night!]; (iii) 'O, du fröhliche O, du selige' [O Thou joyful one, O Thou blessed one]. The MSS also include a separate arrangement for the same forces of the hymn tune 'Grosser Gott', known in English as 'Holy God, we praise thy name'.

Two Ancient Christmas Carols

(i) 'Come see a rose' (or 'It is a rose'), English (Aloys Fleischmann trans. from the German); (ii) 'Resonet in laudibus', Latin. Female-voice choir and organ [= harmonium]. One MS of Resonet in laudibus is dated 'Xmax 1923'.

Veni, veni Emmanuel

'Psalteriolum Cantionum Catholicarum/Cologne 1710' (MS). Latin. Unison voices and organ.

Weihnachts-Wiegenlied [Christmas Cradle Song] 'von Adolf Langsted' (MS) German. Voice and piano.

Cathedral Choir Members
in Fleischmann's Time

Jim Ahern	J. Creedon
Henry Atkins	Tim Creedon
	Jim Crowley
Micheal Baldwin	J.P. Crowley
Seán Barrett	Jim Crockett
J. Barry	D.P. Cummins
Robert Barry	Liam Cunningham
James Bastible	Joe Cunningham
John Bastible	
James Bell	Paddy Daly
Dan Bergin	Simon Daly
Daniel Bevan	W. Daly
Denis Bevan	Delaney
Maurice Bevan	M. Delury
James Blanc	Jerry Dennehy
Donal Buckley	E. Dinan
John Buckley	W. Dinan
P. Buckley	Christy Dineen
Tom Buckley	Donal Dorgan
	J. Doyle
Liam Callaghan	J. Downey
Sean Callaghan	Liam Downey
W. Campion	M. Drinan
G. Canty	D. Duggan
D. Casey	William Dunlea
J. Cashman	
Richard Cassidy	Daniel B. Eaton
J. Cleary	L. Egar
John Clifford	William Egan
Finbarr Conway	Ned Evans
Paddy Cooney	
Anthony Corbett	Hugh Falvey
John Corbett	D.J. Field
J.F. Corkery	Con Fielding
Derry Cotter	Jimmy Finn

Michael Finn
E. Fitzgerald
E. Flynn
J. Flynn
W. Flynn
C. Fogarty
R. Foley
William Foley
T. Forbes

Jerry Galvin
Paddy Geney
Tom Gibney
Bill Griffin

Michael Harrison
P. Hartnett
Cormac Healy
T. Healy
P. Higgins
Denis Hourigan

J. Ivers

J. Jonston

Michael Keane
Paddy Kelleher
Patrick Kelleher
William Kelleher
Aidan Kennedy
P. Kennedy
Karl Kerstein
J. Kiely

Jack Leahy
Larry Leahy
Micheal Lee
W. Lee
Peter Lenehan
S. Linehan
Bill Long
Donie Long
Dan Looney
H. Looney
Bill Luttrell

C. Mahony
P. Mahony

A. Martin
Jack McCabe
D. McCarthy
E. McCarthy
Joe McCarthy
David McInerney
J. Molloy
John Moloney
J. Morrison
Bob Mulcahy
J. Mulchinoch
Donal Mullins
Plunkett Mullins
Bill Murphy
Dan Murphy
J. Murphy
Michael Murphy
Paddy Murphy
Tony Murphy

Seán Neeson
Richard Newman
W. Newton
Noel Noonan

Donal O'Brien
James O'Brien
M. O'Brien
Paddy O'Brien
E. O'Callaghan
Jerome O'Callaghan
D. O'Carroll
J. O'Connor
Patrick O'Connor
Terence O'Connor
Gus O'Donovan
Jack O'Donovan
John O'Donovan
W. O'Flaherty
Donal O'Halloran
Tim O'Halloran
D. O'Keeffe
Gerald O'Keeffe
James O'Keeffe
M. O'Keeffe
Con O'Leary
David O'Leary
Edward O'Leary
J. O'Leary

John O'Leary
Liam O'Leary
P. O'Leary
William O'Leary
Christy O'Mahony
P. O'Regan
Frank O'Reilly
H. O'Reilly
Micheal O'Reilly
Sonny O'Reilly
Thomas O'Reilly
Denis O'Riordan
John O'Riordan
Gerard Shaughnessy
F. O'Shea
Conor O'Sullivan
Denis O'Sullivan
P.T. O'Sullivan
W. O'Sullivan
Seámus Ó Tuama
Seán Óg Ó Tuama

P.J. Power

Tom Quinlan

Ben Rees
T. Reilly
Bill Rice
Patrick Ridgeway

Robert Ridgeway
J. Roche
D. Ryan
Terence Ryan

Fr A. Sanusi
Dan Skidd
Jim Stack
T. Stanton
Tom Sullivan

Colum Toibín
Niall Toibín
J. Twomey

Teddy Vesey
Tom Vesey

T. Wall
Charles Wallace
W. Walsh
John Warren
R. White
Alf Whyte
Frank Whyte
Leo Whyte
Robert Whyte
Dan Williamson
Frank Williamson

Notes and references

INTRODUCTION

1　Fleischmann to his son, undated, mid July 1957. For the text of full letter see Chapter 3, p. 120.

2　Joachim Fischer, *Das Deutschlandbild der Iren 1890–1939* (Heidelberg: C. Winter, 2000) pp. 621–4. It is most unfortunate that this fascinating interdisciplinary 680-page study of Irish perceptions of Germany 1890–1939 has not yet been translated into English.

3　See Axel Klein, *Die Musik Irlands im 20. Jahrhundert* (Hildesheim: 1996), pp. 394–5.

4　See Frederick May, 'The Composer in Ireland' in Aloys Fleischmann (ed.), *Music in Ireland* (Cork: Cork University Press, 1952) pp. 164–6, and Séumas Ó Braonáin, 'Music in the Broadcasting Service', ibid, pp. 198–9.

5　See Bernard Curtis, *Century of the Cork School of Music 1878–1978: Progress of the School 1878–1978* (Cork: 1978), pp. 11–13.

6　Ibid., p. 22.

7　Aloys Fleischmann, 'Music in Cork' in Aloys Fleischmann (ed.), *Music in Ireland*, pp. 269–70.

8　Joachim Fischer in his *Das Deutschlandbild der Iren* provides a detailed description of the project (pp. 238–64); he deplores the fact that this most significant undertaking has been largely ignored by Irish historians.

9　See James M. Doyle, 'Music in the Army' in Aloys Fleischmann (ed.), *Music in Ireland*, pp. 65–6.

10　See Axel Klein, *Die Musik Irlands im 20. Jahrhundert* (Hildesheim: 1996), p. 50, and Gareth Cox and Joseph J. Ryan 'Fritz Brase's Contribution to Irish Musical Life 1923–1940' in Joachim Fischer, Gisela Holfter (Eds.), *Creative Influences: Selected Irish-German Biographies* (Trier: 2009). See too Martin Steffen, 'Wiedersehen mit Dublin, Teil II: Militärmusik in Irland zwischen 1923 und 1947 – Die Ära Brase-Sauerzweig' in *Mit Klingendem Spiel: Zeitschrift der Deutschen Gesellschaft für Militärmusik e.V.* 1/2008, pp. 14–18, 28, which was kindly provided by the author.

11　Duggan in an interview to Joachim Fischer: see *Das Deutschlandbild der Iren*, p. 272.

12　*The Leader*, 7 November 1908: see Joachim Fischer, *Das Deutschlandbild der Iren 1890–1939*, pp. 45, 88. The authors are indebted to Dr Patrick Zuk for drawing their attention to the *Leader* caricature, 29 June 1901, p. 277.

13　*The Germans in Cork*, published anonymously in 1917 by the Unionist Lady Mary Carbery, is analysed by Joachim Fischer in *Das Deutschlandbild der Iren 1890–1939*, pp. 169–78.

14　W.P. Ryan, *The Pope's Green Island* (London: James Nisbet & Co, 1912), pp. 96–7.

15　See Richard O'Donoghue, *Like a Tree Planted: Father O'Flynn of the Loft* (Dublin: Gill, 1967), pp. 34–8.

16　Ibid., p. 207.

17 Raymond Smith, *Father O'Flynn: The Well of Love* (Dublin: Little and McClean, 1964), p. 28.
18 Ibid., p. 57.
19 J.C. O'Flynn, 'The Art of Tragedy', the *Cork Examiner*, 3 May 1930.
20 Aloys Fleischmann junior quoting Father O'Flynn in a letter to the priest of 21 Sept. 1939, written in response to Fr O'Flynn's letter to the Editor, *Cork Examiner*, 19 Sept. 1939 'Eire and Art'.

1. YOUTH IN DACHAU 1880–1906

1 See August Kübler, *Dachau in verflossenen Jahrhunderten* (Dachau: Druckerei und Verlagsanstalt 'Bayerland', 1928), p. 7: *dâha* is Old High German for 'clay', and *ouwe* Middle High German for 'water'.
2 Ibid, p. 101. However, infant mortality came to almost 40 per cent as late as 1868/9 – see Gerhard Hanke and Wilhelm Liebhart, *Der Landkreis Dachau, Kulturgeschichte des Dachauer Landes*, Bd. 1 (Dachau: Kreis Dachau und Verlagsanstalt 'Bayerland', 1992), p. 54. Between 1871 and 1881 the average life expectancy from birth in Germany was 35.6 years for male children and 38.5 for female children; only 30 per cent of the population reached the age of sixty – today 89 per cent of German men and 94 per cent of the women do so: see Statistisches Bundesamt, Sterbetafel 2005/07.
3 Gerhard Hanke, Wilhelm Liebhart, Norbert Göttler, Hans-Günter Richardi, *Geschichte des Marktes und der Stadt Dachau* (Musemsverein Dachau, 1985), p.101.
4 Hans-Günter Richardi, *Dachauer Zeitgeschichtsführer* (Stadt Dachau, 1998), p. 16, and Horst Heres, *Dachauer Gemäldegalerie: Kulturgeschichte des Dachauer Landes*, Bd. 12 (Museumsverein Dachau, 1985), p. 21.
5 August Kübler, *Strassen, Bürger und Häuser in Alt-Dachau* (Münnerstadt: Eigenverlag, 1934), p.149. The Fleischmanns' house was Wieningerstrasse 22. Josef Deger died in 1881; his wife in 1894. To obtain the master-licence, the craftsman had to prove that he owned suitable premises for his workshop – see Ingeborg Rüffelmacher, *Ehrsames Handwerk: Kulturgeschichte des Dachauer Landes*, Bd. 5 (Musemsverein Dachau, 1992), p. 21.
6 Eisolzried had a twelfth-century Gothic castle with a moat by the river; the village was first mentioned in a document of 1220. The castle was enlarged in the eighteenth century, the owner given the right to have a patrimonial court. The building was demolished in the late nineteenth century by its owners. See *Amper-Bote* 2 January 1909, p. 1, and Wilhelm Liebhart and Günther Pölsterl, *Die Gemeinden des Landkreises Dachau: Kulturgeschichte des Dachauer Landes* Band 2 (Musemsverein Dachau, [1992]), p. 42. There is an ancient oak tree just outside the estate which has stood close to the road to Dachau for the past thousand years.
7 See Decision of the Patrimonial Court of Eisolzried of 23 March 1843. Among the Fleischmann papers there is a document of 1813 granting a predecessor of Fleischmann's (Martin Wirt) the right to live and work as barber in Eisolzried house number 4 and outlining his tax and service duties to Franz Xaver Josef Freiherr von Rufin. Regina Kuntz, Rainer Würgau, Alexander Peren and Andreas Bräunling, the Dachau Archivist, very kindly deciphered these handwritten documents, which were written in the old German script.
8 The Eisolzried connection was discovered by Debrett Ancestry Research of Hampshire, who were commissioned by Alan Fleischmann. They traced Franz Xaver Fleischmann back to Fischbach. The Fleischmann family then proceeded to investigate which of the twenty-three Bavarian villages called Fischbach this was. (The name is so common as it simply means: *fish stream*.) The parish priest of the right Fischbach and the Central Episcopal Archive of Regensburg found the answers. Later a genealogical study was found on the internet of the four-house hamlet of Eisolried with their barber-surgeons: Josef Kiening's Bavaria Genealogie.

9   See Ingeborg Rüffelmacher, *Ehrsames Handwerk, Kulturgeschichte des Dachauer Landes* Band 5 (Musemsverein Dachau, 1992), pp.15–16.

10 *Amper-Bote*, 18 January 1902.

11 See Ingeborg Rüffelmacher, *Ehrsames Handwerk*, pp. 153–66.

12 The obituary or 'Nachruf' for Sister Maria Genesia Fleischmann was very kindly provided by Sr M. Consolata Neumann, the archivist of the Munich order, Die Armen Schulschwestern von unserer lieben Frau. She wrote that Anna and Elisabeth (known to the nuns as 'Fleischmann Annerl and Liserl') were taken in as orphans in 1857. However, both parents were then still alive, but in serious trouble due to the contagious illness of the breadwinner. The order was founded to help poor families; the foundress, Maria Therese Gerdinger, was beatified in 1985. The obituaries of the deceased sisters, written solely for the convent records, were the only documents that survived the expulsion of the nuns by the Nazis in 1933 and the bombing of their convent during the war in 1944.

13 See Wilhelm Liebhart, 'Dachau in der frühen Neuzeit' in: Gerhard Hanke, Wilhelm Liebhart, Norbert Göttler, Hans-Günter Richardi, *Geschichte des Marktes und der Stadt Dachau*, p. 79.

14 See Hans-Ulrich Wehler, *Deutsche Gesellschaftsgeschichte*, Bd. 3 1849–1914 (Frankfurt/M: Büchergilde Gutenberg, 1995), pp. 56–8.

15 Maude Barrows Dutton, 'The Night of Wonders (A description of the Manger Plays given at Christmas time by the children of Dachau, Bavaria, under the direction of Alois Fleischmann)' in *The Bookman – An Illustrated Magazine of Literature and Life,* Vol. XXII, No 4 (New York, 1905), p. 318.

16 Prince Ludwig was the son of the Prince Regent; he was king of Bavaria from 1913–18 when he was deposed by the revolution. He died in 1921. During the celebrations of the trade association's twenty-fifth anniversary, Fleischmann sent him a telegram in the name of the assembly thanking him for his visit of 1908 and continued support, receiving a gracious reply the following day. See *Amper-Bote* of 12 January 1910.

17 *Amper-Bote*, 8 January 1910 and 12 January 1910: 'Innungsjubiläum'.

18 But at the end of the year, criticism of the school was voiced in the Corporation, claiming that classes had often been cancelled, that the boys were lazy and not worth the 'hellishly expensive costs of 2,300 marks' (*Amper-Bote*, 15 September 1908). In 1909 the drawing school was said to be doing well: *Amper-Bote*, 8 January 1909.

19 Document No. 8887 of the Bavarian State Library [Bayerische Staatsbibliothek] Munich: Dachau District file [Bezirksamtsakt] of 1911 Number [Signatur] LRA 71795.

20 See obituary of Aloys Fleischmann in the *Amper-Bote*, 24 June 1914 and Andreas R. Bräunling, 'Das verschobene Jubiläum: Zur 1100-Jahr-Feier des Marktes Dachau im Jahre 1908' in *Amperland* Nr 1 2005, p. 27.

21 Ingeborg Rüffelmacher, *Ehrsames Handwerk*, pp. 126–35.

22 Ursula K. Nauderer, 'Die Anfänge der musikalischen Vereine' in Josef Focht, Ursula K. Nauderer, eds., *Musik in Dachau* (Zweckverband Dachauer Galerien und Museen, 2002), pp. 127–8.

23 Hermann Windele, Mayor of Dachau, very kindly supplied copies of the early documents and the 2004 brochure celebrating the choir's 125th anniversary. See too Ursula K. Nauderer, 'Die Anfänge der musikalischen Vereine', p. 128.

24 Ursula Katharina Nauderer, *Hermann Stockmann – Das Heimatpflegerische Wirken des Künstlers* (Dachauer Museumsschriften, Bd. 7, 1987), p. 18, and Ursula Nauderer, 'Die Dachauer Weihnachtsspiele (1903–1906) und ihr Schöpfer Aloys Georg Fleischmann' in *Auf Weihnachten zu: Altdachauer Weihnachtszeit*, (Dachauer Museumsschriften, 2003), pp. 71–2.

25 Andreas R. Bräunling, 'Das verschobene Jubiläum: Zur 1100-Jahr-Feier des Marktes Dachau im Jahre 1908', in *Amperland – Heimatkundliche Vierteljahresschrift für die Kreise Dachau, Freising und Fürstenfeldbruck*, Chefredaktion Prof. Wilhelm Liebhart (Dachau: 2005/1), pp. 29–31.

26 They were officially called *Kleinkinderbewahrungsanstalte* [institutions for the minding of small children].

27 No records of Aloys Fleischmann's schooldays have been found.

28 Fleischmann to Franz Schaehle, 30 September 1953.

29 Ibid.

30 Fleischmann in a letter to his wife, 15 December 1909.

31 Recounted to Hildegard Schaehle and recorded in her diary of her visit to Cork in October 1950.

32 In German Candlemas is called the Feast of Mary's Light, on 2 February.

33 Fleischmann to his mother, 20 March 1909.

34 Fleischmann to his son in Munich, 28 December 1932.

35 Fleischmann to Schaehle, 3 August 1956. The centenary celebration in honour of King Ludwig I took place in Munich on 31 July 1888.

36 Fleischmann to his son in Munich, 20 December 1932

37 Fleischmann to A. Auer, Christmas 1949. Mr Auer's widow and his daughter, Frau Gluck of Dachau, very kindly provided a copy of this letter.

38 Fleischmann's friend, Franz Schaehle, had this letter of Fleischmann's (of 14 August 1953) published in the *Dachauer Nachrichten* of 24/25 October 1953: 'Heimweh nach dem Dachau von einst' [Homesick for the Dachau of long ago].

39 Maude Barrows Dutton, 'The Night of Wonders' in *The Bookman,* Vol. XXII, No. 4 (New York, 1905), p. 318.

40 Maude Barrows Dutton of New York was introduced to Fleischmann by the American consul of Munich in 1904; she had asked to meet him having heard of his stage productions and being interested in Bavarian passion and nativity plays. She spent Christmas 1905 in Dachau, and reviewed at length Fleischmann's nativity play, *Die Nacht der Wunder*, in the New York journal *The Bookman.* There is a photograph in the Fleischmann album of her having a picnic on an Oberammergau mountain with the renowned Passion Play actor Andreas Lang and Fleischmann; two letters from her (written in good German) indicate that she had great respect for him as a musician and much affection as a person. She is to be found on the internet as a writer of tales adapted from Sanskrit.

41 Torquato Tasso was a sixteenth century Italian poet who struggled with madness. Goethe wrote a tragedy based on his life; Lord Byron, among many others, was influenced by him.

42 Fleischmann to his wife in Munich, undated but probably end of March 1910.

43 The work was written in Dachau in 1895 for solo voice, choir and piano and was called: 'Der Versammlung zu Ehren: Vier Lieder', 'Four Songs in Honour of the Gathering'.

44 See Andreas Bräunling, 'Musik der Dachauer Landwehr' in *Musik in Dachau,* p. 50: the two Degers figure in the Register of the Band of the Thirteenth Local Defence Battalion (*Landwehrbataillon*).

45 Programme in honour of Rev. Joh. Winhart 25 June 1900 organised by the Catholic Journeymen's Association of Dachau, conducted by Fleischmann (this information added in his handwriting); programme in honour of the school-master, Anton Ortner, organised by his former pupils 13 November 1904, directed by Fleischmann. The *Amper-Bote* of 7 January 1903 reported that Ortner played for the nativitiy play of 1903.

46 Information from Gertrud Beckmann née Rössler of Dachau, a cousin of Tilly Fleischmann's; letter from Fleischmann to his wife of 22 August 1926 describing his visits to the Zieglers during his holiday in Dachau.

47 Maude Barrows Dutton, 'The Night of Wonders', p. 318.

48 Birgit Schlosser found this information about Fleischmann's studies in the records of the Munich Academy of Music which she presents in her MA thesis 'Aloys Fleischmann: Die Nacht der Wunder – Ein Dachauer Weihnachtsspiel und sein Kontext' [The Night of Wonders – a Dachau Nativity Play and its Context]

submitted to the Institute of Musicology at the Ludwig-Maximilian-University of Munich, Sept. 2004; see pp. 4–5.

49 In an undated letter of July 1954 to his son, Fleischmann wrote: 'In my youth I avidly devoured the writings of Schopenhauer, Nietzsche, Darwin, Haeckel, Kant, Leibnitz, Fichte, Rousseau, Voltaire. They still lie undigested in my stomach. I frequently read [David Friedrich Strauss's] *Life of Jesus* until my conscience started tormenting me and I burnt the heretical book as if it were a depraved witch. I was still living in the Middle Ages. Remorse set in as soon as the book writhed in the flames as if it were a human body in pain.'

50 Norbert Göttler, 'Im Anbruch der Moderne – 1818–1914' in Gerhard Hanke et al., *Geschichte des Marktes und der Stadt Dachau*, p. 124.

51 In a reference of 17 October 1901, the parish priest of Dachau, Johann Winhart, wrote that Fleischmann had first sung in the church choir for many years and 'in recent years' had worked very hard deputising for the sick choirmaster and organist.

52 On the programme for the 'Patrociniums-Feier' of 19 March 1901 Fleischmann added a note: 'Conductor: A. Fleischmann'.

53 Maude Barrows Dutton, 'The Night of Wonders', p. 318.

54 Fleischmann from Oldcastle Camp during his internment to his wife from, 8 July 1916.

55 Hildegard Braceschi-Schaehle recorded this in the diary of her visit to Cork in October 1950.

56 Fleischmann to Franz Schaehle, 17 June 1957.

57 Oskar Panizza's play *Liebeskonzil* of 1895 brought him a year in prison for portraying God the father as a foolish old man and the papal court in Rome as a den of iniquity – see Bernhard Setzwein, *München, Spaziergänge durch die Geschichte einer Stadt* (Stuttgart: Klett-Cotta, 2001), p. 72. Franz Wedekind landed in prison in 1898 over a satirical poem in *Simplizissimus* on Kaiser Wilhelm II's visit to Palestine. See Roger Engelmann, 'Öffentlichkeit und Zensur – Literaur und Theater als Provokation' in Friedrich Prinz und Marita Krauss, *München – Musenstadt mit Hinterhöfen: Die Prinzregentenzeit 1886–1912*, (Munich: Beck Verlag, 1988), p. 270.

58 See Franzpeter Messmer, 'Musikstadt München – Konstanten und Veränderungen' in Friedrich Prinz und Marita Krauss, *München – Musenstadt mit Hinterhöfen*, pp. 288–9.

59 Birgit Schlosser points out in her MA thesis 'Aloys Fleischmann: Die Nacht der Wunder' (p. 5) that the normal course of studies at the Royal Academy lasted four years.

60 Graduation certification of the Royal Academy of Music, 12 Sept. 1901 and notice of appointment as choirmaster and organist in Dachau issued by the Royal Government of Upper Bavaria on 28 November 1901.

61 The *Amper-Bote* of 4 January 1902 commends Alois Fleischmann for the performance at High Mass, which it found 'instrumentally and vocally most successful and for which in the name of the congregation we wish to thank him and express our appreciation'. Ursula Nauderer, director of the Dachau Museum, discovered this and the following two notices in the municipal archives.

62 *Amper-Bote*, 25 June 1902.

63 *Amper-Bote*, 28 June 1902 and 15 November 1902.

64 *Amper-Bote*, 18 April 1903.

65 One of these choral works for male-voice choir, composed before Fleischmann left Dachau for Cork, was a setting of a poem by Börries von Münchhausen. In a letter to Franz Schaehle of 17 February 1950, Fleischmann wrote: 'I set a fairly long poem of his for choir and orchestra. He heard it, liked it, wrote me a flattering letter and asked for a copy of the score. As I only had one left, I promised to let him have one when the work was re-printed. But oh dear. After a long time I received an angry, strongly spiced communication from him about the copyright

of his poem. The sweet tones had disappeared and he signed off with his title as Doctor of Law. I lived in fear and terror. To his misfortune, but my relief, he fell ill and died. Germany lost an outstanding poet.' Münchhausen took his life in 1945 as the Allied forces approached his castle: he had been a member of the National Socialist Party and elected to the Academy due to his support for the regime. It does not emerge from Fleischmann's letter when Münchhausen accused him of breach of copyright, but it must have been while he was still in Dachau. Münchhausen probably did not pursue the issue, or may have been unable to do so as Fleischmann had left for Ireland.

66 The town council paid Fleischmann the nominal sum of forty-six marks for this work, under twenty pfennigs per class. See the Minutes of the Dachau Council meeting of 13 November 1903.

67 *Amper-Bote*, 18 October 1902

68 Ursula Nauderer, 'Die Anfänge der Musikalischen Vereine in Dachau' in Josef Focht und Ursula K. Nauderer, *Musik in Dachau*, p. 133.

69 *Amper-Bote*, 18 October 1902 and Ursula K. Nauderer, 'Die Dachauer Weihnachtsspiele (1903–1906) und ihr Schöpfer Alois Georg Fleischmann' in *Auf Weihnachten zu – Altdachauer Weihnachtszeit* (Bezirksmuseum Dachau: 2003), p. 72. This is the catalogue for the Dachau Museum Association's exhibition 'Christmas in Dachau long ago', 30 November 2003–11 January 2004.

70 On 5 November 1903, Fleischmann appeared before the town council, described his work with the choir school, and requested 350 marks per annum, which would have given him 1,50 per class. The council granted him 200 marks per annum for 'his conscientious and successful efforts' – minutes of the Dachau Council meeting of 13 November 1903. On 16 November 1903, the council asked him to show how the choir school accommodated adults; on 4 December 1903, Fleischmann presented a fifteen-page submission detailing the work of the school, on the basis of which the council granted him 360 marks per annum for his work with the school – minutes of the Dachau Council meeting of 4 December 1903. These documents were discovered by Ursula Nauderer and made available to the authors by the municipal archivist, Andreas Bräunling.

71 Fleischmann to his father, 9 August 1901, written in Heideck near Nuremberg while he was visiting his uncle Philipp and his Nuremberg relations – probably Thomas Deger, who was the administrator of Schloss Kreuth: the castle was one of Prince Oettingen-Spielberg's residences.

72 See Birgit Schlosser, *Aloys Fleischmann: Die Nacht der Wunder* for a detailed account of the passion and nativity play tradition in Bavaria in general and in Dachau in particular. See chapters 2 and 3, pp. 10–19.

73 Ursula K. Nauderer, 'Die Anfänge der Musikalischen Vereine in Dachau', in *Musik in Dachau*, p. 129.

74 *Amper-Bote*, 7 January 1903. The laurel wreath was brought to Ireland and hung on the wall of Fleischmann's drawing room, around a copy of Beethoven's death mask.

75 Maude Barrows Dutton, 'The Night of Wonders', pp. 318–23.

76 An undated newspaper cutting among Fleischmann's papers reports on a concert given by Goldhofer in Dachau: it ends with a mention of the violinist's first public performance in the Dachau Nativity Play with Agnes Straub.

77 Fleischmann to Schaehle, 19 February 1935. In the same letter, Fleischmanns inquires about another equally talented girl who acted the role of Night in the nativity play *Sonnenwende* in 1903: Rosa Schmidlkofer. Her mother had been Schaehle's landlady. But neither Schaehle nor Fleischmann discovered what had become of her: it seems she did not share the good fortune of the other two gifted participants and that her artistic talent was not given a chance to develop.

78 The scores and parts of the nativity plays are with the other Fleischmann compositions in the Archives of University College Cork.

79   *Amper-Bote*, 13 January 1904.
89   *Amper-Bote*, 17 February1904.
81   Tilly Fleischmann, unpublished memoir written on New Year's Eve 1965, circu-
     lated to friends. Kathleen Keyes McDonnell responded on 20 January 1966: 'I am
     sure that Aloys and myself were the only two in Munster who ever met Prince
     Luitpold of Bavaria – a beloved prince. En route to his hunting lodge he always
     called to my school – in Bad Reichenhall – and was a most homely person. When
     he discovered a pupil from Ireland (so far away!) he asked for me. I had very little
     German but with a smattering of English we made headway. All the time I
     addressed him as Sir! This tickled his fancy, and I saw nothing wrong."Königliche
     Hoheit" [Your Royal Highness] was beyond me then.'
82   Fleischmann to Schaehle, 7 March 1959.
83   *Amper-Bote*, 20 July 1904. Ursula Nauderer kindly gave copies to the authors of
     these two press notices, which were not among the Fleischmann papers.
84   Information from Jakob Rössler's great-granddaughter, Gertrud Beckmann née
     Rössler, confirmed what the Fleischmann grandchildren had heard on the
     subject.
85   The booklet by Josef Burghart: St Jakob Dachau, *Zur Geschichte einer uralten
     Pfarrei und eines ehrwürdigen Gotteshauses* (Stuttgart: Libertas Verlag Hubert Baum,
     1962), p. 55, lists Hans Conrad Swertz as church organist from 1878 to 1884: he
     may have taken leave of absence in 1879 and not given notice.
86   For the titles of the Swertz compositions that have survived, see Séamas de Barra,
     Aloys Fleischmann (Dublin: Field Day Publications, 2006), p. 3, note 4.
87   This concert took place on 19 June 1905 in the Academy's large concert hall: the
     Royal Odeon.
88   Selma Lagerlöf, 'Die Heilige Nacht', in *Christuslegenden*, (Munich: Langen Verlag,
     1904), pp.1–9.
89   The journal *Die Jugend* was first published in Munich in 1896 and had a consider-
     able impact during its first decade. It published work by many artists of the Dachau
     painters' colony, and by painters of the *art nouveau* movement such as Böcklin and
     Klimt. The German term for the movement, *Jugendstil*, derives from the journal.
90   *Amper-Bote* 14 January 1905.
91   Ibid.
92   Letters from Langheinrich to Fleischmann of 1 December 1904, 9 December
     1904, from Stockmann to Langheinrich of 17 January 1905.
93   The *Amper-Bote* article of 14 January 1905 gives the names of the financial guar-
     antors of the play with the exception of Mondrion's, saying 'as well as one further
     citizen from here'. Nobody except himself would have omitted Mondrion.
     Furthermore, the writer demanded that those who finance such ventures should
     be shown the text before the music was composed – under the circumstance, only
     Mondrion would have thought of this.
94   Letters from Langheinrich to Fleischmann of 15 September 1904 and 17 October
     1904. Benno Becker, president of the Munich group of painters known as 'The
     Secession', had offered his help with the text; Mondrion had made some changes
     without having been invited to do so.
95   Fleischmann to his son in Munich, 1 May 1934. That incident was remembered by
     some of the musicians. Fleischmann junior met a fellow student whose father
     was a member of the orchestra. On hearing that Aloys junior was from Ireland,
     the student inquired whether he was related to the Fleischmann now living in
     Ireland who was famous for his humour.
96   Maude Barrows Dutton, 'The Night of Wonders', p. 319.
97   *Amper-Bote*, 4 January 1905.
98   *Münchner Stadt-Anzeiger*, 3 January 1905.
99   Fleischmann to his son, 1 May 1934.
100 Maude Barrows Dutton, 'The Night of Wonders', pp. 322–3.

101 See letters from Emil Geyer (not dated) and Franz Langheinrich of 15 November 1906 to Fleischmann.

102 Fleischmann to Schaehle, 7 March 1959.

103 Ibid.

104 Fleischmann to Schaehle, 19 January 1955.

105 Fr Donaghey was from Donegal; after his ordination in 1903, he began work on his doctorate at the University of Munich. He became a good friend of the von Moreaus. He was professor of Physics and Mathematics in Maynooth seminary from 1912–21; he died in San Antonio, Texas in 1949. This information was kindly supplied by his nephew, James E. McAteer of Dublin.

106 The newspaper version of Fleischmann's application was published on 16 Sept. 1905; the petitions in Fleischmann's hand (written in the old German script) of 13 October 1905 and 18 October 1905, and the minutes of 23 October 1905 recording the council's decision are in the Municipal Archives of Dachau. The authors are grateful to Mr Andreas Bräunling, the municipal archivist, for having supplied copies.

107 In the invitation to the founding session of the Musikalisch-Dramatischer Verein Dachau of 15 January 1906 Fleischmann is named as the Musical Director. The Mayor of Dachau, Hermann Windele, kindly provided a copy of this document. The information about the occupations of the founding members of the Society comes from Nauderer, 'Die Dachauer Weihnachtsspiele', p. 83.

108 *Dachauer Anzeiger*, 6 September 1906.

109 *Motu proprio* stipulated in section 13: 'singers in church have a real liturgical office, and . . . therefore women, being incapable of exercising such office, cannot be admitted to form part of the choir'.

110 The information about Swertz's stock-market losses was given by his youngest daughter, Cressie, to her grandnephew, Alan Fleischmann; Tilly Fleischmann entitled an unpublished memoir: 'Unhappy Youth', in which she describes the constant dissension between her parents, 'both excellent people, but of such different temperament that they should never have married'.

111 Copy of Fleischmann's application for the Cork cathedral post, in Tilly Fleischmann's handwriting, signed by him and dated Dachau 29 June 1906.

112 *Dachauer Anzeiger*, 6 September 1906.

113 Article in the *Dachauer Nachrichten* of 24/25 October 1953, 'Heimweh nach dem Dachau von einst' presented by Franz Schaehle.

THE DACHAU SCHOOL OF MUSIC FOR ORCHESTRAL INSTRUMENTS OF 1905

1 Andreas Pernpeintner is a graduate of the music department of the University of Munich. He is currently writing a PhD thesis on Aloys Fleischmann senior.

2 Programme of the nativity play of 1906, Fleischmann Papers.

3 See *Amper-Bote* of 18 October 1902, Municipal Archive Dachau.

4 The plans for the school are well documented; few documents have survived pertaining to its activities. The concert programmes of 1906 describe some of the soloists as teachers in the Dachau school of music. The violinist Anton Riebl continued the school for a time after Fleischmann's departure to Cork in 1906, see *Dachauer Volksblatt*, 9 October 1906, *Amper Bote*, 10 October 1906.

5 See Georg Sowa, *Anfänge institutioneller Musikerziehung in Deutschland 1880–1843* (Regensburg: 1973), p. 103ff.

6 See Leo Kestenberg, 'Volksmusikschule', 'Musikerziehung und Musikpflege' (Leipzig: 1921) reprinted in Dorothea Hemming (ed.), *Dokumente der Geschichte der Musikschule 1902-76* (Regensburg: 1977), p. 30ff.

7 See Georg Sowa, *Anfänge institutioneller Musikerziehung in Deutschland*, pp. 151ff.

8 See Eckhart Nolte, Lehrpläne und Richtlinien für den schulischen Musikunterricht in Deutschland (Mainz: 1975), pp. 19, 22. In the school of music at the Freie

Schulgemeinde Wickersdorf of 1906 many aspects of the subject were emphasised, for instance music appreciation and practical music-making. The main teachers were Gustav Wyneken and August Halm.

9   In the nineteenth century, entrance tests for schools of music were standard practice.

10   Georg Sowa, *Anfänge institutioneller Musikerziehung,* p. 63.

11   See Ursula Nauderer, 'Die Dachauer Weihnachtsspiele (1903–6) und ihr Schöpfer Alois Georg Fleischmann' in Museumsverein Dachau (ed.), *Auf Weihnachten zu. . . Altdachauer Weihnachtszeit* (Dachau: 2003), p. 72.

12   See Georg Sowa, *Anfänge institutioneller Musikerziehung,* pp. 95ff., 128ff. In the course of the process of secularisation, many court orchestras were disbanded, for instance in Passau.

13   Ibid., pp. 179ff. See too Yuko Tamagawa, 'Sozialgeschichte des Klavierunterrichts in der ersten Hälfte des 19. Jahrhunderts' in Hermann Kaiser (Ed.), *Musikpädagogik. Sozialgeschichtliche Aspekte einer wissenschaftlichen Disziplin,* Sitzungsbericht der Wisschaftlichen Sozietät Musikpädagogik (Mainz: 1993), p. 132f.

14   See Wilfried Gruhn, *Geschichte der Musikerziehung* (Hofheim: 2003), pp. 213, 241.

15   See Georg Sowa, *Anfänge institutioneller Musikerziehung,* p. 139. In Aschaffenburg, for instance, poor pupils were given tuition free of charge.

17   Bernd Edelmann, 'Königliche Musikschule und Akademie der Tonkunst in München 1874–1914' in Stefan Schmitt (ed.), *Geschichte der Hochschule für Musik und Theater München von den Anfängen bis 1945* (Tutzing: 2005), p. 117.

18   See Georg Sowa, *Anfänge institutioneller Musikerziehung,* p. 41. Such diverging opinions about women's learning abilities came from the piano teacher Guthmann.

19   That the genre of folk song reached a new level of popularity in the music youth movement is an indication of its strength and of the deeply-rooted need that it satisfied. The same holds good for the revival of domestic music-making at that time.

19   See Eckhart Nolte, *Lehrpläne und Richtlinien für den schulischen Musikunterricht in Deutschland* (Mainz: 1975), p. 19.

20   See Wilfried Gruhn, *Geschichte der Musikerziehung* (Hofheim: 2003), p. 229ff.

Nativity Plays in Dachau

1   Dr Josef Focht is a member of staff of the Music Department of the University of Munich: he directs the project *Lexicon of Bavarian Musicians Online* in co-operation with the Bavarian State Library. The project is funded by the German Research Association, the University and the Bavarian State Library. During a pilot study for the *Lexicon* on musicians in Dachau, he and the director of Dachau's District Museum, Ursula Nauderer, discovered Aloys Fleischmann. He has recently applied for funding for further research into the Fleischmann musicians' legacy and its documentation.

2   Thomas Erlach, *Unterhaltung und Belehrung im Jesuitentheater um 1700. Untersuchungen zu Musik, Text und Kontext ausgewählter Stücke* (Essen: 2006); Ruprecht Wimmer, *Jesuitentheater. Didaktik und Fest* (Frankfurt/Main: 1982).

3   Hermann Bausinger, (ed.), *Schwäbische Weihnachtsspiele* (Stuttgart: 1959) p. 104.

4   Johannes Modesto, 'Ein Münchner Marienlied aus der Barockzeit' in: *Sänger & Musikanten* 46/3, 2003, p. 206–11.

5   Hans Moser, *Volksschaupiel im Spiegel von Archivalien. Ein Beitrag zur Kulturgeschichte Altbayerns* (Munich: 1991), pp. 36f. See too: Hartmann, August, *Weihnachtslied und Weihnachtsspiel in Oberbayern* (Munich: 1875).

6   Gerhard Hanke, 'Die Dachauer Volksschauspiel im 18. und in der ersten Hälfte des 19. Jahrhunderts mit seinen Initiatoren' in *Amperland* 27/4, 1991, p. 211, pp. 207–8.

7   Ursula K. Nauderer, 'Die Anfänge der musikalischen Vereine in Dachau' in Josef

Focht, Ursula K. Nauderer (eds.): *Musik in Dachau. Ausstellungskatalog* (Dachau: 2002), pp. 127–35, in particular 132–3. Ursula K. Nauderer, 'Die Dachauer Weihnachtsspiele (1903–1906) und ihr Schöpfer Alois Georg Fleischmann' in: *Auf Weihnachten zu. . . Altdachauer Weihnachtszeit*, Ausstellungskatalog (Dachau: 2003), pp. 69–86.

8 Stadtarchiv Dachau, Titel VI, Fach 37, Nr. 9a: Musikalisch-dramatischer Verein, 1906.

9 Brigitta Unger-Richter, 'Kontrapunkt und Harmonie. Musik im künstlerischen Schaffen Adolf Hölzels' in Josef Focht, Ursula K. Nauderer (eds.), *Musik in Dachau*, Ausstellungskatalog (Dachau: 2002), pp. 70–85.

Aloys Fleischmann's Home Town Dachau

1 Ursula Nauderer is the director of the District Museum of Dachau. Having discovered Aloys Fleischmann (together with Josef Focht) during the preparations for an exhibition on Dachau musicians, she subsequently featured Fleischmann's nativity plays in an exhibition in 2003 and organised a recital of his songs in the Museum in 2006, the hundredth anniversary of his departure from Dachau to Cork. She is putting on a Fleischmann exhibition in the autumn of 2010 as part of the Dachau Fleischmann Week.

2 1886 to 1912 was the period of the Prince Regency, the rule of Prince Luitpold of Bavaria. Luitpold was the youngest son of King Ludwig I. As prince regent he ruled at first in place of his nephew, Ludwig II, who had been declared a ward of court, and then in place of Ludwig's brother, Otto I, who was insane. The Regency period is frequently uncritically seen as 'the good old days'.

3 Ludwig I ruled from 1825 to 1848. Because of his affair with the dancer, Lola Montez (born Elizabeth Rosanna Gilbert in Grange, Co. Sligo), he had to abdicate during the 1848 revolution. He was succeeded by his son Maximilian II.

4 Munich owes Ludwig I its finest street, Ludwigstrasse. Designed by Leo von Klenze, completed by Gärtner, it was architecturally unified, with the Feldherrnhalle [generals' hall], Siegestor [triumphal arch], the university and State Library, Königsplatz [royal square] with Glyptothek and Propyläen as well as the Ruhmeshalle [hall of fame] with the bronze Bavaria statue, at that time unrivalled in size.

5 Thomas Mann described Munich in the short story 'Gladius' of 1902: 'Art . . . was in power; . . . smiling, she held her sceptre entwined with roses over the city. . . . Munich shone.'

6 See Elisabeth Boser, Ursula K. Nauderer and Bärbel Schäfer, *FreiLichtMalerei. Der Künstlerort Dachau 1870–1914* (Dachau: 2002).

7 Ludwig Thoma, *Erinnerungen* (Munich: 31980), p. 123. Ludwig Thoma was a lawyer by profession, who set up his practice in Dachau. His first publication, *Agricola*, appeared in 1897. In these eleven stories about farmers, he presented a strikingly apt portrait of the rural milieu and farmers of the Dachau countryside. The book brought him literary fame. He abandoned the law, or 'piglet-stabbing', as he contemptuously dubbed it, and lived from then on from his writing. He wrote numerous novels and plays, the models for which he found in Dachau and the surrounding country. In 1897 he moved to Munich. One of the periodicals to which he contributed was *Simplicissimus*, a highly regarded satirical journal. He returned to Dachau every year for the hunting season.

8 Franz Xaver Hartmann, 'Sitten und Gebräuche in den Landgerichtsbezirken Dachau und Bruck' in *Oberbayerisches Archiv zur vaterländischen Geschichte*, Bd. 35 (Munich: 1875), p. 194.

9 The official registration lists of 1891 name twenty artists as visitors. In 1904, for the first time, over 100 and in 1911 almost 200 artists are officially registered as visitors. The real numbers are no doubt very much higher, as visitors who came for the day or for a short stay were not obliged to register. See Gerhard Hanke,

'Die Künstlerkolonie Dachau. Besuche von Künstlern und Angehörigen geistiger Berufe in den Jahren 1891–1918' in Ottilie Stoedtner-Thiemann und Gerhard Hanke, *Dachauer Maler, Die Kunstlandschaft von 1801–1946* (Dachau: 1989), pp. 287–359.

10 See Bärbel Schäfer, 'Künstlerhäuser in Dachau um die Jahrhundertwende' in *FreiLichtMalerei*, pp. 41–57.

11 'When I look back, the best times were those in Dachau,' Thoma wrote at the end of his life about his successful literary career to his friend Maidi von Liebermann: letter of 1 January 1920. Quoted in Anton Keller (ed.), *Ludwig Thoma: Ein Leben in Briefen 1875–1921* (Munich: 1963), p. 408.

12 Cf. Stoedtner-Thiemann/Hanke, *Dachauer Maler*, pp. 357–9.

13 Although the overwhelming majority of Dachau artists were painters, the town nonetheless attracted representatives of other artistic professions such as actors, musicians and in particular literary people (such as Rainer Maria Rilke, Heimito von Doderer and Ludwig Thoma). See Ursula K. Nauderer (ed.), *Literatur in Dachau, Einhorn-Verlag und Schriftsteller im frühen 20. Jahrhundert* (Dachau: 2002).

14 See Ursula K. Nauderer, 'Künstlerleben im alten Dachau' in *FreiLichtMalerei*, pp. 29–40.

15 At that time, taking up residence in Dachau did not automatically bring citizen status and the rights thereof. Only a small number of the artists living in Dachau actually became citizens of the town: Josef Schätz (in 1901), Adolf Hölzel (in 1902), Hermann Stockmann (in 1903), Hans von Hayek (in 1907), Felix Bürgers (in 1908), Karl Hennig (in 1919) and Gustav Friedrichson (in 1919). See Stoedtner-Thiemann/Hanke, *Dachauer Maler*, p. 287.

16 Carl Thiemann, *Erinnerungen eines Dachauer Malers: Beiträge zur Geschichte Dachaus als Künstlerort* (Dachau: 1966), p. 30.

17 See Ursula K. Nauderer, *Hermann Stockmann und das heimatpflegerische Wirken des Künstlers*, Dachauer Museumsschriften Bd. 7 (Dachau: 1987). In contrast to the District Museum, whose collection was soon increased by carefully planned purchases, donations of collections and trusts, the Art Gallery's collection was donated by the artists themselves.

18 Ibid., p. 49

19 Maria Rauffer of Dachau to Aloys Fleischmann junior, 8 February 1971.

20 Hans Seemüller, *Alt-Dachauer Geschichten* (Dachau: n.d.), pp. 11–15.

2. THE FIRST YEARS IN CORK 1906–1914

1 The Reform Bill of 1867 was the result of a concerted working class campaign organised by the unions – in which Irish Fenians were very active – and by the newly founded International Working Men's Association. See A.L. Morton, *A People's History of England* (London: Gollancz, 1938, paperback edn London: Lawrence & Wishart, 1965), pp. 415–18.

2 See Seán Daly's study *Cork: A City in Crisis – A History of Labour Conflict and Social Misery 1870–1872*, (Cork: Tower Books, 1978).

3 Eilis Stack, 'Victorian Cork' in Henry Alan Jefferies, *Cork Historical Perspectives* (Dublin: Four Courts Press, 2004), p. 183.

4 Kevin Hourikan, 'The Evolution and Influence of Town Planning in Cork' in Henry Alan Jefferies, *Cork Historical Perspectives*, pp. 954–5.

5 Henry Alan Jefferies with Eilis Stack, 'Eighteenth-Century Cork', in *Cork Historical Perspectives*, p. 141.

6 S.F. Petit, *The Streets of Cork* (Cork: Studio Publications, 1982), p. 33.

7 Ibid., p. 49.

8 No surname is given for de Paine, who in Fleischmann's *Music in Ireland* is listed as organist in the Cathedral of St Mary and St Anne in Cork in 1889. We are most grateful to Adrian Gebruers who went to much trouble to find information about

de Paine. The student records of the Lemmens Institute of Leuven in Belgium do not mention de Paine, but list one Ernest Depienne, born in Luxemburg in 1875, who began his studies in 1890, graduated in 1894 and is down as having had his first post after graduation in the Catholic Cathedral of Cork. In 1894 Hans Conrad Swertz was cathedral organist and choirmaster in Cork; there is no record of Depienne having worked there. Depienne could not have worked in Cork in 1889 as he was then only fourteen.

9   See Regina Deacy's thesis: 'Continental Organists and Catholic Church Music in Ireland 1860–1960', MLitt thesis, National University of Ireland, Maynooth, 2005. See the register of cathedral organists in Aloys Fleischmann (ed.), *Music in Ireland: A Symposium* (Cork/Oxford: Cork University Press, B.H. Blackwell Ltd., 1952), pp. 160–63, and Paul Collins, 'Strange Voices in the"Land of Song": Belgian and German Organist Appointments to Catholic Cathedrals and Churches in Ireland, 1859–1916' in Michael Murphy and Jan Scmazny (eds.), *Irish Musical Studies 9* (Dublin: Four Courts Press, 2007).

10 See Alicia St Leger, *150 Years at Cork Opera House* (Cork Opera House, 2005), p. 30.
11 Ibid., p. 32.
12 Unpublished account of her childhood by Tilly Fleischmann.
13 Tilly Fleischmann's unpublished account of the ceremony in the cathedral in 1896 celebrating the beatification of Blessed Thaddeus McCarthy; see also Aloys Fleischmann, 'Music and Society' in W.E.Vaughan (ed.), *A New History of Ireland* Vol VI (Oxford: Clarendon Press, 1996), p. 511, and Aloys Fleischmann (ed.), *Music in Ireland*, pp. 268–71.
14 See the *Cork Examiner* and *The Irish Times* 4 July 1883. Joseph Robinson of Dublin conducted the concert.
15 In his book *Parnell to Pearse* (Dublin: Brown and Nolan, 1949), pp. 101–02, John J. Horgan describes the Berlin Philharmonic Orchestra's performance in Cork at the Exhibition: 'For the first time I heard great music nobly played.'
16 The professorship of harmony at the Cork School of Music was advertised in *The Musical Standard* on 6 November 1880, p. 300.
17 See Bernard Curtis, 'The Cork Municipal School of Music' in Aloys Fleischmann (ed.), *Music in Ireland*, p 115.
18 See Peter Murray, 'Art Institutions in Nineteenth-Century Cork' in Patrick O'Flanagan, Cornelius G. Buttimer (eds.), *Cork History and Society* (Dublin: Geography Publications, 1993), pp. 856–9 and 863–4.
19 Janet Egleson Dunleavy and Gareth W. Dunleavy, *Douglas Hyde* (Berkeley: University of California Press, 1991), pp. 210–11.
20 John J. Horgan, *Parnell to Pearse*, p. 115.
21 Eamonn Ó Gallchobhair, 'The Cultural Value of Festival and Feis' in Aloys Fleischmann (ed.) *Music in Ireland*, p. 214.
22 The Instruction approved the French school of thought on Gregorian chant as researched by the Benedictine monks at Solesmes, as against that of the Regensburg College of Church Music.
23 The Bishop of Salford's List was a list of church music approved for use in the diocese; it was the work of an episcopal commission on ecclesiastical music published in 1904. A note at the end states that the catalogue had been 'somewhat hastily arranged' to 'supply immediate necessity' and invites those concerned to suggest further music they wish to have included. The six-part-thirty-eight-page document lists Gregorian chant manuals compiled from the French Solesmes Books; Masses (unison to four-part with or without organ accompaniment) by sixteenth- and seventeenth-century polyphonic composers such as Palestrina, di Lasso, Pergolesi, Scarlatti and Vittoria, together with masses by nineteenth-century German composers of the Cecilian movement published in Regensberg, with occasional works by church musicians working in Britain and in Ireland, including R. Terry, Dr J. Smith and de Prins. In the list of works for use at

benediction the music recommended is mainly that of German Cecilians, but one or two works by Bach, Handl [*sic*], by Mozart, Mendelssohn, Schubert, Gounod, Liszt and Rheinberger are included.

24 Information from Swertz's grandson, Aloys Fleischmann, in a conversation recorded by his son, Alan.

25 See Fleischmann's proposal to the bishop of 1907, 'Skizze Cathedral Society' p. viii. The cathedral in Cork no longer has any of these documents; the Salford List was most kindly sent to the authors by the Diocese of Salford but it has not been possible to discover what nineteenth-century composers Swertz included in his list.

26 Walburga Swertz's father, Jakob Rössler, died in December 1899 aged 86 without ever having seen any of his nine Irish-born grandchildren; his wife, née Walburga Niedermaier, a beer brewer's daughter from Pfaffenhofen, survived him by seven years; she knew her granddaughter Tilly quite well. During her time in Germany, Tilly used to visit both the Rösslers of Dachau and her grandmother's people in Pfaffenhofen, as family photos document.

27 Phyllis Ramsbothom née Scott to Aloys Fleischmann junior, 1 February 1980: she was then 88 years old.

28 See Moirín Chavasse, *Terence MacSwiney* (Dublin: Clonmore and Reynolds, London: Burns and Oates, 1961), pp. 162, 165.

29 MacSwiney worked from 1894 to 1911 as a clerk for Dwyer & Company of Cork, starting at the age of fifteen, ibid., pp. 16–17.

30 Tilly Fleischmann, unpublished memoir.

31 On the title page of MacSwiney's *The Music of Freedom* there is an image of a harp, under which is written: 'I am new-strung/I will be heard'. The author uses the pseudonym Cuireadóir (the Sower); it was published by the Risen Gaedheal Press, Cork in 1907.

32 When in 1891 Corkery saw a notice in a shop window in Barrack Street 'Airgead Síos' (cash down), he thought it was Chinese. See Patrick Maume, *Life that is Exile: Daniel Corkery and the Search for Irish Ireland* (Belfast: Queens University, 1993), p. 6.

33 Ibid., p. 13.

34 Ibid, p. 16.

35 See Fleischmann, *Music in Ireland*, p. 270.

36 Aloys Fleischmann, 'Skizze Cathedral Society', 21 June 1907, p. xxii.

37 Patricia Cox, in Ruth Fleischmann (ed.), *Aloys Fleischmann: A Life for Music in Ireland* (Cork: Mercier Press, 2000), pp. 351–2. Patricia Cox was the daughter of Elsa Swertz and Chris O'Malley-Williams.

38 See Raymond Smith on Father O'Flynn's experience of the north parish in *Father O'Flynn – The Well of Love* (Dublin: Lilmac Books, 1964), pp. 40–45.

39 Michael Weedle, in Ruth Fleischmann (ed.), *Aloys Fleischmann: A Life for Music in Ireland*, p.30.

40 Aloys Fleischmann, 'Skizze Cathedral Society', 21 June 1907, p. II.

41 Letters from Baron and Baroness von Moreau to Fleischmann, 1906–08.

42 Information from Aloys Fleischmann junior. He did not say when his father was offered the post.

43 Fleischmann to Mr Burkley, Treasurer of the Cork Choral Union, 21 May 1909.

44 Tilly Fleischmann's undated draft of a letter to Moirín Chavasse; see also Chavasse, *Terence MacSwiney*, pp. 136–7.

45 This undated text is written in English in Tilly Fleischmann's hand with every second line left free, sometimes a word translated into German and the pronunciation added. This suggests that it was an address to be delivered to the choir. The speech must have been given at the beginning of May 1909 before the controversy started.

46 The calculation instrument used was that of the Institute for the Measurement of Worth founded by Lawrence H. Officer and Samuel H. Williamson, kindly recommended by Patrick Zuk.

47 The residence registration documents of the city of Munich were not destroyed during the bombing of 1944–5 so the date of the Fleischmanns' departure from Amalienstrasse 21 could be ascertained.

48 See Bernard Curtis, *Centenary of the Cork School of Music 1878–1978* (Cork School of Music, 1978), p. 32.

49 Elsa was the third Swertz daughter, Wally the eldest and the Rosa the fourth.

50 Xaver Swertz was educated by the Presentation Brothers, as were the other Swertz boys; he graduated with a degree in Civil Engineering from University College Cork in 1909 and emigrated to America. He was joined some years later by his brother Ferdie.

51 In 1904, Wally Swertz was awarded a second honours BA in English, French and German and an Exhibition or scholarship. She was admitted to the University of Bonn in November 1909 on the basis of her Irish MA and a qualification from the Sorbonne in Paris (see the official document of admission). Her 'Studienbuch' or transcript show that she was enrolled at the University of Bonn until July 1910.

52 Fleischmann to his wife in Munich, 21 November 1909.

53 Wally Swertz in Bonn to her sister Tilly in Munich, 15 April 1910.

54 In a biographical memo, Tilly Fleischmann wrote that she played the organ while her father conducted choir and orchestra during the beatification celebration in the cathedral of Thaddeus McCarthy, a former bishop of Cork. He was beatified in Rome in 1895; on 12 September 1897, a relic was brought to Cork from Turin and enshrined beneath the altar. Swertz wrote an Ecce Sacerdos specially for the occasion. See *The Irish Times*, 13 September 1897. Tilly was then fifteen years old.

55 The Fleischmanns did not keep any of the concert reviews, and only one of the many letters of congratulation they received from friends was found among their papers. The notice which caused them such consternation was found in the Bavarian State Library.

56 In a letter of 2 January 1910, Fleischmann writes to his wife that Frau Hechwig drafted a letter for him to His Excellency Mog, and was going to draft his submission to the Prince Regent. The texts are not among the Fleischmann papers.

57 Information about William Bauress was found on the online Dublin Census of 1911 and kindly confirmed by great-grandson Henry and great-grandnephew Liam Bauress, who were found on the internet.

58 Only five of Fleischmann's organ preludes have survived.

59 Pfeiffer's painting takes its name from the poem depicted in it: 'An die Nacht – Gedicht von Wilhelm Michel'. The text: 'Über allen Dächern stehen/Klar und gross die schönen Sterne./Holde Nacht, lass mich vergehen/Tief in deiner samtnen Ferne/Wie ein Lied vergeht am Hügel,/Wie ein Wind verweht im Baum,/Hüll mich ein in deine Flügel,/Nimm mich auf in deinen Traum.' Fr Pat MacSwiney translated the poem for the recital programme of 7 June 1934 when the Fleischmann song was performed by Rita Horgan: 'High above the housetops twinkling,/Big and bright the starry sky./Kindly Night, my gaze is sinking/Lost in thy deep velvet eye,/As a song fades o'er the hill,/As the wind plays around a tree,/Fold thy wing about me still,/Waft me up in dreams of thee.'

60 This letter shows that Fleischmann got Pfeiffer's picture in March 1910; it is not certain that he immediately wrote his song based on it: he might have sent Tilly some other song for her name-day, possibly 'Dream in a Dream'.

61 Aloys Fleischmann's birth certificate states that he was born on 13 April 1910 at 8 p.m. in Adalbertstrasse 36, which was the address given of the midwife, Babette Leibl, who registered the birth.

62 Fleischmann to his son for his thirty-fifth birthday on 13 April 1945.

63 Fleischmann to his wife, undated, third week of April 1910.

64 Hildegard Schaehle heard this from Tilly Fleischmann during the former's visit to the Fleischmanns in October 1950.

65 Information from Catriona Mulcahy of the University College Cork Archives. In his book *The College – A History of Queen's/University College Cork* (Cork University Press, 1995), John A. Murphy lists Wally Swertz as Professor of German in 1909 (p. 376). If that were so, she would have been the first woman professor in the United Kingdom, but she was in fact studying and teaching in Bonn at that time.
66 The concert programme gives Terence MacSwiney as the translator of the work; Walter Henley is named on the mansucript as the translator. There may have been two versions, but only that of MacSwiney has survived.
67 Review by A.W.P. in *Musical News* of 18 November 1911, p. 462.
68 Moirín Chavasse, *Terence MacSwiney*, p. 98.
69 Lacaduv was the home of John J. Horgan and his wife Mary Windle, not far from the Fleischmann's Holmkliffe (the spelling used in Guy's Directory) on the Lee Road.

3. Internment during World War I

1 Tilly Fleischmann noted this information on the envelope containing her father-in-law's death notice.
2 On 18 August 1914, Rev John Russell, Curate to St Mary's Cathedral, and Fleischmann's friend, John J. Horgan, solicitor and deputy-coroner for the County of Cork, signed a declaration (which is in John J. Horgan's hand) bearing witness to Fleischmann's good character and taking responsibility for his good behaviour. Fleischmann promised good conduct and compliance with all police instructions. On 20 August he received a pass from the Commandant of the Cork Detention Barracks (now Collins Barracks) stating that he was deemed 'a person in no way dangerous to the safety of the realm'. On 22 August he was granted an Alien Permit of Residence.
3 Under the Aliens Restriction Order, Section 19.
4 See Fleischmann's Petition to the Home Office of 27 May 1915 in which he recounts what happened the previous year, and the letter of 12 September 1914 from the General Officer commanding the Queenstown Defences permitting Fleischmann's return to Cork.
5 The petition of 27 May 1915 is among the Fleischmann Papers together with a 'Memorandum re Aloys Fleischmann' drawn up by the solicitor John J. Horgan in January 1916 in an attempt to have him released from Oldcastle.
6 Mary Kirkpatrick in London to Tilly Fleischmann, 5 January 1916.
7 Today the term 'prisoner of war' is used for military personnel captured during hostilities; during the First World War, it was used in that sense, but also for civilian internees. See Yvonne M. Cresswell (ed.), *Living with the Wire: Civilian Internment in the Isle of Man during the two World Wars* (Douglas: Manx National Heritage, 1994), p. 7.
8 See Oliver Cougan, *Profiles of War in Co. Meath 1913–1973* (Dublin, 1983)
9 Statement in John J. Horgan, 'Memorandum re Aloys Fleischmann' of January 1916.
10 Geraldine Neeson's memoirs: *In My Mind's Eye – The Cork I Knew and Loved* (Dublin: Prestige Books, 2001), p. 58.
11 See Fleischmann's letter to his wife, 27 May 1918.
12 Grace O'Brien (a relation of Smith O'Brien of the 1848 rising), who had been in Stavenhagen's masterclass with Tilly and Märchen; Mary Horgan, John J. Horgan's wife.
13 Fleischmann to his wife, 26 January 1916.
14 Fleischmann to his wife, 16 January 1916.
15 This letter to Muriel Murphy is part of Fleischmann's letter home of 22 January 1916.
16 Fleischmann to his wife, 26 January 1916

17 Magdalena Fleischmann in Dachau to her son, not dated.
18 'Schermen' – a playful imitation of the German pronunciation of her French name. Fleischmann to his wife, 15 April 1917.
19 Fleischmann to his wife, 28 October 1917.
20 Fleischmann to his wife, 4 August 1916.
21 Fleischmann to his wife, 29 August 1917.
22 Fleischmann to his wife, 28 October 1917.
23 Fleischmann to his wife, 16 December 1917.
24 Fleischmann to his wife, 23 December 1917.
25 Vincenz Goller (who used the pseudonym, Hans von Berchthal) was an Austrian composer and church musician; he studied in Regensburg in the late 1890s. Fleischmann was in Germany in 1913; if he was able to accept Goller's invitation to visit him in Salzburg, no documentation of the visit has survived.
26 Fleischmann to his wife, 30 December 1917.
27 Fleischmann to his wife, 5 April 1918.
28 Fleischmann to his wife, 12 May 1918.
29 Information from W. Thirkettle, assistant archivist of the Manx Museum, Douglas, Isle of Man, 12 February 1996.
30 Fleischmann to Canon O'Sullivan, 15 July 1918.
31 Fleischmann to his wife, 27 May 1918.
32 The magazine *John Bull* published an article on 29 May 1915 entitled: 'The Huns' Paradise – bands, concerts and picnics for Isle of Man aliens'.
33 B.E. Sargeaunt, *The Isle of Man and the Great War* (London: Royal United Services Institution, 1920), see Chapter 3, especially pp. 67, 68, 74, 78.
34 Cresswell (ed.), *Living with the Wire*, p. 102.
35 Fleischmann to his wife, 30 May 1918.
36 The drawing by Fritz Koch-Gotha was published as the frontispiece of the *Berliner Illustrierte Zeitung*, 8 June 1919, title: 'Vier Jahre!' or 'Four Years!'.
37 Fleischmann to his son, 1 September 1918.
38 Fleischmann obituary by Seán Neeson in *The Irish Times*, 4 January 1964.
39 See Cresswell, *Living with the Wire*, p. 19.
40 Margery West, *Island at War* (Laxey: Western Books, 1986), p. 100, and information from Andreas Lang's grandson, Florian Lang, of Oberammergau, who very kindly provided the authors with photographs of some of his grandfather's work.
41 Fleischmann to his wife, 18 June 1918.
42 Fleischmann to his wife, 30 May 1918.
43 When Fleischmann junior was introduced to Winter in Munich in 1932, Winter told him he had been interned with his father and gave permission for him to attend all orchestral rehearsals – letter to his father, 28 September 1932.
44 Fleischmann told the Neesons that during his imprisonment, he kept hearing the chord of A major: Geraldine Neeson, *In My Mind's Eye*, p. 58.
45 There is only one letter from Goller among the Fleischmann papers: Fleischmann asked his wife to send him the letters, no doubt to show to Dr Ertl. He probably had to leave them behind when he was sent back to Germany. Only seven letters have survived which were sent to him in the camp: they are from his son.
46 Fleischmann to his son, undated, mid July 1957.
47 Margery West, *Island at War*, p. 104.
48 Fleischmann to his wife, 24 July 1918, 8 August 1918.
49 Fleischmann to Franz Schaehle, 19 September 1960.
50 Ibid.
51 Fleischmann to his son, undated, mid July 1957.
52 This information came from W. Thirkettle, assistant archivist of the Manx Museum in Douglas (letter of 12 February 1996). She wrote that there is no register of prisoners detained in Knockaloe and only one for Douglas, in which Fleischmann is listed. So the date when Fleischmann was sent to London is not known.

53 Fleischmann to Schaehle, 6 July 1950.
54 Ibid.
55 Undated letter from Fleischmann to the administrator of the Cathedral, Canon Ahern, written in the early 1950s.
56 Gerhard Hanke, Wilhelm Liebhart, Norbert Göttler, Hand-Günter Richardi, *Geschichte des Marktes und der Stadt Dachau,* pp. 138–51.
57 Communication from the British Consulate General in Munich, on behalf of the Home Office of Whitehall, dated 3 August 1920. It was signed: 'Your obedient servant [!], John Pedder'.
58 There is a photograph of Aloys and Tilly Fleischmann having tea in Kew Gardens with Tony Swertz and his wife in September 1920, as the inscription under the picture states.

4. LIFE IN THE FREE STATE 1920–34

1 Information from Máirín O'Rourke.
2 The Fleischmanns at that time lived in 2 Clifton Villas, Montenotte.
3 Fleischmann to his son, 13 April 1945.
4 Fleischmann junior to his grandmother in Dachau, 31 July 1923.
5 Daniel Corkery, letter to the editor, the *Cork Examiner,* 26 January 1924.
6 See Michael Lenihan and Kieran McCarthy, *Cork: A Pictorial Journey* (Cork: 2001), p. 7, and Cormac Ó Gráda, *Ireland: A New Economic History 1780–1939* (Oxford: Clarendon Press, 1994, reprinted 2001), p. 438.
7 Fleischmann to the cathedral administrator, Canon Ahern, undated, early 1950s.
8 Ibid.
9 Fleischmann gives the date as being 22 November 1922. However, Herr Gerhard Walcker-Meyer informed the authors that the year of installation of the Cork Walcker organ recorded in the company's books is 1923. The printed programme for the cathedral service on the feast of St Cecilia with Dr Beecher of Maynooth as preacher is dated 23 November 1924. Fleischmann mentioned in a letter that a planned second recital on the new organ had to be cancelled due to the death of Cardinal Logue – the Cardinal died in November 1924.
10 Fleischmann to Canon Ahern, undated, early 1950s.
11 Information kindly given by Herr Gerhard Walcker-Meyer in March 2007.
12 The cost of the organ was never divulged, but in a letter to Canon O'Keeffe written in the early 1940s, Fleischmann intimates that it came to just under £1,500. It is not clear whether this figure includes the new seats and balustrade put up around the choir area, work carried out by a Cork firm which came to almost as much as the price of the organ.
13 Dublin's Catholic cathedral is called the 'Pro-Cathedral'. The term means 'substitute for the cathedral'. The original cathedral of the city, Christ Church, constituted during the reign of Archbishop St Laurence O'Toole (1128–80), was taken over during the Reformation by the established Protestant Church of Ireland. This has never been officially recognised by the Catholic bishops of Ireland and they have therefore never requested the Pope to designate a different church as the city's Catholic cathedral.
14 Edward Martyn (1859–1924) was a landlord of Norman descent whose family settled in the west of Ireland in the twelfth century. His family were unique in being both powerful as well as popular with their tenants: they were dispensed by the Crown from the sanctions of the Penal Laws and remained both Catholic and people of property. Edward became a nationalist on reading Lecky's *History of Ireland,* joined the cultural movement, was one of the founders of the Abbey Theatre, wrote plays, became president of Sinn Fein, patronised the arts and in particular church music and art. See John J. Horgan, *Parnell to Pearse,* pp. 112–18.

15 Canon Daniel Cohalan was cathedral administrator from 1929–37; he was a nephew of Bishop Daniel Cohalan, bishop of Cork 1916–52.

16 Fleischmann to Canon O'Keeffe, undated, probably 1945.

17 Undated letter from Fleischmann to the Cathedral administrator, Canon O'Keeffe, written around 1945. The same idea is also expressed briefly at the end of his 'Ten Precepts' for the Cathedral Choir, a copy of which was given to the Head of the School of Music, Carl Hardebeck, in the early 1920s, but which may have been drawn up during Fleischmann's first years in Cork.

18 Michael Drinan to Tilly Fleischmann, 21 January 1964.

19 Geraldine Neeson, *In My Mind's Eye – The Cork I Knew and Loved*, p. 58.

20 Liam Ó Murchú remembers another recruiter for the cathedral choir: 'Up the street on Pope's Quay lived little "Tonny" Curtis who, with his son, taught music to the starved urchins of Blarney Street Christian Brothers and the Rock Steps National School. "Tonny" would steer likely improvers towards Aloys Fleischmann's Cathedral Choir or George Brady's on Pope's Quay. He was a discerning mentor who, over the years, saw to it that the choir-stalls were well filled. The recruiting station for the Turners Cross church choir was the nearby public house, the "Mountain", where there was excellent singing; the priest, Father Tackum, had a regular client divert singers of talent to his choir.' ('Sweet Singing in the Choir' in *Ireland's Own*, 29 February 2008).

21 The Honans were Cork grain merchants who were benefactors of the university. Money from their legacy was used to build the Honan Chapel, at the dedication of which Tilly Fleischmann conducted the Cathedral Choir in November 1916. The chapel is a product of the Gaelic Revival with Hiberno-Romanesque architecture and stained glass windows by Harry Clarke and Sarah Purser in an original Irish *art nouveau* style. See Virginia Teehan and Elisabeth Wincott Heckett, *The Honan Chapel: A Golden Vision* (Cork: University Press, 2004).

22 Jack Lynch, 'Tanora and a Motor Car with Lights' in *Magill* Magazine, 1977.

23 The feast of Pentecost celebrates the descent of the Holy Ghost on the apostles fifty days after the resurrection – the name derives from the Greek for fiftieth. Whitsun means 'white Sunday' from the white robes worn by those baptised on that day.

24 The feast of Corpus Christi celebrates the Eucharist; it was instituted in the thirteenth century. The ceremonies could not be practised in Ireland while the penal laws against Catholicism were in force; the feast was reinstated by Cardinal Cullen in the second half of the nineteenth century as a public demonstration of faith.

25 Niall Toibín, *Smile and be a Villain* (Dublin: Town House, 1995), pp. 52–4.

26 Seán Barrett of Dublin to Ruth Fleischmann, 2 February 1999.

27 See *The Irish Independent* of 15 July 1929, p. 10. The aerial photographs show huge crowds.

28 Bernard Curtis, *Centenary of the Cork School of Music 1878–1978*, p. 72; see too Richard O'Donoghue, *Like a Tree Planted: Father O'Flynn of the Loft* (Dublin: Gill, 1967), pp. 55–6, and Raymond Smith, *Father O'Flynn – The Well of Love*, p. 47.

29 See Seán Neeson's obituary of Fleischmann, *The Irish Times*, 4 January 1964.

30 See Bernard Curtis, *Centenary of the Cork School of Music 1878–1978*, p. 57.

31 The *Cork Examiner*, 20 June 1923.

32 A reply to the secretary, Frank Giltinan, drafted in the hand of Father Pat MacSwiney, explains that Fleischmann had undertaken to find a rehearsal hall with the knowledge and consent of the school supervisor, Miss Barker, who was out sick due to an accident, and that he had himself paid for the advertisement. He was clearly upset that, instead of being thanked for his commitment, he had been rebuked, and announced his resignation from the consultive committee.

33 Father Daniel J. Burns to Ruth Fleischmann, 18 March 1997.

34 James Good, 'A Tribute to the two Fleischmanns', *The Fold*, September 1992.

35 Michael MacDonald wrote this account of Fleischmann in February 1999.

36 Father Pat Walsh in J.C. Walsh, *Farranferris: The Heritage of St. Finbarr 1887–1987* (Cork: Tower Books, 1987). When Fleischmann's son was asked to provide a photograph, he sent one taken with Arnold Bax in 1933. Father Diarmuid Linehan, who was in charge of the lay-out, decided to omit Bax. He wrote to thank Fleischmann Jun. for his help, adding: 'Without a doubt, that photo really IS your father. I trust there won't be any ill-feeling between them in the heavenly choirs when Arnold Bax discovers the omission!'

37 See W.F.P. Stockley, 'Church Singing in Ireland', *Irish Ecclesiastical Record* 1930, p. 262.

38 Mary Sheppard (born in 1912) wrote this account for us in 2005. Her father was a first cousin of Terence MacSwiney and of Fr Pat MacSwiney. She has passed her interest in music on to her family. Her grandson, John O'Brien, directed the revival of Fleischmann's nativity play, *The Night of Wonders*, which was performed in her presence in Cork City Library on 6 January 2010. Kitty Buckley, director of the Music Library, had the idea; Liz O'Connor of Dublin's Rockmount Choir made it possible by digitally typesetting the fragile score.

39 A tierce is a third of a cask – the old term was in use in Cork at this time.

40 Neither the programme nor the press report mention the composer of *The Pied Piper of Hamelin*. The German operas composed in 1879 by Viktor Nessler and in 1880 by Adolf Neuendorff had German librettists.

41 M.C. Gillington (1829–1910) was an English organist and composer; Florian Pascal was the pseudonym of Joseph Williams Junior (1850–1923), a music publisher and composer of songs and operettas.

42 There is a photograph of a Miss Crowley with the Fleischmanns and Bax of 1937; Anne Crowley was interviewed for the Northern Ireland BBC Bax programme of 2005: it is no doubt the same person.

43 Among the Fleischmann papers there is an undated and incomplete newspaper article announcing the classes, inviting those interested to enrol.

44 In March 1995, the two surviving members of this choir, Richard Downing and Michael Deasy, were awarded the papal medal, Benemerente, both of whom having spent more than sixty years singing in the choir. Richard Downing was then eighty-eight years old, and still working in his own tailor shop in Bandon.

45 Herr Gleitsmann-Wolf returned to Munich in the early 1930s and was succeeded by Miss Daughton and Miss Troy. Fleischmann assisted both in training the choir during Canon Murphy's lifetime.

46 There is a form among the Fleischmann papers headed: Eaglais Naomh Phádraig, Droichead na Banndan (St Patrick's Church, Bandon), Choir, which was probably addressed to the parents of children selected for choir membership, with the following text: 'Dear . . ., . . . has been examined in Singing by Professor Fleischmann and passed for the . . . Choir. . . . is a good . . . and will have a fine voice when trained. If you kindly sign and return form enclosed, . . . will be taught music and trained for the Choir. Yours faithfully, M. Canon Murphy, P.P. 193. . .

47 2RN is said to have been a chiffre for 'To Éireann'.

48 See Séumas Ó Braonáin, 'Music in the Broadcasting Service', in Aloys Fleischmann (ed.) *Music in Ireland*, pp. 197–8.

49 Seán Barrett to Ruth Fleischmann, 2 February 1999. None of the former choir members the authors spoke to can explain where the name 'Bert' came from, nor do they think it likely that it might have been a reference to Albert, Queen Victoria's German consort.

50 The Feis Ceoil, or Music Festival, emerged out of the Irish National Literary Society and Gaelic League in order to promote Irish music and was founded by Annie Patterson; the first Feis was held in Dublin in 1897. It was part of an tOireachtas [assembly] founded the same year to provide a forum for creative work in all branches of Irish culture. The Feis Maitiú was founded in 1927 in Cork by the Capuchins and had 2,250 entries that year. See Fleischmann, *Music in Ireland*, pp. 214–16.

51 See Tilly Fleischmann, 'Some Memories of Arnold Bax', published in the *British Music Society Newsletter* No. 86, London, June 2000, editor Rob Barnett, and thereafter placed on the Bax website by Richard Adams. She writes that Bax first came to adjudicate in 1928: he in fact came the following year, as Séamas de Barra has established. See his article: 'Arnold Bax, the Fleischmanns and Cork', *Journal of Music in Ireland*, 5, 1 (January/February, 2005), p. 4, note 7.

52 Carl Hardebeck to Tilly Fleischmann, 12 November 1919.

53 See Bernard Curtis, *Centenary of the Cork School of Music*, p. 62.

54 Fleischmann to Canon O'Keeffe about the bad condition of the organ, undated, around 1945.

55 For an account of Fleischmann Junior's *The Four Masters*, see Séamas de Barra, *Aloys Fleischmann* (Dublin: Field Day, 2006), pp. 73–8.

56 The relationship with the housekeepers seems to have been good. Julia, referred to in a letter by the ten-year old Aloys Junior to his father in 1920, remained with the Fleischmanns until 1927, when she went to London. She corresponded with Aloys junior, collected stamps for him, and was taken to the cinema when she came back to Cork on holiday – Aloys Fleischmann jun. often refers to her in his *Diary of Myself and my Actions 1926*. Madge was with the family for several years, she accompanied them on the train to Cobh to see Aloys junior off when he set out for Germany in 1932, and wept with them on the way back having watched the liner sail off out of sight. She corresponded with him when he was studying in Munich. Hannah Hurley of Ovens, County Cork was the Fleischmanns' house-keeper from the early 1940s until she retired twenty years later. Her name for the head of the household, 'the Boss', was adopted by his wife and son. She tended the grandchildren when they were infants, came to mind them in the evenings if their parents were out, baked brown bread for them, prayed for them if they went into their piano lessons without having practised properly and comforted them tactfully afterwards if the prayers had not been effective. The Irish ballads she recited for them in front of the fire on winter evenings were their introduction to the 'hidden Ireland' which they will never forget.

57 Tilly Fleischmann, *Some Memories of Arnold Bax*, p. 1.

58 Elisabeth Schumann (1888–1952) was one of the foremost opera and *lieder* singers of the early twentieth century. She sang in Hamburg from 1909 to 1919, and subsequently for twenty years at the State Opera of Vienna under all the great conductors. At her lieder recitals she was frequently accompanied by Gerald Moore.

59 Fleischmann to Schaehle, mid May 1955. At an earlier concert, given at the Clarence Hall in Cork on 10 March 1926, Fleischmann also accompanied Rita Horgan Wallace. She sang, among other songs, a setting of Tagore's 'Do not Go, my Love' by the Dutch-American composer Richard Hageman.

60 Aloys Fleischmann Jun. in Munich to his mother, 3 May 1933, and Tilly Fleischmann to him, 27 March 1934. Rita Wallace proposed that Joyce Sullivan, a pupil of Tilly's, accompany her at a recital of Fleischmann Senior's songs; he agreed.

61 In March 1928 Fleischmann had to undergo surgery twice for a deep-seated abscess in his hip, after which he spent several weeks convalescing in Bantry with his friend Canon Murphy (see letters from Aloys Óg to his grandmother in Dachau of 1 and 11 April 1928).

62 Seán Barrett to Ruth Fleischmann, 2 February 1999.

63 Aloys Óg to his grandmother in Dachau, 6 September 1925. The six subjects in which he received honours were Irish, English, Geography, German, History and Latin. Music was not an examination subject.

64 Fleischmann's inaugural lecture to the Art Society is discussed in Séamas de Barra, *Aloys Fleischmann* (Dublin: Field Day, 2006), pp. 18–19.

65 Hans Conrad Swertz to Tilly Fleischmann, 10 January 1927.

66 See Charlotte H. Fallon, *Soul of Fire* (Cork: Mercier Press, 1986), p. 88.

67 See the *Cork Examiner*, 28 November 1923. Máirín O'Rourke most kindly undertook an extensive search of the 1922 and 1923 volumes of the newspaper to find this report.

68 Mary MacSwiney eventually had to drop the case. See Charlotte H. Fallon, *Soul of Fire*, p. 108.

69 Tilly Fleischmann to her son in Munich, 20 January 1933.

70 See Geraldine Neeson, *In My Mind's Eye: The Cork I Knew and Loved*, p. 57.

71 Máire Brugha in Ruth Fleischmann (ed.), *Aloys Fleischmann (1910–1992): A Life for Music in Ireland* (Cork: Mercier Press, 2000), p. 350, and Máire MacSwiney Brugha, *History's Daughter*, p. 61.

72 See Moirín Chavasse, *Terence MacSwiney*, p. 162, and Máire MacSwiney Brugha, *History's Daughter* (Dublin: O'Brien Press, 2005), p. 64.

73 This is based on the account by Máire MacSwiney Brugha of how she came back to Ireland written in response to her mother's representation, which she refutes. Her friend Máirín O'Rourke very kindly sent the authors a copy, with Máire MacSwiney Brugha's permission.

74 See the *Cork Examiner*, 30 November 1923, researched by Máirín O'Rourke.

75 See the *Pilgrim's Newsletter Aylesford*, May 1972 No. 113 by Carmelite priest Malachy Lynch, master of novices in the Kinsale monastery in Father Pat's time. This was kindly given to the authors by Máirín O'Rourke. See too Father Pat's obituary by John J. Horgan in the *Cork Historical and Archaeological Society*, July–December 1940, pp. 39–40.

76 Geraldine Neeson, 'Meeting the Fleischmanns', the *Cork Examiner*, 29 March 1977.

77 Geraldine Neeson, *In My Mind's Eye – The Cork I Knew and Loved*, p. 58.

78 Ibid., p. 105.

79 Lord Monteagle in London to Tilly Fleischmann, 28 February 1934.

80 Fleischmann to Franz Schaehle, 19 February 1935.

81 Fleischmann to Syvia Duff Knight, Arthur Duff's daughter, 10 August 1982.

82 Harry Scully in London to Tilly Fleischmann, August 1933.

83 Nicola Gordon Bowe, *The Life and Works of Harry Clarke* (Dublin: Irish Academic Press, 1989), p. 154.

84 Daniel A. Veresmith was born in Ohio in 1861 as the son of an immigrant German tailor named Wehrschmidt. As a young man he was invited by Hubert von Herkomer, a renowned German portrait painter living in England, to work in his art school in Hertfordshire, and was one of the artists chosen by him to illustrate Thomas Hardy's novel *Tess of the Durbervilles*. Veresmith exhibited his work in the Royal Academy. During the First World War he anglicised his name. He was a member of the Royal Society of Portrait Painters; his portrait of Robert Scott hangs in the National Portrait Gallery of London; the National Gallery of Canada owns two of his works.

85 Daniel Veresmith to Fleischmann, 10 June 1929.

86 Ibid.

87 Sean O'Faolain, *Vive Moi! An Autobiography* (London: Rupert Hart-Davis, 1965), p. 129.

88 See O'Faolain's preface to his play, *She Had to Do Something* (London: Jonathan Cape, 1938), p. 7. In the play, the Frenchwoman is married to a church musician. The idea for the play may have come from an incident in Cork in 1929, when a small visiting ballet company was deprived of audiences at the Opera House after being denounced in a number of the city's Catholic churches. The play was greeted on the first night, O'Faolain writes, 'with a storm of boos and hisses'.

89 Ibid., p. 134.

90 Frank O'Connor, *An Only Child* (London: 1961, paperback by Pan Books, 1970), p. 55.

91 Daniel Corkery to Aloys Fleischmann, 19 February 1958.

92 Frank O'Connor, *An Only Child*, pp. 152–3.
93 Ludwig Berberich to Fleischmann, undated: unclear London postmark, December 1923.
94 Fleischmann to his wife, 22 August 1926.
95 The press notice welcoming Fleischmann was not found among the Fleischmann papers, but in the Dachau archive.
96 Ibid.
97 Ibid.
98 Fleischmann in Munich to his wife, 22 August 1926.
99 Harold White (1872–1943) was an Irish composer, teacher and music critic.
100 John J. Horgan's son, Ivor, had decided to study at the Academy of Art and was still in Munich when Aloys Junior came to the Academy of Music in 1932. Ivor subsequently qualified as a solicitor.
101 Agnes Straub's stage career began in 1909 in Vienna, then she worked in Heidelberg, Bonn, Königsberg and from 1916 in Berlin, where she directed the Agnes Straub Theatre from 1936. She acted strong women characters in countless classical and contemporary dramas and also in films.
102 Fleischmann to his son, undated, 16 September 1932.
103 Fleischmann to his son in Munich, 26 October 1932.
104 Fleischmann to his son, 2 November 1932.
105 Fleischmann to his son, 26 October 1932.
106 Fleischmann to his son, 2 November 1932.
107 Fleischmann to his son, 20 December 1932.
108 Ibid.
109 The car, bought before Aloys Óg had left for Munich, was somewhat antiquated and was soon sold as the bills for repairs became excessive.
110 Fleischmann to his son, 28 December 1932.
111 Ibid.
112 Ibid.
113 Fleischmann to his son, undated, May 1934.

5. HANDING ON THE TORCH 1934–64

1 Fleischmann Junior interview with Tomás Ó Canainn, *The Cork Review* (Cork: Triskel Arts Centre, 1992) p. 16. The passage Fleischmann refers to is sung by Tristan towards the end of Act I: 'Wohl kenne ich die irische Königin' [Indeed I know the Irish queen]. The text of the interview is on the Fleischmann website, courtesy of Tomás Ó Canainn and the director of the Triskel Arts Centre, Tony Sheehan.
2 Fleischmann Junior's *Sreath do Phiano*, or Suite for Piano was performed at a concert of the State Academy of Music in 1934 (published by Chester the following year) and his motet *Illumina Occulos Meos* in June 1934 by the choir of the Munich cathedral under Monsignor Prof. Ludwig Berberich.
3 R. Purcell of Killagh to Tilly Fleischmann, 13 March 1936.
4 'Memorandum from the Musical Association of Ireland' of 1939 in Aloys Fleischmann (ed.), *Music in Ireland*, p. 91.
5 Sister Marie Collins wrote this account in 2003.
6 The first man from the Irish Presentation Order to study music was Brother Lewis, Michael A. Mac Eoin, who took his BMus in University College Cork under Fleischmann Junior and studied the piano with Tilly Fleischmann. From Northern Ireland, he returned there to teach, founding school choirs and bands. He arranges music and composes; the works in his *Cór Gaelach* (published in 2000) have been performed and broadcast all over Ireland and the UK.
7 Michael Weedle studied with Fleischmann senior in the late 1940s, and began his university studies in Cork in 1951. He wrote this account in 1999.
8 See the UCC Summer School programmes of 1938 and 1939. Seán Neeson invited the dancer Joan Denise Moriarty to participate in the Irish section of the

1938 Summer School with a performance on the war pipes. This was the occasion of her first meeting with the Fleischmanns.

9 See Aloys Fleischmann junior's article on Séamus Murphy, 'A Munster Phidias', *The Cork Review*, Paul Durcan (ed.) (Cork: Triskel Arts Centre, 1980), p. 24.

10 Adolf Mahr was a native of South Tyrol, which had been handed over to Italy under the Treaty of Versailles in 1919. This may have been one of the reasons why he became a supporter of Hitler's. He is now known to have been the leader of the National Socialist party organisation in Dublin, secretly relaying information to the German government and organising support for the Nazi cause in Ireland. Having realised that he was being observed by the Irish police, he left Dublin for Vienna in July 1939 – according to the information in this Fleischmann letter, probably on 25 July. Austria had been incorporated into the German Reich the previous year. Mahr was in charge of the German broadcasts to Ireland during the war; two Celtic scholars, Hans Hartmann and Ludwig Mühlhausen broadcast regularly in Irish. See David O'Donoghue, *Hitler's Irish Voices: The Story of German Radio's Wartime Irish Service* (Belfast: Beyond the Pale Publications, 1998), chapters 2 and 5. See too the accounts of Fritz Brase in German military journals: Alix Koenig, 'Deutsche Militärmusik in Irland' in *Die Woche*, 1931 and the obituary by Dr Georg Kandler, 'Ein führender Auslandspionier der deutschen Militärmusik: Oberst Professor Brase' in *Deutsche Militär-Musiker-Zeitung*, 25 January1941, copies of which were kindly provided by Martin Steffen.

11 Fleischmann to his family in Cork; the letter is not dated but internal evidence shows it was written at the end of July 1939.

12 Hitherto.

13 Daniel Corkery to Tilly Fleischmann, 22 February 1933.

14 Seán Neeson to Aloy Fleischmann Junior November 1937.

15 Fleischmann to Canon O'Keeffe, probably 1945. Fleischmann Junior wrote to Jim Hurley, Secretary of UCC, on 2 November 1957 that the losses from his orchestral concerts over the first six years came on average to £35 per annum. Cheques made out to Fleischmann Senior for 1951 and 1957 were recently discovered in the cathedral, copies of which were kindly made available to us. In the 1950s Fleischmann received £300 per annum, paid in three-monthly instalments. This was the remuneration for his work in the cathedral and in the Seminary of Farranferris.

16 William Martin in conversation with Anne Fleischmann, August 2006.

17 Peter F. Lenihan to Fleischmann, 15 June 1934.

18 J.P. Cronin from Gibraltar to Tilly Fleischmann, 15 January 1964 in a letter of condolence after her husband's death.

19 Canon Bastible to Aloys Fleischmann Junior, 6 January 1964, in a letter of condolence on the death of his father.

20 Bob Barry wrote this account in 2003.

21 William Martin's father died when he was a child, and his mother had to bring up the four children on her own. William had a fine voice, so she managed to have him taught music and later sent him to the cathedral choir. He had to give up his piano classes after missing the Third Grade examination, which could not be repeated. The exam was on a Saturday morning, but there were two hours of school on Saturdays. At school on the Saturday of the examination, he gave his teacher, a Christian Brother at the North Monastery, a letter from his mother asking that he be allowed leave early to take the examination in the School of Music. The letter was thrown into the bin. When William asked for permission to go, the teacher called him up to the front of the class and beat him on the back of the fingers of both hands so that he was unable to play. His resolute mother went straight to the headmaster. The Brother was removed from the school that week – and transferred to St Patrick's Boys' Industrial School at Upton. There the Brother was safe from intervening parents, as the pupils had been committed to the

residential school by the courts on grounds of lack of proper guardianship. As William Martin put it: 'If he could do that to me, what chance did the poor children down there have?' In 1959, the Mayor of Cork, Gus Healy, complained to the Taoiseach, Jack Lynch, about conditions in Upton. An inspection was arranged, the institution informed in advance of the visit, after which the investigation was dropped. The school was closed in 1966; it has since been proven that many of the children there suffered serious abuse. See *www.paddydoyle.com/historyofneglect.html*.

22 Dom Clancy to Fleischmann, 26 March 1937.

23 Seán Óg Ó Tuama to Fleischmann, 27 February 1936.

24 Sister M. Dympna to Tilly Fleischmann, 28 February 1936.

25 Daniel C. Eaton in Edinburgh to Fleischmann, 17 December 1936.

26 Patrick Jeffery to Fleischmann, 13 June 1938.

27 Robert Whyte in Dublin to Leo Whyte in Cork, 28 June 1942 about a Cork cathedral choir broadcast of 25 June 1942. Leo must have passed part of the letter on to Fleischmann. (Leo became bursar in UCC in 1965.)

28 The press notice was copied in Fleischmann's hand; source and date are not given: probably February 1936.

29 Ernest de Regge to Fleischmann, 28 February 1936.

30 T.C. Smiddy, now resident in Belvedere, Dalkey, Dublin, 1 March 1936 to Tilly Fleischmann

31 L.G. Clarke of Carrick-on-Shannon, Co. Leitrim to Fleischmann, 12 June 1938.

32 Herbert Hughes was born in Belfast in 1882, studied in London under Stanford at the Royal College of Music, graduating in 1901. He was editor of the Irish Folk Song Society's journal, from 1911–32 music critic of *The Daily Telegraph*. Like Carl Hardebeck, he used folk songs as material for his own compositions; many folk songs owe their popularity to his arrangements. See Axel Klein, *Die Musik Irlands im 20. Jahrhundert* (Hildesheim: Georg Olms Verlag, 1996), pp. 162–5, 420–1.

33 *The Irish Press*, 20 March 1936. The newspaper erroneously attributed Herbert Hughes' praise to the choir of Cork's Protestant cathedral, which had not given a broadcast on the date in question.

34 Sir Richard Terry was born in 1865. When the Catholic cathedral of Westminster was built in 1901, he became musical director, a post he held until 1924, when he resigned after controversy with the new administration regarding his choice of music. He edited and published the forgotten MSS of Tudor church music; he was knighted in 1922 for his achievement.

35 Sir Richard Terry to Fleischmann, undated, probably November 1936.

36 Fleischmann to Sir Richard Terry, undated, probably November 1936.

37 Ibid.

38 E.J. Moeran's father was a clergyman who was born in Dublin but grew up in England. His son sustained a serious head injury during the war in 1917 from which he never quite recovered.

39 BBC: 'The Golden Age has Passed', made to commemorate the thirtieth anniversary of Bax's death in 1983. The transcript of the interview is to be found on the Bax website.

40 Arnold Bax, Forword to Aloys Fleischmann (ed.), *Music in Ireland: A Symposium* (Cork University Press, 1952), iii.

41 See Tilly Fleischmann, 'Some Memories of Arnold Bax', MS 1955, available on the Bax website.

42 Fleischmann to Mrs Bax, 16 May 1937.

43 See Gölz Aly, *Hitlers Volksstaat: Raub, Rassenkrieg und nationaler Sozialismus* (Frankfurt a.M.: S. Fischer Verlag, 2005) Teil III: Die Enteignung der Juden, pp. 209–310.

44 David O'Donoghue, *Hitler's Irish Voices*, pp. 12–13.

45 See the Martin Niemöller Trust website (*Martin-Niemöller-Stiftung: das Zitat*). The parson was in the camp in Dachau 1941–5.

46 NSDAP: National-Sozialistische Deutsche Arbeiterpartei or National Socialist German Workers' Party.
47 Information given to the family by Gerald Y. Goldberg, one of the organisers of the protest.
48 Annette Kolb's lecture, 'Die International Rundschau und der Krieg', was delivered in Dresden on 29 January 1915, and published in *Die weissen Blätter* (Leipzig: Verlag der Weissen Bücher, März 1915), pp. 269–84.
49 Ludwig Mühlhausen in Hamburg to Fleischmann, 15 March 1933.
50 See Máire MacSwiney Brugha, *History's Daughter, A Memoir from the only child of Terence MacSwiney* (Dublin: O'Brien Press, 2005), p. 191, and J.J. Lee, *Ireland 1912–1985: Politics and Society* (Cambridge: Cambridge University Press, 1989), pp. 219–24.
51 Germaine Stockley to Fleischmann, undated, 1944.
52 Information from a descendant of de la Main's, Constantin Roman of Chelsea. Professor Roman cites as his source: Caulfield, Richard (ed.), *Gentleman's Magazine*, Sept. 1855. (Richard Caulfield (1823–87) was librarian and custodian of the Royal Cork Institution and librarian of Queen's College Cork.)
53 Fleischmann to his son, 13 April 1945.
54 Dan Donovan to Ruth Fleischmann, 5 Sept. 2006 outlining the story of the Cork Little Theatre. The account continues: 'They were also joined by many of the experienced players of the Good Companions from our separated brethren, who used the Gregg Hall in the South Mall and were anxious to spread their wings in a bigger and better civic context. These included Cecil Marchant (manager of Piggotts), his wife Bettie, Alan Shouldice and his wife Joyce, Harry Bogan and others. The producers were Jim Stack, Geraldine Neeson, Eddie Golden and Cecil Marchant. The actors were strictly amateur but there was a moderate honorarium for the producer and this subsequently became a source of some little disunity and squabbling. I was invited to join its ranks sometime in the middle forties as was Der Breen, who produced at least one show for them. We and others were recruited to fill the ranks when (believe it or not!) there was a split, when Jim Stack opted to break away, taking many of the old players with him to found his own company on a more professional basis. This was a great success and continued till Jim's death. Eddie Golden was soon to follow him to pursue a professional career mainly in the Abbey. The Society held within itself the seeds of its own ultimate destruction. It had some wonderful successes when the leading people pulled together creatively. But by the late forties it was in a parlous state and came to an end by the early fifties.'
55 Aloys Fleischmann, *Music in Ireland*, p. 274.
56 *The Standard*, [mid] April 1944.
57 Ibid.
58 Moirin Chavasse to Fleischmann, 12 July 1944. She (née Fox) had married Claud Chavasse, an Englishman with relatives in Ireland, who was an enthusiastic supporter of all things Gaelic. His summer school, Scoil Acla (1910–14) provided classes for Irish and Irish culture. He liked to wear a saffron kilt and cloak and refused to speak anything but Irish. In 1916 he was arrested and fined five pounds in Macroom Court for speaking Irish to a policeman stationed in Ballingeary, an Irish-speaking area. He was at that time president of the Oxford branch of the Gaelic League. During the Civil War he spent a year interned in the Curragh camp. In 1925 they bought the Martins' home, Ross House in Killannin, Co. Galway (see the local history website of Carrowmoreknock).
59 Patrick Hennessy to Fleischmann, undated, 1944.
60 Fleischmann to his son, 13 April 1945.
61 Ibid.
62 No accounts of the liberation of the camp have been found among Fleischmann's papers. In 1945 he could receive no letters or newspapers from Germany and he

did not live to see the establishment of the Memorial Site, in which the arrival of the American troops is documented. The soldiers were so appalled by what they saw that their initial relative friendliness to the citizens of the town was replaced by bitter hostility. Huge numbers of prisoners from other concentration camps had been dispatched to Dachau during the last months of the war as the Allied forces advanced. The extreme overcrowding, lack of food and a typhus epidemic had decimated the prisoners. During the last days of their control of the camp the SS guards had forced nearly 7,000 prisoners to leave the camp and set out on foot for a destination remote from the approaching Allied forces. The fate of the Dachau 'death march' prisoners is unknown. See Wolfgang Benz, Barbara Distel (eds.), *Dachauer Hefte I, Studien und Dokumente zur Geschichte der nationalsozialistischen Konzentrationslager* (Dachau: Comité International de Dachau, 1985), pp. 3–11, 61–87.

63 Fleischmann was surprised to find his Dachau nativity plays, which ended in 1906, presented in an American magazine thirty-eight years later as victims of Nazi oppression. He described it to Franz Schaehle in a letter of 19 January 1955: 'What war propaganda can make of things! An article with a strikingly large title appeared in the well-known New York magazine *Coronet* (which was sent to me) in December 1944: 'The Man Who Murdered Christmas'. Here are just a few sentences: 'A.F. started the festival with the sixteenth century miracle plays and drew enormous crowds. They became an institution. (!!) He was successful beyond his dreams. The festival had become celebrated throughout the world. (!!!)' etc. and then: 'Hitler and his supporters destroyed it and set up in its place the most horrible concentration camp in Europe.'

64 Franz Schaehle to Fleischmann, 31 March 1949.

65 Franz Schaehle to Fleischmann, 16 June 1949.

66 The *Münchner Merkur* was the second paper in Munich to be licensed by the American military government; it began publishing in 1946. As all newpapers and radio stations had been under Nazi control, they were closed down by the Allies in 1945.

67 Fleischmann wrote a long letter on 29 December 1949 to one of the 'four musical evangelists' who had performed his tower music for wind ensemble, Mr Auer, whose mother had been a school friend of his mother's. A copy of this letter was most kindly sent to Ruth Fleischmann by Mr Auer's daughter, Frau Glück of Wieningerstrasse, Dachau – they had met by chance in Dachau in the vicinity of Fleischmann's old home.

68 One of the German aristocrats stranded on the shores of Ireland after the war was Gräfin Vera von Zedtwitz. The Asch branch of the von Zedtwitz family (which goes back to the thirteenth century) originated in Zedtwitz near Hof in Bavaria and settled in Moravia (Slovakia) and Duppau (Bohemia) in the nineteenth century. After the Second World War, they were expelled and expropriated and are now scattered all over the world.

69 Fleischmann to Schaehle, 19 January 1955.

70 See Ruth Fleischmann (ed.), *Joan Denise Moriarty: Founder of Irish National Ballet* (Cork: Mercier Press, 1998).

71 Ibid, p. 31.

72 Sister M. Peter to Fleischmann, 27 September 1955.

73 Seán Barrett to Ruth Fleischmann, 2 February 1999.

74 J.P. Cronin in Gibraltar to Tilly Fleischmann, 15 January 1964.

75 Jack O'Donovan in a conversation with Anne Fleischmann on 27 October 2009.

76 David MacInerny wrote this account in July 2003.

77 Fleischmann to Terence O'Connor, 27 November 1947.

78 Fleischmann to Schaehle, 6 July 1950.

79 Fewer than half a dozen of the 163 letters of congratulation on the papal honour of 1954 have survived.

80 Fleischmann's rendering of the broad Bavarian dialect: 'Woast mei Liaber, hie und do a Rausch ham is was Schönes. Do kriagt me wieder a Schneid. De Mensch muss wos ham vom Leben, net wohr?'

81 Fleischmann to Schaehle, 5 November 1956.

82 Fleischmann to Schaehle, 2 November 1950.

83 Prince Georg Timo (etc.) of Saxony was born 22 December 1923 in Munich. His father, Prince Ernst Heinrich of Saxony, was the youngest son of the last king of Saxony, Frederick Augustus III, and the Archduchess Louise of Austria. Prince Georg's mother was Princess Sophie of Luxembourg. Prince Georg died on 22 April 1982 in Emden, northern Germany. The meeting with the prince is described by Fleischmann in a letter to Schaehle of 27 January 1951.

84 Arnold Bax speaking in *The Golden Age Has Passed: A Centenary Celebration of Arnold Bax*, by Michael Oliver, BBC Radio 3, 1983. The transcript is on the Bax website. See also Bax, *Farewell, My Youth*, p. 48.

85 Arnold Bax, Foreword to *Music in Ireland*, ed. Aloys Fleischmann, p. iii.

86 Aloys Fleischmann interviewed for the BBC Bax programme, *The Golden Age Has Passed*.

87 At the Bax memorial service in St Martin-in-the-Fields, London on 20 October 1953, John Churchill played Elgar's *Prelude to the Kingdom*; the BBC Chorus (conducted by Leslie Woodgate) sang Bax's motet 'This Worldes Joie', the Aeolian String Quartet played the slow movement from Bax's String Quartet No. 1; Eric Gillett read Revelation xxi, 1–7; the BBC Chorus sang Holst's Anthem 'Turn back, O Man' (words by Clifford Bax); the organist of St. George's Chapel, Windsor, W.H. Harris, played Bax's Nunc Dimittis, and Bach's Fugue in E flat.

88 Fleischmann to Schaehle, 12 July 1949.

89 Fleischmann to his son, 12 July 1949.

90 Fleischmann to Schaehle, 24 June 1956.

91 Fleischmann to his son, undated, mid July 1957.

92 Aloys Óg mentioned the 1957 London Symphony Orchestra's concert of Irish works in a letter to Brian Boydell, 1 August 1957, saying that the fine performance of his *Clare's Dragoons* had been marred by 'ferocious cymbal playing and a misbeat at the start of the pipes' first entry, which resulted in a twenty-bar shambles'. The authors are grateful to Dr Patrick Zuk, who transcribed the letter found among the Boydell papers in Trinity College Dublin.

93 Fleischmann to his son, undated, 16 June 1957.

94 Fleischmann to his wife, 2 April 1956.

95 The Jewish community of Cork made the Tóstal visit of the Vienna Philharmonic Orchestra possible through its sponsorship – see Fleischmann Junior's letter of thanks to Gerald Y. Goldberg, 14 May 1956.

96 Fleischmann to Franz Schaehle, 9 April 1957.

97 See Donnchadh Ua Braoin, 'Music in the Primary Schools', in Fleischmann (ed.), *Music in Ireland*, pp. 37–44.

98 Fleischmann allowed Pilib Ó Laoghaire to join the cathedral choir at the age of six – the youngest ever admitted. The boy had no trouble reading the music, though he still had some difficulty with the words. He studied in Scotland with Sir Hugh Roberton, and graduated from the music department of UCC in 1958, where he subsequently lectured in choral music. See the article by his daughters, Colom and Íde Ní Laoghaire, in Ruth Fleischmann (ed.), *Cork International Choral Festival 1954–2004: A Celebration* (Cork: Glen House Press, 2004), pp. 32–42.

99 Fleischmann to Franz Schaehle, 17 May 1954.

100 Fleischmann to Franz Schaehle, 24 May 1960.

101 Fleischmann to Franz Schaehle, 21 Nov. 1960.

102 Hans Waldemar Rosen to Fleischmann Junior, 12 January 1960. Rosen wrote that the singers 'simply loved' Fleischmann Senior's setting of Mörike's 'Zum Neuen Jahr'.

103 John O'Riordan, honorary secretary of the cathedral choir, letter to the editor of the *Cork Examiner*, 16 January 1964 in response to Denis Gwynn's obituary.
104 See 'In grateful appreciation', *Cork Examiner*, 21 May 1963.
105 Bob Barry's account of his time in the cathedral choir, written in 2003.
106 Fleischmann's *A Child is Born in Bethlehem* was broadcast by Radio Éireann in December 1966. For forty years there was no further performance of his music until a recital of his *Lieder* was given in Dachau in July 2006 on the hundredth anniversary of his departure from the town.
107 James Blanc to Tilly Fleischmann, 15 February 1966.
108 Donal Twomey in London to Tilly Fleischmann, 21 January 1966.
109 Brother T.J. Cronin from Gibraltar to Tilly Fleischmann, 15 January 1964.

THE MUSIC OF ALOYS GEORG FLEISCHMANN   ·

  1 In 1954 Fleischmann submitted the second of the Tagore songs with orchestra (presumably in the piano version), *He came and sat by my side*, for a competition that was organised by the Arts Council and adjudicated by John F. Larchet. The song was awarded a prize of £15.
  2 See Maurice Gorham, *Forty Years of Irish Broadcasting* (Dublin, 1967), p. 75.

Bibliography

Barra, Séamas de, 'Aloys Fleischmann and the Idea of an Irish Composer' *Journal of Music in Ireland*, September/October 2005

—— 'Arnold Bax, the Fleischmanns and Cork', *Journal of Music in Ireland*, January/February 2005

—— 'Into the Twilight: Arnold Bax and Ireland', *Journal of Music in Ireland*, March/April 2004

—— 'Music and Nationalism', *Journal of Music in Ireland*, November/December 2003

—— *Aloys Fleischmann* (Dublin: Field Day Publications, 2006)

Bausinger, Hermann (ed.), *Schwäbische Weihnachtsspiele* (Stuttgart: Jäckh Verlag, 1959)

Bax, Arnold, *Farewell, My Youth* (London, Longmans, Green & Co, 1943)

Benz, Wolfgang and Distel, Barbara (eds.), *Dachauer Hefte I, Studien und Dokumente zur Geschichte der nationalsozialistischen Konzentrationslager* (Dachau: Comité International de Dachau, 1985)

Boser, Elisabeth; Nauderer, Ursula K.; and Schäfer, Bärbel, *FreiLichtMalerei. Der Künstlerort Dachau 1870–1914* (Dachau: Dachauer Galerien und Museen/Selbstverlag, 2002)

Bräunling, Andreas R., 'Das verschobene Jubiläum: Zur 1100–Jahr–Feier des Marktes Dachau im Jahre 1908', in Wilhelm Liebhart (ed.), *Amperland – Heimatkundliche Vierteljahresschrift für die Kreise Dachau, Freising und Fürstenfeldbruck* (Dachau, 2005/1)

Bräunling, Andreas, 'Musik der Dachauer Landwehr' in Josef Focht, and Ursula K. Nauderer, (eds.), *Musik in Dachau* (Dachau: Zweckverband Dachauer Galerien und Museen, 2002)

Brown, Terence, *Ireland: A Social and Cultural History 1922–79* (London, Fontana 1981)

Burghart, Josef, *St Jakob Dachau: Zur Geschichte einer uralten Pfarrei und eines ehrwürdigen Gotteshauses* (Stuttgart: Libertas Verlag Hubert Baum, 1962)

Chavasse, Moirín, *Terence MacSwiney* (Dublin: Clonmore and Reynolds; London: Burns and Oates, 1961)

Collins, Paul, 'Strange Voices in the "Land of Song"– Belgian and German Organist Appointments to Catholic Cathedrals and Churches in Ireland, 1859–1916' in Michael Murphy and Jan Scmazny (eds.), *Music in Nineteenth Century Ireland*, Irish Musical Studies 9 (Dublin: Four Courts Press, 2006)

Corkery, Daniel, *The Hidden Ireland* (Dublin, 1924; rpt Dublin: Gill & Macmillan, 1967)

Cougan, Oliver, *Profiles of War in County Meath 1913–1973* (Dublin, 1983)

Cox, Gareth and Klein, Axel, *Irish Music in the Twentieth Century*, Irish Musical Studies 7 (Dublin, Four Courts Press, 2003)

Cox, Patricia, 'Aloys Fleischmann' in Ruth Fleischmann (ed.), *Aloys Fleischmann: A Life for Music in Ireland* (Cork: Mercier Press, 2000)

Cresswell, Yvonne M. (ed.), *Living with the Wire: Civilian Internment in the Isle of Man during the two World Wars* (Douglas: Manx National Heritage, 1994)

Cuireadóir [Terence MacSwiney], *The Music of Freedom* (Cork: Risen Gaedheal Press, 1907)

Cunningham, Joseph P., 'The Herr and Cork's Most Famous Choir' in *The Holly Bough*, Christmas, 1994

Curtis, Bernard, *Centenary of the Cork School of Music 1878–1978: Progress of the School 1878–1978* (Cork School of Music, 1978)

—— 'The Cork Municipal School of Music' in Aloys Fleischmann (ed.), *Music in Ireland – A Symposium* (Cork: Cork University Press ; Oxford: Blackwell, 1952)

Dachau und das Konzentrationslager: Ein Beitrag der Grossen Kreisstadt Dachau zum 50. Jahrestag der Befreiung am 29. April 1945 (Dachau, 1995)

Daly, Kieran A., *Catholic Church Music in Ireland, 1878–1903: The Cecilian Reform Movement* (Dublin: Four Courts Press, 1995)

Daly, Seán (*Cork: A City in Crisis – A History of Labour Conflict and Social Misery 1870–1872* (Cork: Tower Books, 1978)

Deacy, Regina, '*Continental Organists and Catholic Church Music in Ireland 1860– 1960*' (MLitt thesis, National University of Ireland, Maynooth, 2005).

De Giacomo Albert, 'Remembering T.C. Murray', *Irish University Review*, Autumn/Winter 1995

Dunleavy, Janet Egleson and Dunleavy, Gareth W., *Douglas Hyde* (Berkeley, University of California Press, 1991)

Edelmann, Bernd, 'Königliche Musikschule und Akademie der Tonkunst in München 1874–1914' in Stephan Schmitt, (ed.), *Geschichte der Hochschule für Musik und Theater München von den Anfängen bis 1945* (Tutzing: Hans Schneider Verlag, 2005)

Elsner, Andreas, *Zur Geschichte des musikwissenschaftlichen Lehrstuhls an der Universität München* (Munich: doctoral thesis presented to the Ludwig Maximilian University, 1982)

Engelmann, Roger, 'Öffentlichkeit and Zensur – Literaur und Theater als Provokation' in Friedrich Prinz und Marita Krauss, *München – Musenstadt mit Hinterhöfen: Die Prinzregentenzeit 1886–1912* (Munich: Beck Verlag, 1988)

Erlach, Thomas, *Unterhaltung und Belehrung im Jesuitentheater um 1700. Untersuchungen zu Musik, Text und Kontext ausgewählter Stücke* (Essen: Die Blaue Eule, 2006)

Fallon, Brian, *An Age of Innocence – Irish Culture 1930–1960* (Dublin: Gill and Macmillan, 1999)

Fallon, Charlotte H., *Soul of Fire: A Biography of Mary MacSwiney* (Cork: Mercier Press, 1986)

Fischer, Joachim, *Das Deutschlandbild der Iren 1890–1939* (Heidelberg: C. Winter, 2000)

Fischer, J. and Holfter, G. (eds.), *Creative Influences – Selected Irish-German Biographies* (Trier: Wissenschaftlicher Verlag, 2009)

Fleischmann, Aloys, 'A Munster Phidias', *The Cork Review* (Cork: Triskel Arts Centre, 1980)

——'Music and Society 1850–1921' in W.E. Vaughan (ed.), *A New History of Ireland*, Vol. VI (Oxford: Clarendon Press, 1996)

——*Music in Ireland – A Symposium* (Cork: Cork University Press; Oxford: Blackwell, 1952)

Fleischmann, Ruth (ed.), *Joan Denise Moriarty: Founder of Irish National Ballet* (Cork: Mercier Press, 1998)

——(ed.), *Aloys Fleischmann (1910–1992): A Life for Music in Ireland* (Cork: Mercier Press, 2000)

Fleischmann, Tilly, 'Some Memories of Arnold Bax', in Robert Barnett (ed.), *British Music Society Newsletter*, No 86 (London: June 2000)

Focht, Josef and Nauderer, Ursula K., *Musik in Dachau* (Dachau, Zweckverband Dachauer Galerien und Museen, 2002)

Gillen, Gerard and Johnstone, Andrew (eds.), *An Historical Anthology of Irish Church Music*, Irish Musical Studies 6 (Dublin, Four Courts Press, 2001)

Gillen, Gerard and White, Harry, *Music and Irish Cultural History*, Irish Musical Studies 3 (Dublin, Four Courts Press, 1995)

——'Musicology in Ireland', *Irish Musical Studies 1* (Dublin, Four Courts Press, 1990)

——(eds.), *Music and the Church,* Irish Musical Studies 2 (Dublin: Four Courts Press, 1993

Good, James, 'A Tribute to the two Fleischmanns', *The Fold*, Sept. 1992

Gordon Bowe, Nicola, *The Life and Works of Harry Clarke* (Dublin: Irish Academic Press, 1989)

Göttler, Norbert, 'Im Anbruch der Moderne – 1818–1914' in Gerhard Hanke et al., *Geschichte des Marktes und der Stadt Dachau* (Dachau: Musemsverein, 1985)

Gruhn, Wilfried, *Geschichte der Musikerziehung. Eine Kultur- und Sozialgeschichte vom Gesangsunterricht der Aufklärungspädagogik zu ästhetisch-kultureller Bildung* (Hofheim, Wolke Verlag, 2003)

Hanke, Gerhard, 'Die Dachauer Volksschauspiel im 18. und in der ersten Hälfte des 19. Jahrhunderts mit seinen Initiatoren' in *Amperland* 27/4 (Große Kreisstadt Dachau), 1991

——'Die Künstlerkolonie Dachau. Besuche von Künstlern and Angehörigen geistiger Berufe in den Jahren 1891–1918' in Ottilie Stoedtner-Thiemann und Gerhard Hanke, *Dachauer Maler, Die Kunstlandschaft von 1801–1946* (Dachau, Verlagsanstalt 'Bayerland', 1989)

Hanke, Gerhard and Liebhart, Wilhelm, *Der Landkreis Dachau*, Kulturgeschichte des Dachauer Landes Bd. 1 (Dachau: Kreis Dachau und Verlagsanstalt 'Bayerland', 1992)

Hanke, Gerhard et al., *Geschichte des Marktes und der Stadt Dachau* (Dachau: Musemsverein, 1985)

Hartmann, August, *Weihnachtslied und Weihnachtsspiel in Oberbayern* (Munich: Kaiser, 1875)

Hartmann, Franz Xaver, 'Sitten und Gebräuche in den Landgerichtsbezirken Dachau und Bruck' in *Oberbayerisches Archiv zur vaterländischen Geschichte*, Bd. 35 (Munich: Historischer Verein von Oberbayern/Selbstverlag, 1875)

Heres, Horst, *Dachauer Gemäldegalerie*, Kulturgeschichte des Dachauer Landes, Bd. 12 (Dachau: Musemsverein Dachau, 1985)

Horgan, John J., 'Father Patrick MacSwiney' [Obituary] (Cork *Historical and Archaeological Society Journal*, July–December 1940

—— *Parnell to Pearse* (Dublin: Brown and Nolan, 1949)

Hourikan, Kevin, 'The Evolution and Influence of Town Planning in Cork' in Henry Alan Jefferies, *Cork Historical Perspectives* (Dublin: Four Courts Press, 2004)

Keller, Anton (ed.), *Ludwig Thoma: Ein Leben in Briefen 1875–1921* (Munich: Piper Verlag, 1963)

Kestenberg, Leo, 'Volksmusikschule'(n.d.) and 'Musikerziehung und Musik-pflege' (Leipzig: 1921) repr. in Dorothea Hemming (ed.), *Dokumente zur Geschichte der Musikschule (1902–1976)* (Regensburg: Gustav Bosse Verlag, 1977)

Kiberd, Declan, *Inventing Ireland: The Literature of the Modern Nation* (London: Jonathan Cape, 1995)

Klein, Axel, *Die Musik Irlands im 20. Jahrhundert,* Hildesheimer Musikwissen-schaftliche Arbeiten, Bd. 2 (Hildesheim: Georg Olms Verlag, 1996)

Kolb, Annette, 'Die International Rundschau und der Krieg' in *Die weissen Blätter* (Leipzig, Verlag der Weissen Bücher, March 1915)

Kübler, August, *Dachau in verflossenen Jahrhunderten* (Dachau, Druckerei und Verlagsanstalt 'Bayerland', 1928)

—— *Strassen, Bürger und Häuser in Alt-Dachau* (Münnerstadt: Eigenverlag, 1934)

Lagerlöf, Selma, 'Die Heilige Nacht', in *Christuslegenden* (Munich: Langen Verlag, 1904)

Lee, Joseph, *The Modernisation of Irish Society 1848–1918,* The Gill History of Ireland 10 (Dublin: Gill and Macmillan, 1973)

Lee, Joseph J., *Ireland 1912–1985: Politics and Society* (Cambridge, Cambridge University Press, 1989)

Lenihan, Michael and McCarthy, Kieran, *Cork: A Pictorial Journey* (Cork: 2001)

Liebhart, Wilhelm and Pölsterl, Günther, 'Die Gemeinden des Landkreises Dachau', *Kulturgeschichte des Dachauer Landes, Bd. 2* (Dachau: Musemsverein, [1992])

Lynch, Jack, 'Tanora and a Motor Car with Lights' in *Magill Magazine,* 1977

Lynch, Malachy, *Pilgrim's Newsletter Aylesford,* No. 113, May 1972

Lyons, F.S.L., *Culture and Anarchy in Ireland 1890–1939* (Oxford: Oxford University Press), 1979

MacSwiney Brugha, Máire, *History's Daughter: A memoir from the only child of Terence MacSwiney* (Dublin: O'Brien Press, 2005)

Mark, Graham, *Prisoners of War in British Hands during World War 1 – A study of the history, the camps and their mails* (The Postal History Society, 2007)

Maume, Patrick, '*Life that is Exile' – Daniel Corkery and the Search for Irish Ireland'*, (Belfast: Institute of Irish Studies, 1993)

Messmer, Franzpeter, 'Musikstadt München – Konstanten und Veränderungen' in Friedrich Prinz und Marita Krauss, *München – Musenstadt mit Hinterhöfen: Die Prinzregentenzeit 1886–1912* (Munich: Beck Verlag, 1988)

Modesto, Johannes, 'Ein Münchner Marienlied aus der Barockzeit' in *Sänger & Musikanten* 46/3, (Munich: Deutscher Landwirtschaftsverlag, 2003)

Morton, A.L., *A People's History of England* (London: Gollancz, 1938; paperback edition, London: Lawrence & Wishart, 1965)

Moser, Hans, *Volksschauspiel im Spiegel von Archivalien. Ein Beitrag zur Kulturgeschichte Altbayerns* (Munich: Kommission für Bayerische Landesgeschichte der Bayerischen Akademie der Wissenschaften, 1991)

Murphy, John A., *The College – A History of Queen's/University College Cork* (Cork: Cork University Press, 1995)

Murphy, Michael and Smaczny, Jan (eds.), *Music in Nineteenth-Century Ireland*, Irish Musical Studies 9 (Dublin: Four Courts Press, 2006)

Murphy, Seamas, *Stone Mad* (Dublin: Golden Eagle Books, 1950)

Murray, Peter, 'Art Institutions in Nineteenth-Century Cork' in Patrick O'Flanagan and Cornelius G. Buttimer (eds.), *Cork History and Society* (Dublin: Geography Publications, 1993)

Nauderer, Ursula K., *Auf Weihnachten zu: Altdachauer Weihnachtszeit* (Dachau: Museumsverein, 2003)

Nauderer, Ursula K., 'Die Anfänge der musikalischen Vereine in Dachau' in Josef Focht and Ursula K. Nauderer (eds.), *Musik in Dachau. Ausstellungskatalog* (Dachau: Bezirksmuseum, Zweckverband Dachauer Galerien und Museen, 2002)

Nauderer, Ursula K., *Hermann Stockmann und das heimatpflegerische Wirken des Künstlers, Dachauer Museumsschriften Bd. 7* (Dachau: Verlagsanstalt 'Bayerland', 1987)

Nauderer, Ursula K. (ed.), *Literatur in Dachau, Einhorn-Verlag und Schriftsteller im frühen 20. Jahrhundert* (Dachau: Dachauer Galerien und Museen/Selbstverlag, 2002)

Neeson, Geraldine, *In My Mind's Eye* (Dublin: Prestige Books, 2001)

Ní Laoghaire, Colom and Íde; and Ó Laoghaire, Pilib, in Ruth Fleischmann (ed.) *Cork International Choral Festival 1954–2004: A Celebration* (Cork: Glen House Press, 2004)

Nolte, Eckhard, *Lehrpläne und Richtlinien für den schulischen Musikunterricht in Deutschland vom Beginn des 19. Jahrhunderts bis in die Gegenwart. Eine Dokumentation* (Mainz: Schott, 1975)

Ó Braonáin, Séumas, 'Music in the Broadcasting Service' in Aloys Fleischmann (ed.), *Music in Ireland – A Symposium* (Cork: Cork University Press ; Oxford: Blackwell, 1952).

O'Brien, Grace, 'The Music of the Nativity: A Cork Musician's Christmas Play', *The Irish Press*, 20 December 1934.

Ó Canainn, Tomás, Interview with Aloys Fleischmann, *The Cork Review* (Cork: Triskel Arts Centre, 1992)

Ó Gallchobhair, Éamonn, 'The Cultural Value of Festival and Feis', in Aloys Fleischmann (ed.), *Music in Ireland – A Symposium* (Cork: Cork University Press ; Oxford: Blackwell, 1952)

Ó Gráda, Cormac, *Ireland: A New Economic History 1780–1939* (Oxford: Clarendon Press, 1994; repr. 2001)

Ó Murchú, Liam, 'Sweet Singing in the Choir', *Ireland's Own*, 29 February 2008

O'Connor, Frank, *An Only Child* (1958, repr. London: Pan Books, 1971)

O'Donoghue, David, *Hitler's Irish Voices: The Story of German Radio's Wartime Irish Service* (Belfast: Beyond the Pale Publications, 1998)

O'Donoghue, Richard, *Like a Tree Planted: Father O'Flynn of the Loft* (Dublin: Gill, 1967)

O'Faolain, Sean, *She Had to Do Something* (London: Jonathan Cape, 1938)

—— *Vive Moi! An Autobiography* (London: Rupert Hart-Davis, 1965)

Petit, Seán F., *The Streets of Cork* (Cork: Studio Publications, 1982)

Pine, Richard (ed.), *Music in Ireland 1848–1998*, Thomas Davis Lectures (Cork: Mercier Press, 1998)

Reitmeier, Lorenz Josef, *Dachau: Ansichten und Zeugnisse aus zwölf Jahrhunderten* (Dachau: 1976)

——*Dachau: Ansichten und Zeugnisse aus zwölf Jahrhunderten. Der Andere Teil* (Dachau: 1979)

——*Dachau: Ansichten und Zeugnisse aus zwölf Jahrhunderten. Der Letzte Teil der Trilogie* (Dachau: 1982)

——*Dachau: Ansichten und Zeugnisse aus zwölf Jahrhunderten. Nachtrag zur Trilogie* (Dachau: 1986)

——*Dachau: ein Kunstbilderbuch* (Dachau: 1995)

Richardi, Hans-Günter, *Dachauer Zeitgeschichtsführer* (Dachau: Stadt Dachau, 1998)

Rüffelmacher, Ingeborg, *Ehrsames Handwerk, Kulturgeschichte des Dachauer Landes*, Bd. 5 (Dachau: Musemsverein, 1992)

Ryan, Joseph, 'Nationalism and Music in Ireland', (PhD Dissertation, University College Dublin, 1991)

Ryan, Vera and Donovan, Dan, *An Everyman's Life* (Cork: Collins Press, 2008)

Ryan, William Patrick, *The Pope's Green Island* (London: James Nisbet & Co., 1912)

Sargeaunt, B.E., *The Isle of Man and the Great War* (London: Royal United Services Institution, 1920)

Schäfer, Bärbel, 'Künstlerhäuser in Dachau um die Jahrhundertwende' in Boser, Elisabeth, Nauderer, Ursula K. and Schäfer, Bärbel, *FreiLichtMalerei. Der Künstlerort Dachau 1870–1914* (Dachau: Dachauer Galerien und Museen/Selbstverlag, 2002)

Schlosser, Birgit, 'Aloys Fleischmann: Die Nacht der Wunder – Ein Dachauer Weihnachtsspiel und sein Kontext' (MA thesis submitted to the Institute of Musicology at the Ludwig-Maximilian-University of Munich, September 2004)

Seemüller, Hans, *Alt-Dachauer Geschichten* (Dachau:Hans Zauner Verlag, n.d. [1970])

Setzwein, Bernhard, *München, Spaziergänge durch die Geschichte einer Stadt* (Stuttgart: Klett-Cotta, 2001)

Smith, John, 'The Oldcastle Internment Camp' in John Smith, *Oldcastle Centenary Book: A History of Oldcastle Commemorating St Brigid's Church 1904–2004* (Oldcastle Centenary Committee, 2005)

Smith, John, 'The Oldcastle Prisoner of War Camp 1914–1918' in Séamus Mac Gabhann (Hon. Ed.), *Ríocht na Midhe: Records of Meath Archaeological and Historical Society,* Vol XXI, 2010

Smith, Raymond, *Father O'Flynn – The Well of Love* (Dublin: Little & McClean, 1964)

Sowa, Georg: *Anfänge institutioneller Musikerziehung in Deutschland (1800–1843). Pläne, Realisierung und zeitgenössische Kritik, mit Darstellung der Bedingungen und Beurteilung der Auswirkungen* (Regensburg, Gustav Bosse Verlag, 1973)

St Leger, Alicia, *Melodies and Memories – 150 Years at Cork Opera House* (Cork Opera House, 2005)

Stack, Eilis, 'Victorian Cork' in Henry Alan Jefferies, *Cork Historical Perspectives* (Dublin: Four Courts Press, 2004)

Stockley, W.F.P., 'Church Singing in Ireland', *Irish Ecclesiastical Record*, 1930

Stoedtner-Thiemann Ottilie and Hanke, Gerhard, *Dachauer Maler, Die Kunstland-schaft von 1801–1946* (Dachau: Verlagsanstalt 'Bayerland', 1989)

Tamagawa, Yuko, 'Sozialgeschichte des Klavierunterrichts in der ersten Hälfte des 19. Jahrhunderts', in Kaiser, Hermann J. (ed.), *Musikpädagogik. Sozialgeschicht-liche Aspekte einer wissenschaftlichen Disziplin, Sitzungsbericht 1989 der Wissenschaftlichen Sozietät Musikpädagogik* (Mainz: Schott, 1993)

Teehan, Virginia and Wincott Heckett, Elisabeth, *The Honan Chapel: A Golden Vision* (Cork: Cork University Press, 2004)

Thiemann, Carl, *Erinnerungen eines Dachauer Malers: Beiträge zur Geschichte Dachaus als Künstlerort* (Dachau: Hans Zauner Verlag, 1966)

Thoma, Ludwig, *Erinnerungen* (Munich: Piper Verlag, 3rd edition, 1980)

Toibín, Niall, *Smile and be a Villain* (Dublin: Town House, 1995)

Ua Braoin, Donnchadh, 'Music in the Primary Schools' in Fleischmann, Aloys (ed.), *Music in Ireland – A Symposium* (Cork: Cork University Press; Oxford: Blackwell, 1952)

Unger-Richter, Brigitta, 'Kontrapunkt und Harmonie. Musik im künstlerischen Schaffen Adolf Hölzels' in Josef Focht, Ursula K. Nauderer (eds.), *Musik in Dachau*. Exhibition Catalogue (Dachau: Bezirksmuseum, Zweckverband Dachauer Galerien und Museen, 2002)

Walsh, Fr Patrick, 'Farranferris – Music Voluntary' in J.C. Walsh (ed.), *Farranferris: The Heritage of St Finbarr 1887–1987* (Cork: Tower Books, 1987)

Weedle, Michael, 'Aloys Fleischmann' in Ruth Fleischmann (ed)., *Aloys Fleischmann: A Life for Music in Ireland Remembered by Contemporaries* (Cork: Mercier Press, 2000)

Wehler, Hans-Ulrich, *Deutsche Gesellschaftsgeschichte*, Bd. 3 1849–1914 (Frankfurt am Main: Büchergilde Gutenberg, 1995)

West, Margery, *Island at War* (Laxey: Western Books, 1986)

White, Harry, *The Keeper's Recital – Music and Cultural History in Ireland, 1770–1970* (Cork: Cork University Press, 1998)

—— 'Heinrich Bewerunge and the Cecilian Movement in Ireland' in *The Keeper's Recital – Music and Cultural History in Ireland 1770–1970* (Cork: Cork University Press, 1998)

—— , *The Progress of Music in Ireland* (Dublin: Four Courts Press, 2005)

White, Harry and Murphy, Michael, *Musical Constructions of Nationalism: Essays on the History and Ideology of European Musical Culture 1800–1945* (Cork: Cork University Press, 2001)

Wichmann, Siegfried, *Dachau: Ansichten aus zwölf Jahrhunderten in elf Themen* (Dachau:Stadt Dachau, n.d.)

Wimmer, Ruprecht, *Jesuitentheater. Didaktik und Fest* (Frankfurt am Main: Klostermann, 1982)

Zuk, Patrick, 'Music and Nationalism' Part 1, *Journal of Music in Ireland* (Dublin January/February 2002)

—— 'Music and Nationalism' Part 2, *Journal of Music in Ireland* (Dublin: March/April 2002)

—— 'Music and Nationalism: The Debate Continues', *Journal of Music in Ireland*, July/August 2003

Index